Improving Consumer Engagement in Digital Marketing Through Cognitive AI

Hamed Nozari
Bio10, Dubai, UAE

Sepideh Samadi
Heriot-Watt University, UAE

Stavroula Kalogeras
Heriot-Watt University, UAE

IGI Global
Scientific Publishing
Publishing Tomorrow's Research Today

Vice President of Editorial Melissa Wagner
Director of Acquisitions Mikaela Felty
Director of Book Development Jocelynn Hessler
Production Manager Mike Brehm
Cover Design Jose Rosado

Published in the United States of America by
IGI Global Scientific Publishing
701 East Chocolate Avenue
Hershey, PA, 17033, USA
Tel: 717-533-8845 | Fax: 717-533-7115
Website: https://www.igi-global.com E-mail: cust@igi-global.com

Library of Congress Cataloging-in-Publication Data

Names: Nozari, Hamed, 1984- editor | Samadi, Sepideh, 1985- editor | Kalogeras, Stavroula editor
Title: Improving consumer engagement in digital marketing through cognitive AI / [edited by] Hamed Nozari, Sepideh Samadi, Stavroula Kalogeras.
Description: Hershey, PA : IGI Global Scientific Publishing, [2026] | Includes bibliographical references and index. | Summary: "This book aims to present a well-rounded exploration of how cognitive AI can be applied to strengthen consumer engagement in digital marketing"-- Provided by publisher.
Identifiers: LCCN 2025019278 (print) | LCCN 2025019279 (ebook) | ISBN 9798337337753 hardcover | ISBN 9798337337760 paperback | ISBN 9798337337777 ebook
Subjects: LCSH: Telemarketing | Artificial intelligence | Consumer behavior
Classification: LCC HF5415.1265 .I47 2026 (print) | LCC HF5415.1265 (ebook) | DDC 658.8/720285--dc23/eng/20250708
LC record available at https://lccn.loc.gov/2025019278
LC ebook record available at https://lccn.loc.gov/2025019279

British Cataloguing in Publication Data
A Cataloguing in Publication record for this book is available from the British Library.

Table of Contents

Detailed Table of Contents

This study examines the role of AI-based simulators in experiential marketing education. By designing an interactive conceptual model, it is shown how the combination of intelligent algorithms with experiential learning theory can enhance student engagement, improve marketing decision analysis, and personalize the learning path. The benefits, challenges, and implementation dimensions of this technology are also analyzed, and suggestions are made for effective utilization in the higher education system.

This research investigates and evaluates an adaptive neural marketing system based on ubiquitous artificial intelligence (AIoE). The proposed system uses biometric, behavioral, and environmental data to identify users' emotions and adapt marketing content in real time. The results showed that the system is able to identify users' emotions with high accuracy and significantly increase users' engagement with personalized content. This research shows that AIoE can lead to improved performance of personalized marketing systems.

This study examines the role of the Internet of Everything (IoE) in the evolution of intelligent marketing. Using IoE, brands are able to collect and analyze real-time data from connected devices and can create personalized and dynamic marketing experiences for their customers. By reviewing the basic concepts, designing intelligent marketing infrastructures, and providing case studies from various industries, this study examines the practical applications of this technology and analyzes the challenges and solutions associated with its implementation. The findings show that IoE can improve marketing efficiency and effectiveness.

This chapter examines how artificial intelligence (AI) and Industry 4.0 technologies are transforming sports marketing. As traditional methods for analyzing fan behavior lose relevance, AI provides advanced tools to understand preferences, emotions, and purchase patterns. The chapter details the roles of machine learning (ML) for predictive analysis, natural language processing (NLP) for social media sentiment, and computer vision (CV) for visual engagement. It also explores AI integration with blockchain for secure fan data management and the use of virtual and augmented reality (VR/AR) for immersive experiences. These technologies enhance decision-making, marketing personalization, financial risk reduction, and operational efficiency. Ethical concerns, including data privacy and algorithmic bias, are also addressed. The chapter offers practical insights for marketers, analysts, and researchers on using AI to build more personalized and sustainable relationships with the evolving generation of tech-savvy sports fans.

This research designs and implements an AI-based educational system for sentiment analysis in marketing texts. The system uses advanced natural language processing models such as BERT and LSTM to identify consumer sentiment and provide students with real-time feedback. The goal of this system is to improve students' sentiment analysis skills and gain a deeper understanding of consumer behavior. The results showed that this system helped improve students' analytical skills and provided them with an interactive and effective learning experience. This system can be used as an effective tool in marketing education.

This study explored social media monetization policy in Nigeria as a potential avenue for a new social contract as a digital economy development indicator and entrepreneurship sustainability. By examining existing monetization policy, regulatory challenges, and the socio-economic implications for digital content creators and stakeholder's engagement, the paper highlights the urgent need for policies that balance profitability with targeted digital marketing campaign and consumer protection with artificial intelligence (AI). The study adopted a random sampling technique, 10 real estate companies were selected from the 15 medium scale real estate companies in the study area. Of the completed questionnaires, 75% were recovered and deemed valuable for the data analysis. The results of the study indicated that significant portion of medium scale real estate investment companies generated between 20million and 100million in revenue after implementing data-driven product engineering digital marketing, which is more than they did in the year before digital marketing implementation.

This research presents an intelligent framework for analyzing and optimizing customer interactions in smart cities, which is based on the combination of real-time Internet of Things (IoT) data and recurrent neural networks (RNN). By synchronizing multi-source data and utilizing the LSTM model, it is possible to predict consumer behavior and design personalized marketing campaigns. The results show that the proposed framework is capable of extracting spatial-temporal behavioral patterns with high accuracy and can be used as a basis for real-time marketing decision-making in smart cities.

messaging. Actual-time communique is made feasible via AI, which guarantees activate solutions to customer questions.

Preface

In today's dynamic world, marketing is no longer just about delivering messages to the audience; it also requires intelligent interactions, timely responses, and personalized experiences that can be embedded in the minds and hearts of consumers. As the boundary between the physical and digital spaces becomes increasingly blurred, consumer expectations are becoming more complex, informed, and sometimes volatile. In such an environment, traditional marketing tools are no longer responsive to new challenges and opportunities. The need to evolve approaches and use emerging technologies is felt more than ever.

Cognitive AI, with its ability to understand context, analyze intent, and predict consumer behavior, has opened up new horizons in digital interaction. This technology not only analyzes data, but is also able to identify hidden patterns and allow marketers to create a unique, tailored, and more human experience in real time. Focusing on engagement, not just advertising, is the essence of this approach; and cognitive AI plays a role as a bridge between data and emotion.

This book is an attempt to answer questions that have occupied the minds of many marketing professionals, researchers, and business owners: How can we increase consumer engagement in the digital space? How can we turn data into insights and insights into action? And finally, how can we use cognitive AI to create an authentic, empathetic, and effective experience for the audience?

It is hoped that this book can be a useful, inspiring, and practical guide for all those who are on the path to reinventing the consumer experience in the digital age. Reading this work is not just a conceptual review, but an invitation to rethink the nature of human interaction in today's technology-driven world.

Hamed Nozari
Bio10, Dubai, UAE

Sepideh Samadi
Heriot-Watt University, UAE

Stavroula Kalogeras
Heriot-Watt University, UAE

Chapter 1
AI-Powered Simulations for Experiential Marketing Education

Stavroula Kalogeras
Heriot-Watt University, Dubai, UAE

ABSTRACT

This study examines the role of AI-based simulators in experiential marketing education. By designing an interactive conceptual model, it is shown how the combination of intelligent algorithms with experiential learning theory can enhance student engagement, improve marketing decision analysis, and personalize the learning path. The benefits, challenges, and implementation dimensions of this technology are also analyzed, and suggestions are made for effective utilization in the higher education system.

1- INTRODUCTION

In today's fast-paced world, higher education is facing numerous challenges in adapting to technological developments and the expectations of a new generation of learners. One of the areas that needs innovation in educational methods more than any other is marketing education in business and management schools. Marketing education inherently requires experience, a real understanding of consumer behavior, market analysis, competitiveness, and ultimately the ability to make strategic decisions under uncertainty. However, most of the common methods in universities – such as theoretical lectures, case studies, and group presentations – are somewhat

DOI: 10.4018/979-8-3373-3775-3.ch001

distant from these needs and focus more on the transfer of explicit knowledge than the development of practical capabilities (Troy, 2025).

In such a context, experiential learning has been proposed as an effective approach in management and marketing education. This method is based on David Kolb's theory, which emphasizes that learning will be more effective when the learner is involved in the learning process through direct experience, intellectual reflection, conceptualization, and active experimentation. However, implementing experiential learning in marketing classrooms, especially on a large scale, is fraught with difficulties. Designing field projects, connecting with real markets, and providing opportunities for customer interaction require resources, time, and extensive coordination that are not practical for many educational institutions (Shrotri, Tiwari, Karthikeya, Ahmed, & Shukla, 2024).

In recent years, the emergence of intelligent technologies, especially artificial intelligence (AI), has provided a new perspective to overcome the limitations of traditional education. By utilizing capabilities such as natural language processing, reinforcement learning, and behavioral data analysis, AI can create interactive and dynamic educational environments in which learners can make their decisions in quasi-realistic conditions and observe and analyze their consequences in real time. In the meantime, AI-based marketing simulators have emerged as one of the most efficient tools for combining digital education and experiential learning (Nozari, Ghahremani-Nahr, & Szmelter-Jarosz, 2024).

Marketing simulators create a virtual space in which students play the role of marketing manager, market analyst, or brand manager and interact with a simulated market that includes intelligent customers, competitors, and environmental fluctuations by making decisions on key variables such as pricing, advertising budget, product development, and distribution. Unlike educational games or older systems, AI-based simulators use real or simulated data and use dynamic models to generate different scenarios based on student performance. This feature ensures that each student has a unique experience that matches their learning style (Chew & Gilani, 2024).

In this research, with the aim of examining the potential of this technology in the transformation of marketing education, a conceptual model for designing an AI-based marketing simulator is presented. This model is designed based on the connection of experiential learning theory with the architecture of AI algorithms and attempts to show how the combination of these two areas can be used to improve the level of learning, analysis, and strategic thinking of students. In addition, in this study, the advantages, capabilities, and challenges facing the implementation of such simulators have also been analyzed and evaluated to provide a comprehensive view of the theoretical and practical dimensions of the subject.

The necessity of addressing this issue is not only due to educational and technological needs, but also due to fundamental changes in the behavior and expectations of the new generation of students. Today's learners, who have grown up in a digital environment, are more inclined towards interactive, experience-based, and personalized learning. Therefore, rethinking marketing education methods and utilizing new technological tools is not a choice, but an inevitable necessity for universities and higher education institutions around the world.

In the following, this article first reviews the relevant literature and related theories, then introduces the conceptual model of the intelligent marketing simulator and explains the functioning of its components. Next, the advantages and challenges of implementing this approach are analyzed, and finally, with a discussion and conclusion, future directions for the development of this technology in marketing education will be outlined.

2- LITERATURE REVIEW

Marketing education has witnessed transformations in recent decades, stemming from fundamental changes in educational environments, new technologies, and the needs of a new generation of learners. Initially, marketing education was largely based on traditional methods such as lectures, case study analysis, and classroom presentations; methods that focused more on transferring theoretical knowledge than on improving analytical and decision-making skills (Movahed, Movahed, & Nozari, 2024). Although these methods were useful for initial understanding of concepts, they faced limitations in developing practical capabilities, creativity, and understanding the complexities of the real market.

In response to these limitations, new approaches such as experiential learning entered the field of marketing education. These approaches emphasize the active interaction of the learner with the learning environment and believe that effective learning is formed in the process of engaging with real problems, reflecting on experiences, and applying concepts (Aliahmadi, Nozari, Ghahremani-Nahr, & Szmelter-Jarosz, 2022). In these models, education is transformed from a passive to a participatory and interactive process, with the learner playing an active role in discovering and applying knowledge. Despite the effectiveness of this approach, its practical implementation, especially in academic environments, has been accompanied by challenges such as resource limitations, difficulty in designing real experiences, and inconsistency with the educational calendar (Mishra, Afaq, Mishra, & Mathur, 2025).

In this context, digital technologies, and in particular artificial intelligence, entered the education space as transformative tools. The application of artificial intelligence in education initially began in the form of intelligent learning systems, interactive chatbots, and learner performance analysis, but later it also included areas such as content personalization, learner behavior modeling, and the design of simulated environments (Nozari, Tavakkoli-Moghaddam, & Gharemani-Nahr, 2022). This technology has provided the ability to analyze a large volume of data, predict learning patterns, and generate adaptive scenarios for learners. For this reason, artificial intelligence gradually became a key tool in skill training such as marketing, which requires decision-making in dynamic conditions, interaction with real data, and multidimensional performance measurement.

One of the prominent applications of artificial intelligence in marketing education is the design of interactive marketing simulators. These simulators create an artificial but realistic environment in which learners can assume the role of marketing decision-makers, experience different scenarios, and observe and analyze the results of their choices. Studies have shown that the use of intelligent simulations in marketing classes increases participation, strengthens analytical skills, and significantly improves understanding of strategic marketing concepts (Zheng, Shen, Chen, Che, & Zhu, 2024). Unlike traditional educational software, these simulators use advanced machine learning algorithms to simulate market behavior, competitor reactions, and customer decisions. This feature makes the learning environment dynamic and adaptive to the learner's performance (Nozari & Edalatpanah, 2023).

Another advantage of this technology is the ability to personalize the learning path. Unlike static methods, in smart simulators, the difficulty level of scenarios, the type of feedback, and even the educational progress are adjusted based on the behavior and performance of the student in real time (Semwal et al., 2024). This level of adaptability is in line with new approaches to adaptive learning, which personalize the content and educational experience for each individual based on continuous analysis of learner data. Empirical evidence suggests that this type of learning significantly increases the effectiveness of education compared to traditional standardized models (More & Unnikrishnan, 2024).

Despite these advantages, a significant part of the literature has also examined the limitations and challenges of implementing these technologies in educational settings. Some studies have pointed to the high costs of developing AI-based simulators, which can be a barrier for educational institutions, especially in developing countries (Rahmaty & Nozari, 2023). Also, cultural and organizational barriers such as the resistance of some professors to accepting new technologies, the lack of technical knowledge in educational teams, and the lack of educational policies compatible with digital transformation are among the challenges highlighted in the literature (Dai, 2023).

In addition, some research has addressed ethical issues and data security. As intelligent simulators collect and analyze behavioral and performance data of students on a large scale, concerns have been raised about privacy, algorithmic transparency, and the possibility of automated bias in the analyses (Nozari, 2023). Solutions such as designing ethical frameworks, codes of conduct, and human oversight of the data analysis process are among the suggestions made to manage these challenges.

Overall, the literature review shows that the use of AI-based marketing simulators in marketing education is a novel and productive approach that can overcome many of the educational limitations of the past. However, the successful exploitation of this technology requires careful design, appropriate infrastructure, ongoing training of professors, and attention to ethical and technical requirements. There are also gaps in the literature, including the lack of coherent conceptual models for designing interactive simulators, the lack of long-term empirical studies, and the lack of integrated evaluation frameworks for analyzing the effectiveness of these technologies in the field of marketing learning. The present study seeks to fill part of this scientific gap by presenting a conceptual model and analyzing the practical dimensions and challenges of these simulators.

3- THEORETICAL FRAMEWORK

Marketing education has always sought ways to make the connection between theoretical knowledge and the complex realities of the market more tangible for students. In this regard, the Experiential Learning Theory, first proposed by David Kolb, provides a solid foundation for understanding the active learning process. This theory is based on the principle that effective learning occurs when an individual is engaged in a dynamic cycle through practical experience, intellectual reflection, abstract conceptualization, and active experimentation. In other words, students learn best when the experientialist plays a central role in the learning process.

In this regard, the emergence of new technologies, especially artificial intelligence, has provided unprecedented opportunities to redefine teaching and learning processes. Artificial intelligence, with capabilities such as Natural Language Processing (NLP), Reinforcement Learning, and Agent-Based Modeling, is able to create interactive and dynamic environments in which students find themselves within a real marketing scenario and actively participate in decision-making.

Combining experiential learning theory with the capabilities of artificial intelligence provides a platform in which marketing education is transformed from a traditional lecture-based and case-study-based mode to an immersive and interactive experience. In such an environment, intelligent simulators are able to dynamically play the roles of customers, competitors, the market, and even social media. This allows students to not only apply marketing concepts in practice, but also to observe and analyze the consequences of their decisions in real time.

In addition, artificial intelligence allows the simulator's difficulty level to be adjusted according to the student's performance. In other words, the training process is personalized for each individual and adjusted to their needs, abilities, and learning style. This feature not only increases the effectiveness of training, but also strengthens the students' sense of intrinsic motivation and cognitive engagement.

Finally, the theoretical framework of this research is based on the link between experiential learning and artificial intelligence technologies. This approach believes that the use of intelligent simulators can transform the marketing learning process into a meaningful, dynamic experience that is in line with the developments of the digital age.

4- CONCEPTUAL MODEL OF ARTIFICIAL INTELLIGENCE-BASED MARKETING SIMULATORS

With the developments that have emerged in the field of artificial intelligence in the last decade, new opportunities have been provided in higher education, especially in applied fields such as marketing. One of these opportunities is the design of advanced simulators that can play a substitute role for real market experience and recreate the decision-making environment in real market conditions for students. These simulators operate based on a conceptual model in which the interaction between the learner, artificial intelligence, the simulated market environment, and the intelligent feedback system is designed in a cyclical and dynamic manner.

In this model, the student plays the main role and acts as a decision maker in the marketing space. He can make decisions on various elements of the marketing mix such as price, product, distribution and advertising. These decisions are processed in the simulation engine and the results are reflected in the virtual market environment which is composed of complex factors such as consumer behavior, competitors, environmental fluctuations and economic conditions. The artificial intelligence system used in this process not only helps in simulating the market but also uses reinforcement learning algorithms and natural language processing to analyze decisions, identify patterns and provide personalized feedback to the student.

As can be seen in Figure 1, the conceptual model consists of five key components that work in interaction with each other. These components include the student decision-making input, the AI-based simulation engine, the virtual market, the intelligent feedback system and the educational analytics dashboard. Each of these components plays a specific role in the experiential learning process and ultimately leads to deeper learning of marketing concepts in an interactive and data-driven environment.

Figure 1. Conceptual model of an AI-based marketing simulator

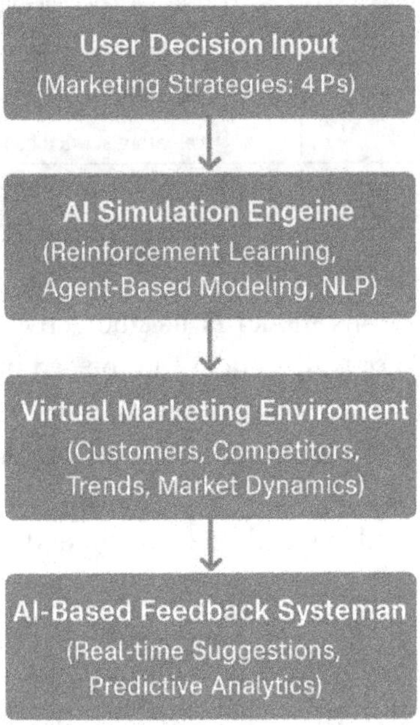

In this model, the simulation engine plays the role of the brain of the system. This engine analyzes the student's input data and simulates the market reaction based on a series of dynamic rules that are developed in a self-learning and intelligent manner. These reactions are manifested in the form of changes in sales volume, market share, brand awareness, competitor behavior, and even emotional changes in customers to the decisions made. In order to evaluate the effects of decisions, analytical and explanatory feedback is provided to the student, which can include visual reports, analytical predictions, and optimization suggestions.

Along with this structure, Table 1 shows some of the key variables and indicators that can be viewed in the AI dashboard. In addition to displaying the student's performance in different scenarios, this dashboard provides users with the possibility of trend, comparative, and cause-and effect analysis. Such a level of analysis takes the student to a higher level of understanding of marketing concepts and helps them strengthen their strategic decision-making and analytical thinking skills.

Table 1. Performance indicators in the AI-based marketing simulator dashboard

KPI	Unit	Analytical Purpose in Learning
Market Share	%	Analyzing effectiveness of pricing and competitive positioning
Return on Investment	%	Assessing efficiency of marketing investments
Customer Churn Rate	%	Evaluating service quality and customer retention
Brand Awareness Index	Composite Score	Measuring the impact of communication and advertising efforts

The important point of this model is its interactive and personalized nature. In many traditional simulators, all students are placed in uniform conditions with predetermined scenarios; but in smart simulators, the level of difficulty, the type of market reaction, and even the speed of change are adjusted based on the performance and decision-making style of each student. This flexibility increases the cognitive engagement of students with the content and improves the effectiveness of the training process.

In summary, the presented conceptual model not only enables the implementation of experiential marketing training in a safe and risk-free environment, but also transforms learning from a passive state into an active, data-driven, and dynamic experience by using the analytical and predictive power of artificial intelligence. Such a structure can chart a new path for designing marketing training courses in the digital age.

5- ADVANTAGES AND CHALLENGES OF USING AI-BASED MARKETING SIMULATORS

The use of intelligent simulators in marketing education is an innovative and transformative approach that can overcome many of the limitations of traditional educational methods. This approach, relying on modern technologies, especially artificial intelligence, is able to create a dynamic, interactive, and data-driven environment for learning. However, the implementation and use of such simulators also comes with challenges that require careful examination and analysis. In this section, the most important advantages and challenges of this approach are discussed in detail.

The first and perhaps most important advantage of these simulators is the creation of a learning environment based on real experience. Unlike common methods such as theoretical teaching, slide presentations and case studies, in AI-based simulators, the student is placed in a real decision-making situation and sees the consequences of his decisions in the form of dynamic results. This practical experience activates critical thinking, strengthens decision-making ability and deepens the student's understanding of key marketing concepts. In fact, the student is not only involved in learning concepts, but also faces real challenges such as unexpected market reactions, competitive pressure, resource constraints and complex consumer behavior (Nozari, Ghahremani-Nahr, & Najafi, 2023).

The second significant advantage of this technology is the possibility of personalizing the education process. Through machine learning capabilities, these simulators are able to analyze the student's behavioral patterns and adjust educational scenarios according to his abilities, academic background and learning style. For example, if a student is strong in pricing decisions but weak in advertising, the simulator will gradually design scenarios focused on advertising to strengthen his or her weaknesses. This level of adaptability increases intrinsic motivation, active participation, and reduces burnout rates in students.

Other notable benefits include analytics and providing intelligent and real-time feedback. In these simulators, unlike traditional systems where feedback is usually provided at the end of the educational activity and in general, students see the analysis of the results of their decisions in real time and accurately. This feedback usually includes indicators such as return on investment, market share, customer retention rate, and brand awareness, which are displayed in the form of graphs and analytical reports. This feature enhances learning not only at the cognitive level, but also at the practical and analytical level.

However, implementing such simulators comes with challenges, some of which are rooted in the nature of technology and others in educational structures. One of the important challenges is the high cost of developing and implementing intelligent educational systems. Designing a simulation engine that has the ability to analyze decisions, simulate market behavior, and provide intelligent feedback requires significant financial, specialized, and infrastructure resources. This may be a serious obstacle to the widespread use of this technology, especially for educational institutions in developing countries.

Another challenge is the resistance of some teachers and educational administrators to the adoption of new technologies. In many traditional educational systems, technological approaches are seen as a threat to the role of the teacher. However, such technologies not only do not replace the teacher, but can also strengthen his role as a facilitator of learning and an analyst of the educational process. Creating a technological culture, training teachers and raising awareness about the benefits of smart simulators are essential steps to overcome this resistance (Niyozov, Saburov, Ganiyev, & Olimov, 2023).

Another important point to consider is the ethical issues and transparency in data analysis. Since simulators collect, analyze, and store student performance data, it is important to observe ethical principles in the use of data, maintain privacy, and prevent algorithmic bias. If appropriate monitoring and security mechanisms are not designed, student trust in the system may be undermined and the learning experience may be weakened.

Finally, it should not be forgotten that although AI-based simulators have extraordinary capabilities, they are impossible to completely replace field experience. In other words, these technologies should be used as a powerful complement to other methods of marketing education, not an absolute replacement. Designing hybrid models that use digital and field learning capacities synergistically can guide marketing education towards greater quality, depth, and effectiveness.

6- DISCUSSION

The conceptual and analytical findings presented in this study indicate that the use of AI-based marketing simulators can change the trajectory of marketing education from a traditional and static approach to an interactive, personalized, and data-driven model. This transformation is not only in line with the educational needs of a new generation of students, but also with technological developments and the requirements of the labor market in the digital age.

The conceptual model presented in this paper provides a coherent and applicable structure for designing an intelligent learning environment in which the interaction between the learner, the AI system, the simulated market environment, and the immediate feedback mechanism is organized into a dynamic and continuous cycle. This cycle not only strengthens students' practical skills in the field of marketing, but also increases their capacity to analyze data, understand customer behavioral trends, and make strategic decisions.

On the other hand, one point that became clear during the research is the key role of AI in adapting the educational process to the individual needs of students. While traditional educational systems often have a uniform and convergent approach, intelligent simulators, relying on machine learning algorithms, can adjust the learning path based on the performance, preferences, and strengths and weaknesses of each student. This feature enables a type of adaptive learning that can lead to significant improvements in learning outcomes.

At the same time, the analysis of the challenges showed that the practical realization of this model requires several groundwork. Among the most important of them, we can mention the need for technological infrastructure, training and empowerment of professors, and management of organizational resistance to digital changes. Without considering these factors, even if the theoretical model is very powerful and forward-looking, it will not be possible to successfully exploit it in real school environments.

From a comparative perspective, it can be said that the smart simulator model is several steps ahead of other modern marketing education methods such as case studies, management games, or real projects. The reason for this superiority lies in three basic features: first, the possibility of experiencing complex and risky scenarios without facing real consequences; second, the ability to analyze multidimensional student performance data in real time; and third, the model's ability to simulate human and market behaviors based on real or simulated data using artificial intelligence.

Also, it is worth noting the potential for interdisciplinary development of this model in other areas of business education. The presented simulator structure is not limited to marketing, but can also be implemented in strategic management education, consumer behavior, innovation, and even entrepreneurship. This shows that the future horizons of this research can be much broader than the limited field of marketing and can be proposed as a comprehensive model in the design of intelligent education systems in 21st century universities.

In conclusion, it can be said that the link between experiential learning theories, artificial intelligence technologies, and the interactive structure of simulators is a new starting point for the transformation of marketing education. Although its implementation path is accompanied by obstacles, with careful planning, investment in infrastructure, and human capital empowerment, its significant benefits can be enjoyed in order to improve the quality and effectiveness of education.

7- CONCLUSIONS AND SUGGESTIONS

The present study aimed to investigate the role and function of AI-based simulators in marketing education and to present a conceptual model for their implementation. The findings of this study showed that combining AI with experiential learning principles provides a unique opportunity for transformation in marketing education. In this model, instead of playing a passive role in traditional classes, students are placed in real decision-making positions and can test their marketing strategies in a simulated environment with real market conditions and receive instant feedback. This experience deepens learning, strengthens analysis and decision-making skills, and improves learners' self-confidence.

The conceptual model designed in this study forms a complete and dynamic learning cycle by utilizing an intelligent simulation engine, a virtual market environment, an analytical feedback system, and a learning dashboard. This cycle is designed to provide a personalized learning process for each student, continuously analyze their performance, and guide them towards deeper learning through intelligent feedback. Such a model is not only compatible with the educational needs of the new generation, but also responds to technological developments and professional requirements of the labor market.

However, the results of the discussions and analyses showed that the use of this model also faces challenges. The cost of designing and implementing such systems, the need for advanced technology infrastructure, training and empowering professors, and dealing with cultural resistance to educational changes are among the obstacles that need to be considered in planning. Also, issues related to ethics in artificial intelligence, protecting student data, and transparency of algorithms are among the challenges that should not be overlooked.

Accordingly, the following suggestions are presented for researchers, educational policymakers, and universities:

- Targeted investment in technological infrastructure in order to develop and implement advanced educational simulators, especially in applied fields such as marketing;
- Designing educational programs to empower professors in using modern teaching-learning technologies and changing their approach from instructor to facilitator;
- Establishing clear ethical and legal frameworks for managing student data, ensuring algorithmic fairness, and preventing bias in simulations;
- Encouraging empirical research in academic settings to test the impact of intelligent simulators on student learning performance compared to traditional methods;
- Expanding the application of this model to other management subjects, such as entrepreneurship, organizational behavior, and strategy, in order to more comprehensively exploit the capabilities of AI in education.

Finally, it should be emphasized that AI-based marketing simulators should not be seen as a complete replacement for field experience, but as a powerful complement to the higher education system. This technology allows for the structuring of learning through data, experience, and analytics, and can play an important role in preparing the next generation of marketing professionals to face the complexities and uncertainties of the real world.

REFERENCES

Aliahmadi, A., Nozari, H., Ghahremani-Nahr, J., & Szmelter-Jarosz, A. (2022). Evaluation of key impression of resilient supply chain based on artificial intelligence of things (AIoT). *arXiv preprint arXiv:2207.13174*.

Chew, P., & Gilani, H. (2024). Artificial Intelligence in Marketing Education. In *Decolonizing Marketing Theory and Practice* (pp. 218–236). Routledge. DOI: 10.4324/9781032698083-15

Dai, C. P. (2023). *Enhancing learning achievements and self-efficacy for preservice teachers using model-based support in simulation-based learning with artificial intelligence-powered virtual agents*. The Florida State University.

Mishra, S., Afaq, A., Mishra, T. K., & Mathur, N. (2025). Integrating Generative AI-Driven Learning Programs to Enhance Marketing Skills. In *Generative Artificial Intelligence and Ethics: Standards, Guidelines, and Best Practices* (pp. 189-226). IGI Global.

More, A., & Unnikrishnan, R. (2024). AI-Powered Analytics in Product Marketing Optimizing Customer Experience and Market Segmentation. *Journal Of Multidisciplinary*, *4*(11), 12–19.

Movahed, A. B., Movahed, A. B., & Nozari, H. (2024). Opportunities and challenges of smart supply chain in Industry 5.0. *Information Logistics for Organizational Empowerment and Effective Supply Chain Management*, 108-138.

Niyozov, N., Saburov, S., Ganiyev, S., & Olimov, S. (2023). AI-powered learning: revolutionizing technical higher education institutions through advanced power supply fundamentals. In *E3S Web of Conferences* (Vol. 461, p. 01092). EDP Sciences. DOI: 10.1051/e3sconf/202346101092

Nozari, H. (Ed.). (2023). *Building Smart and Sustainable Businesses with Transformative Technologies*. IGI Global. DOI: 10.4018/979-8-3693-0210-1

Nozari, H., & Edalatpanah, S. A. (2023). Smart systems risk management in IoT based supply chain. In *Advances in reliability, failure and risk analysis* (pp. 251–268). Springer Nature Singapore. DOI: 10.1007/978-981-19-9909-3_11

Nozari, H., Ghahremani-Nahr, J., & Najafi, E. (2023). The role of Internet of things and Blockchain in the development of agile and sustainable supply chains. In *Digital Supply Chain, Disruptive Environments, and the Impact on Retailers* (pp. 271-282). IGI Global. DOI: 10.4018/978-1-6684-7298-9.ch015

Nozari, H., Ghahremani-Nahr, J., & Szmelter-Jarosz, A. (2024). AI and machine learning for real-world problems. [). Elsevier.]. *Advances in Computers*, *134*, 1–12. DOI: 10.1016/bs.adcom.2023.02.001

Nozari, H., Tavakkoli-Moghaddam, R., & Gharemani-Nahr, J. (2022). A neutrosophic fuzzy programming method to solve a multi-depot vehicle routing model under uncertainty during the covid-19 pandemic. *International Journal of Engineering*, *35*(2), 360–371.

Rahmaty, M., & Nozari, H. (2023). Optimization of the hierarchical supply chain in the pharmaceutical industry. *Edelweiss Applied Science and Technology*, *7*(2), 104–123. DOI: 10.55214/25768484.v7i2.376

Semwal, R., Tripathi, N., Rana, A., Dafouti, B. S., Bairwa, M. K., & Mathur, V. (2024, May). AI-Powered Personalization and Emotional Intelligence Integration for Enhanced Service Marketing in Transformative Tourism Experiences. In *2024 International Conference on Communication, Computer Sciences and Engineering (IC3SE)* (pp. 1851-1856). IEEE. DOI: 10.1109/IC3SE62002.2024.10592909

Shrotri, N. V., Tiwari, A., Karthikeya, E., Ahmed, S., & Shukla, P. (2024, December). Effective Use of AI Tools for Engineering and Management Education for Experiential Learning. In *2024 IEEE International Conference on Teaching, Assessment and Learning for Engineering (TALE)* (pp. 1-7). IEEE. DOI: 10.1109/TALE62452.2024.10834327

Troy, L. C. (2025). Enhancing Marketing Student Success with AI-Guided Experiential Learning: A Case Study.

Zheng, K., Shen, Z., Chen, Z., Che, C., & Zhu, H. (2024). Application of AI-empowered scenario-based simulation teaching mode in cardiovascular disease education. *BMC Medical Education*, *24*(1), 1003. DOI: 10.1186/s12909-024-05977-z PMID: 39272041

Chapter 2
Adaptive Neuromarketing Through AIoE

Sepideh Samadi
https://orcid.org/0000-0002-1689-5596
Heriot-Watt University, Dubai, UAE

ABSTRACT

This research investigates and evaluates an adaptive neural marketing system based on ubiquitous artificial intelligence (AIoE). The proposed system uses biometric, behavioral, and environmental data to identify users' emotions and adapt marketing content in real time. The results showed that the system is able to identify users' emotions with high accuracy and significantly increase users' engagement with personalized content. This research shows that AIoE can lead to improved performance of personalized marketing systems.

1- INTRODUCTION

In recent decades, the rapid growth of digital technologies and artificial intelligence has dramatically transformed marketing practices. Digital marketing, once limited to displaying simple advertisements on websites and social networks, has now evolved into a complex and multidimensional approach that includes user data analysis, content personalization, and the use of advanced artificial intelligence algorithms (Lee, Broderick, & Chamberlain, 2007). One such new approach is neuromarketing, which studies and analyzes users' emotional and cognitive responses to marketing content. Using biometric data such as heart rate, electrical skin activity, and facial expressions, neuromarketing can help identify users' emotions and tailor

DOI: 10.4018/979-8-3373-3775-3.ch002

marketing content accordingly (Duque-Hurtado, Samboni-Rodriguez, Castro-Garcia, Montoya-Restrepo, & Montoya-Restrepo, 2020).

With the advent of Artificial Intelligence of Everything (AIoE), it is possible to use more diverse and comprehensive data to analyze user behavior. AIoE refers to a set of intelligent technologies that can seamlessly interact with various devices and systems and collect and analyze a variety of data, including biometric, behavioral, environmental, and textual data (Movahed, Movahed, & Nozari, 2024). By connecting smart devices, sensors, and data processing systems to a single network, this technology enables the collection and analysis of user information in real time. In the meantime, AIoE-based adaptive neuromarketing has been proposed as a new approach that can change marketing content in real time based on users' emotions and reactions (Mileti, Guido, & Prete, 2016).

Neuromarketing has traditionally relied on analyzing users' biometric data, such as heart rate, electrical skin activity, and facial expressions. This data can provide important information about users' emotional states. For example, increased heart rate and electrical skin activity are commonly interpreted as signs of excitement or stress, while calmness and decreased electrical skin activity may indicate a state of relaxation (Nozari, Irani, & Rahmaty, 2023). Using this data, marketing systems can tailor the content displayed to users based on their emotions and improve the user experience. However, several challenges have always been raised, such as accurate emotion recognition, complex data analysis, and user privacy (Nozari, Szmelter-Jarosz, & Ghahremani-Nahr, 2021).

Artificial Intelligence of Everything (AIoE) can help address these challenges by combining intelligent technologies and connecting different devices into a single network. This technology allows for the collection and analysis of diverse data from different sources simultaneously. For example, an AIoE-based neural marketing system can simultaneously collect and analyze users' biometric data (such as heart rate), behavioral data (such as clicks and content viewing time), and environmental data (such as temperature and light) (Ariely & Berns, 2010). This multidimensional analysis can help the system more accurately identify users' emotions and dynamically adapt marketing content in a personalized way.

Previous studies have shown that the use of adaptive marketing systems can lead to increased user engagement with marketing content (Nozari & Samadi, 2025). For example, one study found that AI-based marketing systems can increase user engagement with video content by 30% by analyzing users' emotions (Nozari, 2025). Another study found that the use of biometric data such as heart rate and electrical skin activity can help improve the accuracy of user emotion recognition by up to 85% (Meshrarm & Bekouni, 2021). These findings suggest that combining biometric data and artificial intelligence can lead to improved performance of marketing systems.

However, many current neuromarketing systems rely only on analyzing users' biometric data and neglect users' environmental and behavioral data. This can reduce the accuracy of sentiment analysis and content personalization. In contrast, the use of AIoE can overcome this limitation and allow the system to use diverse data to analyze users' sentiments. The AIoE-based adaptive neuromarketing system introduced in this study, by combining biometric, behavioral, and environmental data, is able to identify users' sentiments more accurately and dynamically adapt marketing content in real time.

This study investigates and evaluates the effectiveness of this adaptive system, and the results show that the proposed system can effectively identify users' sentiments and change marketing content according to these sentiments. The results of this study not only help to clarify the capabilities of artificial intelligence in identifying users' sentiments, but also can help to develop personalized marketing systems in various industries. In particular, this approach can also be used in other areas such as education, healthcare, and customer service, where personalized interactions are of great importance.

2- LITERATURE REVIEW

Neuromarketing, as a new branch of marketing, uses biometric data and cognitive science to analyze and understand consumer behavior. This approach, with the help of advanced technologies such as biometric sensors, facial recognition cameras, and EEG devices, can examine users' emotional and cognitive responses to marketing content (Nozari, Abdi, & Rafiei, 2025). Numerous studies have shown that biometric data such as heart rate, electrical skin response (ESR), and facial expression can effectively identify users' emotions and predict their reactions to advertising content (Ulman, Cakar, & Yildiz, 2015).

One of the first applications of neuromarketing was the use of EEG devices to examine users' brain activity while viewing advertisements. This method allowed researchers to directly measure users' cognitive responses and gain a better understanding of the emotional effects of advertising content (Movahed, Movahed, & Nozari, 2024). For example, increased alpha brainwave activity has been shown to indicate a user's state of relaxation, while increased beta brainwave activity can indicate excitement or increased focus (Fugate, 2008).

In addition to EEG data, the use of biometric data such as heart rate and electrical skin activity have also been proposed as effective methods of emotion detection. Heart rate is known to be an indicator of excitement and stress, and changes in it can indicate a user's emotional reactions to content (Irani & Nozari, 2024). Electrical skin response (GSR) has also been used as an indicator of physiological responses to emotional stimuli. This data can be collected and analyzed in real time, allowing marketing systems to adapt the content displayed based on users' reactions (Javor, Koller, Lee, Chamberlain, & Ransmayr, 2013).

In recent years, with the advancement of artificial intelligence, the use of deep learning and natural language processing (NLP) algorithms in neuromarketing has received widespread attention. Deep learning allows systems to automatically analyze complex biometric data such as facial images or biometric signals (Najafi, Nozari, & Edalatpanah, 2022). For example, convolutional neural network (CNN) models are able to identify different facial expressions such as happiness, sadness, surprise, and anger. On the other hand, recurrent neural networks (RNN) can analyze continuous signals such as heart rate and identify patterns related to users' emotions (Ait Hammou, Galib, & Melloul, 2013).

One of the main challenges of neuromarketing systems is the accuracy of identifying users' emotions. Studies have shown that using biometric data alone may not be accurate enough, especially when complex emotions such as a combination of happiness and sadness are simultaneously evoked in the user (Nozari & Chobar, 2024). To address this challenge, researchers have proposed using a combination of biometric and behavioral data to improve the accuracy of emotion analysis. For example, combining heart rate data, electrical skin activity, and facial analysis can improve the accuracy of emotion recognition by up to 90% (Bercea, 2012).

In the meantime, artificial intelligence of all kinds (AIoE) has been proposed as a new approach that can help improve the performance of neural marketing systems. AIoE refers to a set of intelligent technologies that seamlessly connect to various devices and systems and enable the collection and analysis of diverse data (Abdi & Nozari, 2025). This technology can collect biometric, behavioral, and environmental data simultaneously, allowing marketing systems to analyze users' reactions more accurately. For example, an AIoE-based neural marketing system can simultaneously analyze a user's heart rate, facial expression, ambient temperature, and light level and adapt marketing content based on this data (Nozari, Szmelter-Jarosz, & Rahmaty, 2024).

Several studies have investigated the effectiveness of AIoE-based adaptive marketing systems. In one such study, it was found that the use of AIoE can lead to increased user engagement with marketing content. For example, one study showed that AIoE-based marketing systems can increase click-through rates (CTR) by up to 40% by analyzing users' emotions (Alsharif, Salleh, Abdullah, Khraiwish, & Ashaari, 2023). This increased engagement is due to the system's ability to personalize content based on users' emotions and display content relevant to their emotional state.

Another important aspect of AIoE in neuromarketing is the ability to use environmental data to improve the user experience. For example, an AIoE-based marketing system can measure ambient temperature, light, and sound levels in real time and adjust marketing content based on this data. For example, in a dimly lit environment, the system can display content with higher brightness and clearer text to improve the user experience (Kalogeras, 2025). This approach not only helps to improve the accuracy of emotion recognition, but also can improve the user experience.

However, there are also several challenges in using AIoE in neuromarketing. First, the issue of user privacy is one of the fundamental challenges of this approach. The collection and analysis of users' biometric and behavioral data can raise concerns about their privacy (Garcia & Saad, 2008). To overcome this challenge, the use of data encryption techniques, federated learning, and data processing in an anonymous manner has been proposed (Alsharif, Salleh, Baharun, & Safaei, 2020). Second, the complexity of analyzing biometric and environmental data can also be a serious challenge for neuromarketing systems. These systems must be able to analyze diverse data in real time and display appropriate content (Nozari, Rahmaty, & Szmelter-Jarosz, 2024).

Finally, studies have shown that the combination of AIoE and neuromarketing can lead to the creation of adaptive marketing systems with high accuracy and dynamic personalization capabilities. These systems can help improve user experience and increase user engagement with marketing content (Kumar & Singh, 2015). This research aims to develop and evaluate an AIoE-based adaptive neural marketing system that attempts to improve the accuracy and efficiency of marketing systems by combining biometric, behavioral, and environmental data.

3- CONCEPTUAL FRAMEWORK

The conceptual framework of this research is based on the combination of Adaptive Neuromarketing and Artificial Intelligence of Everything (AIoE). This framework shows how the proposed system is able to dynamically and personalized adjust and optimize marketing interactions using biometric, behavioral, and environmental data. The framework consists of four main modules that operate in continuous interaction with each other: data collection, data analysis, decision making, and content presentation. These relationships are shown in Figure 1.

Figure 1. Conceptual framework of AIoE-based adaptive neuromarketing system

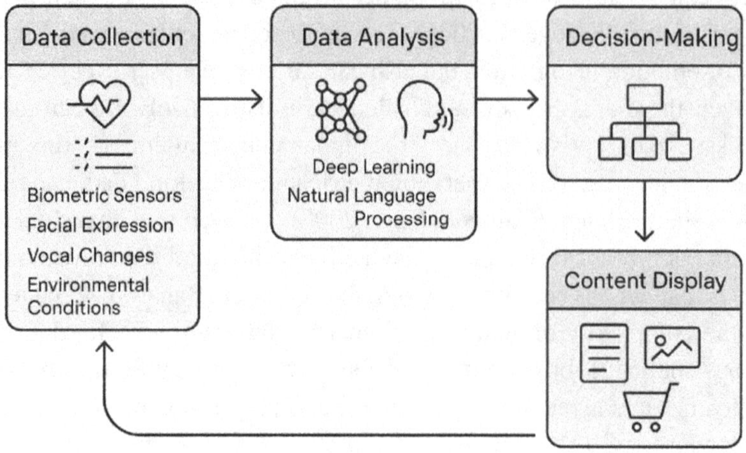

The data collection module uses biometric sensors (such as wearable devices, facial recognition cameras, and smart microphones). These sensors are capable of collecting various information, including heart rate, electrical skin activity, facial expression, voice changes, and even environmental conditions (such as temperature and light). This data is transmitted to the system in real time and provides the necessary information base for analyzing user behavior.

In the data analysis module, the system analyzes the collected information using deep learning and natural language processing algorithms. These algorithms are capable of identifying the user's emotions by analyzing biometric signals and examining the tone and content of their speech. For example, changes in heart rate or electrical skin activity can be interpreted as signs of the user's stress or excitement. The system can also use recurrent neural network (RNN) models to sequentially analyze this data and better understand the user's reactions.

In the decision-making module, the results of data analysis are transferred to an intelligent decision-making system. This system automatically selects appropriate marketing content based on the user's reactions and environmental conditions. For example, if the user shows a state of excitement or satisfaction, the system can display relevant shopping suggestions or advertising content. Conversely, if signs of fatigue or discomfort are detected, the system can provide more relaxing suggestions, such as music or educational content.

In the content display module, the user is presented with tailored content. This content can include text, images, video, or even purchase suggestions. Using AIoE technology, the system can dynamically change the displayed content. For example, in a video ad, the system can change the sound, image, or even the text of the video to match the user's emotional state.

This conceptual framework enables users to be presented with a fully personalized and real-time experience by creating a closed loop of data collection, analysis, decision-making, and content display. It can also be extended to other areas such as education, healthcare, and customer service, as it can continuously learn from new data and improve its performance.

4- RESEARCH METHODOLOGY

This study was designed and implemented to investigate the effectiveness of an adaptive neural marketing system based on ubiquitous artificial intelligence (AIoE). The system was developed to provide personalized and dynamic marketing content to users and its performance was evaluated in a controlled laboratory environment. The research methodology of this study was designed in such a way that all steps, from the collection of biometric and behavioral data to data analysis and display of marketing content, were carefully examined and documented. The steps of this research methodology are schematically shown in Figure 2.

Figure 2. Research method process

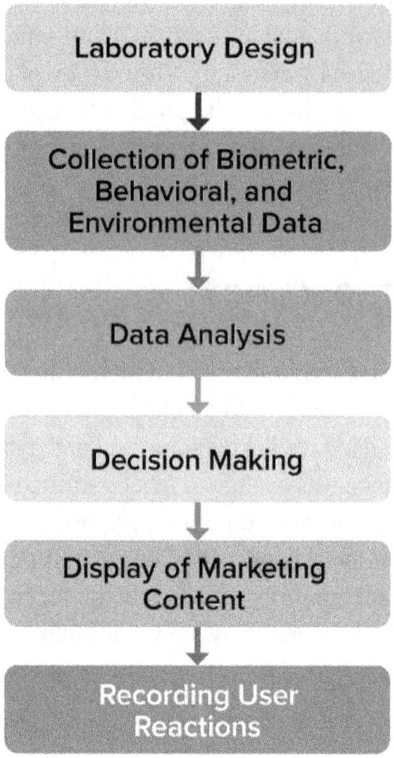

This study is designed as a laboratory experiment, which includes a sample of 100 digital users with a variety of age, gender, and digital usage histories. These users are randomly selected to represent a wide range of user behaviors. The laboratory environment of this study includes wearable devices for biometric measurement, facial recognition cameras, smart microphones, and advertising displays connected to an adaptive neural marketing system. These devices allow for the collection of a variety of biometric, behavioral, and environmental data.

The collected data includes three main categories. First, biometric data, which includes users' heart rate, electrical skin activity, facial expressions, voice changes, and eye movements. This data is recorded in real time using advanced sensors and wearable devices and is used as input to the system. Second, behavioral data, which includes clicks, content viewing time, and user interaction responses such as likes or comments. This data helps the system to analyze user reactions to the displayed content. Third, environmental data, which includes information such as temperature, lighting, and environmental conditions, helps to better analyze user reactions.

In the data analysis phase, the system uses deep learning and natural language processing algorithms to identify user emotions and behaviors. First, biometric data is preprocessed to remove noise and possible anomalies. Then, features related to user emotions, such as increased heart rate or changes in skin electrical activity, are extracted. These features are used as input to deep learning models, including convolutional neural networks (CNN) for analyzing facial images and recurrent neural networks (RNN) for analyzing continuous signals such as heart rate. Also, to analyze users' verbal emotions, natural language processing techniques are used and the tone and content of their speech are examined.

The results of the data analysis are transmitted to an intelligent decision-making system that uses a combination of a rule-based system and reinforcement learning to select the best marketing content for each user. This system is able to display appropriate content in real time based on the user's emotional reactions. For example, if the user shows signs of excitement or satisfaction, the system displays advertising content with special offers. Conversely, if signs of fatigue or discomfort are detected, the system can provide more relaxing content such as music or educational content.

The selected content is displayed to the user and their reaction to this content (such as viewing time, clicks, and interactions) is automatically recorded. These reactions are returned to the system as feedback data and used to improve the analysis and decision-making models. This process allows the system to improve its accuracy in identifying emotions and tailoring marketing content over time, using more data.

To assess the effectiveness of the system, several key metrics were examined. First, the accuracy of the system in correctly identifying users' emotions based on biometric data was examined. Also, the increase in user engagement with personalized content was measured compared to static content. This comparison shows that thc proposcd systcm is ablc to improvc uscr cngagcmcnt. In addition, thc dcgrcc of content personalization was also evaluated, meaning the extent to which the displayed content matched the users' emotions and reactions.

Finally, the user experience of the system has also been examined. Users have voluntarily provided feedback on their experience using the system. This feedback has shown that most users had a positive and interactive experience and found the displayed content to be in line with their emotions.

5- RESULTS

This study aimed to investigate the effectiveness of an adaptive neural marketing system based on AIoE. The results of the system implementation and the analysis of the collected data show that the system is able to effectively identify users' emotions and display marketing content dynamically and personalized. This section presents the key findings of the study, including the system's accuracy in identifying emotions, the level of user interaction with the adapted content, and the user feedback on the experience of using the system.

First, the system's accuracy in identifying users' emotions was investigated. As shown in Figure 3, the system was able to identify different emotions of users with high accuracy by using deep learning and natural language processing (NLP) algorithms. Specifically, the analysis of biometric data including heart rate, electrical skin activity, and facial expression showed that the system is able to accurately identify emotional states such as happiness, sadness, excitement, and fatigue. The system's accuracy in identifying emotions ranged from 85 to 92 percent, depending on the type of data and testing conditions.

Figure 3. Emotion detection accuracy

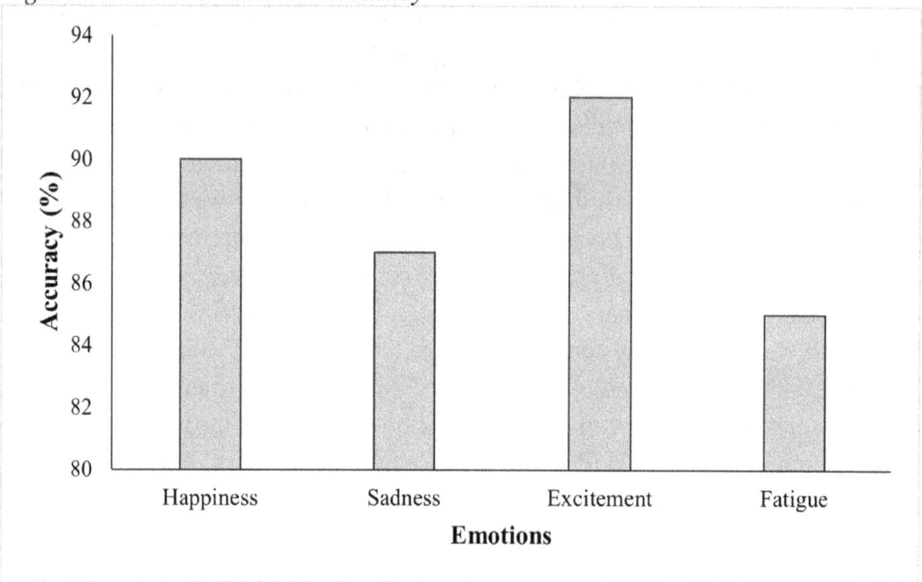

Next, the level of user engagement with the adapted content was examined. As can be seen in Figure 4, the system was able to display appropriate marketing content based on the emotional reactions of the users. A comparison between the experimental group (which used the adaptive system) and the control group (which viewed static content) showed that the level of user engagement was significantly higher in the experimental group. The click-through rate (CTR) in the experimental group was 38 percent, while in the control group it was only 27 percent.

Figure 4. Comparison of click-through rate

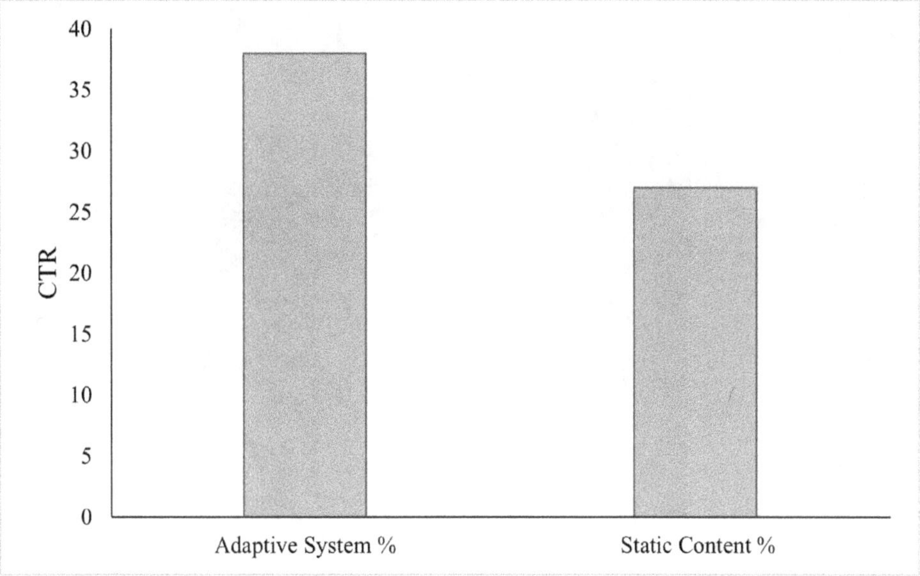

Additionally, the duration of content viewing by users was also examined. As shown in Figure 5, users in the experimental group viewed the adapted content for an average of 75 seconds, while this duration was only 57 seconds for users in the control group. These findings indicate the positive impact of the adaptive system on increasing user attention and engagement.

Figure 5. Average view time comparison

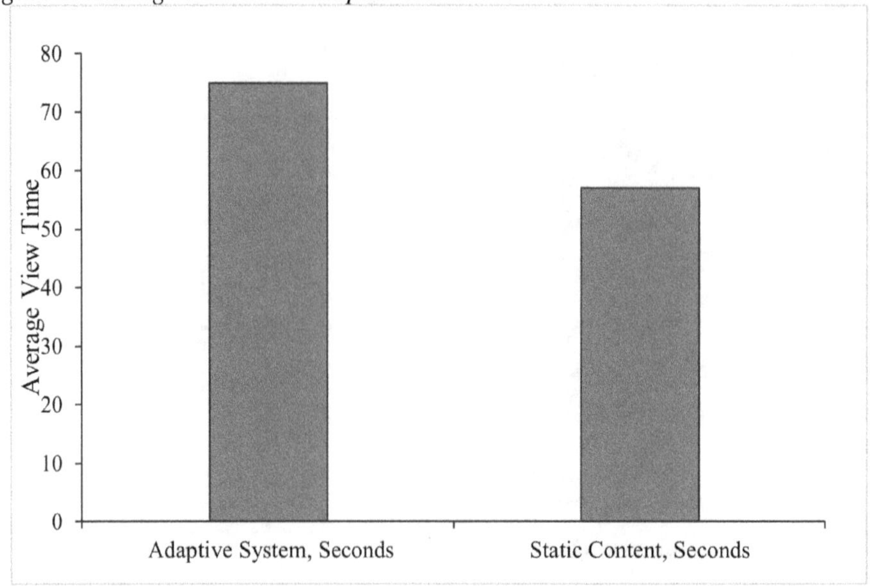

User feedback was also collected and analyzed qualitatively. Users voluntarily provided their opinions about their experience using the system. The feedback showed that most users rated the experience of using the system positively and stated that the content displayed was close to their emotions. Some users mentioned the system's ability to quickly adapt content to their emotional state, while a small number of users mentioned cases of inaccuracy in recognizing emotions. This feedback is presented in Table 1.

Table 1. User Feedback on Adaptive System

User Feedback
Positive experience, felt the content matched emotions.
Impressed with the system's ability to adapt content.
Found the system engaging and relevant.
Noted a few inaccuracies in emotion recognition.

These results clearly show that the AIoE-based adaptive neuromarketing system is not only capable of identifying user emotions with high accuracy, but also can improve user experience and increase user engagement with marketing content.

6- DISCUSSION AND ANALYSIS

This research aimed to develop and evaluate an adaptive neural marketing system based on Artificial Intelligence of All-Around (AIoE). The results of this research show that this system is capable of accurately identifying users' emotions and adapting marketing content to these emotions. In this section, the results obtained are analyzed and compared with the findings of previous studies. Also, challenges, limitations, and future opportunities for improving this system are discussed.

One of the important findings of this research was the high accuracy of the system in identifying users' emotions based on biometric data. Using deep learning and natural language processing (NLP) algorithms, the system was able to identify emotional states such as happiness, sadness, excitement, and fatigue with an accuracy of between 85 and 92 percent. This high accuracy shows that the models used in biometric data analysis, including convolutional neural networks (CNN) and recurrent neural networks (RNN), are effectively capable of analyzing complex data. This finding is consistent with previous studies that have shown that using deep learning can significantly increase the accuracy of sentiment analysis.

In addition, the adaptive neural marketing system was able to significantly increase user engagement with marketing content. The click-through rate (CTR) in the experimental group, which used the adaptive system, reached 38%, while the rate in the control group, which viewed static content, was only 27%. This 11% increase indicates the effectiveness of the system in attracting users' attention. Also, the average duration of viewing content in the experimental group was 75 seconds, while this duration was only 57 seconds in the control group. These results indicate that the adaptive system was able to improve the user experience and encourage users to interact more with the content. These findings are consistent with previous research in the field of adaptive marketing, which has shown that personalized content can increase user engagement.

On the other hand, user feedback also indicated their satisfaction with the system. Many users positively evaluated the experience of using the system and stated that the displayed content was close to their emotions. These feedbacks show that the system was able to meet users' expectations and create an interactive and engaging experience for them. However, some users pointed out cases of inaccuracy in emotion recognition. This issue could be caused by two factors: first, the quality of biometric data, which may be affected by noise or environmental conditions. Second, the limitations of deep learning algorithms, which may make errors in analyzing certain emotions.

One of the important challenges of this research is the issue of user privacy. Although the use of biometric and behavioral data of users helps the accuracy of the system, it can raise concerns about user privacy. To address this challenge, the use of privacy-preserving techniques such as data encryption, federated learning, and anonymous data processing is proposed. These techniques can ensure that user data is collected and analyzed securely.

Technically, one of the limitations of this study was the use of a controlled laboratory environment for data collection. Although this method allows for better control of the variables and experimental conditions, the behavior of users in this environment may differ from their behavior in real-world situations. To increase the accuracy and generalizability of the results, it is suggested that the system be tested in real-world environments with real-time data. Also, the use of more sophisticated biometric data such as EEG (electroencephalography) can help improve the accuracy of emotion recognition.

On the other hand, the adaptive decision-making system in this study, which was designed based on a combination of Reinforcement Learning and Rule-Based System, showed good performance in adapting marketing content. This approach allows the system to dynamically change marketing content based on users' reactions. However, the use of more advanced models such as Attention Mechanisms can help improve the system's performance in emotion recognition and analysis. These models are able to pay more attention to key features of the data and increase the accuracy of the analysis.

Overall, this research showed that the AIoE-based adaptive neural marketing system can effectively increase users' engagement with marketing content. By combining biometric data, deep learning, and adaptive decision-making, the system enables the delivery of personalized and dynamic marketing experiences. However, for future developments, the use of more diverse data, improving the accuracy of algorithms, and ensuring user privacy should be considered. This system can be used as a novel solution in the digital marketing industry and even in other fields such as education and healthcare.

7- CONCLUSION

This research aimed to develop and evaluate an adaptive neural marketing system based on ubiquitous artificial intelligence (AIoE). The proposed system dynamically and in real time adapted marketing content based on users' emotions by utilizing biometric, behavioral, and environmental data. The results of this research showed that the proposed adaptive system is able to identify users' emotions with an accuracy of between 85 and 92 percent and modify marketing content based on these emotions. These findings indicate that the use of deep learning and natural language processing (NLP) algorithms can significantly increase the accuracy of sentiment analysis.

Comparing the user engagement rate with adapted content and static content showed that the adaptive system can significantly increase user engagement. The click-through rate (CTR) in the experimental group reached 38 percent, while this rate was only 27 percent in the control group. Also, the average viewing time for the experimental group was 75 seconds, while the control group only spent 57 seconds. These findings indicate that the adaptive system is not only able to identify users' emotions, but also can improve the user experience and encourage users to engage more with marketing content.

User feedback also indicated their satisfaction with the system. Most users rated the experience of using the system positively and stated that the content displayed was close to their emotions. This feedback indicates that the system was able to create an interactive and personalized experience for users. However, some users noted cases of inaccuracy in emotion recognition, which could be due to the quality of the biometric data or the limitations of the deep learning algorithms.

In addition to providing an adaptive neuromarketing system, this research has helped to shed light on the capabilities of AI in identifying users' emotions and personalizing content. This system can be used as a new solution in the digital marketing industry and improve the user experience. In addition, this approach can also be used in other areas such as education, healthcare, and customer service, where personalized interactions are of great importance.

However, this research was accompanied by some limitations. First, the users' biometric and behavioral data were collected in a controlled environment, which may not fully reflect the real conditions of the users. Also, the performance of the system depends on the accuracy and quality of the collected data, and the use of more advanced sensors can improve its accuracy. The issue of user privacy is also one of the main challenges of this system. To overcome this challenge, the use of data encryption techniques and federated learning can help protect users' privacy.

As a suggestion for future research, the use of more sophisticated biometric data such as EEG or multisensory data can help improve the accuracy of the system. Also, developing the system to adapt content based on temporal data (such as time of day or season) or dynamic environmental conditions can increase its capabilities. The use of more advanced deep learning models such as Attention Mechanisms can also help improve the accuracy of the system in identifying users' emotions.

As a new step in the field of AIoE-based adaptive neuromarketing, this research can help improve the user experience and increase users' interactions with marketing content. The proposed system showed that AI-based adaptive approaches can effectively play a role in improving the performance of marketing campaigns and lead to the creation of a personalized and dynamic experience for users.

REFERENCES

Abdi, H., & Nozari, H. (2025). Blockchain-Powered Multiobjective Portfolio Optimization under Uncertainty. *Journal of Future Digital Optimization*, *1*(1), 62–70.

Ait Hammou, K., Galib, M. H., & Melloul, J. (2013). The contributions of neuromarketing in marketing research. *Journal of Management Research*, *5*(4), 20. DOI: 10.5296/jmr.v5i4.4023

Alsharif, A., Salleh, N., Baharun, R., & Safaei, M. E. H. D. I. (2020). Neuromarketing approach: An overview and future research directions. *Journal of Theoretical and Applied Information Technology*, *98*(7).

Alsharif, A. H., Salleh, N. Z. M., Abdullah, M., Khraiwish, A., & Ashaari, A. (2023). Neuromarketing tools used in the marketing mix: A systematic literature and future research agenda. *SAGE Open*, *13*(1), 21582440231156563. DOI: 10.1177/21582440231156563

Ariely, D., & Berns, G. S. (2010). Neuromarketing: The hope and hype of neuroimaging in business. *Nature Reviews. Neuroscience*, *11*(4), 284–292. DOI: 10.1038/nrn2795 PMID: 20197790

Bercea, M. D. (2012, August). Anatomy of methodologies for measuring consumer behavior in neuromarketing research. In *Proceedings of the Lupcon Center for Business Research (LCBR) European Marketing Conference*. Ebermannstadt, Germany.

Duque-Hurtado, P., Samboni-Rodriguez, V., Castro-Garcia, M., Montoya-Restrepo, L. A., & Montoya-Restrepo, I. A. (2020). Neuromarketing: Its current status and research perspectives. Estudios gerenciales, 36(157), 525-539.

Fugate, D. L. (2008). Marketing services more effectively with neuromarketing research: A look into the future. *Journal of Services Marketing*, *22*(2), 170–173. DOI: 10.1108/08876040810862903

Garcia, J. R., & Saad, G. (2008). Evolutionary neuromarketing: Darwinizing the neuroimaging paradigm for consumer behavior. *Journal of Consumer Behaviour*, *7*(4-5), 397–414. DOI: 10.1002/cb.259

Irani, H. R., & Nozari, H. (Eds.). (2024). *Smart and Sustainable Interactive Marketing*. IGI Global. DOI: 10.4018/979-8-3693-1339-8

Javor, A., Koller, M., Lee, N., Chamberlain, L., & Ransmayr, G. (2013). Neuromarketing and consumer neuroscience: Contributions to neurology. *BMC Neurology*, *13*(1), 1–12. DOI: 10.1186/1471-2377-13-13 PMID: 23383650

Kalogeras, S. (2025). A Smart Framework for Making Stories Smarter through Transmedia and Real User Interaction. *Applied Innovations in Industrial Management, 5*(2), 59–66. DOI: 10.63630/aiim.52.59

Kumar, H., & Singh, P. (2015). Neuromarketing: An emerging tool of market research. [IJEMR]. *International Journal of Engineering and Management Research, 5*(6), 530–535.

Lee, N., Broderick, A. J., & Chamberlain, L. (2007). What is 'neuromarketing'? A discussion and agenda for future research. *International Journal of Psychophysiology, 63*(2), 199–204. DOI: 10.1016/j.ijpsycho.2006.03.007 PMID: 16769143

Meshrarm, D., & Bekouni, A. (2021). Prediction and classification of customer behavior in electronic marketing using data mining and neural network (A case study of network marketing companies). *Applied Innovations in Industrial Management, 1*(2), 1–7.

Mileti, A., Guido, G., & Prete, M. I. (2016). Nanomarketing: A new frontier for neuromarketing. *Psychology and Marketing, 33*(8), 664–674. DOI: 10.1002/mar.20907

Movahed, A. B., Movahed, A. B., & Nozari, H. (2024). Opportunities and challenges of marketing 5.0. Smart and Sustainable Interactive Marketing, 1-21.

Movahed, A. B., Movahed, A. B., & Nozari, H. (2024). Marketing 6.0 Conceptualization. In Advanced Businesses in Industry 6.0 (pp. 15-31). IGI Global.

Najafi, S. E., Nozari, H., & Edalatpanah, S. A. (2022). Investigating the key parameters affecting sustainable IoT-based marketing. In *Computational Intelligence Methodologies Applied to Sustainable Development Goals* (pp. 51–61). Springer International Publishing. DOI: 10.1007/978-3-030-97344-5_4

Nozari, H. (2025). Cognitive Targeting and Neuromarketing Applications in AI-Driven Digital Advertising. *Applied Innovations in Industrial Management, 5*(2), 52–58. DOI: 10.63630/aiim.52.52

Nozari, H., Abdi, H., & Rafiei, K. (2025). Edge Computing and Marketing in the Smart Economy: Processing Consumer Data in Real-Time. In Nozari, H. (Ed.), *Dynamic and Safe Economy in the Age of Smart Technologies* (pp. 191–208). IGI Global Scientific Publishing., DOI: 10.4018/979-8-3693-4369-2.ch012

Nozari, H., & Chobar, A. P. (2024). The Dimensions and Components of Marketing 5.0: Introduction to Marketing 6.0. In Advanced Businesses in Industry 6.0 (pp. 75-86). IGI Global.

Nozari, H., Irani, H. R., & Rahmaty, M. (2023, November). Investigating Critical Success Factors in IoT-Based Marketing Systems. In International Conference on Optimization and Data Science in Industrial Engineering (pp. 259-271). Cham: Springer Nature Switzerland.

Nozari, H., Rahmaty, M., & Szmelter-Jarosz, A. (2024). A framework for AIoT-based smart sustainable marketing system. In *Artificial Intelligence of Things for Achieving Sustainable Development Goals* (pp. 255–271). Springer Nature Switzerland. DOI: 10.1007/978-3-031-53433-1_13

Nozari, H., & Samadi, S. (2025). Digital Twin-Enhanced Sentiment Analysis for Targeted Marketing Optimization. In Dynamic and Safe Economy in the Age of Smart Technologies (pp. 121-138). IGI Global Scientific Publishing. DOI: 10.4018/979-8-3693-4369-2.ch008

Nozari, H., Szmelter-Jarosz, A., & Ghahremani-Nahr, J. (2021). The ideas of sustainable and green marketing based on the internet of everything—The case of the dairy industry. *Future Internet*, *13*(10), 266. DOI: 10.3390/fi13100266

Nozari, H., Szmelter-Jarosz, A., & Rahmaty, M. (2024). Smart marketing based on artificial intelligence of things (AIoT) and Blockchain and evaluating critical success factors. In *Smart and Sustainable Interactive Marketing* (pp. 68–82). IGI Global Scientific Publishing. DOI: 10.4018/979-8-3693-1339-8.ch005

Ulman, Y. I., Cakar, T., & Yildiz, G. (2015). Ethical issues in neuromarketing:"I consume, therefore I am!". *Science and Engineering Ethics*, *21*(5), 1271–1284. DOI: 10.1007/s11948-014-9581-5 PMID: 25150848

Chapter 3
Building Smart Marketing Infrastructures With IoE

Maryam Rahmaty
https://orcid.org/0000-0003-3772-4216
Islamic Azad University, Chalous, Iran

ABSTRACT

This study examines the role of the Internet of Everything (IoE) in the evolution of intelligent marketing. Using IoE, brands are able to collect and analyze real-time data from connected devices and can create personalized and dynamic marketing experiences for their customers. By reviewing the basic concepts, designing intelligent marketing infrastructures, and providing case studies from various industries, this study examines the practical applications of this technology and analyzes the challenges and solutions associated with its implementation. The findings show that IoE can improve marketing efficiency and effectiveness.

1- INTRODUCTION

The rapid developments in information and communication technology in recent decades have led to the emergence of a more comprehensive and complex concept than the Internet of Things (IoT), called the Internet of Everything (IoE). Unlike IoT, which focuses only on connecting devices to the Internet and communicating with each other, IoE integrates four basic elements: people, objects, data, and processes, creating a dynamic and intelligent network in which all elements interact seamlessly with each other (Aliahmadi & Nozari, 2023). This concept allows brands

DOI: 10.4018/979-8-3373-3775-3.ch003

to analyze and improve customer experience, optimize marketing processes, and increase operational efficiency.

Marketing, as one of the main areas affected by IoE, has witnessed a profound transformation in the ways of interacting with customers and managing advertising campaigns. In the past, marketing was mainly based on one-way and general communications, but with the advent of IoE, brands have been able to collect real-time data from customers and analyze this data to provide personalized offers (Najafi, Nozari, & Edalatpanah, 2022). Data collected from connected devices, including mobile phones, wearables, sensors, and smart cameras, allows brands to more accurately identify customer needs and preferences and create unique marketing experiences for them.

For example, in the retail industry, smart stores use sensors and wearables to track and analyze customer behavior in stores. This data allows brands to provide personalized offers to each customer and automatically optimize inventory management (Nozari, Abdi, & Rafiei, 2025). Similarly, in the hospitality industry, the use of IoE devices, such as smart temperature, lighting, and music control systems in hotel rooms, improves the guest experience and provides personalized services to them (Nozari, Fallah, Szmelter-Jarosz, & Krzemiński, 2021). In the automotive industry, IoE allows manufacturers to collect real-time data on vehicle performance and use this data to provide preventive services and improve vehicle quality (Nozari, Szmelter-Jarosz, & Ghahremani-Nahr, 2022).

But the use of IoE in marketing is not limited to improving the customer experience. This technology also allows for the optimization of marketing processes and increased operational efficiency. Brands can use the collected data to predict consumer behavior and dynamically adjust their marketing strategies. For example, machine learning and artificial intelligence algorithms can analyze IoE data to identify customer behavior patterns and automatically send them promotional offers (Aliahmadi, Nozari, Ghahremani-Nahr, & Szmelter-Jarosz, 2022). In addition, content management platforms (CMS) and customer management systems (CRM) allow brands to improve the customer experience in a personalized and continuous manner (Rahmaty & Nozari, 2023).

However, the use of IoE in marketing also comes with several challenges. One of the most important challenges is protecting the privacy and security of consumers' data. As the number of connected devices and the volume of data collected increase, the risk of data theft and privacy breaches also increases significantly. Brands should use security standards such as data encryption, multi-factor authentication, and the use of advanced security protocols to protect users' information (Nozari, Fallah, Kazemipoor, & Najafi, 2021). Also, establishing transparent policies for data collection and use and educating consumers about their rights can help build customer trust (Movahed, Movahed, & Nozari, 2024).

Another challenge is related to the scalability of IoE systems and coordination between connected devices. Given the diversity of devices and different communication protocols, integrating these devices into a unified system can lead to technical complexities (Nozari, Szmelter-Jarosz, & Ghahremani-Nahr, 2021). The use of standard communication protocols such as MQTT, HTTP, and WebSocket and the use of cloud computing and edge computing systems can help improve the efficiency of these systems (Nozari, 2023).

This study comprehensively examines the role of the Internet of Everything (IoE) in the design and implementation of smart marketing infrastructures. First, the basic concepts and key technologies of IoE are introduced. Then, smart marketing structures based on IoE are designed and analyzed. Next, the challenges and solutions related to the implementation of IoE in marketing are examined and finally, by presenting case studies from different industries, the practical applications of this technology in various fields are explained. The aim of this study is to provide a deep understanding of the effects of IoE on marketing and introduce the best methods for effectively utilizing this technology to enhance customer experience and improve brand performance.

2- LITERATURE REVIEW

In recent decades, the digital transformation has fundamentally transformed marketing, especially with the emergence of new technologies such as the Internet of Things (IoT) and the Internet of Everything (IoE). The research literature in this area shows that IoE enables the delivery of personalized and interactive marketing experiences by combining real-time data, artificial intelligence, and connected devices.

Several studies have examined the role of IoE in marketing. For example, a systematic review of 52 scientific articles published between 2011 and 2020 analyzed the role of IoT in improving marketing and business processes. The study shows that IoT can help companies provide better services and make strategic decisions by collecting and analyzing consumer data (Movahed, Movahed, & Nozari, 2024).

One of the prominent applications of IoE in marketing is the personalization of the customer experience. Using data collected from connected devices, brands can identify customer needs and preferences and provide tailored offers. This approach not only increases customer satisfaction but also strengthens their loyalty to the brand (Nozari, Najafi, Fallah, & Hosseinzadeh Lotfi, 2019).

In addition, the integration of IoE with artificial intelligence enables predictive analysis of consumer behavior. Machine learning algorithms can identify customer behavior patterns and make predictions about their future needs. This information helps brands dynamically adjust their marketing strategies (Nozari, 2024).

However, the use of IoE in marketing also comes with challenges. One of the most important challenges is the protection of consumer privacy and data security. As the number of connected devices and the volume of data collected increase, the risk of privacy breaches also increases. To address this challenge, it is essential to use advanced security standards and establish transparent policies for data collection and use (Nozari, Ghahremani-Nahr, & Szmelter-Jarosz, 2024).

In addition, the integration of different systems and coordination between connected devices can also create complexities. To overcome this challenge, the use of standard communication protocols and the use of cloud and edge computing systems can be effective (Nozari, Abdi, & Jahangard, 2025).

Overall, the research literature shows that IoE has great potential for marketing transformation. However, to effectively exploit this technology, brands need to pay special attention to the challenges related to security, privacy, and system integrity. Future research can help expand the applications of IoE in marketing by focusing on the development of ethical frameworks, technical standards, and implementation strategies.

3- FUNDAMENTAL CONCEPTS AND KEY TECHNOLOGIES

In the digital age, the concept of the Internet of Everything (IoE) is recognized as a major revolution in the world of technology and marketing. Unlike the Internet of Things (IoT), which only refers to the connection of devices to the Internet network and their communication with each other, IoE goes beyond and encompasses a more comprehensive concept that includes the connections between people, data, processes and objects. This concept allows marketers to use the countless data generated by connected devices, users and digital environments to create intelligent and optimized marketing strategies. In this section, we will examine the basic concepts and key technologies of IoE in marketing (Nozari, Ghahremani-Nahr, & Szmelter-Jarosz, 2023).

As a complex system, IoE consists of four basic elements: people, things, data and processes. People, as the main part of this system, are connected to the network through smartphones, mobile phones and wearables. These connections allow brands to interact directly with consumers and understand their needs and preferences more accurately. Things also include a wide range of physical devices such as sensors, cameras, smart home appliances and wearables that connect to the internet and provide valuable data for analysis. These devices continuously record information such as location, temperature, user behavior and environmental conditions and send it to data management systems.

Data, the third fundamental pillar of IoE, plays a vital role in intelligent marketing. Data collected from connected devices can be structured (such as users' personal information and purchase history) or unstructured (such as images, videos, and audio). This data is analyzed using data processing and machine learning techniques and transformed into valuable insights that can be used to design targeted and personalized marketing campaigns. IoE data analytics involves real-time processing and prediction of consumer behavior using machine learning algorithms and artificial neural networks. These technologies allow brands to predict consumer behavior and identify their needs before they are explicitly expressed.

Figure 1 summarizes the relationship between these four key elements (people, things, data, and processes) along with the key technologies used in IoE marketing. These technologies include Artificial Intelligence (AI), Cloud Computing, Real-Time Analytics, and Data Security, which act as supporting elements in data processing and management. Communication between these elements is established through communication protocols such as Wi-Fi, Bluetooth, Zigbee, and 5G, which enable real-time data transmission.

Figure 1. Conceptual model of IoE in smart marketing infrastructure

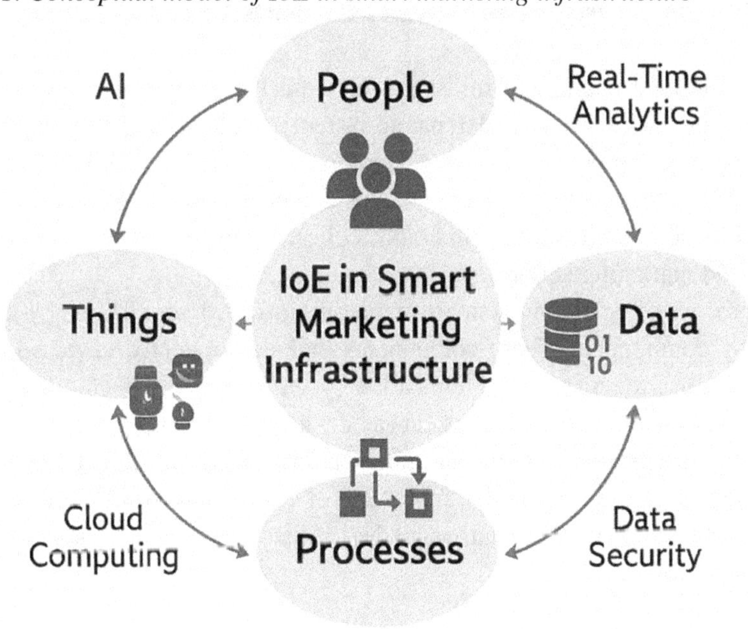

Processes, as the fourth element of IoE, also play a key role in transforming data into marketing actions. Processes include a set of instructions, algorithms, and automated systems that allow brands to use collected data to create dynamic experiences tailored to the individual needs of consumers. These processes can include sending personalized messages, providing special offers based on past user behavior, or setting up dynamic advertising campaigns in real time. Using content management systems (CMS) and customer relationship management (CRM) platforms, brands can automate and intelligently execute these processes (Nozari & Samadi, 2025).

Finally, data security is a key challenge in using IoE in marketing. As the number of connected devices and the volume of data generated increase, security and privacy risks also increase significantly. Brands should use security standards such as data encryption, multi-factor authentication, and advanced security protocols to protect user information. These measures not only ensure data security, but also build consumer trust and enable sustainable use of IoE in marketing (Nozari, 2025a).

Overall, the Internet of Everything (IoE) combines real-time data, connected devices, and artificial intelligence technologies to provide an intelligent and dynamic infrastructure for marketing. This technology allows brands to engage with customers more effectively and purposefully, creating personalized and differentiated experiences for them.

4- DESIGNING SMART MARKETING INFRASTRUCTURES

Designing smart marketing infrastructures using the Internet of Everything (IoE) means creating an integrated and dynamic system that allows brands to engage with consumers in real time and deliver personalized experiences. This infrastructure includes a set of connected devices, data management systems, AI algorithms, and communication protocols that help brands collect, analyze, and translate user data into targeted marketing actions.

The process of designing a smart marketing infrastructure begins by identifying its key components. These components include connected devices (sensors, wearables, smart devices), communication systems (Wi-Fi, Bluetooth, 5G), and data management and AI platforms. These devices continuously record data such as location, user behavior, biometric information, and environmental conditions. Figure 2 shows an overview of the components of an IoE-based intelligent marketing infrastructure, which includes data input devices, storage systems, and analysis and execution platforms.

Figure 2. Key components of an IoE-based intelligent marketing infrastructure

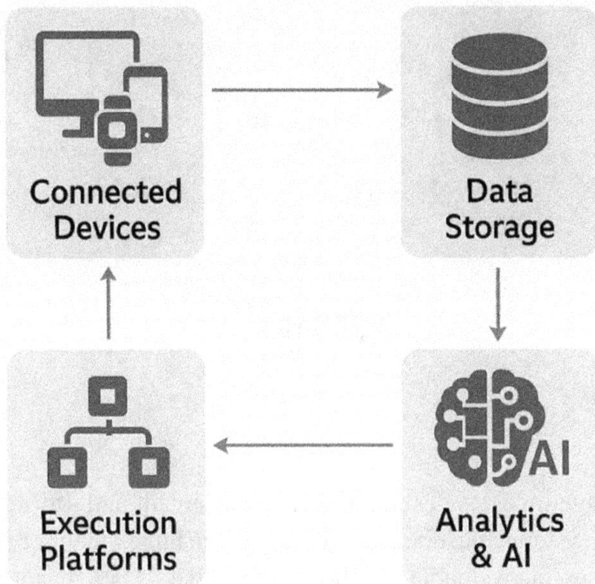

After identifying the components, the next step is to design the communications between them. These communications must be designed in such a way that data is transferred in real time from the connected devices to the data processing systems. Various communication protocols such as MQTT, HTTP, WebSocket, and CoAP can be used to transfer data between devices. These protocols are suitable for IoE data transfer due to their high speed and efficiency. Figure 3 shows how connected devices are connected to the processing and storage systems through communication protocols.

Figure 3. Communication architecture of IoE devices in smart marketing infrastructure

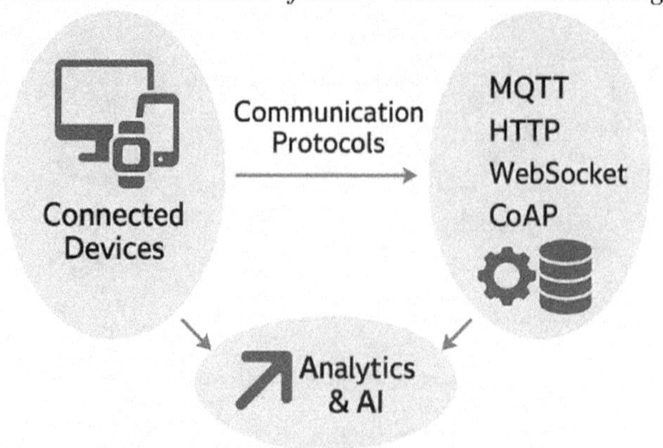

The third stage involves designing data management and artificial intelligence systems. These systems must be able to analyze the huge amount of collected data in real time and extract valuable insights from this data. Data management systems (DMP) and cloud computing platforms can be used to store and process the data. Artificial intelligence algorithms such as machine learning and deep learning can also analyze the collected data to predict consumer behavior. These artificial intelligence models can identify user behavior patterns and send them personalized recommendations. Figure 4 schematically shows the data processing process in an intelligent marketing infrastructure.

Figure 4. Data processing and intelligent analytics process in IoE marketing infrastructure

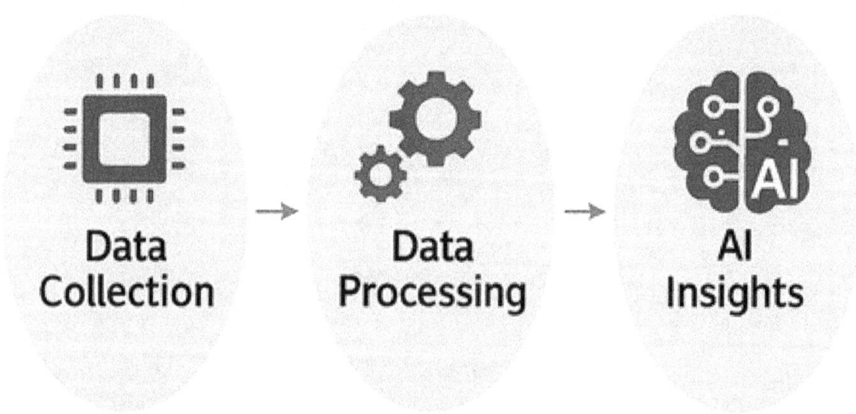

Finally, the final step involves implementing automated systems to execute marketing campaigns based on IoE data. These systems can include content management systems (CMS), customer relationship management (CRM) platforms, and automated messaging tools. These systems allow brands to respond dynamically and in real time to consumer behavior and create personalized marketing experiences for them.

These intelligent marketing infrastructures using IoE allow brands to use user data to create dynamic, personalized, and real-time experiences. These infrastructures not only help improve the customer experience, but also increase customer loyalty and marketing efficiency.

5- CHALLENGES AND SOLUTIONS

In the process of designing and implementing smart marketing infrastructures based on the Internet of Everything (IoE), brands face several challenges that can negatively impact the performance and effectiveness of these infrastructures. These challenges include technical issues, data security, consumer privacy, data analysis complexities, and system integration. This section examines the most important challenges in this area and provides practical solutions for each (Nozari, 2025b).

One of the main technical challenges in designing smart marketing infrastructures based on the IoE is the scalability and coordination of connected devices. As the number of devices connected to the network increases, data management, real-time analysis, and coordination of these devices becomes a complex issue. This challenge is especially evident when brands try to integrate various systems such as wearables, sensors, and smart devices with data analytics platforms and customer relationship management (CRM) systems. The solution to this challenge is to use standard communication protocols such as MQTT, HTTP and WebSocket, which enable secure and optimized communication between devices. In addition, the use of cloud computing and edge computing systems can help reduce data processing latency and increase system efficiency.

Another challenge is data security and consumer privacy. Given the large volume of data collected from connected devices, the risk of data theft, privacy violations and misuse of consumers' personal information increases significantly. This is important not only from a technical perspective but also from a legal and ethical perspective. Brands should use security standards such as data encryption, multi-factor authentication and the use of advanced security protocols such as TLS and SSL. Also, establishing transparent policies for data collection and use, educating consumers about their privacy rights, and providing users with data management options can help build consumer trust.

Another major challenge is the complexity of analyzing IoE data. Data collected from connected devices is usually recorded in real-time and in various formats (structured and unstructured). This data includes text, audio, video, and biometric information, the analysis of which requires the use of advanced technologies such as machine learning and deep learning. Brands should use data management platforms (DMPs) and artificial intelligence systems to automatically analyze this data. In addition, the use of data preprocessing techniques such as noise filtering, dimensionality reduction, and data classification can improve the efficiency of data analysis.

The fourth challenge is related to system integration and coordination between different devices and platforms. In IoE infrastructures, different devices use different protocols and standards, which can lead to inconsistencies and inconsistencies. This is especially true when connecting devices from different manufacturers to data management systems and marketing platforms. The solution to this challenge is to use unified device management platforms and standard APIs that allow brands to easily connect different devices to their IoE network. Also, creating a modular and scalable architecture can help brands adapt quickly to technological changes.

Finally, one of the strategic challenges of using IoE in marketing is to adjust advertising campaigns in real time and personalized. Given the high speed of data collection and processing, brands must use automated systems to analyze consumer behavior and execute advertising campaigns. The solution to this challenge is to use machine learning algorithms and automated content management systems (CMS) that can send advertising messages dynamically and based on user needs.

Overall, the challenges of using IoE in marketing are not only technical, but also ethical and strategic. To succeed in this area, brands must use advanced technologies for data management, consumer privacy, and IoE data analytics. This approach will allow them to create personalized and effective marketing experiences for their customers.

6- CASE STUDIES: PRACTICAL APPLICATIONS OF IoE IN SMART MARKETING INFRASTRUCTURES

In this section, we will examine three case studies of the use of the Internet of Everything (IoE) in intelligent marketing across three different industries. These studies include the retail industry, the hospitality industry, and the automotive industry, each of which faced its own unique challenges, goals, and solutions, and achieved impressive results using IoE infrastructures. These studies demonstrate how IoE can improve the customer experience, increase operational efficiency, and strengthen brand loyalty.

Case Study 1: Smart Retail

In a large chain store, an IoE-based smart marketing system is designed to track and analyze customer behavior in the store in real time. Smart sensors at the entrance and exit of the store record the number of customers and their movement patterns. Wearable devices and the store's mobile app allow customers to receive personalized special offers. In addition, shelf sensors monitor inventory and are connected to the inventory management system, so that best-selling products are automatically reordered. The system analyzes real-time data and predicts customer purchasing patterns using machine learning algorithms.

Figure 5. IoE application in smart retail

Case Study 2: Smart Hospitality

In a luxury hotel, an IoE system is designed to deliver a unique and personalized customer experience. Hotel rooms are equipped with smart sensors that adjust temperature, lighting, and music based on guests' preferences. Guests' wearable devices are connected to the hotel management system, allowing them to request services via a mobile app. The hotel's energy management system uses IoE data to optimize energy consumption, such as automatically turning off heating and lighting when guests leave the room. The hotel also uses real-time data to provide guests with personalized offers, such as restaurant discounts and spa services.

Figure 6. Application of IoE in Smart Hospitality

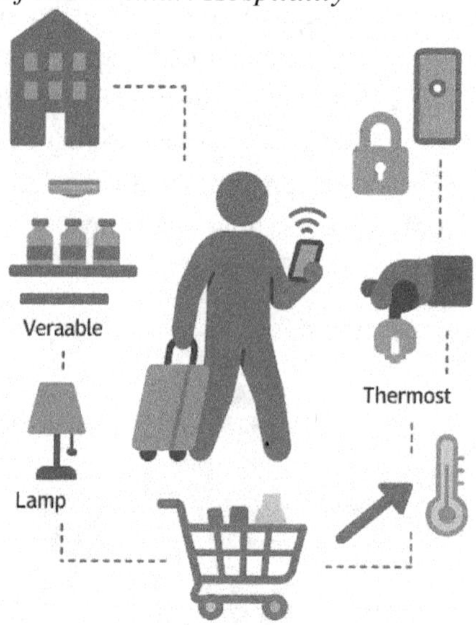

Case Study 3: Smart Automotive

In an automobile manufacturing plant, the IoE infrastructure is seamlessly integrated with production, quality control, and supply chain systems. Smart sensors on the production line monitor the status of machinery, temperature, pressure, and quality of manufactured parts. This data is sent to the production management system, and if any defects are detected, an alert is issued in real time. In the sales department, smart cars are connected to the IoE system and collect data related to driver behavior, fuel consumption, and service needs and send it to after-sales service centers. This data allows the automobile company to provide proactive after-sales service and improve the customer experience.

Figure 7. Application of IoE in smart automotive

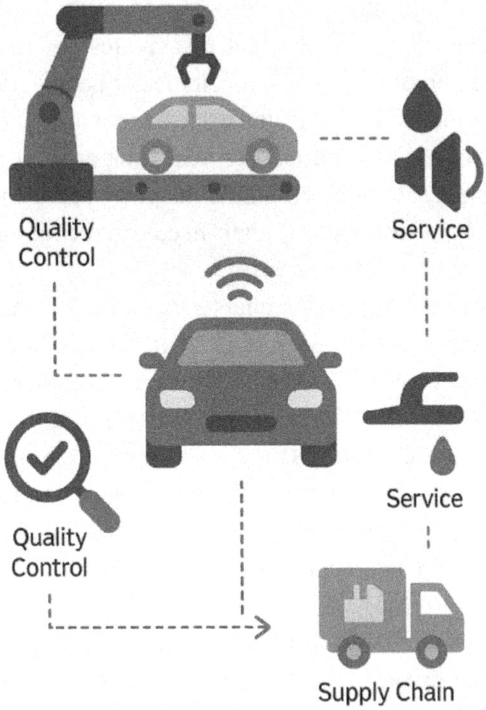

These three case studies demonstrate how IoE can be used across industries to improve customer experience, increase operational efficiency, and improve resource management. From a retailer offering a personalized shopping experience to customers, to a hotelier using IoE to provide convenience and special services to guests, to the automotive industry improving quality and customer satisfaction through real-time monitoring and predictive after-sales service, these studies clearly demonstrate that IoE is not just a new technology, but also a strategic tool for transforming industries.

7- CONCLUSION AND FUTURE PROSPECTS

As one of the most innovative technologies of the last decade, the Internet of Everything (IoE) has been able to fundamentally transform the marketing infrastructure. By combining data collected from connected devices, intelligent analytics, and automated systems, brands can create fully personalized and real-time marketing experiences for their customers. This technology not only helps brands interact with customers more effectively, but also improves operational efficiency and the effectiveness of marketing campaigns.

The analysis in this chapter shows that IoE creates an integrated and dynamic marketing system by combining four main elements: people, things, data, and processes. These four elements are connected to each other using key technologies such as artificial intelligence, cloud computing, real-time analytics, and data security, transforming consumer data into actionable insights. These insights allow brands to predict consumer behavior, identify their needs, and continuously improve customer experiences.

The case studies presented in this chapter demonstrate that IoE offers unique capabilities in various industries, including retail, hospitality, and automotive. In the retail industry, IoE enables personalized recommendations and automated inventory management by collecting real-time data from sensors and wearables. In the hospitality industry, IoE improves the guest experience by intelligently adjusting room temperature, lighting, and music, and providing personalized services. In the automotive industry, IoE improves efficiency and service quality by monitoring the quality of manufactured parts, managing the supply chain, and providing proactive after-sales services.

However, the use of IoE in marketing also brings with it several challenges. Data security and consumer privacy are among the most important concerns for brands and customers. Brands must use advanced security standards such as data encryption, multi-factor authentication, and information security management systems to gain consumer trust. In addition, technical challenges related to the coordination of connected devices, system scalability, and the complexity of data analysis also require technological solutions such as the use of cloud computing and machine learning algorithms.

From a futures perspective, the use of IoE in marketing is expected to continue to grow with technological advances. One of the important future trends is the expansion of the use of artificial intelligence and deep learning to analyze IoE data. Advanced machine learning algorithms will be able to analyze the collected data with greater accuracy and predict consumer behavior. Also, with the development of 5G technology and satellite internet, the speed and stability of IoE communications will improve, which will allow brands to process and analyze real-time data more quickly.

Another trend is using IoE to create dynamic and immersive customer experiences. Brands can use connected devices to deliver interactive marketing experiences. For example, in smart retail stores, customers can access special offers and interact with products using their wearable devices and smartphones. IoE systems can also provide customers with personalized shopping experiences based on their shopping patterns.

In the hospitality industry, IoE is expected to lead to more personalized and intelligent experiences. Smart rooms will be designed to automatically adjust to guests' preferences. On the other hand, hotels can use IoE data to predict guest needs and provide special services such as special discount offers or spa services.

In the automotive industry, IoE will also lead to improve after-sales service quality and intelligent production management with the spread of autonomous vehicles and smart connectivity systems. IoE-connected vehicles can send their performance data to after-sales service centers in real time, thereby predicting the need for service and repairs. Also, manufacturing plants can use IoE data to automatically monitor and control the quality of manufactured parts.

Finally, another important future trend is the increasing use of IoE for emotional and psychological marketing. Brands can use wearables to track consumers' emotional states and deliver emotional, personalized marketing experiences based on this data. For example, fashion and beauty brands can recommend products to consumers based on their emotional states.

In short, the Internet of Everything (IoE) creates an intelligent and dynamic infrastructure for marketing by connecting people, things, data, and processes. To get the most out of this technology, brands must not only use intelligent and automated systems, but also pay special attention to issues of data security, consumer privacy, and advanced data analytics. The future of marketing with IoE is moving towards fully personalized, dynamic, and real-time experiences, and brands that can strategically and securely apply this technology will achieve greater success.

REFERENCES

Aliahmadi, A., & Nozari, H. (2023, January). Evaluation of security metrics in AIoT and blockchain-based supply chain by Neutrosophic decision-making method. In Supply chain forum: an international journal (Vol. 24, No. 1, pp. 31-42). Taylor & Francis. DOI: 10.1080/16258312.2022.2101898

Aliahmadi, A., Nozari, H., Ghahremani-Nahr, J., & Szmelter-Jarosz, A. (2022). Evaluation of key impression of resilient supply chain based on artificial intelligence of things (AIoT). arXiv preprint arXiv:2207.13174.

Movahed, A. B., Movahed, A. B., & Nozari, H. (2024). Opportunities and challenges of marketing 5.0. Smart and Sustainable Interactive Marketing, 1-21.

Movahed, A. B., Movahed, A. B., & Nozari, H. (2024). Marketing 6.0 Conceptualization. In Advanced Businesses in Industry 6.0 (pp. 15-31). IGI Global.

Najafi, S. E., Nozari, H., & Edalatpanah, S. A. (2022). Investigating the key parameters affecting sustainable IoT-based marketing. In *Computational Intelligence Methodologies Applied to Sustainable Development Goals* (pp. 51–61). Springer International Publishing. DOI: 10.1007/978-3-030-97344-5_4

Nozari, H. (Ed.). (2023). *Building Smart and Sustainable Businesses with Transformative Technologies*. IGI Global. DOI: 10.4018/979-8-3693-0210-1

Nozari, H. (2024). Green Supply Chain Management based on Artificial Intelligence of Everything. *Journal of Economics and Management*, *46*, 171–188. DOI: 10.22367/jem.2024.46.07

Nozari, H. (Ed.). (2025). *Dynamic and Safe Economy in the Age of Smart Technologies*. IGI Global. DOI: 10.4018/979-8-3693-4369-2

Nozari, H. (2025). Cognitive Targeting and Neuromarketing Applications in AI-Driven Digital Advertising. *Applied Innovations in Industrial Management*, *5*(2), 52–58. DOI: 10.63630/aiim.52.52

Nozari, H., Abdi, H., & Jahangard, S. (2025). Quantum Cognitive Intelligence Network Q-CIN as a Transformative Framework for Industry 6.0. *ALL Bioscience*, *1*(1), 27–37.

Nozari, H., Abdi, H., & Rafiei, K. (2025). Edge Computing and Marketing in the Smart Economy: Processing Consumer Data in Real-Time. In Dynamic and Safe Economy in the Age of Smart Technologies (pp. 191-208). IGI Global Scientific Publishing.

Nozari, H., Fallah, M., Kazemipoor, H., & Najafi, S. E. (2021). Big data analysis of IoT-based supply chain management considering FMCG industries. *Бизнес-информатика*, *15*(1, 1 (eng)), 78–96. DOI: 10.17323/2587-814X.2021.1.78.96

Nozari, H., Fallah, M., Szmelter-Jarosz, A., & Krzemiński, M. (2021). Analysis of security criteria for IoT-based supply chain: a case study of FMCG industries. Central European Management Journal, 29(4).

Nozari, H., Ghahremani-Nahr, J., & Szmelter-Jarosz, A. (2023). A multi-stage stochastic inventory management model for transport companies including several different transport modes. *International Journal of Management Science and Engineering Management*, *18*(2), 134–144. DOI: 10.1080/17509653.2022.2042747

Nozari, H., Ghahremani-Nahr, J., & Szmelter-Jarosz, A. (2024). AI and machine learning for real-world problems. [). Elsevier.]. *Advances in Computers*, *134*, 1–12. DOI: 10.1016/bs.adcom.2023.02.001

Nozari, H., Najafi, E., Fallah, M., & Hosseinzadeh Lotfi, F. (2019). Quantitative analysis of key performance indicators of green supply chain in FMCG industries using non-linear fuzzy method. *Mathematics*, *7*(11), 1020. DOI: 10.3390/math7111020

Nozari, H., & Samadi, S. (2025). Digital Twin-Enhanced Sentiment Analysis for Targeted Marketing Optimization. In Dynamic and Safe Economy in the Age of Smart Technologies (pp. 121-138). IGI Global Scientific Publishing. DOI: 10.4018/979-8-3693-4369-2.ch008

Nozari, H., Szmelter-Jarosz, A., & Ghahremani-Nahr, J. (2021). The ideas of sustainable and green marketing based on the internet of everything—The case of the dairy industry. *Future Internet*, *13*(10), 266. DOI: 10.3390/fi13100266

Nozari, H., Szmelter-Jarosz, A., & Ghahremani-Nahr, J. (2022). Analysis of the challenges of artificial intelligence of things (AIoT) for the smart supply chain (case study: FMCG industries). *Sensors (Basel)*, *22*(8), 2931. DOI: 10.3390/s22082931 PMID: 35458916

Rahmaty, M., & Nozari, H. (2023). Optimization of the hierarchical supply chain in the pharmaceutical industry. *Edelweiss Applied Science and Technology*, *7*(2), 104–123. DOI: 10.55214/25768484.v7i2.376

Chapter 4
Predicting the Next Wave of Sports Fans Through Artificial Intelligence in the Future of Sports Marketing:
AI in Sports Marketing

Sajjad Pashaie
https://orcid.org/0000-0002-3933-146X
Department of Sports Management, University of Tabriz, Iran

Sardar Mohammadi
https://orcid.org/0000-0001-7078-956X
University of Kurdistan, Iran

Mike Rayner
https://orcid.org/0000-0001-7793-8687
School of Psychology, Sport, and Health Sciences, UK

ABSTRACT

This chapter examines how artificial intelligence (AI) and Industry 4.0 technologies are transforming sports marketing. As traditional methods for analyzing fan behavior lose relevance, AI provides advanced tools to understand preferences, emotions, and purchase patterns. The chapter details the roles of machine learning (ML) for predictive analysis, natural language processing (NLP) for social media sentiment, and computer vision (CV) for visual engagement. It also explores AI integration with blockchain for secure fan data management and the use of virtual

DOI: 10.4018/979-8-3373-3775-3.ch004

and augmented reality (VR/AR) for immersive experiences. These technologies enhance decision-making, marketing personalization, financial risk reduction, and operational efficiency. Ethical concerns, including data privacy and algorithmic bias, are also addressed. The chapter offers practical insights for marketers, analysts, and researchers on using AI to build more personalized and sustainable relationships with the evolving generation of tech-savvy sports fans.

PART I: INTRODUCTION

Artificial intelligence (AI) is making waves in the sports industry by enhancing athlete performance and fan engagement. From tracking player statistics to optimizing team strategies and delivering personalized experiences for fans, AI is helping to transform the way sports are played and consumed (Xu & Baghaei, 2025). The rapid advancement of AI has significantly transformed the sports industry over the past decade. The impact of AI on fan engagement has been profound, enabling highly personalized content and recommendations that create a stronger connection between fans and their favorite teams or athletes. Using AI-based algorithms, ticket pricing strategies are optimized, resulting in increased ticket sales and revenue. AI-based performance evaluation tools help sports managers make informed decisions about team composition and tactics (Xu & Baghaei, 2025).

As AI technologies, including sensors, processors, and algorithms, continue to evolve, they will enhance the spectator experience, making competitions more engaging for audiences. With billions of fans worldwide and increasing competition, sports managers and coaches are actively seeking innovative methods to improve performance and attract larger fan bases. The integration of AI into various facets of sports is becoming indispensable, reflecting a shift that cannot be ignored (Pashaie, Mohammadi, & Golmohammadi, 2024). Predictions suggest that AI could achieve human-level intelligence by 2029, with the ability to self-improve, further revolutionizing the industry. Over the past two decades, the rapid expansion of sports has transformed it into a dynamic industry, leading to significant advancements in fields like physical education and sports science. These changes present numerous opportunities for adolescents and young adults, fostering new experiences, enhancing skills, promoting social interactions, and supporting personal development. Historically, AI has played a role in sports, providing researchers with a unique environment to develop systems that assist in complex decision-making processes (Shayeg, 2023).

In this evolving sports landscape, the convergence of technology and marketing has introduced both opportunities and challenges for organizations striving to engage their audiences effectively. One of the most significant advancements is the incorporation of AI into sports marketing, which has become essential as fan behaviors and preferences grow increasingly complex due to digital media and globalization. The integration of generative AI into sports marketing is fundamentally changing fan engagement by enabling hyper-personalization and real-time content adaptation. AI-based technologies, including machine learning (ML), natural language processing (NLP), predictive analytics (PA), and automated content generation (ACG), have introduced new ways to improve fan experiences while optimizing business strategies. These advances are driving innovation in content delivery, audience segmentation, and behavioral prediction, helping to develop more inclusive and interactive sports consumption models (Westerbeek, 2025).

AI-driven predictive analytics can be utilized to anticipate future trends in fan behavior, uncover growth opportunities, and optimize marketing campaigns for the greatest effectiveness. AI algorithms can also deliver real-time insights into fan engagement, sentiment, and behavior, enabling marketers to make swift adjustments to their campaigns and messaging. Given that AI can gather large volumes of data rapidly, fans are likely to encounter more personalized marketing in the future. For instance, sports applications like the ESPN mobile app illustrate this concept. When a user creates an account, AI can be employed to collect data about them. This could lead to articles related to the user's favorite teams or players being highlighted more prominently in their feed. Additionally, it might result in targeted advertisements for tickets to their favorite teams' games or promotions for merchandise related to their favorite players.

For some consumers, the notion of more personalized marketing may be appealing as their interests are catered to. However, others may raise ethical concerns regarding the extent of data being collected about them. There is a fine line between gathering data for the enhancement of marketing and infringing on users' privacy. The future of AI remains uncertain as it continues to evolve, but it is crucial that its application is ethical and fair (Sylvia IV, 2024).

This chapter focuses particularly on the next wave of fans, a digitally native, tech-savvy generation of sports consumers whose engagement is shaped by AI-driven platforms, immersive technologies, and data-personalized interactions. Furthermore, we will explore how AI enhances fan experiences through personalized content delivery and interactive environments, leveraging technologies like virtual reality (VR), augmented reality (AR), and blockchain. The synergy of these technologies is redefining fan engagement and the future of sports marketing.

This chapter is designed for a wide range of readers, including sports marketing managers, business strategists, data analysts, students, and academics. Sports marketers will benefit from practical insights on how to use AI-driven tools for predicting purchasing behavior, customizing fan engagement strategies, and protecting financial resources. Data scientists and analysts will gain an understanding of how to apply AI algorithms in sports-specific contexts, while researchers will find suggestions for future exploration in areas such as ethical AI, fan segmentation, and technology integration. Policymakers and legal experts may also find value in discussions about ethical challenges, data privacy concerns, and the need for regulatory frameworks in AI adoption.

By the end of this chapter, readers will be able to answer key questions such as:

How can AI improve the prediction of fan behavior and preferences in a dynamic digital environment?
What specific AI tools and techniques are most effective in enhancing sports marketing strategies?
How can organizations use AI to reduce financial risks and detect fraud in sports operations?
What are the ethical considerations and challenges associated with AI in the sports industry?
How does the integration of AI with other emerging technologies like blockchain, VR, and AR transform the fan experience?

Ultimately, this chapter not only sheds light on the current uses of AI in sports marketing but also provides a forward-looking perspective on how organizations can adapt to the digital transformation of the industry. Through a blend of theoretical foundations, real-world applications, and ethical reflection, we aim to equip readers with the knowledge and tools necessary to embrace AI as a critical asset in shaping the future of sports marketing.

PART II: METHODOLOGY

This chapter employs a conceptual and integrative methodology aimed at exploring how AI and Industry 4.0 technologies are transforming the field of sports marketing. The methodology consists of three main components: literature selection, thematic synthesis, and theoretical contextualization.

1. Literature Selection

A structured literature review was conducted using academic databases such as SpringerLink, IGI Global Scientific, Scopus, Web of Science, and Google Scholar. Keywords used in the search included: artificial intelligence, sports marketing, machine learning, fan behavior, predictive analytics, virtual reality, blockchain, risk management in sports, and digital transformation. Preference was given to peer-reviewed articles, book chapters, and conference proceedings published between 2015 and 2025. Seminal works outside this range were also included for foundational concepts.

2. Thematic Synthesis

After collecting and reviewing relevant sources, a thematic synthesis approach was used to identify core themes across disciplines. These themes include:

- The role of AI tools (e.g., ML, NLP, CV) in predicting fan behavior
- Financial risk mitigation through AI
- Personalized fan engagement
- Integration of emerging technologies (e.g., VR, AR, blockchain)
- Ethical and legal considerations

The synthesis aimed to bridge the gap between technological capabilities and sports marketing strategies, offering a multi-layered perspective on the subject.

3. Theoretical Contextualization

Findings were framed using relevant theories and models from marketing and information systems literature, such as the Theory of Reasoned Action (TRA), the Technology Acceptance Model (TAM), and risk assessment frameworks. These models helped interpret how AI adoption influences fan behavior prediction and marketing decision-making in sports organizations.

Overall, this methodology provides a robust framework for analyzing existing knowledge, identifying innovation trends, and proposing strategic insights for practitioners, researchers, and policy-makers in the field of sports marketing.

PART III: THE USE OF AI IN PREDICTING FAN BEHAVIOR AND MANAGING FINANCIAL RISKS IN SPORTS MARKETING

In the rapidly evolving landscape of sports marketing, understanding fan behavior is crucial for organizations seeking to optimize their strategies and enhance profitability. AI has emerged as a transformative tool, enabling marketers to analyze vast amounts of data and extract actionable insights regarding fan preferences, engagement patterns, and purchasing behaviors. By leveraging AI technologies, sports marketers can predict future trends and behaviors, allowing them to tailor their offerings and communication strategies more effectively. Furthermore, AI plays a pivotal role in managing financial risks associated with unpredictable market dynamics and shifting consumer interests. By implementing advanced predictive analytics, organizations can make informed decisions, allocate resources efficiently, and ultimately safeguard their financial investments in a competitive industry. This section explores the significance of AI in revolutionizing fan engagement and risk management within the realm of sports marketing.

- **The importance of forecasting in sports marketing and its role in reducing financial risks**

As the modern economy evolves, traditional sports industry enterprises have also expanded their financial operations. One of the challenges that sports companies face is ensuring information security and managing financial risks. Risk assessment involves utilizing mathematical models to evaluate the risk factors identified in earlier stages in order to forecast potential risks (Zhao, 2021). The advancement of science and technology has facilitated the modernization of sports. Innovations in technology and engineering have contributed to enhanced sports performance. Online gaming, blogs, and virtual sports clubs have transformed the way sports are observed and engaged with (Vieira et al., 2021).

The emergence of financial services within the industrial framework of sports enterprises and financial institutions aims to ensure that the financial sector supports the real economy. However, there are inherent risks associated with financial activities (Verma et al., 2020). Risk management involves understanding the evolution of events and the surrounding environment, as well as the personnel, policies, and regulations involved. The primary goal of risk management is to identify potential risk factors and implement appropriate preventive measures (Zhao, 2021). Typically, risk management employs a blend of qualitative and quantitative approaches to safeguard the integrity and normal progression of activities while ensuring that economic benefits are preserved (Scullen et al., 2020). By organizing, implementing, coordinating, and controlling activities in a structured manner, sports operations can be conducted in a planned, precise, orderly, and safe manner. Current literature on supply chain risk identification indicates that qualitative research predominates, while quantitative research is less prevalent (Sinnett et al., 2016). Rautaray and Agrawal (2015) characterized sports risk management as the process of anticipating and mitigating threats that could have severely negative impacts on an organization or its assets. This process also encompasses the examination of organizational processes and decision-making to take appropriate actions. According to Vesper et al. (2015), the tasks involved in risk management include analyzing financial conditions and the initial insights gained from efforts to control productivity and minimize business losses. The growth of financial services supports the advancement of the real economy. Risk management typically utilizes a combination of qualitative and quantitative methods to ensure the safety and proper development of activities, thereby safeguarding their economic benefits (Tang et al., 2016). Through organized planning, implementation, coordination, and control, activities can proceed according to a predetermined, accurate, orderly, and secure operation. Current research on supply chain risk identification highlights that qualitative research is more prevalent compared to quantitative studies. Tang et al. (2016) categorized supply chain risks based on their source and whether they fall within a controllable range. In the process of identifying supply chain risks, Rao further classified these risks into external macroenvironmental risks, industry systemic risks, corporate internal risks, and operational risks (Jana, 2016).

- **Challenges of traditional methods of predicting fan behavior in the digital age**

Considering issues such as globalization, urbanization, and the emergence of new information and communication technologies, it can be stated that the new generation is facing a different world that transforms its values, norms, and culture. If generational gaps are overlooked, it may lead to the emergence of a social issue that results in generational divides and their consequences (Fathi & Motlag, 2011).

The sports industry is a dynamic field continuously shaped and transformed by technological innovations. The digitalization process has brought significant changes to various aspects of sports management. Digitalization has transformed conventional strategies for engaging fans, providing tailored and interactive experiences that enhance the emotional connections between supporters and sports organizations (Bayindir, 2024).

The challenges of traditional methods for predicting fan behavior in the sports industry have significantly increased in the digital age due to major changes brought about by technology and social media (Fazeli et al., 2024). In the past, analyzing fan behavior in sports was usually based on historical data and limited surveys (Shahpar Tofigh et al., 2022). However, with the emergence of digital platforms, fan behavior patterns have become markedly more complex. Information gathered from social media, online interactions, and big data highlights the need for new and more accurate methods for analyzing fan behavior (Pashaie & Golmohammadi, 2024). For example, fans can easily share their opinions about teams and games, and these opinions can influence management decisions and marketing strategies. Additionally, rapid changes in fans' interests and preferences, which are easily swayed by current trends and digital content, further complicate the challenges of accurate prediction. For this reason, sports organizations must turn to advanced technologies and innovative methods to better understand and predict their fans' behavior, enabling them to establish more effective communication with fans and provide a better experience for them.

- **Introducing AI and its sub-branches as a new tool in risk management**

Two of the most significant strategies for research, development, and transformation in leading companies are planned journey strategies and hill-climbing strategies, which stand in contrast to each other in terms of methodology. In a planned journey, the destination and the route to reach it are clearly defined. In this scenario, strategists have a clear vision of their objectives and the path that needs to be followed, allowing them to specify the steps necessary to achieve their goals. They develop a detailed plan that includes methods, timelines, and required resources, serving as a foundation for the managers responsible for implementing the transformation within the organization. Conversely, in the hill-climbing strategy, the destination remains uncertain. It resembles a tourist navigating an unknown environment, following the footprints of those who have passed through before, in hopes of reaching a remarkable destination. In this context, specialists explore new technologies with the aim of discovering how they can be utilized and what potential outcomes may be achieved. Interestingly, research from reputable institutions indicates that this second approach, the hill-climbing strategy, has garnered more interest among companies and has demonstrated greater returns. These studies reveal that innovative firms tend to engage in research on new technologies even when they do not have a clear idea of how to apply them within their business, focusing on the methods of implementation instead. Technologies such as the Internet of Things, fourth-generation automation, and artificial intelligence are among those that frequently represent key options in companies' hill-climbing strategies. Currently, services related to artificial intelligence have emerged as a thriving new business sector, with several knowledge-based companies in our country defining their mission as aiding the decision-making processes of large enterprises through data analysis and the provision of valuable managerial insights derived from that data. This trend is highly desirable, as it not only has the potential to play a significant role in fostering entrepreneurship among skilled professionals but also contributes to enhancing the managerial maturity and decision-making capabilities of companies in our nation. However, naturally, wherever there are substantial benefits, there are also significant risks. If these risks are not acknowledged, it is likely that important resources will be wasted. Given that this industry is still in its infancy, it is crucial to remind stakeholders in this field of these risks. Additionally, as such services expand, it is essential to establish appropriate regulations that align with their growth (Norian, 2021).

Many organizations have now come to recognize that artificial intelligence systems can significantly enhance their economic returns and that this technology has the potential to shape the businesses of the future. However, the implementation of this technology is accompanied by risks that some leading companies have already encountered, or they have utilized risk analysis methods to evaluate these challenges and identify effective approaches. The published results of these analyses indicate the existence of considerable hazards in this field. Furthermore, it is neither feasible to avoid artificial intelligence nor to simply overlook its associated risks and challenges. Therefore, companies must engage not only with technical research and development teams but also establish groups consisting of risk analysis and legal experts to comprehensively examine all aspects of the development and application of artificial intelligence. These teams should rigorously assess the initial processes related to artificial intelligence, including data collection, analysis, and feedback provision, and conduct a transparent and comprehensive analysis of the associated technical, strategic, and legal risks. Additionally, various types of risks related to this technology have been analyzed in detail, and it is important to note that, depending on the nature and application of these systems, other risks may also pose threats to companies (Norian, 2021; Rahimi Kolour & Ghasemi Hamedani, 2023).

- **Providing a framework for using AI in predicting fan behavior and managing financial risk**

In recent times, AI has become a fundamental element across all industries, and the financial sector is no exception. From banks and insurance companies to stock markets and investment firms, all these areas are increasingly leveraging AI algorithms to predict risks, conduct automated trading, and even detect fraud. These advancements not only enhance efficiency and accuracy in financial processes but also have implications for the sports industry. For instance, sports clubs can utilize this technology to analyze player performance data, manage financial risks, and optimize investment strategies, ultimately leading to improved overall performance in this sector.

With the continuous changes in our surrounding world, the sports industry is also undergoing transformation. The new generation of athletes and fans has compelled clubs and sports organizations to adopt innovative approaches in managing and conducting sports businesses. The exponential increase in data has provided leaders in the business sector with access to broader informational resources than ever before, and the globalization of trade has brought new opportunities, challenges, and situations. Over the past half-century, significant changes have occurred in the responsibilities of financial managers, including the definition of business strategies, risk management, and the role of information technology in financial management.

These developments reflect the profound impact of finance on all aspects of business. In the digital age, staying updated with technological advancements is of particular importance for businesses, as it aids them in competing with others and achieving their goals quickly and effectively (Sharifan, 2023).

-Risk management with AI

One of the most significant applications of AI in the financial sector is risk prediction. These systems employ machine learning algorithms to analyze large datasets, enabling them to forecast customer behavior and market fluctuations. For instance, banks utilize these tools to assess customer profiles and conduct credit evaluations. In this context, if a customer demonstrates a history of considerable financial volatility, AI systems can predict a higher likelihood of default or improper repayment. This capability is not only essential for financial institutions but also has relevance in the sports industry. Sports organizations can leverage similar AI-driven risk assessment techniques to evaluate player contracts, manage investment risks in player acquisitions, and enhance overall financial stability, ensuring more informed decision-making within their operations (Rahimi Kolour & Ghasemi Hamedani, 2023).

-Fraud detection and enhanced eecurity

Fraud detection is a crucial area of research in online banking, as cybercriminals continuously devise increasingly sophisticated fraud schemes. This ongoing threat necessitates the development of innovative detection techniques by researchers. Within the financial sector, fraud detection exemplifies a significant application of AI. Many companies and banks encounter daily risks associated with cyberattacks and financial fraud, and AI plays a vital role in identifying and preventing these incidents. AI systems are particularly effective at recognizing anomalous behaviors; when suspicious transactions or unusual activities occur within a bank account, these systems promptly notify the user or the financial institution (Akbarossadat & Esmaeilpour, 2022).

For instance, if an individual typically engages in online purchases from Iran and suddenly initiates a large transaction from a different country, such as the United States, the AI system will quickly assess this abnormal change in behavior and issue a warning. This capability is equally relevant in the sports industry, where organizations can implement AI-driven fraud detection mechanisms to safeguard against financial misconduct, ticket fraud, or unauthorized access to sensitive information. By employing these technologies, sports entities can enhance their security protocols, ensuring the integrity of their financial transactions and protecting their assets.

-Data analysis and support for informed decision-making

AI today not only facilitates data analysis but also assists companies and financial institutions in making informed decisions. For example, deep learning algorithms can process vast amounts of data in minimal time. This capability enables banks and investment firms to identify optimal investment strategies. Furthermore, this technology can uncover hidden patterns within datasets, providing financial analysts with valuable insights that enhance their decision-making processes (Karimi et al., 2025).

In the context of the sports industry, similar applications of AI can be observed. Sports organizations can utilize advanced data analytics to assess player performance, evaluate team strategies, and optimize resource allocation. By leveraging AI-driven insights, teams can make data-informed decisions regarding player acquisitions, training regimens, and game strategies, ultimately leading to improved performance and competitive advantage in the sports arena.

-Personal banking and customer experience enhanced by AI

It is likely that you have encountered chatbots and intelligent banking assistants. These tools, developed using AI, are designed to assist customers with transactions, answer inquiries, and even provide financial recommendations. For instance, a chatbot can facilitate tasks such as checking account balances, obtaining loan information, or addressing questions related to investments. Such services have significantly improved the customer experience within banks and financial institutions, making it more convenient and efficient (Manzouri & Khalili, 2023).

In the realm of sports, similar AI-driven innovations can be applied to enhance fan engagement and improve the overall experience. Sports organizations can implement chatbots to assist fans with ticket purchases, provide real-time updates on games, and offer personalized recommendations for merchandise. By employing AI technology, these organizations can create a more seamless and interactive experience for their customers, ultimately fostering greater loyalty and satisfaction among fans.

-AI and the future of finance

It is anticipated that the utilization of AI in the financial sector will significantly increase in the coming years, potentially extending into areas that are currently difficult to envision. For example, we may see the emergence of fully automated brokerage services that eliminate the need for human intervention. Additionally, AI may enhance the accuracy of market volatility predictions, thereby enabling more precise and lower-risk investment strategies. As these advancements unfold, the landscape of finance is likely to undergo transformative changes, reshaping how financial services are delivered and experienced (Bholat et al., 2018).

-Challenges and potential issues of AI in finance

Despite the numerous advantages, the application of AI in the financial sector presents several challenges and issues. Some of these challenges include:

Security and Privacy: The implementation of AI requires extensive data collection and analysis, which may pose risks to individual privacy.
Prediction Errors: While AI is advancing rapidly, it is still susceptible to inaccuracies in predictions. Financial markets are inherently complex, and it is not always possible to forecast outcomes with complete precision.
Impact on Employment: The increasing reliance on AI may lead to a decline in certain job roles, such as bank tellers and financial analysts, potentially resulting in job displacement for some individuals.

Artificial intelligence is rapidly transforming the landscape of finance. From automated trading algorithms to risk prediction tools, this technology is enabling banks, investment firms, and users to engage with financial services in a more efficient and secure manner. However, it is essential to recognize that AI still requires further enhancement and development, and its implementation must be approached with careful consideration of ethical, security, and privacy challenges (Bholat et al., 2018).

PART IV: THEORETICAL FOUNDATIONS OF AI IN PREDICTING FAN BEHAVIOR

- **The evolution of analytical methods in sports marketing**

Today, AI has become an integral part of the sports industry, and it is projected that its market value will reach $19.2 billion by 2030 (Mohammadi, Pashaie, et al., 2025a). The importance of studies in sports marketing is highlighted by the evolving relationship between sports and marketing strategies, which has changed significantly over the years. This transformation is largely due to the growing recognition of sports as a powerful marketing platform, resulting in an increase in research within this area. Sports marketing is identified as a dynamic field that connects academic research, marketing professionals, and public policy makers, showcasing its complex nature and the variety of consumer behaviors it addresses. Moreover, the incorporation of marketing strategies in the sports sector has become crucial for organizations seeking to capitalize on the booming global sports industry, which has seen a rise in sporting events and consumer participation (Moradi, 2025).

The sports industry is now commonly referred to as the sports entertainment industry, where financial considerations have significantly advanced beyond just on-field entertainment and action. The evolution of digital technology and customer satisfaction has also played a crucial role in supporting and enhancing the sports sector. Successful teams in today's sports landscape primarily utilize analytics for two main objectives. Firstly, they enhance their engagement and interaction with fans, spectators, and consumers by leveraging various platforms to connect with their supporters and grow their audience. Secondly, analytics can be applied to improve their performance through competitor analysis and by monitoring and evaluating their own players' gameplay. Key elements in this field include social media analytics and their impact on the team, business, and performance metrics. Teams are increasingly employing online methods to gauge fan sentiment and understand what supporters want, aiming to build closer relationships with them. Over the past 2–3 years, there has been a rise in digital marketing campaigns, allowing clubs and leagues to be more extravagant and distinctive. Additionally, sports management has unlocked the potential for variable and dynamic ticket pricing through analytics. By identifying which games fans are willing to pay more for, teams can adjust ticket prices accordingly. Thus, analytics have empowered clubs to leverage their popularity and grow their fan bases (Jaiwant & Kureethara, 2024).

The field of marketing is continuously evolving due to its commercial objectives and the cultural context surrounding customer needs. To ensure customer satisfaction and attraction, marketing must inevitably employ effective and efficient tools. In recent years, marketing has transcended its traditional approaches, significantly transformed by technological advancements and the digital landscape. Artificial Intelligence Marketing (AIM) represents a novel approach to market management, utilizing cutting-edge technology to enhance customer experiences and identify their needs. This type of marketing bridges the gap between data science and marketing by analyzing vast amounts of data. In today's world, smart marketing has revolutionized the market and is considered the core of business. The emergence of artificial intelligence in marketing holds the potential to assist managers in various areas, such as lead generation, market research, and social media management. Utilizing competitive intelligence systems and market data can facilitate effective strategic planning and organization within the sales domain. Recent studies indicate that current research in marketing has primarily focused on structures with measurable variables, with the methodology largely grounded in statistics, mathematical calculations, and artificial intelligence. This trend has led to many aspects of smart marketing being overlooked by some researchers. AIM emerges as an innovative research domain that connects neuroscience with subconscious structures, potentially contributing to the expansion of knowledge boundaries in marketing management. Research in marketing encompasses marketing research, marketing strategies, marketing plans, marketing actions, and marketing performance as outcomes of applying artificial intelligence in the field. Additionally, the antecedents of AI usage in marketing include technological, organizational, environmental, behavioral, and individual factors. Furthermore, companies can expand their businesses through new marketing methods, including smart marketing. It is also noted that marketing efforts are unlikely to yield fruitful results without the presence of smart marketing and effective tools (Fekrat & Jaberi, 2024).

Sports marketing involves a variety of activities designed to promote sports events, teams, and products by tapping into the emotional bonds fans have with their favorite sports and athletes. This combination of promotion and emotional engagement is essential for comprehending consumer behavior within the sports industry, which has evolved into a multi-billion-dollar global market. The development of sports marketing mirrors broader shifts in consumer behavior, advancements in technology, and the globalization of sports, highlighting the need for marketers to continuously research and adapt to meet evolving consumer expectations and preferences (Moradi, 2025).

- **Theoretical frameworks for risk assessment in sport marketing decision making**

Risk management has become a key priority for sports organizations in light of the growing complexity of their operations, governance issues, and unforeseen events like the COVID-19 pandemic. These organizations encounter a variety of risks, such as financial instability, legal liabilities, and operational disruptions, among others. Implementing effective risk management—entailing the identification, assessment, and mitigation of potential threats to an organization's goals—is essential for maintaining their resilience and ensuring long-term sustainability. A thorough understanding of the current landscape of risk management in this context is crucial for formulating strategies that tackle these diverse challenges (Genovard et al., 2025).

Risk management, traditionally a strategy used in financial organizations, has now expanded into other areas, particularly sports marketing. The complex and dynamic conditions of today's market significantly impact sports companies and create a need for business transparency as a prerequisite for effective management of various resources, including financial and human resources. As sports organizations increasingly conduct their business transactions based on market principles, they naturally expose themselves to various types of risks. This situation heightens the necessity for capable sports managers in the marketing field—individuals who can develop, implement, and evaluate appropriate management strategies to address current challenges. The growing exposure of sports organizations to multiple risks has paved the way for the emergence of a new profession in sports management, emphasizing the importance of risk management in the success and sustainability of these organizations. Thus, risk management not only aids in improving the financial and operational performance of sports organizations but can also contribute to attracting and retaining audiences and sponsors, which in turn strengthens the brand and reputation of sports entities (Ghafarzadeh Malasi & Ismaili Shahzandi, 2022).

Numerous articles and chapters from reference books are dedicated to marketing risks. Some of these focus on elements of promotional programs and strategies, while others are concerned with product development, packaging, branding, and product rejection. Additionally, some resources address pricing maneuvers, product reduction versus price reduction, pricing lines, or price levels. Meanwhile, other sources focus on distribution issues, such as sales representatives or direct sales forces, and the use of dedicated distributors with direct sales. While these topics encompass both strategic and tactical components and may occupy a significant amount of decision-makers' time, two factors that have a greater impact on risk are market share and familiarity with the market (Shah & LaPlaca, 1981).

The theoretical frameworks for assessing risk in sports marketing decision-making refer to a set of models and approaches that assist in analyzing and managing risks associated with marketing activities in the sports industry. These frameworks typically include economic theories, decision-making models, and risk analysis approaches that enable sports managers to examine various factors such as market fluctuations, consumer behavior, and existing competition. By utilizing these frameworks, managers can identify potential risks and develop appropriate strategies to mitigate them. Additionally, these frameworks help decision-makers to design more effective marketing actions through a more accurate evaluation of market conditions, ultimately leading to better outcomes in audience engagement and increased revenues for sports organizations. Ultimately, these approaches not only contribute to improving the financial performance of sports organizations but can also enhance the brand and reputation of these organizations in the competitive sports market.

Adventure sport coaches operate in environments that are both dynamic and high-risk, encompassing both perceived and actual dangers. The inherent risks tied to these activities, along with individuals' reactions and the optimal management of these factors, make risk management in adventure sports more intricate and perilous compared to traditional sports, where the focus is primarily on risk minimization. A crucial aspect of this process is the ability of adventure sports coaches to make informed judgments about risk levels, potential benefits, and possible outcomes. Understanding this decision-making process should be fundamental to coaching practices and coach education within this complex and ever-changing field (Collins & Collins, 2013). Risk assessment can provide valuable information for decision-making in the field of risk reduction, optimization of control systems, and planning for the desired response.

- Risk management in sports organisations

In recent years, numerous sports scandals have jeopardized the sustainability and integrity of the industry. Prominent instances include the FIFA corruption scandal, where officials engaged in bribery and racketeering (Verver, 2015), and the Rio 2016 Olympics, which encountered significant infrastructure failures and public health concerns associated with the Zika virus (Halchin & Rollins, 2017). Additionally, the 2010 match-fixing scandal in cricket, involving several Pakistani players, underscored the serious risks related to integrity in sports (Gross, 2006). Furthermore, the Lance Armstrong doping scandal, in which the cyclist was found guilty of using performance-enhancing drugs during his seven Tour de France victories, raised important questions about governance and ethics in the sport (Dimeo, 2014). While media coverage has predominantly spotlighted high-profile incidents within major organizations, it is important to acknowledge that all sports entities, regardless of their size or type, are vulnerable to risks (Genovard et al., 2025).

The COVID-19 pandemic has recently intensified these challenges, resulting in significant socioeconomic repercussions such as revenue losses for organizations, decreased economic liquidity, workforce reductions, volunteer attrition, and a drop in workforce participation (Mohammadi et al.; Zhong et al., 2021). The unfolding of these events has revealed serious concerns regarding the effectiveness of risk assessment and management practices within sports organizations (Young & Wendit, 2017). The lack of strong risk management frameworks makes sports entities prone to considerable vulnerabilities, thus jeopardizing their sustainability and operational integrity in an increasingly unstable environment (King, 2016).

As a result, risk management has become a crucial pillar that includes cultural, procedural, and structural elements aimed at optimal management of potential opportunities and associated challenges (Laroche & Corbett, 2010). Consequently, effective risk management enables entities to take well-prepared actions when considering objectives and planning strategic pathways, ultimately leading to improved governance of sports organizations. Despite the growing interest in risk management applications and its established link to good governance practices, along with the numerous advantages it offers sports entities—such as minimizing the time spent reacting to risks and fostering a more proactive approach to strategy, or assisting organizations in decision-making, achieving goals, and formulating informed strategies the implementation of risk management has not yet achieved widespread acknowledgment within the sports and leisure sectors (Genovard et al., 2025).

- **Convergence of AI and fan data management**

Currently, with the emergence of technologies such as artificial intelligence (AI), virtual reality (VR), augmented reality (AR), and data visualization (DV), we are witnessing significant changes in the world of sports. These technologies assist in improving sports performance analysis, automating data collection, and creating effective training environments, thereby enhancing decision-making processes. Traditional methods of sports performance analysis typically relied on manual data collection, subjective observations, and limited statistical models; however, recent advancements in technology have transformed this process into an objective and up-to-date one. For example, AI has revolutionized the field by simplifying data collection, processing large datasets, and automating sports analysis. Virtual reality enables training in highly realistic environments, allowing athletes to enhance their skills in controlled conditions. Augmented reality provides digital information within the real sports environment, facilitating the tactical planning process. Additionally, data visualization techniques represent complex data visually, improving the understanding of performance metrics. This convergence of AI and fan data management helps create new, personalized experiences for fans. AI can analyze fan data and identify their behavioral patterns, allowing teams to establish better connections with fans and provide more engaging experiences for them. As a result, these technologies not only contribute to improving sports performance but also strengthen the relationships between teams and their fans (Kiani, 2024; Mahmoudian et al., 2024).

The rapid growth of widespread data, connectivity, and services poses significant challenges, especially in relation to the rigorous demands of the IoT. To find more effective solutions and enhance information retrieval, AI acts as a powerful force, significantly aiding in data analysis and decision-making processes. It plays a vital role in advancing digital and intelligent services (Shi et al., 2020).

PART V: AI TOOLS IN RISK FORECASTING AND MANAGEMENT

By utilizing machine learning algorithms and big data analysis, artificial intelligence can identify hidden patterns in data and provide more accurate predictions of potential events. Important applications of AI in this area include predicting equipment failures, identifying safety hazards in work environments, optimizing operational processes, and effectively managing crises. Evidence suggests that investing in the development and implementation of AI-based systems can significantly reduce costs associated with incidents, improve productivity, and enhance safety levels across various industries. It also confirms that AI can aid in more accurate risk prediction and better decision-making by analyzing complex data and learning from past experiences. However, challenges such as data quality, human-machine interaction, and ethical issues also exist in this field, which will be addressed in the continue chapter of the book (Karimi, 2025).

Figure 1. AI tools

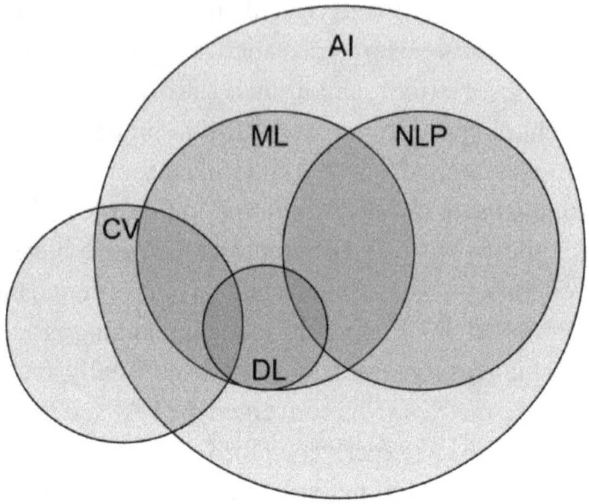

Source: Baker et al. (2024)

Note: *AI is a broad term with many interconnected concepts. While machine learning (ML) and natural language processing (NLP) are separate fields, they both leverage tools from each other, including deep learning (DL). Similarly, computer vision (CV) utilizes ML and DL but also many tools outside of the AI umbrella.*

- **Machine learning in predicting purchasing behavior**

Predicting customer behavior is one of the biggest challenges facing businesses today. In this competitive environment, companies must quickly respond to changes and customer demands, and the ability to predict their behavior can provide a significant competitive advantage. Accurate predictions of customer behavior can assist businesses in making strategic decisions, developing products and services, and managing customer relationships. One of the most important tools and techniques used in this area is artificial intelligence algorithms and neural networks. These tools have the ability to analyze large volumes of data and can extract complex patterns that may be overlooked in predictive models. Therefore, utilizing these algorithms for predicting customer behavior can lead to more accurate and effective models (Ghorbani Ghader et al., 2024).

In the world of sports marketing, personalizing the experience for fans and customers is just as important as in e-commerce (Pashaie & Nasirpour, 2024). Utilizing machine learning (ML) can help sports teams and brands analyze the behaviors and interests of their fans and offer tailored recommendations and special content accordingly. For example, by analyzing data related to past purchases and fan interactions with the brand, teams can create a unique and personalized experience for each fan, such as offering exclusive tickets, discounts, or special content based on their interests. This approach can not only increase the conversion rate of ticket and merchandise sales but also strengthen the relationships between sports brands and their fans, ultimately enhancing their loyalty to the brand (Mohammadi, Pashaie, et al., 2025a).

ML, a branch of artificial intelligence, identifies customer behavior patterns through data analysis and provides accurate predictions. These patterns can include purchase history, customer preferences, repeat behaviors, and responses to marketing campaigns. With this technology, online stores can provide specific offers and products to each customer individually, which helps increase customer engagement and loyalty (Segun-Falade et al., 2024).

Predictive analytics is essential for comprehending and forecasting customer behavior, allowing businesses to make informed decisions and adjust their strategies to align with changing market demands. By examining historical data, companies can recognize patterns and trends that offer insights into future customer actions, preferences, and needs. However, traditional methods of predictive analytics often encounter challenges related to accuracy and scalability. ML significantly improves these capabilities by employing advanced algorithms capable of processing large datasets with enhanced accuracy. Unlike standard statistical techniques, ML algorithms learn from data and evolve over time, refining their predictions as they receive more information. This adaptive learning process facilitates more precise forecasts of customer behavior and empowers businesses to proactively address emerging trends. The integration of ML with predictive analytics provides numerous advantages for studying customer behavior. ML algorithms can reveal intricate patterns and relationships that traditional methods might overlook, resulting in deeper insights and a more nuanced understanding. This synergy improves the ability to effectively segment customers, tailor marketing strategies, and enhance customer interactions. Moreover, ML-driven predictive models can adjust to shifts in customer behavior in real-time, ensuring that businesses remain flexible and responsive in a rapidly changing market environment (Segun-Falade et al., 2024).

In summary, the fusion of ML and predictive analytics offers a powerful resource for gaining a competitive advantage in the analysis of customer behavior.

By utilizing these advanced methodologies, companies can achieve more precise predictions, deepen their understanding of customers, and ultimately drive more successful business outcomes.

- The concept of behavior prediction

The concept of predicting customer behavior refers to the process of identifying and analyzing behavioral patterns and preferences of customers in order to forecast their future needs, desires, and behaviors. Accurate predictions of customer behavior can help companies design more effective marketing strategies and provide more personalized services. These predictions may include identifying products that customers are likely to be interested in, forecasting their future needs, simulating their reactions to price changes or advertisements, and other factors that influence their behavior (Ghorbani Ghader et al., 2024).

- The importance of predicting customer behavior

The world of business is changing, and predicting customer behavior is regarded as a competitive tool for organizations. By utilizing customer behavior predictions, companies can adopt more targeted marketing strategies, allocate resources more efficiently, and make smarter decisions. Consequently, this leads to reduced costs, increased sales, improved customer experience, and ultimately greater profitability (Ghorbani Ghader et al., 2024).

- AI algorithms and their application in predicting customer behavior

AI, as a technology capable of automatically analyzing information without human intervention, has seen significant growth in recent years. This technology encompasses various machine learning algorithms that can identify patterns in data and utilize them for outcome predictions. In predicting customer behavior, artificial intelligence algorithms analyze historical data, customer behaviors, and characteristics to provide forecasts about their future behavior (Ghorbani Ghader et al., 2024).

- Machine learning algorithms in predicting sport customer behavior

The rapid emergence of AI and its derivative ML tools has been embraced with enthusiasm in sport consumer behavior research lately (Du et al., 2023). ML algorithms fall into various categories, including supervised learning, unsupervised learning, and reinforcement learning. In predicting customer behavior, supervised learning is often used because these algorithms utilize labeled data to train models.

One of the commonly used algorithms in this area is the decision tree algorithm, which simulates human decision-making and can assist in identifying customer behavioral patterns (Ghorbani Ghader et al., 2024).

Machine learning algorithms play a crucial role in predicting customer behavior in the sports industry by analyzing vast amounts of data to uncover patterns and trends. These algorithms, such as decision trees, support vector machines, and neural networks, can process information from various sources, including ticket purchases, membership renewals, and fan engagement on social media. By employing supervised learning techniques, organizations can build predictive models that identify factors influencing customer loyalty, attendance, and spending habits. As a result, sports clubs and organizations can tailor their marketing strategies, enhance customer experiences, and improve retention rates, ultimately driving revenue growth and fostering a stronger connection with their fan base. This data-driven approach empowers decision-makers to make informed choices and implement strategies that resonate with their audience, ensuring long-term success in a competitive market.

- **Natural language processing in fan feedback analysis**

The behavior of sports fans is one of the most common and universal activities in people's leisure time. These behaviors range from purchasing tickets and merchandise to discussing team performance on social media, creating a deep connection between fans and their favorite teams, which leads to a variety of diverse behaviors. In many cases, the behavior of fans who directly influence the policies of a sports organization has drawn the attention of numerous researchers in the sports industry (Moradipour et al., 2021).

In recent years, various techniques and tools from AI, including machine learning, natural language processing (NLP), random decision forests (RDF), neural networks (NN), deep learning (DL), and text mining (TM) have emerged. These can assist in better analyzing complex phenomena and provide deeper insights. In particular, text mining techniques can reveal key concepts, trends, and hidden relationships within texts by extracting meaning. Existing studies in sports management have utilized text mining techniques to analyze the sentiments of fans' tweets during Super Bowl games (which consist of unstructured data). NLP is a subfield of AI that helps machines understand and process human language. This technology enables the automated execution of repetitive tasks and has a close relationship with the fields of ML and DL. The implementation and execution of NLP require the use of models and algorithms from both machine learning and deep learning (Heidari et al., 2024).

Figure 2. Natural language processing (NLP)

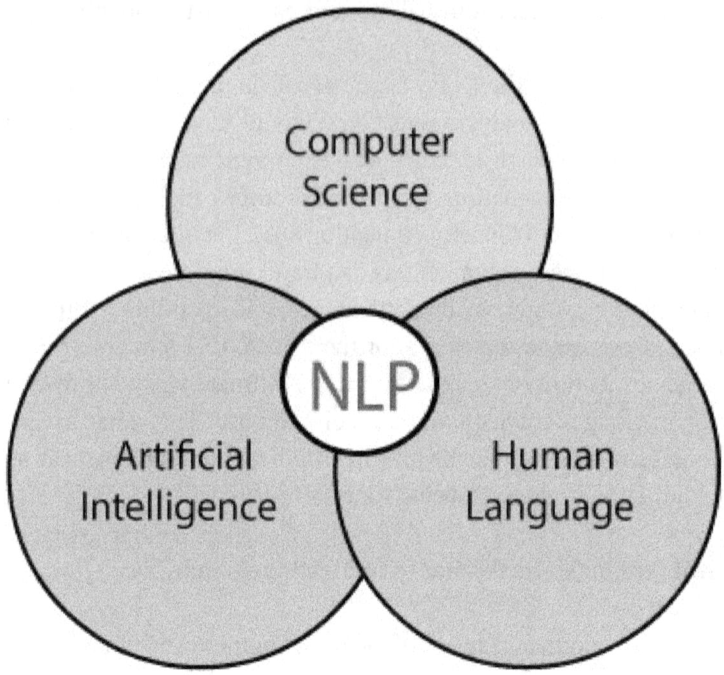

The evolution of NLP can be traced back to the early 1950s. In his seminal paper titled "Computing Machinery and Intelligence," Alan Turing discusses the concept of machine thinking capable of simulating human conversations (Turing, 2009), laying the groundwork for what would later become one of the most dynamic fields in AI. With the increase in computational power and access to data, NLP has made significant strides, evolving from simple language processing tasks to complex systems capable of engaging in human-like conversations. Today, these advanced systems are recognized as a fundamental part of AI. From the early natural language processing models to modern neural network-based models like GPT (Generative Pre-trained Transformer) (Deshpande et al., 2024), designed to produce human-like text, and BERT (Bidirectional Encoder Representations from Transformers) (Mohammed & Ali, 2021), which is utilized for a better understanding of sentence context, this field has experienced remarkable growth in capabilities and applications.

The advancement of NLP has been a rapid and transformative journey, evolving from early rule-based systems to sophisticated models designed to understand, interpret, generate, and process human language in a meaningful and effective manner. These models represent a significant step toward creating machines capable of communicating in human language, effectively bridging the gap between human cognition and computational processing. The primary goal of NLP is to enable computers to comprehend, interpret, and produce human language. Achieving this requires a multidisciplinary approach that integrates fields such as linguistics, computer science, and artificial intelligence, allowing machines to replicate the understanding and generation of human language.

- **Computer vision in assessing fan engagement**

Artificial intelligence and computer vision (CV) play a significant role in sports marketing and fan engagement. In light of the COVID-19 pandemic, these technologies are rapidly evolving, allowing sports marketers to create more personalized experiences for fans. Smart fitness programs powered by AI can help fans improve their home workouts and establish a stronger connection with their favorite teams. Additionally, analyzing data and fan behavior through these technologies enables marketers to design more effective strategies for attracting and retaining fans. Overall, artificial intelligence is recognized as a key factor in the sports technology industry, helping to strengthen the connections between teams and fans and enhance their overall experience (Mohammadi, Pashaie, & Ghaffarisadr, 2025; Pashaie, Golmohammadi, & Zakhirani, 2024).

Sports and technology are intricately linked in various aspects. Athletes are constantly looking for innovative methods to enhance their performance, coaches strive to leverage all available data for a competitive edge, and broadcasters work to deliver a distinctive and improved experience for their audiences. Recent developments in CV technology have significantly transformed sports analysis and visualization (Gade et al., 2024). Cutting-edge data collection technologies, computational methods, and advanced algorithms have transformed sports analytics across multiple dimensions, affecting everything from athlete performance to fan interaction. Technologies such as CV and DL are essential for analyzing video footage to predict player behavior and game scenarios; however, their effectiveness hinges on the volume and quality of training data, particularly in sports characterized by distinct dynamics and camera perspectives. Each sport presents its own unique challenges (Istasse et al., 2023).

- **Deep learning in sport marketing**

The rapid evolution of Internet technology has established a unified platform for sports organizations to leverage in developing innovative business models within the industry. As the number of athletes and support staff continues to increase, this growth generates data at an unprecedented pace, resulting in a substantial volume of sports-related information. Effectively analyzing and predicting trends from such extensive data presents a formidable challenge that conventional methods struggle to address (Lv et al., 2022).

In this context, the digital revolution has become a fundamental force driving all facets of commerce, particularly in marketing. Nowadays, it is nearly impossible to find a company in any industry that does not employ digital marketing strategies to engage with customers, and the sports sector is no exception. The increasing prevalence of digitalization has significantly transformed the fan experience, allowing fans to engage more deeply with both the game and its surrounding elements (Sbrighi, 2024a). This expansion of marketing data is simultaneously fostering a greater reliance on deep learning (DL) techniques, further enhancing marketing strategies in the sports industry (Liu, 2023).

Deep learning, which is a subset of ML and AI, is now recognized as a foundational technology of the Fourth Industrial Revolution (4IR or Industry 4.0). Its ability to learn from data, stemming from artificial neural networks (ANN), has made DL a prominent subject in computing. This technology is extensively utilized across diverse fields, including healthcare, visual recognition, text analytics, and cybersecurity. So, ML and DL are specific methods within the broader field of AI, contributing to the automation of intellectual tasks performed by humans (Kufel et al., 2023). In the realm of sports marketing, the application of DL can significantly enhance data analysis and consumer engagement strategies, allowing organizations to better understand fan preferences and optimize marketing efforts effectively (Mohammadi, Pashaie, et al., 2025a).

PART VI: STRATEGIES TO OVERCOME AI CHALLENGES IN SPORTS MARKETING

Artificial intelligence technology has immense potential to enhance efficiency, decision-making, and user experience across various fields. However, its implementation can also lead to ethical dilemmas (Pashaie, Mohammadi, & Golmohammadi, 2024). To ensure that AI serves as a positive force, it is essential to pay attention to the following ethical challenges:

- ***Ethical Laws and Regulations***

Before deploying AI, stakeholders must have a comprehensive understanding of its ethical dimensions. This includes the impact of AI on privacy, security, bias, discrimination, and overall human welfare (Feijóo et al., 2020; Modi, 2023). Policymakers, developers, and organizations should collaborate to establish guidelines that align AI development with social values.

In the realm of AI ethics, international cooperation is crucial (Ala-Pietilä & Smuha, 2021). Policymakers must work together to create global standards for the development and use of AI (Shen, 2024). Initiatives like the Montreal Declaration and partnerships in AI have laid the groundwork for global collaboration in AI governance.

AI systems can produce unintended consequences that may harm individuals or groups (Smuha, 2021). Therefore, considering human rights in the development and application of AI systems is vital. This includes ensuring that AI systems are not used to discriminate against individuals or groups.

Countries around the world are developing national AI strategies to harness the potential of AI while addressing ethical concerns. These strategies focus on research, innovation, talent development, data management, and the responsible deployment of AI technologies (Feijóo et al., 2020).

- ***Responsible System Design***

If AI algorithms are not carefully designed and tested, they can perpetuate bias and discrimination. Implementing fair practices throughout the AI development process is crucial to minimizing bias and ensuring impartial decision-making. Techniques such as data preprocessing to eliminate biases, utilizing diverse training datasets, and conducting regular audits of AI systems can help reduce discrimination (Varona & Suárez, 2022).

Transparency is essential for building trust in AI systems (Thalpage, 2023; Von Eschenbach, 2021). Users and stakeholders need to understand how AI makes decisions. Employing interpretable AI models, providing explanations for decisions, and delivering clear documentation of AI processes are vital for achieving transparency.

Addressing privacy concerns is a critical aspect of developing ethical AI. The collection, processing, or storage of personal data can lead to privacy-related issues. Ensuring that AI systems comply with data protection regulations is essential. Additionally, safeguarding the collection and processing of personal data to protect individuals' privacy is of utmost importance (Mohammadi, Pashaie, et al., 2025b).

- ***Human Oversight***

AI technologies should be designed to take responsibility for the decisions they make. As AI systems grow increasingly complex, opaque, and autonomous, ensuring responsible use becomes a formidable challenge. This requires establishing clear lines of accountability and ensuring human oversight in critical decision-making processes (Holzinger et al., 2024). In cases of negative outcomes, it must be clear who is responsible for addressing and resolving the issues. Ethics review boards can provide valuable guidance and oversight throughout the AI development process.

These boards consist of interdisciplinary experts who evaluate and assess the ethical implications of AI projects.

Training employees on the ethical implications of AI and educating them on how to develop and utilize ethical AI is essential. This ensures that all staff involved in the development or use of AI systems understand the importance of ethical considerations. Additionally, training helps employees recognize and mitigate potential ethical issues.

Collaborating with ethical providers who consider your values and can assist in developing and implementing ethical AI is crucial. Seek out providers that prioritize diversity and inclusion, transparency, and human rights in the development and use of AI systems.

Overall, in the realm of sports marketing, the integration of artificial intelligence can significantly enhance customer engagement and data-driven decision-making. However, it is crucial to address the ethical implications of using AI, such as data privacy concerns and the potential for biased marketing strategies. For instance, while AI can analyze consumer behavior to create targeted ads, it must do so without invading personal privacy or perpetuating stereotypes. By emphasizing ethical principles like fairness and transparency, sports marketers can build trust with their audience, ensuring that AI tools are used responsibly to foster a more inclusive and equitable sports environment.

PART VII: ETHICAL CONSIDERATIONS IN AI

AI is revolutionizing the sports industry, addressing its challenges and limitations is essential. Ensuring data accuracy, affordability, privacy, and ethical implementation will be key to unlocking its full potential. As AI continues to advance, its influence on sports is set to expand, driving innovation and enhancing various aspects of the industry (Rahmani et al., 2024). Emerging technologies continue to reshape the landscape of data privacy. For instance, AI and machine learning present both new opportunities and significant challenges (Fakeyede et al., 2023). Different countries have various laws on data privacy, AI ethics, and technology use. These differences create major challenges for international sports organizations trying to apply AI solutions consistently across regions. Following local regulations while keeping a unified AI strategy is a significant obstacle (Pashaie, Mohammadi, & Golmohammadi, 2024). AI enables tools to perform cognitive tasks that were previously handled by humans, with high accuracy, while minimizing or even eliminating the role of humans. The guidelines developed in laboratories, which form the foundation of AI, are quickly moving beyond the lab and are being implemented at all levels of society. Such widespread adoption of AI may lead to negative consequences, including greater racial and gender discrimination due to hidden biases in input data, the loss of human agency, the rise of cybercrimes, misuse of big data, privacy violations, job displacement, unchecked political influence by multinational corporations, and the concentration of wealth and power in the hands of a few groups (Bolboli Qadikolaei & Parsania, 2023). A comprehensive approach to risk management is essential for effective data privacy governance. This requires embedding data privacy risk assessments into broader risk management strategies and promoting cross-departmental collaboration to achieve a holistic understanding of risks and mitigation measures. Furthermore, organizations should leverage emerging technologies like AI and blockchain to strengthen data protection while considering ethical implications and ensuring compliance with privacy principles (Fakeyede et al., 2023).

AI-powered platforms are now essential for success in modern e-commerce. In digital marketing, AI plays a pivotal role by facilitating data-driven decision-making through deep learning methods, allowing businesses to forecast user behavior throughout the entire buying process. In sports marketing, AI helps organizations improve fan engagement, boost operational effectiveness, and unlock new opportunities for growth. It strengthens the performance of existing business systems, speeding up daily operations and workflows (Pashaie, Golmohammadi, & Zakhirani, 2024).

Digital transformation and the integration of e-CRM in the sports industry present significant opportunities alongside numerous ethical challenges. A primary concern is the protection of fan privacy and the security of their data (Dehghanpouri et al., 2020). The extensive collection and analysis of customer data raise issues related to surveillance, informed consent, and unauthorized information use (Karimi et al., 2025). To address these concerns, sports organizations must implement transparent policies, empower users with options to manage their consent, and adhere to stringent security standards to safeguard personal information. Moreover, the introduction of artificial intelligence to personalize fan experiences may trigger resistance from fans who are sensitive to algorithmic recommendations and targeted advertising. To navigate this challenge, organizations should strike a balance between personalization and privacy by offering options for users to control their privacy settings and clarifying the automated decision-making processes involved (Pashaie, Golmohammadi, & Zakhirani, 2024)

This growing complexity in technology is mirrored by an evolving regulatory landscape. The emergence of the Internet and digital platforms has turned data into a powerful global asset, yet it has also highlighted significant privacy challenges. Governments are now faced with critical decisions about whether existing privacy laws sufficiently protect personal data online. The United States and the European Union, as leaders in both technological advancement and privacy legislation, are under scrutiny to establish effective standards in data protection (Choi, 2020).

In the age of digital transformation, safeguarding personal data has become a major priority, leading to the implementation of strict regulations like the General Data Protection Regulation (GDPR) and the California Consumer Privacy Act (CCPA) (Fakeyede et al., 2023).

The European Union's Data Policy Directive, enacted in 1995, was the first regulation requiring member states to create regulatory frameworks for privacy. However, it restricted the transfer of data outside the European Economic Area unless the receiving countries had adequate protective measures—criteria that even the United States struggled to meet. Due to its non-binding nature, the directive's impact was limited. In response to these challenges, the European Parliament introduced the General Data Protection Regulation (GDPR), which outlines rules for protecting individuals' personal data and facilitates the free movement of such data. This regulation offers more robust mechanisms for data transfer outside the EU and mandates compliance from all 28 member states while respecting national sovereignty (Bradley, 2024).

Similarly, in the United States, the California Legislature enacted the California Consumer Privacy Act (CCPA) in 2020 to empower consumers with greater rights over their data. The CCPA grants rights such as: (1) knowing what personal information is collected and how it is used; (2) requesting deletion of collected personal information (with certain exceptions); (3) opting out of the sale or sharing of personal information; and (4) non-discrimination for exercising these rights. Following this, the California Privacy Rights Act (CPRA) was passed in 2020, with most provisions becoming effective in January 2023, further enhancing consumer data privacy rights. The CPRA introduced additional rights, including (5) the right to correct inaccurate personal information and (6) the right to limit the use and disclosure of sensitive personal information (Bradley, 2024). The CPRA is referenced as an amendment to the CCPA, underscoring the evolving legal framework for data protection in California.

From a legal standpoint, different countries have developed diverse frameworks for protecting personal data. Regulations like the GDPR in the European Union and the CCPA in the United States impose strict requirements on the collection, storage, and processing of user information. Sports organizations that operate internationally must remain vigilant and align their internal policies with these regulations to ensure compliance.

PART VIII: FUTURES STUDIES AND EMERGING TRENDS

- **New technologies and their impact on predicting sports fan behavior**

Today, sports have become one of the most important aspects of modern industrial societies, with a significant portion of the population in each country engaging with them in various ways. Among these, sports spectators constitute a considerable percentage of the audience. For this reason, sports have transformed into a global economic industry. In the realm of global commerce, sports are unique because they have customers who pay to watch rather than to purchase or consume the products directly. Professional clubs utilize various methods and resources to secure funding, including attracting sponsors, promoting commercial goods, selling players, and selling tickets and sports products, as well as offering ancillary services.

Fans are the spirit of sports, and therefore, they play a crucial role in the success of sporting competitions. The empty seats in the stadiums of premier leagues indicate that sports are not genuinely appealing and popular. In fact, the behavioral intentions of fans of sports teams and football are highly diverse and varied. Whether customers are inclined to use a company's services or not is indicative of their behavioral intentions and may lead them to turn to another provider. Thus, by better understanding customer behavior, managers and marketers can develop appropriate marketing strategies and more effectively present their products and services (Esmaeili et al., 2021).

Wang and Tang (2018) believe that positive behavioral intentions are associated with the ability to provide services that lead customers to express positive things about them, recommend them to other customers, remain loyal (i.e., the intention to return), purchase a product or service after consumption, provide verbal information about a product or service to someone else, and gather information for future purchases (Anthony et al., 2020)

In fact, a customer-centric approach is essential in today's era, which emphasizes quality in business and economic activities. Therefore, paying attention to customer behavioral intentions is of great importance. The foundation of all activities relies on understanding these intentions, as many significant research studies indicate that if behavioral intentions are measured correctly, they can effectively predict actual behaviors (Esmaeili et al., 2021).

The "Theory of Reasoned Action" suggests that attitudes lead to a positive or negative intention regarding a supplier, which is likely to influence actual behavior. For example, a positive attitude combined with the intention to act can determine behavior through intentions that directly lead to action (Black & Hibbeln, 2019). According to this theory, attitudes are predictive of actual behavior, and a positive attitude towards a supplier is likely to lead to a repeat purchase (Shah Alam & Mohamed Sayuti, 2011).

Innovative performance is considered one of the key criteria for measuring success in business companies. Innovation is recognized as the most important source of competitive advantage because it can lead to the production of new products that more effectively meet the needs of sports fans. Additionally, innovation can improve the quality of existing products or reduce the production costs of in-demand products. The use of modern technologies is essential for better understanding the behavior of sports fans and predicting their intentions. In fact, the continuous collection and integration of new knowledge through digital technologies can lead to innovation in this field. Innovative performance, by generating the necessary knowledge for the development of new products and production processes or improving existing processes, can significantly enhance the experience of fans. Thus, a better understanding of fan behavior and the use of modern technologies can lead to the formation of more effective strategies for attracting and retaining fans (Malekmahmoodi et al., 2022).

- **Convergence of AI with other technologies such as Virtual Reality (VR), Augmented Reality (AR) and blockchain in sports marketing**

In recent years, AI has demonstrated its dominance across multiple sectors, particularly in various entertainment games, and its application in the sports industry has significantly grown. The emergence of new digital technologies has sparked a transformation in sports marketing, similar to what has occurred in other industries, resulting in the evolution of digital sports marketing (Nalbant & Aydın, 2022; Pashaie, Golmohammadi, & Zakhirani, 2024). Blockchain technology is recognized as an effective tool for maintaining the integrity and security of information due to its prominent features such as decentralized architecture and high security. Alongside this, AI, with its advanced capabilities in pattern recognition and predictive analytics, extracts valuable and useful information from extensive data sets. Consequently, many scientists, technology companies, and governmental organizations are exploring and planning the integration of these two technologies to enhance security, efficiency, and productivity in dynamic business environments. One significant application of the integration of blockchain and artificial intelligence, particularly in the realm of sports marketing, is observed in supply chain management. This collaboration effectively enhances efficiency, transparency, and flexibility. Artificial intelligence plays a key role in pattern recognition and process optimization, while blockchain provides reliability and traceability of information. Together, these technologies facilitate improved data management and critical decision-making within the supply chain.

Moreover, the predictive capabilities of artificial intelligence can assist in forecasting demand and supply, while blockchain automates processes and fosters trust among stakeholders. Additionally, AI-equipped sensors can provide real-time tracking and predictive alerts, whereas blockchain ledgers contribute to accurate and auditable information tracking. This integration enables sports marketing professionals to manage conditions effectively and anticipate and evaluate disruptions. Furthermore, artificial intelligence aids in risk reduction, while the permanent records of blockchain and smart contracts enhance preventive measures against fraud and manipulation. This collaboration can lead to the formation of more effective sports marketing strategies that not only improve fan experiences but also foster more sustainable relationships between brands and customers.

Blockchain technology is emerging with remarkable potential across various sectors, including sports marketing. Cryptocurrencies, smart contracts, and NFTs are gradually finding diverse applications within the sports industry, possessing the capability to significantly impact the entire sports ecosystem. As blockchain technology matures, it will play a pivotal role in the future of sports marketing. The integration and development of blockchain across different industries is an inevitable trend that can not only bring about technological revolutions but also alter production relationships and business models, reconstruct the social value system, and redefine the value paradigm within sports marketing (Alidoust Ghahfarokhi & Dehghan Ghahfarokhi, 2024).

Virtual Reality (VR) is a technology that immerses users in computer-generated environments, going beyond the limits of physical reality to enhance their experiences and engagement through visual, auditory, and tactile stimuli. It includes several system categories, such as Non-Immersive, Semi-Immersive Projection, and Fully Immersive systems. In contrast, Augmented Reality (AR) is defined as a dynamic blend of the virtual and real worlds, allowing for the real-time integration of virtual entities within actual environments and enabling user interaction across both realms (Cossich et al., 2023).

The origins of VR trace back to the 1960s when Morton Heilig, an American cinematographer, developed the Sensorama, a mechanical device designed to deliver a multisensory experience through stereoscopic 3D visuals, sounds, smells, and vibrations (Gutierrez, 2023). In the late 1960s and early 1970s, Ivan Sutherland created what is often regarded as the first genuine head-mounted display (HMD) system, known as the "Sword of Damocles" (Sutherland, 1968). However, it was not until the 1980s and 1990s that VR technology began to take a more defined form, driven by advancements in computer graphics, display technology, and interaction devices. The term "virtual reality" was first coined in the 1990s by Jaron Lanier (Lanier, 1992). Additionally, the 1990s saw the introduction of Computer Automatic Virtual Environment (CAVE) systems, which provided a fully immersive environment (Cruz-Neira et al., 1992). This technology allows users to fully engage with and navigate 3D computer-generated environments within a spacious cube created by multiple display screens. As users physically enter this projection cube, they become completely surrounded by the virtual environment, resulting in a more natural and realistic sense of presence (Neumann et al., 2018).

Similarly, the concept of AR has its roots in the 1950s, with the term itself being introduced by Tim Caudell and David Mizell in 1990 (Berryman, 2012). AR systems can be either head-mounted see-through or monitor-based video systems. Although there are some theoretical distinctions between VR and AR, both technologies aim to enhance user experiences by expanding possibilities beyond the physical realm through seamless and integrated interactions. In fact, some suggest that both should be encompassed within a single comprehensive framework referred to as 'Extended Reality (XR),' where X serves as a placeholder for any form of reality (Rauschnabel et al., 2022).

It is clear that the evolution of both VR and AR is deeply intertwined with emerging technologies. Consequently, the widespread adoption of these technologies depends on the commercial availability of the related devices. In recent decades, considerable advancements have been made in the VR and AR landscape, resulting in a diverse array of devices that cater to various levels of immersion and functionality. From the early initiatives of SEGA VR and Google Glass to the more current Microsoft HoloLens and Meta Quest 2 & 3, as well as the newly launched Apple Vision Pro, these devices have the potential to revolutionize how we perceive and engage with both the virtual and real worlds, creating opportunities for innovative applications across fields such as medicine and physiotherapy, manufacturing, entertainment, sport, and education (Cossich et al., 2023).

The convergence of artificial intelligence with emerging technologies such as VR, AR, and blockchain is creating a significant transformation in how brands engage with fans and customers in sports marketing. AI enables athletes and teams to create more personalized content and experiences for their supporters by analyzing large data sets and identifying behavioral patterns. Meanwhile, VR and AR provide immersive and interactive experiences, allowing fans to participate directly in sports events and activities, fostering a deeper connection with brands. Additionally, blockchain, as a secure and transparent technology, can play a crucial role in managing digital rights, ticket sales, and building loyalty among fans. This convergence not only enhances user experience but also allows brands to communicate more effectively with their audiences, ultimately delivering added value to the sports industry.

- **Transforming sports marketing business models with AI**

The rise and growth of advanced technologies linked to the Fourth Industrial Revolution (IR4) and the advancement of information and communication technologies (ICT) have significantly transformed the sports industry. These transformations have positioned the sports sector as one of the most vibrant and competitive markets, underscoring the necessity for innovative and effective strategies to attract and retain customers. In this landscape, AI has emerged as a key player in revolutionizing and enhancing sports marketing processes. Furthermore, researchers anticipate a growing trend in labor market transformations due to the ongoing development and widespread adoption of AI (Pashaie, Golmohammadi, & Zakhirani, 2024).

AI facilitates the collection, analysis, and interpretation of vast amounts of data from various sources, enabling sports organizations to manage their marketing strategies more effectively. Nonetheless, much of the existing research has concentrated on conventional marketing approaches and general digital practices, with less focus on the role of AI in enhancing personalization (IP) and customer interaction (IC). Implementing AI in sports marketing allows for the delivery of unique and targeted marketing experiences through the analysis of customer data and the creation of personalized profiles, ultimately improving business performance in attracting and retaining clients. Personalization is a critical element of digital marketing that directly influences customer experience. By analyzing consumer behavior data and profiles, AI tailors marketing messages and experiences to specific needs and preferences, adjusting targeted advertisements and product recommendations for distinct consumer segments. This not only enhances the customer experience but also boosts satisfaction and loyalty (Pashaie, Golmohammadi, & Zakhirani, 2024)..

Customer interaction, a fundamental principle of successful marketing, plays a crucial role in enhancing customer motivation and engagement in sports activities while driving sales and revenue for companies. AI can facilitate the creation of targeted and customized advertising campaigns that cater to customer needs by analyzing data related to purchasing behavior. For example, sports clubs have successfully utilized AI to provide personalized recommendations to their fans, resulting in heightened engagement and increased revenue from ticket and merchandise sales. Therefore, the integration of AI in digital sports marketing enriches customer experience and fosters satisfaction and loyalty.

AI also contributes to boosting sales, expanding exports, and enhancing profitability for organizations and businesses. Recent studies have indicated that sports teams employing AI in their marketing strategies have experienced a notable increase in return on investment (ROI). In the realm of sports marketing, AI develops more precise strategies by analyzing fan behavior and preferences, which enhances the fan experience, strengthens their engagement with brands and sports teams, and ultimately leads to increased marketing revenues. For instance, sports clubs improve fan experience and create more targeted advertising campaigns by examining ticket purchase data and fans' online behavior (Pashaie, Golmohammadi, & Zakhirani, 2024).

Research shows that AI can identify behavioral patterns and offer personalized suggestions that increase customer engagement and satisfaction by analyzing user data (Rane, 2023). This technology, with its advanced capabilities, predicts that sports marketing will undergo substantial transformations (Sbrighi, 2024b). The results indicate that concepts such as customer, social, industry, tourism, and brand are emphasized in digital marketing, while concepts like club, social, and competitive are highlighted in articles related to sports and digital marketing (Golmohammadi et al., 2025). The use of AI in digital sports marketing plays an essential role in enhancing service personalization and increasing customer engagement (Bag & Wood, 2022). By utilizing big data analysis and advanced algorithms, AI can identify customer behavior patterns and provide suggestions tailored to their needs and preferences (Pereira et al., 2022). Moreover, studies show that using intelligent chatbots on sports platforms has led to increased user engagement and improved post-sales services (Krishnan et al., 2022). However, specific capabilities and skills are required to fully exploit IR4 technologies (Bag et al., 2021). On the other hand, a substantial limitation of previous research has been the lack of sufficient attention to the long-term effects of AI on customer behavior and loyalty (Prentice et al., 2020).

PART IX: SUMMARY

This chapter examines the transformative impact of artificial intelligence (AI) on sports marketing, emphasizing its innovative capabilities to predict fan behavior, manage financial risks, and enhance engagement strategies. In an increasingly competitive and complex sports landscape, traditional marketing methods such as surveys and historical trend analysis, are proving inadequate due to their limitations in scope and predictive power. AI, utilizing technologies like machine learning (ML), natural language processing (NLP), and computer vision, offers real-time insights into fan preferences and behaviors, enabling sports organizations to shift from reactive to proactive decision-making.

Machine learning models can identify patterns in ticket demand, personalize merchandise offerings, and facilitate dynamic pricing strategies, while NLP techniques analyze fan sentiment across social media platforms. Additionally, computer vision tools provide insights into fan engagement during events, helping refine strategies to enhance the overall fan experience. In terms of financial risk management, AI can predict potential pitfalls by analyzing performance data and fan behavior, while also playing a crucial role in fraud detection and secure ticketing systems. By integrating predictive analytics with operational data, sports managers can significantly reduce uncertainty and improve strategic planning.

The chapter also explores the integration of AI with emerging technologies such as blockchain, virtual reality (VR), and augmented reality (AR). This convergence allows for deeper fan immersion and personalized experiences. Blockchain ensures data transparency and security, particularly in ticketing and loyalty programs, while VR and AR enhance virtual fan experiences. Deep learning, a subset of AI, further supports real-time decision-making and consumer behavior forecasting, which is invaluable in the fast-paced sports environment.

However, the implementation of AI raises ethical considerations that cannot be overlooked. The authors stress the importance of data privacy, algorithmic transparency, and accountability, cautioning against biases in AI systems. They advocate for regulatory frameworks to guide the ethical deployment of AI, particularly when handling fan data.

To effectively harness the power of artificial intelligence in sports marketing, managers should focus on building a solid data infrastructure that enables robust systems for collecting and managing fan data across various platforms, such as ticketing systems, social media, and customer relationship management (CRM) tools. Additionally, adopting AI tools for personalization is crucial; machine learning models can analyze fan behavior to tailor communication, offers, and content, while natural language processing (NLP) can facilitate real-time sentiment tracking. Furthermore, predictive analytics should be utilized for risk management, aiding in financial planning through demand forecasting and investment analysis related to player contracts and event planning. It is also essential to integrate AI with fan experiences by exploring augmented and virtual reality (AR/VR) to enhance engagement, and leveraging blockchain technology for secure transactions and loyalty programs. Lastly, prioritizing ethical AI use is vital; establishing internal review boards, ensuring transparency in data utilization, and complying with data protection regulations like GDPR or CCPA will foster trust and accountability.

To advance the understanding of AI's role in sports marketing, future research should explore cross-cultural fan behavior models to assess how AI tools perform across different cultural and regional contexts. Longitudinal studies examining the long-term effects of AI-driven personalization on fan loyalty and organizational revenue are also needed. Additionally, developing ethical frameworks for AI design, specifically focused on bias mitigation and transparent decision-making, should be a priority. Research should also investigate the application of AI in grassroots sports to support marketing and fan development in amateur and semi-professional contexts. Finally, exploring models of human-AI collaboration can provide insights into how human decision-makers and AI tools can effectively work together in strategic marketing planning. This chapter serves as a comprehensive roadmap for understanding and leveraging AI in sports marketing, addressing both practical challenges and strategic opportunities.

Ultimately, this chapter highlights AI's potential to revolutionize sports marketing by providing accurate predictions of fan behavior, identifying new opportunities, and mitigating financial risks. By leveraging AI, sports organizations can optimize marketing strategies, enhance customer experiences, and ensure more informed decision-making in an industry characterized by fluctuating fan loyalty and constrained financial resources. The chapter aims to offer a practical framework for employing AI in predicting fan behavior and navigating the complexities of the modern sports marketing landscape.

Declaration of generative AI and AI-assisted technologies in the writing process

During the preparation of this work the authors used ChatGPT, and Grammarly in order to improve language, and readability of certain parts of the book chapter.

REFERENCES

Akbarossadat, S. M., & Esmaeilpour, B. (2022). An Overview of Bankruptcy Detection Methods Using Artificial Intelligence. *Intelligent Knowledge Exploration and Processing*, *2*(6), 20–41. DOI: 10.30508/kdip.2022.349333.1044

Ala-Pietilä, P., & Smuha, N. A. (2021). A framework for global cooperation on artificial intelligence and its governance. *Reflections on artificial intelligence for humanity*, 237-265. https://doi.org/DOI: 10.1007/978-3-030-69128-8_15

Alidoust Ghahfarokhi, E., & Dehghan Ghahfarokhi, A. (2024). (in press). Blockchain Technology and the Future of Sports Industry. *New Approaches in Sports Mmanagement. Articles.* Advance online publication. DOI: 10.22034/ntsmj.2024.2030428.1028

Anthony, D. R., Gordon, S., & Gucciardi, D. F. (2020). A qualitative exploration of mentally tough behaviour in Australian football. *Journal of Sports Sciences*, *38*(3), 308–319. DOI: 10.1080/02640414.2019.1698002 PMID: 31783717

Bag, S., Pretorius, J. H. C., Gupta, S., & Dwivedi, Y. K. (2021). Role of institutional pressures and resources in the adoption of big data analytics powered artificial intelligence, sustainable manufacturing practices and circular economy capabilities. *Technological Forecasting and Social Change*, *163*, 120420. DOI: 10.1016/j.techfore.2020.120420

Bag, S., & Wood, L. C. (2022). Guest editorial: Human resource development in the digital age: recent issues and future research directions. *International Journal of Manpower*, *43*(2), 253–262. DOI: 10.1108/IJM-05-2022-561

Baker, C. R., Pease, M., Sexton, D. P., Abumoussa, A., & Chambless, L. B. (2024). Artificial intelligence innovations in neurosurgical oncology: A narrative review. *Journal of Neuro-Oncology*, *169*(3), 489–496. DOI: 10.1007/s11060-024-04757-5 PMID: 38958849

Bayindir, M. (2024). The Role of Mobile Applications and Social Media in Increasing Fan Loyalty. *Turkish Journal of Sports Informatics and Technology*, *1*(1), 1–13.

Berryman, D. R. (2012). Augmented reality: A review. *Medical Reference Services Quarterly*, *31*(2), 212–218. DOI: 10.1080/02763869.2012.670604 PMID: 22559183

Bholat, D., Gharbawi, A., & Thew, O. (2018). Artificial intelligence and the future of finance. *Bank of England Quarterly Bulletin*, *58*(3), 1–12.

Black, D., & Hibbeln, M. (2019). Sport and contemporary international political economy. *The Palgrave Handbook of Contemporary International Political Economy*, 651-665. https://doi.org/DOI: 10.1057/978-1-137-45443-0_40

Bolboli Qadikolaei, S., & Parsania, H. (2023). A systematic review of the ethical implications of using artificial intelligence in digital technologies and its relationship with the ethics of flourishing. *Socio-Cultural Strategy*, *12*(3), 771–798. DOI: 10.22034/scs.2022.160772

Bradley, S. (2024). Comparative Analysis of Two Data Privacy Regulatory Schemes: The GDPR and the CCPA.

Choi, K. H. M. (2020). *A Critical Juncture in Data Protection Standards: Comparing Data Protection Legislation in the United States and the European Union*].

Collins, L., & Collins, D. (2013). Decision making and risk management in adventure sports coaching. *Quest*, *65*(1), 72–82. DOI: 10.1080/00336297.2012.727373

Cossich, V. R., Carlgren, D., Holash, R. J., & Katz, L. (2023). Technological breakthroughs in sport: Current practice and future potential of artificial intelligence, virtual reality, augmented reality, and modern data visualization in performance analysis. *Applied Sciences (Basel, Switzerland)*, *13*(23), 12965. DOI: 10.3390/app132312965

Cruz-Neira, C., Sandin, D. J., DeFanti, T. A., Kenyon, R. V., & Hart, J. C. (1992). The CAVE: Audio visual experience automatic virtual environment. *Communications of the ACM*, *35*(6), 64–73. DOI: 10.1145/129888.129892

Dehghanpouri, H., Soltani, Z., & Rostamzadeh, R. (2020). The impact of trust, privacy and quality of service on the success of E-CRM: The mediating role of customer satisfaction. *Journal of Business and Industrial Marketing*, *35*(11), 1831–1847. DOI: 10.1108/JBIM-07-2019-0325

Deshpande, S. B., Velrani, K. S., Bhagyalakshmi, A., Vani, M. S., Ananthi, S., & Sahu, D. (2024). Neural Networks for Natural Language Processing. 2024 Asian Conference on Intelligent Technologies (ACOIT), Dimeo, P. (2014). Why Lance Armstrong? Historical context and key turning points in the 'cleaning up'of professional cycling. *The International Journal of the History of Sport*, *31*(8), 951–968. DOI: 10.1080/09523367.2013.879858

Du, J., Pifer, N. D., & Gulavani, S. S. (2023). Harnessing the power of machine learning in sport consumer behavior research. In *Sports Sponsorship and Branding* (pp. 165–183). Routledge., DOI: 10.4324/9781003458890-12

Esmaeili, A., Mohammadi, N., & Emami, F. (2021). A Model of Factors Affecting the Behavioral Intentions of Premier League Football Fans Using Grounded Theory. *Strategic Studies on Youth and Sports*, *20*(53), 93–112. DOI: 10.22034/ssys.2021.458

Fakeyede, O. G., Okeleke, P. A., Hassan, A., Iwuanyanwu, U., Adaramodu, O. R., & Oyewole, O. O. (2023). Navigating data privacy through IT audits: GDPR, CCPA, and beyond. *International Journal of Research in Engineering and Science*, *11*(11).

Fathi, S., & Motlag, M. (2011). Globalization and Generation Gap (A social study of generation gap by focusing on information and communication technologies). *Strategic Studies of public policy, 2*(5), 145-177. https://sspp.iranjournals.ir/article_2481_e28e739c320baaac1ca139e35ddbc449.pdf

Fazeli, F., Mahmoudi, A., & Askarian, F. (2024). (in press). Blockchain Technology: Advantages, Challenges, and Development Strategies in the Sports Industry Services Sector. *Sport Management Journal. Articles*. Advance online publication. DOI: 10.22059/jsm.2024.373644.3269

Feijóo, C., Kwon, Y., Bauer, J. M., Bohlin, E., Howell, B., Jain, R., Potgieter, P., Vu, K., Whalley, J., & Xia, J. (2020). Harnessing artificial intelligence (AI) to increase wellbeing for all: The case for a new technology diplomacy. *Telecommunications Policy*, *44*(6), 101988. DOI: 10.1016/j.telpol.2020.101988 PMID: 32377031

Fekrat, A., & Jaberi, A. (2024). Phenomenology of the role of artificial intelligence marketing on increasing sales and exports of Iranian sports goods. *Sports Marketing Studies*, *5*(2), 1–15. DOI: 10.22034/sms.2024.139803.1254

Gade, R., Merler, M., Thomas, G., & Moeslund, T. B. (2024). The (Computer) Vision of Sports: Recent Trends in Research and Commercial Systems for Sport Analytics. *Computer Vision*, 296-311. https://doi.org/DOI: 10.1201/9781003328957-14

Genovard, F., Muñoz, J., Petchamé, J., & Solanellas, F. (2025). Risk management approaches in sports organisations: A scoping review. *Heliyon*, *11*(3), e42270. Advance online publication. DOI: 10.1016/j.heliyon.2025.e42270 PMID: 39968147

Ghafarzadeh Malasi, M. R., & Ismaili Shahzandi, M. R. (2022). *Risk management in sports and sports organizations* The 8th National Conference of Sport Sciences and Physical Education of Iran, Tehran. https://civilica.com/doc/1649667

Ghorbani Ghader, A., Hashemi Nasab, M., & Hedayati, M. S. (2024). Designing a Customer Behavior Prediction Model Using Artificial Intelligence Algorithms and Neural Networks. *Journal of Intelligent Strategic Management*, *3*(2), 39–56. https://doi.org/bumara.3.2.15564.35879841478

Golmohammadi, H., Ghadami, S., Pashaie, S., & Zolfi, H. (2025). Identification and Analysis of Prominent Concepts in Digital Marketing and Sports. *Sports Marketing Studies, 5*(4), -. https://doi.org/DOI: 10.22034/sms.2024.140983.1328

Gross, M. (2006). 'Not cricket': A'nexus of silence'over the cricket match-fixing scandal.

Gutierrez, N. (2023). The ballad of morton heilig: On VR's mythic past. *JCMS: Journal of Cinema and Media Studies*, *62*(3), 86–106. DOI: 10.1353/cj.2023.0027

Halchin, L. E., & Rollins, J. W. (2017). The 2016 Olympic Games: Health, security, environmental, and doping issues. *Current Politics and Economics of South and Central America, 10*(2), 203–249.

Heidari, L., Aghaei, N., & Akbari Yazdi, H. (2024). The Role of Team Identification and Sentiment Analysis of Iranian Football Clubs' Fans in Twitter Social Media with Natural Language Processing. *Journal of Intelligent Marketing Management*, *5*(4), 77–97. https://doi.org/Jabm.3.2.15564.35887879085849695

Holzinger, A., Zatloukal, K., & Müller, H. (2024). Is Human Oversight to AI Systems still possible? *New Biotechnology*, *85*(25), 59–62. DOI: 10.1016/j.nbt.2024.12.003 PMID: 39675423

Istasse, M., Somers, V., Elancheliyan, P., De, J., & Zambrano, D. (2023). Deep-Sportradar-v2: A multi-sport computer vision dataset for sport understandings. Proceedings of the 6th International Workshop on Multimedia Content Analysis in Sports, Jaiwant, S. V., & Kureethara, J. V. (2024). Sports Marketing Analytics: Digital Evolution in Shaping the Sports Industry. In *Sports Analytics: Data-Driven Sports and Decision Intelligence* (pp. 221-235). Springer. https://doi.org/DOI: 10.1145/3606038.3616160

Jana, A. K. (2016). Dynamic simulation, numerical control and analysis of a novel bottom flashing scheme in batch distillation. *Computers & Chemical Engineering*, *89*, 166–171. DOI: 10.1016/j.compchemeng.2016.04.010

Karimi, J., Pashaie, S., & Golmohammadi, H. (2025). Artificial Intelligence (AI) and the Future of Sports Marketing: Exploring New Challenges and Opportunities. *Journal of Advanced Sport Technology*. https://doi.org/DOI: 10.22098/jast.2025.15830.1374

Karimi, M. (2025). The Role of Artificial Intelligence in Reducing Risks and Managing Risk in the Futured. *Research in Safety, Health and Environment Quarterly, 2*(7), 63-71. https://hse.ihu.ac.ir/article_209704_ac817f999c644467abd07373a78f934d.pdf

Kiani, M. S. (2024). An in-depth look at the future of sports with artificial intelligence, virtual reality, and data visualization to improve athlete performance analysis. *Intelligent Knowledge Exploration and Processing*, *4*(12), 8–35. DOI: 10.30508/kdip.2024.451951.1100

King, N. (2016). *Sport governance: An introduction*. Routledge. DOI: 10.4324/9781315623313

Krishnan, C., Gupta, A., Gupta, A., & Singh, G. (2022). Impact of artificial intelligence-based chatbots on customer engagement and business growth. In *Deep learning for social media data analytics* (pp. 195–210). Springer., DOI: 10.1007/978-3-031-10869-3_11

Kufel, J., Bargieł-Łączek, K., Kocot, S., Koźlik, M., Bartnikowska, W., Janik, M., Czogalik, Ł., Dudek, P., Magiera, M., Lis, A., Paszkiewicz, I., Nawrat, Z., Cebula, M., & Gruszczyńska, K. (2023). What is machine learning, artificial neural networks and deep learning?—Examples of practical applications in medicine. *Diagnostics (Basel)*, *13*(15), 2582. DOI: 10.3390/diagnostics13152582 PMID: 37568945

Lanier, J. (1992). Virtual reality: The promise of the future. *Interactive Learning International*, *8*(4), 275–279. DOI: 10.5555/155259.155263

Laroche, D., & Corbett, R. (2010). . Risk management guide for community sport organizations. *2010 Legacies Now*.

Liu, X. (2023). Deep learning in marketing: A review and research agenda. *Artificial Intelligence in Marketing*, 239-271. https://doi.org/DOI: 10.1108/S1548-643520230000020014

Lv, C., Wang, Y., & Ma, Y. (2022). Construction of business innovation model for sports industry using a deep learning algorithm. *Soft Computing*, *26*(20), 10753–10763. DOI: 10.1007/s00500-022-06962-8

Mahmoudian, A., Mohammadi, S., & Wang, W. (2024). Fan Engagement Management: Fan Response to Brand Image Attributes of Professional Athletes on Instagram. *Journal of Global Sport Management*, 1-19.

Malekmahmoodi, V., Mondalizadeh, Z., & Zohrevandian, K. (2022). The Effect of Innovation Capability on Innovative Performance of Sport Clubs [Research]. *New Trends in Sport Management, 9*(35), 29-44. http://ntsmj.issma.ir/article-1-1462-fa.html

Manzouri, H., & Khalili, A. J. (2023). Investigating the effect of perceived convenience, personalization and improvement of service quality on the formation of customers' experience of using artificial intelligence through the mediating variable of trust. *Management Science in Industry*, *2*(1), 227–239.

Modi, T. B. (2023). Artificial Intelligence Ethics and Fairness: A study to address bias and fairness issues in AI systems, and the ethical implications of AI applications. *Revista Review Index Journal of Multidisciplinary*, *3*(2), 24–35. DOI: 10.31305/rrijm2023.v03.n02.004

Mohammadi, S., Pashaie, S., & Ghaffarisadr, S. I. (2025). Aesthetics and Football: Aesthetics. In *Global Perspectives on Soccer and the Media and Entertainment Industry* (pp. 237-282). IGI Global Scientific Publishing. https://doi.org/DOI: 10.4018/979-8-3693-4298-5.ch009

Mohammadi, S., Pashaie, S., Ghaffarisadr, S. I., & Rayner, M. (2025a). Opportunities and Challenges of Leveraging Artificial Intelligence (AI) in Sport Marketing. *Advancing the Marketing Technology (MarTech). Advances in Marketing, Customer Relationship Management, and E-Services*, •••, 233–272. DOI: 10.4018/979-8-3693-4361-6.ch009

Mohammadi, S., Pashaie, S., Ghaffarisadr, S. I., & Rayner, M. (2025b). Opportunities and Challenges of Leveraging Artificial Intelligence (AI) in Sport Marketing. In *Advancing the Marketing Technology (MarTech) Revolution* (pp. 233-272). IGI Global Scientific Publishing. https://doi.org/DOI: 10.4018/979-8-3693-4361-6.ch009

Mohammadi, S., Siani, M. G., Abdolmaleki, H., & Sato, M. COVID-19 Pandemic and Sporting Events: Tokyo 2020 Olympics–Challenges and Solutions. In *Crisis Management and Sports* (pp. 182-195). Routledge.

Mohammed, A. H., & Ali, A. H. (2021). (in press). Survey of bert (bidirectional encoder representation transformer) types. Journal of Physics: Conference Series, Moradi, E. (2025). Tracing the Evolution of Sport Marketing and Sponsorship: A Bibliometric Analysis of Trends and Scholarly Impact in a Leading Journal. *Sports Business Journal. Articles.* Advance online publication. DOI: 10.22051/sbj.2025.49152.1194

Moradipour, T., Nikbakhsh, R., Farahani, A., & Safani, A. M. (2021). Investigating the cognitive and social behaviors of fans and the effect of these behaviors on their enthusiasm to attend the stadium. *New Trends in Sport Management*, *9*(34), 85–99.

Nalbant, K. G., & Aydın, S. (2022). Literature review on the relationship between artificial intelligence technologies with digital sports marketing and sports management. *Indonesian Journal of Sport Management*, *2*(2), 135–143. DOI: 10.31949/ijsm.v2i2.2876

Neumann, D. L., Moffitt, R. L., Thomas, P. R., Loveday, K., Watling, D. P., Lombard, C. L., Antonova, S., & Tremeer, M. A. (2018). A systematic review of the application of interactive virtual reality to sport. *Virtual Reality (Waltham Cross)*, *22*(3), 183–198. DOI: 10.1007/s10055-017-0320-5

Norian, H. (2021). *Artificial Intelligence and its Management Risks*. hosseinnourian.com

Pashaie, S., & Golmohammadi, H. (2024). Exploring the Influence of E-CRM on the innovation capabilities of sports venues: The moderating role of covid-19. *Sports Marketing Studies*, *4*(3), 108–128. DOI: 10.22034/sms.2024.139773.1253

Pashaie, S., Golmohammadi, H., & Zakhirani, E. (2024). Digital Transformation in Sports Marketing: The Impact of Artificial Intelligence on Personalization and Customer Engagement. *International Journal of Innovation in Management. Economics and Social Sciences*, *4*(4), 42–58. DOI: 10.59615/ijimes.4.4.42

Pashaie, S., Mohammadi, S., & Golmohammadi, H. (2024). Unlocking athlete potential: The evolution of coaching strategies through artificial intelligence. *Proceedings of the Institution of Mechanical Engineers, Part P: Journal of Sports Engineering and Technology*, 17543371241300889. https://doi.org/DOI: 10.1177/17543371241300889

Pashaie, S., & Nasirpour, M. (2024). (in press). The Impact of Observability and Compatibility on Consumers' Attitudes Towards AI-Generated Sports Marketing Content and Its Effect on Purchase Intent. *Sports Marketing Studies. Articles*. Advance online publication. DOI: 10.22034/sms.2024.141529.1367

Pereira, A. M., Moura, J. A. B., Costa, E. D. B., Vieira, T., Landim, A. R., Bazaki, E., & Wanick, V. (2022). Customer models for artificial intelligence based decision support in fashion online retail supply chains. *Decision Support Systems*, *158*, 113795. DOI: 10.1016/j.dss.2022.113795

Prentice, C., Dominique Lopes, S., & Wang, X. (2020). The impact of artificial intelligence and employee service quality on customer satisfaction and loyalty. *Journal of Hospitality Marketing & Management*, *29*(7), 739–756. DOI: 10.1080/19368623.2020.1722304

Rahimi Kolour, H., & Ghasemi Hamedani, I. (2023). Investigating the role of artificial intelligence-based risk management in increasing the agility and capabilities of supply chain reengineering. *Science and Technology Policy Letters*, *13*(3), 5–23.

Rahmani, M., Majedi, N., Hemmatinejad, M., & Jamshidi, A. (2024). Application of Artificial Intelligence in the Sports Industry: A Review Article. *AI and Tech in Behavioral and Social Sciences*, *2*(2), 20–27. DOI: 10.61838/kman.aitech.2.2.4

Rane, N. (2023). Enhancing customer loyalty through Artificial Intelligence (AI), Internet of Things (IoT), and Big Data technologies: improving customer satisfaction, engagement, relationship, and experience. *Internet of Things (IoT), and Big Data Technologies: Improving Customer Satisfaction, Engagement, Relationship, and Experience*. https://doi.org/DOI: 10.2139/ssrn.4616051

Rauschnabel, P. A., Felix, R., Hinsch, C., Shahab, H., & Alt, F. (2022). What is XR? Towards a framework for augmented and virtual reality. *Computers in Human Behavior*, *133*, 107289. DOI: 10.1016/j.chb.2022.107289

Rautaray, S. S., & Agrawal, A. (2015). Vision based hand gesture recognition for human computer interaction: A survey. *Artificial Intelligence Review*, *43*(1), 1–54. DOI: 10.1007/s10462-012-9356-9

Sbrighi, A. (2024a). *Leveraging The Power Of Deep Tech Within The Realm Of Digital Marketing: An Explorative Insight Into The Relationship Between Artificial Intelligence And Sports Fan Engagement* Università Ca' Foscari]. Italy.

Sbrighi, A. (2024b). Leveraging The Power Of Deep Tech Within The Realm Of Digital Marketing: An Explorative Insight Into The Relationship Between Artificial Intelligence And Sports Fan Engagement. https://doi.org/DOI: 10579/26168

Scullen, T., Amenta, P. S., Nerva, J. D., & Dumont, A. S. (2020). Commentary: Predicting long-term outcomes after poor-grade aneurysmal subarachnoid hemorrhage using decision tree modeling. *Neurosurgery*, *87*(3), E293–E295. DOI: 10.1093/neuros/nyaa074 PMID: 32195548

Segun-Falade, O. D., Osundare, O. S., Kedi, W. E., Okeleke, P. A., Ijomah, T. I., & Abdul-Azeez, O. Y.Osinachi Deborah Segun-FaladeOlajide Soji OsundareWagobera Edgar KediPatrick Azuka OkelekeTochukwu Ignatius IjomahOluwatosin Yetunde Abdul-Azeez. (2024). Utilizing machine learning algorithms to enhance predictive analytics in customer behavior studies. *International Journal of Scholarly Research in Engineering and Technology*, *4*(1), 1–18. DOI: 10.56781/ijsret.2024.4.1.0018

Shah, K., & LaPlaca, P. J. (1981). Assessing risks in strategic planning. *Industrial Marketing Management*, *10*(2), 77–91. DOI: 10.1016/0019-8501(81)90001-8

Shah Alam, S., & Mohamed Sayuti, N. (2011). Applying the Theory of Planned Behavior (TPB) in halal food purchasing. *International Journal of Commerce and Management, 21*(1), 8–20. DOI: 10.1108/10569211111111676

Shahpar Tofigh, A., Deldar, E., Eghbali, K., & Aflatoon, S. (2022). Identification and ranking of socio-cultural factors affecting making culture in sport of Iran. *Applied Research in Sport Management, 10*(4), 49–61. DOI: 10.30473/arsm.2022.8957

Sharifan, M. S. (2023). Providing a framework for reducing artificial intelligence risks in finance and banking (with considerations of passive defense). In *Proceedings of the 7th National Conference on New Horizons in Management.* Economics, and Computer Science., https://civilica.com/doc/2015030

Shayeg, M. M. (2023). Future research on artificial intelligence in the sports industry. *Paya Shahr Specialized Scientific Monthly, 1*, 1–17.

Shen, A. (2024). AI Ethics and Governance at International Standards. *International IT Journal of Research, ISSN: 3007-6706, 2*(1), 8-14.

Shi, F., Ning, H., Huangfu, W., Zhang, F., Wei, D., Hong, T., & Daneshmand, M. (2020). Recent progress on the convergence of the Internet of Things and artificial intelligence. *IEEE Network, 34*(5), 8–15. DOI: 10.1109/MNET.011.2000009

Sinnett, A., Ho, C., & Malcolm, B. (2016). Expanding a dairy business affects business and financial risk. *Animal Production Science, 57*(10), 2167–2174. DOI: 10.1071/AN15041

Smuha, N. A. (2021). Beyond the individual: Governing AI's societal harm. *Internet Policy Review, 10*(3). Advance online publication. DOI: 10.14763/2021.3.1574

Sutherland, I. E. (1968). A head-mounted three dimensional display. Proceedings of the December 9-11, 1968, fall joint computer conference, part I, Sylvia IV, J. (2024). The Data Renaissance: Analyzing the Disciplinary Effects of Big Data, Artificial Intelligence, and Beyond. DOI: 10.1145/1476589.1476686

Tang, C. S., Bai, J., So, K. C., Chen, X. M., & Wang, H. (2016). Coordinating supply and demand on an on-demand platform: Price, wage, and payout ratio. SSRN *Electronic Journal.* DOI: 10.2139/ssrn.2831794

Thalpage, N. (2023). Unlocking the black box: Explainable artificial intelligence (XAI) for trust and transparency in ai systems. *J. Digit. Art Humanit, 4*(1), 31–36. DOI: 10.33847/2712-8148.4.1_4

Turing, A. M. (2009). *Computing machinery and intelligence.* Springer. DOI: 10.1007/978-1-4020-6710-5_3

Varona, D., & Suárez, J. L. (2022). Discrimination, bias, fairness, and trustworthy AI. *Applied Sciences (Basel, Switzerland), 12*(12), 5826. DOI: 10.3390/app12125826

Verma, N., Mishra, P., & Purohit, N. (2020). Development of a knowledge based decision tree classifier using hybrid polarimetric SAR observables. *International Journal of Remote Sensing, 41*(4), 1302–1320. DOI: 10.1080/01431161.2019.1666314

Verver, J. (2015). Lessons from the FIFA corruption scandal. *Risk Management, 62*(7), 16–18.

Vesper, H. W., Wang, Y., Vidal, M., Botelho, J. C., & Caudill, S. P. (2015). Serum total testosterone concentrations in the US household population from the NHANES 2011–2012 study population. *Clinical Chemistry, 61*(12), 1495–1504. DOI: 10.1373/clinchem.2015.245969 PMID: 26510959

Vieira, M., Paulo, H., Pinto-Varela, T., & Barbosa-Póvoa, A. P. (2021). Assessment of financial risk in the design and scheduling of multipurpose plants under demand uncertainty. *International Journal of Production Research, 59*(20), 6125–6145. DOI: 10.1080/00207543.2020.1804638

Von Eschenbach, W. J. (2021). Transparency and the black box problem: Why we do not trust AI. *Philosophy & Technology, 34*(4), 1607–1622. DOI: 10.1007/s13347-021-00477-0

Wang, M. C.-H., & Tang, Y.-Y. (2018). Examining the antecedents of sport team brand equity: A dual-identification perspective. *Sport Management Review, 21*(3), 293–306. DOI: 10.1016/j.smr.2017.07.010

Westerbeek, H. (2025). Algorithmic fandom: How generative AI is reshaping sports marketing, fan engagement, and the integrity of sport. *Frontiers in Sports and Active Living, 7*, 1597444. DOI: 10.3389/fspor.2025.1597444 PMID: 40406423

Xu, T., & Baghaei, S. (2025). Reshaping the future of sports with artificial intelligence: Challenges and opportunities in performance enhancement, fan engagement, and strategic decision-making. *Engineering Applications of Artificial Intelligence, 142*, 109912. DOI: 10.1016/j.engappai.2024.109912

Young, P. C., & Wendit, J. T. (2017). GOVERNANCE IN SPORTS GOVERNING BODIES: A RISK MANAGEMENT PERSPECTIVE. *International Sports Law Review Pandektis, 12*.

Zhao, Y. (2021). [Retracted] Sports Enterprise Marketing and Financial Risk Management Based on Decision Tree and Data Mining. *Journal of Healthcare Engineering, 2021*(1), 7632110. DOI: 10.1155/2021/7632110 PMID: 34691380

Zhong, Y., Li, Y., Ding, J., & Liao, Y. (2021). Risk management: Exploring emerging Human Resource issues during the COVID-19 pandemic. *Journal of Risk and Financial Management*, *14*(5), 228. DOI: 10.3390/jrfm14050228

Chapter 5
Emotion-Driven Marketing Education With AI Sentiment Analysis

Zornitsa Yordanova
http://orcid.org/0000-0002-6056-8445
University of National and World Economy, Bulgaria

ABSTRACT

This research designs and implements an AI-based educational system for sentiment analysis in marketing texts. The system uses advanced natural language processing models such as BERT and LSTM to identify consumer sentiment and provide students with real-time feedback. The goal of this system is to improve students' sentiment analysis skills and gain a deeper understanding of consumer behavior. The results showed that this system helped improve students' analytical skills and provided them with an interactive and effective learning experience. This system can be used as an effective tool in marketing education.

1- INTRODUCTION

Marketing, as one of the most important branches of management, has always sought new ways to better understand consumer behavior and establish effective relationships with them. One of the key aspects of marketing is the analysis of consumer sentiment. Emotions play an important role in consumer decision-making and can influence their attitudes, preferences, and purchasing behavior (Habbat, Nouri, Anoun, & Hassouni, 2023). For this reason, sentiment analysis has been considered as an effective tool in developing marketing strategies. With the advent of artificial intelligence and natural language processing (NLP), the possibility of

DOI: 10.4018/979-8-3373-3775-3.ch005

automatic sentiment analysis in marketing texts has become available, and these technologies have become powerful tools for identifying and analyzing consumer sentiment (Murthy, Allu, Andhavarapu, Bagadi, & Belusonti, 2020).

Sentiment analysis in marketing means identifying and classifying different emotions in marketing-related texts such as customer reviews, product reviews, social media posts, and advertisements. This analysis can include identifying positive, negative, and neutral emotions, and in more advanced cases, it can even lead to the detection of complex emotions such as happiness, anger, sadness, fear, and satisfaction (Movahed, Movahed, & Nozari, 2024a). There are various methods for sentiment analysis, including lexical-based approaches, machine-based analysis, and deep learning. Lexical-based methods are limited to identifying specific words and attributing them to specific sentiments, while machine-based and deep learning methods use more complex models such as convolutional neural networks (CNN), long-term memory networks (LSTM), and attention-based models such as BERT (Kalogeras, 2021).

Despite significant advances in sentiment analysis, one of the major challenges in this field is the use of this technology in educational settings. Teaching sentiment analysis to marketing students helps them become familiar with the concept of emotions in marketing and improve their skills in analyzing and interpreting these emotions. However, traditional marketing education methods often involve providing static and non-interactive content and do not provide students with the opportunity to experience sentiment analysis in practice (Kalogeras, 2025). These limitations have led to the use of artificial intelligence-based educational systems as a new solution for teaching sentiment analysis. These systems are able to provide students with an active and dynamic learning experience by providing interactive exercises, real-time feedback, and sentiment analysis in marketing texts (Nozari, 2025a).

In this study, an artificial intelligence-based educational system for sentiment analysis in marketing is designed and implemented. This system uses advanced natural language processing models such as BERT (Bidirectional Encoder Representations from Transformers) and LSTM (Long Short-Term Memory) to analyze sentiment in marketing texts. These models are able to identify different sentiments in input texts and display the analysis results to students in a visual and interactive way (Movahed, Aliahmadi, Parsanejad, & Nozari, 2023). Using this system, students can analyze different marketing texts and improve their sentiment analysis skills by receiving real-time feedback.

The educational system designed in this study is designed in a way that, in addition to providing accurate analyses, allows students to become familiar with various sentiment analysis concepts in a practical way. The user interface of this system includes a text input section, displaying sentiment analysis results, and providing educational feedback to students. Students can enter various texts into the system, view the sentiment analysis results, and develop their abilities in sentiment analysis by receiving feedback. By providing visual analyses and textual explanations, this system helps students to better understand the semantic context of texts and be able to identify mixed and contradictory sentiments (Diekson et al., 2023).

The importance of this research is that by using artificial intelligence, sentiment analysis training can be done to marketing students in a more effective and interactive way. This educational system not only helps to improve students' technical skills, but also familiarizes them with the importance of sentiment analysis in marketing strategies. Also, the use of advanced artificial intelligence models such as BERT and LSTM has led to increased accuracy and efficiency of the system (Nozari & Edalatpanah, 2023). This educational system can be used as an effective tool for teaching sentiment analysis in marketing courses and prepares students to face the practical challenges of sentiment analysis in real marketing environments.

In the following, this research will first review the research background and concepts related to sentiment analysis and its applications in marketing. Then, the research methodology will be explained, including the design of the educational system, the configuration of artificial intelligence models, and the training and evaluation process. In the implementation section, the operation of the system and the structure of the user interface will be explained in detail. Finally, the results obtained from using the educational system and their analysis will be presented, and solutions for improving the system and suggestions for future research will be stated.

2- LITERATURE REVIEW

Sentiment analysis has received widespread attention in recent years as one of the important applications of artificial intelligence and natural language processing (NLP). This method refers to the identification, classification, and analysis of emotions expressed in various texts, which can include positive, negative, and neutral emotions (Kalogeras, 2019). Applications of sentiment analysis can be seen in various fields such as marketing, customer service, social network analysis, customer feedback analysis, and even education (Rahmaty & Nozari, 2023). In the field of marketing, sentiment analysis helps marketers to gain a better understanding of consumers' attitudes and feelings towards products and services and optimize their strategies based on this information (Nozari, Ghahremani-Nahr, & Najafi, 2023).

There are various methods for sentiment analysis that can be divided into three general categories: vocabulary-based methods, machine learning-based methods, and deep learning-based methods. Vocabulary-based methods involve the use of lists of emotional words and attributing these words to specific emotions (Ayyappa et al., 2023). Although these methods are simple and understandable, they do not perform well in analyzing complex texts and identifying composite emotions. Machine learning-based methods include classification algorithms such as Support Vector Machine (SVM), Random Forest, and Artificial Neural Networks (Nozari, 2023a). These algorithms are trained using labeled training data and are able to identify emotional patterns in text. However, these methods also have limitations in identifying semantic context and composite emotions.

In recent years, the use of deep learning methods has become popular as an advanced approach in sentiment analysis. Deep learning models such as convolutional neural networks (CNN), long-term memory networks (LSTM), and attention-based models such as BERT (Bidirectional Encoder Representations from Transformers) are able to analyze the semantic context of text and identify complex sentiments (Aliahmadi & Nozari, 2023). Due to its bidirectional structure, the BERT model is able to understand the semantic relationship between words and sentences in a text, and therefore performs better in analyzing complex marketing texts (Movahed, Movahed, & Nozari, 2024b). The LSTM model is also able to identify sequential patterns of sentiment in text due to its time-sequence structure, but it is less accurate compared to BERT (Nozari, 2024). These models are trained using large and labeled datasets and are able to identify different emotions such as happiness, anger, sadness, fear, and satisfaction (Akpatsa et al., 2022).

Sentiment analysis in marketing is used as a powerful tool to identify consumer emotions and improve marketing strategies. One of the most important applications of sentiment analysis in marketing is the analysis of customer feedback. Customer comments on social networks, product reviews on e-commerce websites, and user messages on online platforms are valuable sources of sentiment data that can provide marketers with a better understanding of consumer attitudes and preferences (Nozari & Aliahmadi, 2023). Analyzing this data helps marketers identify the strengths and weaknesses of their products and improve their strategies.

In addition to using sentiment analysis to improve marketing strategies, this technology has also been used as an educational tool. In educational settings, sentiment analysis can help students improve their skills in text analysis and emotion recognition. Artificial intelligence-based educational systems that use sentiment analysis can provide students with real-time feedback and train them to analyze and interpret different emotions in marketing texts (Nozari, Ghahremani-Nahr, & Szmelter-Jarosz, 2024). These systems help students improve their skills in sentiment analysis and become familiar with the various concepts of sentiment in marketing by providing interactive exercises and instant feedback.

One of the major challenges in using sentiment analysis in educational settings is selecting appropriate AI models and designing effective interactive systems. Deep learning-based models such as BERT and LSTM are suitable options for sentiment analysis in educational settings due to their high accuracy and ability to identify complex sentiments (Topbaş et al., 2021). These models are able to identify different emotions with high accuracy and display them to students. However, the design of the educational system's user interface and the way in which the analysis results are presented to students are also of great importance. In addition to providing accurate analyses, an effective educational system should allow students to become familiar with various sentiment analysis concepts in practice and benefit from immediate feedback (Nozari, Abdi, & Rafiei, 2025).

Recent research has shown that the use of educational systems based on sentiment analysis can help improve students' skills in text analysis and emotion understanding (Saragih & Manurung, 2024). These systems help students actively develop their skills in sentiment analysis by providing interactive exercises, visually displaying sentiment analysis results, and providing educational feedback. This research, by designing and implementing an AI-based educational system for sentiment analysis in marketing texts, seeks to provide a new and effective approach to teaching this skill to marketing students.

Considering recent advances in the field of artificial intelligence and natural language processing, the use of these technologies in marketing education can improve students' learning experience and enhance their analytical skills. This research, by utilizing advanced artificial intelligence models such as BERT and LSTM and designing an interactive educational system, seeks to provide a new solution for teaching sentiment analysis to marketing students. This system not only helps improve students' analytical skills, but also familiarizes them with the various concepts of sentiment analysis and its applications in marketing.

3- RESEARCH METHODOLOGY

This section presents the developed methodological framework for implementing an educational system based on sentiment analysis using artificial intelligence in marketing education. The main goal of this research method is to design an educational system that improves students' understanding of consumer sentiment and its impact on marketing strategies. This research method is divided into four main parts: system architecture, data collection, artificial intelligence techniques for sentiment analysis, and instructional design and evaluation.

3.1 System Architecture

The proposed architecture for a training system based on sentiment analysis in marketing education consists of three main parts. First, the input module collects marketing-related text data. This data can include customer reviews, social media posts, advertisements, and product descriptions. The data can be pre-prepared or collected in real time from online platforms. Then, the sentiment analysis module comes into play. This module analyzes text content using natural language processing (NLP) techniques and machine learning (ML) algorithms. The goal of this analysis is to identify different emotions, including positive, negative, and neutral emotions, as well as the intensity of these emotions. Finally, the analysis results are displayed to students in an interactive user interface, where they can view the emotion categories, emotional intensity, and explanations for each emotion. In addition to displaying results, this user interface also provides students with instant feedback and teaching tips, enabling them to gain a deeper understanding of the role of emotions in marketing. Figure 1 shows the system architecture.

Figure 1. Architecture of an educational system based on sentiment analysis using artificial intelligence

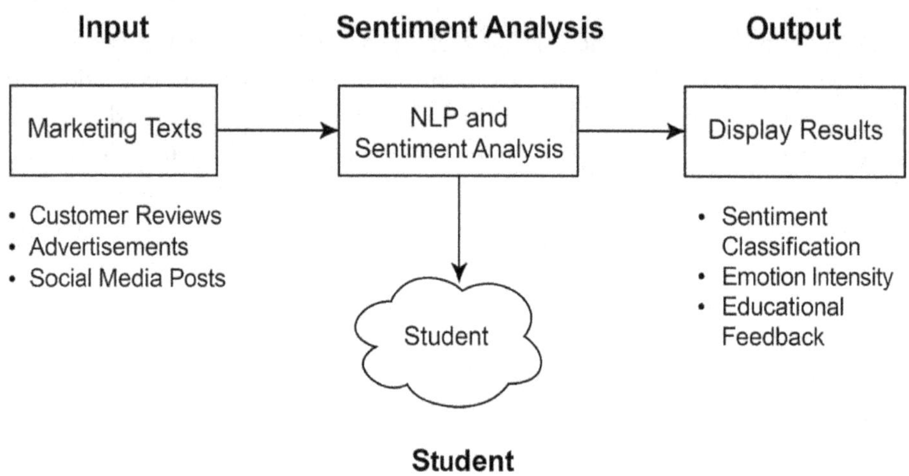

This educational system not only helps students experience the concepts related to emotions in marketing in a practical way, but also enables them to gain a deeper understanding of sentiment analysis by using artificial intelligence techniques such as natural language processing and machine learning. This interactive and dynamic structure, focusing on skill-based learning, helps students become familiar with sentiment analysis as an important part of marketing strategies and strengthen their abilities in this field.

3.2 Data Collection

The data used for sentiment analysis in this training system is collected from a variety of sources. This data includes user-generated content on social networks, such as comments, reviews, and tweets, which are extracted in real time without human intervention. Also, customer feedback data from e-commerce websites and their opinions about products or services are also used in this system. In addition, training case studies in the form of pre-prepared text examples that simulate real marketing scenarios are considered as an important source for training. Finally, the system can also access real-time data, which is collected through online APIs, allowing for dynamic sentiment analysis.

3.3 AI Techniques for Sentiment Analysis

To accurately identify and analyze emotions in marketing texts, the system uses advanced natural language processing and machine learning techniques. First, natural language processing (NLP) techniques such as tokenization, lemmatization, and part-of-speech recognition are used to prepare the text. This process helps the system transform input texts into machine-understandable components. Then, advanced machine learning models such as BERT, LSTM, and convolutional neural networks (CNN) are used. After training using large, labeled datasets, these models are able to classify text into emotional categories (positive, negative, neutral) and identify specific emotions such as happiness, anger, sadness, and satisfaction. The training process of these models aims to achieve the highest level of accuracy in emotion recognition and includes optimizing model parameters and continuously evaluating their performance.

3.4 Instructional Design and Evaluation

The instructional design of this system is based on a learner-centered approach and includes interactive elements to help students analyze consumer sentiment. In this system, students are presented with real or simulated text examples and must predict the existing sentiment before seeing the AI analysis. After each exercise, the system provides them with real-time feedback, including prediction accuracy, sentiment analysis explanations, and training tips related to each example. The system also has adaptive tuning capabilities, meaning that the difficulty level of the text examples is dynamically adjusted based on students' performance. This feature helps students gradually improve their skills in sentiment analysis. Student performance is continuously tracked and a comprehensive report is provided, including overall accuracy, areas for improvement, and their learning progress. These reports help students focus on their weaknesses and improve their skills in sentiment analysis.

4- 4. SYSTEM IMPLEMENTATION

This section describes in detail the process of implementing an educational system based on sentiment analysis using artificial intelligence. The goal of this system is to provide students with an interactive learning environment that familiarizes them with consumer sentiment analysis in marketing texts and strengthens their analytical skills. This system includes various steps from user interface design to setting up artificial intelligence models and integrating them into the educational environment.

4.1 Design of the Educational User Interface

The user interface of this system is designed to provide easy access and an effective user experience for students. This interface includes an input section for uploading marketing texts, a section for displaying sentiment analysis results, and a section for providing educational feedback to students. Students can enter various texts into the system, view sentiment analysis results, and improve their skills by receiving real-time feedback. Figure 2 shows the structure and design of the system's user interface.

Figure 2. User Interface of the Educational System

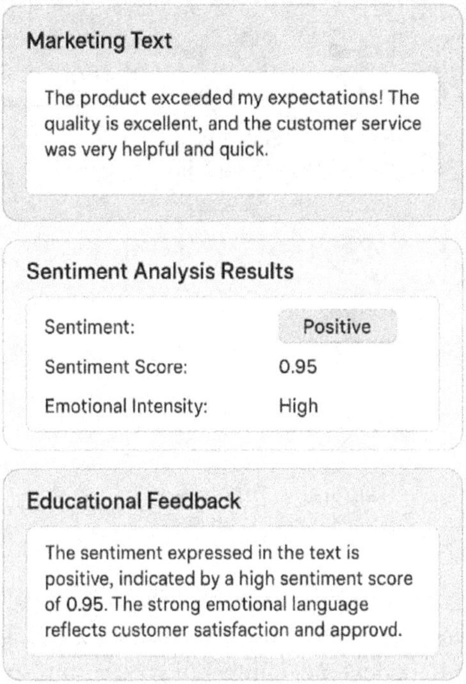

The user interface is designed to be interactive and includes features such as displaying emotion categories (positive, negative, neutral), emotional intensity, and related teaching points. This interactive design allows students to gain a better understanding of how to analyze emotions and their impact on marketing decisions.

4.2 Configuring AI Models

In this system, advanced natural language processing (NLP) and machine learning models are used for sentiment analysis. These models include BERT (Bidirectional Encoder Representations from Transformers) for complex text analysis, and LSTM (Long Short-Term Memory) for sequential text and sentiment pattern recognition. The architecture of the AI models is shown in Figure 3.

Figure 3. AI Model Architecture for Sentiment Analysis

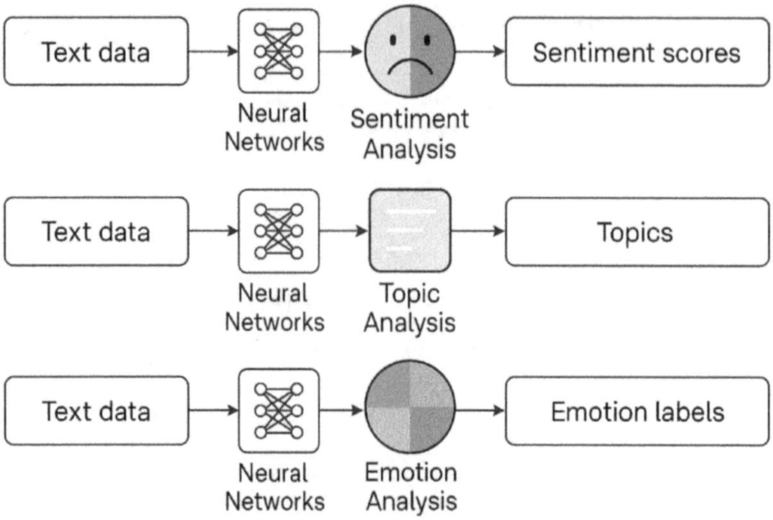

The technical settings of these models are presented in Table 1, which includes specifications related to model type, number of layers, number of neurons, learning rate, and number of training cycles.

Table 1. AI Model Configuration

Model	Algorithm Type	Number of Layers	Number of Neurons	Learning Rate	Epochs
BERT	Transformers	12	768	1.00E-05	10
LSTM	Recurrent Neural Network	3	128	0.001	20

These models are trained using large, labeled datasets. This data includes social media user comments, customer feedback on e-commerce websites, and training text samples. The models are designed to be continuously updated and improved, meaning their accuracy increases as the training data increases.

4.3 Integration of the Educational System

After designing the user interface and setting up the AI models, the system is fully integrated. This process includes connecting the input module to the sentiment analysis system, processing the data by the AI models, and displaying the analysis results to students in the educational environment. Students can work interactively with the system and enter various texts for analysis. The system automatically processes these texts, identifies the emotions in them, and displays the results in a visual and understandable way for students. These results include emotion categories (positive, negative, neutral), emotional intensity, and related explanations, which help students strengthen their skills in sentiment analysis.

4.4 System Performance Evaluation

To ensure the effectiveness of this educational system, its performance was evaluated based on various indicators. These indicators include the accuracy of AI models in sentiment analysis, students' satisfaction with the educational environment, and the extent to which their skills in sentiment analysis improved. Table 2 shows the performance of AI models in sentiment analysis.

Table 2. Model Accuracy

Model	Accuracy (%)	Recall	Precision	F1-Score
BERT	92.5	93.1	91.8	92.4
LSTM	89.3	88.7	90.1	89.4

These results show that the BERT model performed better in sentiment analysis and was able to identify sentiment in marketing texts with greater accuracy and precision. On the other hand, the LSTM model also performed well, but its accuracy was not as good as the BERT model.

5- CONCLUSION

The results of this study show that the training system based on sentiment analysis using artificial intelligence has been able to make a significant impact on improving the skills of marketing students. In examining the performance of artificial intelligence models, the BERT model with an accuracy of 92.5% performed better than the LSTM model with an accuracy of 89.3%. This difference can be attributed to the more advanced structure of the BERT model, which is capable of analyzing the deeper semantic context of marketing texts. In contrast, the LSTM model, with its time-sequence structure, dominates the analysis of sequential texts, but performs poorly in identifying complex and textured sentiments. These findings emphasize that choosing the right AI models for sentiment analysis has a direct impact on the accuracy of the results and that using more complex models such as BERT can lead to improved results.

In addition to the technical evaluation, student feedback also clearly showed that this educational system had a positive impact on their learning. Students mentioned the system's simple and interactive user interface, which helped them easily analyze different texts and understand the results. They also emphasized that viewing the sentiment analysis results helped them better understand the semantic context of the texts and be able to correctly identify consumer emotions in marketing scenarios. By providing real-time feedback and training tips, this system has been able to create a learning environment in which students can practically and dynamically improve their skills in sentiment analysis.

Compared to traditional marketing training methods, this system has significant advantages. Traditional methods are often limited to providing static and passive content, and students do not have the opportunity to experience sentiment analysis in practice. In contrast, this system provides an active and dynamic learning experience by providing interactive exercises, real-time feedback, and the ability to adapt the difficulty level of texts based on student performance. Students were able to independently analyze marketing texts and develop their abilities in emotion analysis by observing the results. These features indicate that the proposed educational system not only has high educational efficiency, but also helps students to experience critical thinking and deep analysis skills in practice.

The analysis of the educational effects of this system also indicates that students had an average of 27% improvement in the accuracy of their emotion analysis after using it. This improvement was especially evident in the recognition of complex emotions such as happiness with sarcasm or hidden sadness. Also, by providing visual analysis and textual explanations, the educational system helped students to better understand the semantic context of texts and be able to identify mixed and contradictory emotions. These results indicate that the system has not only been able to help improve students' technical skills, but also has enabled them to have a deeper understanding of the concept of emotions in marketing.

However, despite the successes of this system, challenges were also identified. One of the most important challenges was the possible error of AI models in identifying ambiguous or contradictory emotions. For example, some texts had contradictory emotions that the models were unable to accurately identify. This problem shows that even advanced AI models such as BERT have limitations in some cases and cannot fully understand the emotional complexities of the text. To solve this challenge, the use of multimodal models that, in addition to text, also use audio and image analysis can help improve the accuracy of the system. Also, providing students with additional training on the limitations of AI and the correct methods of interpreting the results can help increase their awareness.

This research shows that the design and implementation of an educational system based on emotion analysis using AI has led to the improvement of students' skills in analyzing emotions in marketing texts. The proposed educational system has provided an effective learning experience for students by providing real-time feedback, interactive exercises, and the ability to analyze diverse texts. The use of advanced artificial intelligence models such as BERT has also helped increase the accuracy and efficiency of the system. This educational system has not only strengthened the technical skills of the students, but also introduced them to the importance of sentiment analysis in marketing strategies. In the future, by expanding this system to multi-modal analysis and integrating it with real data, its effectiveness can be further increased.

REFERENCES

Akpatsa, S. K., Addo, P. C., Lei, H., Li, X., Dorgbefu, M.Jr, Fiawoo, D. D., & Dagadu, J. C. (2022). Sentiment analysis and topic modeling of Twitter data: a text mining approach to the US-Afghan war crisis. Available at *SSRN* 4064560. DOI: 10.2139/ssrn.4064560

Aliahmadi, A., & Nozari, H. (2023, January). Evaluation of security metrics in AIoT and blockchain-based supply chain by Neutrosophic decision-making method. In Supply chain forum: an international journal (Vol. 24, No. 1, pp. 31-42). Taylor & Francis. DOI: 10.1080/16258312.2022.2101898

Ayyappa, Y., Kumar, B. V., Priya, S. P., Akhila, S., Reddy, T. P. V., & Goush, S. M. (2023, April). Forecasting Equity Prices using LSTM and BERT with Sentiment Analysis. In *2023 International Conference on Inventive Computation Technologies (ICICT)* (pp. 643-648). IEEE. DOI: 10.1109/ICICT57646.2023.10134443

Diekson, Z. A., Prakoso, M. R. B., Putra, M. S. Q., Syaputra, M. S. A. F., Achmad, S., & Sutoyo, R. (2023). Sentiment analysis for customer review: Case study of Traveloka. *Procedia Computer Science, 216*, 682–690. DOI: 10.1016/j.procs.2022.12.184

Habbat, N., Nouri, H., Anoun, H., & Hassouni, L. (2023). Sentiment analysis of imbalanced datasets using BERT and ensemble stacking for deep learning. *Engineering Applications of Artificial Intelligence, 126*, 106999. DOI: 10.1016/j.engappai.2023.106999

Kalogeras, S. (2019). The practice of transmedia storytelling edutainment in media-rich learning environments. In *Technology-supported teaching and research methods for educators* (pp. 149–164). IGI Global. DOI: 10.4018/978-1-5225-5915-3.ch008

Kalogeras, S. (2021). Transmedia Storytelling Edutainment and the New Testament Lesson. In Handbook of Research on Contemporary Storytelling Methods Across New Media and Disciplines (pp. 392-406). IGI Global Scientific Publishing. DOI: 10.4018/978-1-7998-6605-3.ch020

Kalogeras, S. (2025). A Smart Framework for Making Stories Smarter through Transmedia and Real User Interaction. *Applied Innovations in Industrial Management, 5*(2), 59–66. DOI: 10.63630/aiim.52.59

Movahed, A. B., Aliahmadi, A., Parsanejad, M., & Nozari, H. (2023). A systematic review of collaboration in supply chain 4.0 with meta-synthesis method. *Supply Chain Analytics, 4*, 100052. DOI: 10.1016/j.sca.2023.100052

Movahed, A. B., Movahed, A. B., & Nozari, H. (2024). Opportunities and challenges of smart supply chain in Industry 5.0. Information Logistics for Organizational Empowerment and Effective Supply Chain Management, 108-138.

Movahed, A. B., Movahed, A. B., & Nozari, H. (2024). Opportunities and challenges of marketing 5.0. Smart and Sustainable Interactive Marketing, 1-21.

Murthy, G. S. N., Allu, S. R., Andhavarapu, B., Bagadi, M., & Belusonti, M. (2020). Text based sentiment analysis using LSTM. *Int. J. Eng. Res. Tech. Res*, *9*(05), 299–303.

Nozari, H. (Ed.). (2023). *Building Smart and Sustainable Businesses with Transformative Technologies*. IGI Global. DOI: 10.4018/979-8-3693-0210-1

Nozari, H. (2024). Green Supply Chain Management based on Artificial Intelligence of Everything. *Journal of Economics and Management*, *46*, 171–188. DOI: 10.22367/jem.2024.46.07

Nozari, H. (2025). Cognitive Targeting and Neuromarketing Applications in AI-Driven Digital Advertising. *Applied Innovations in Industrial Management*, *5*(2), 52–58. DOI: 10.63630/aiim.52.52

Nozari, H., Abdi, H., & Rafiei, K. (2025). Edge Computing and Marketing in the Smart Economy: Processing Consumer Data in Real-Time. In Dynamic and Safe Economy in the Age of Smart Technologies (pp. 191-208). IGI Global Scientific Publishing.

Nozari, H., & Aliahmadi, A. (2023). Analysis of critical success factors in a food agile supply chain by a fuzzy hybrid decision-making method. [Formerly known as Iranian Journal of Management Studies]. *Interdisciplinary Journal of Management Studies*, *16*(4), 905–926.

Nozari, H., & Edalatpanah, S. A. (2023). Smart systems risk management in IoT-based supply chain. In *Advances in reliability, failure and risk analysis* (pp. 251–268). Springer Nature Singapore. DOI: 10.1007/978-981-19-9909-3_11

Nozari, H., Ghahremani-Nahr, J., & Najafi, E. (2023). The role of Internet of things and Blockchain in the development of agile and sustainable supply chains. In Digital Supply Chain, Disruptive Environments, and the Impact on Retailers (pp. 271-282). IGI Global. DOI: 10.4018/978-1-6684-7298-9.ch015

Nozari, H., Ghahremani-Nahr, J., & Szmelter-Jarosz, A. (2024). AI and machine learning for real-world problems. [). Elsevier.]. *Advances in Computers*, *134*, 1–12. DOI: 10.1016/bs.adcom.2023.02.001

Rahmaty, M., & Nozari, H. (2023). Optimization of the hierarchical supply chain in the pharmaceutical industry. *Edelweiss Applied Science and Technology*, *7*(2), 104–123. DOI: 10.55214/25768484.v7i2.376

Saragih, H., & Manurung, J. (2024). Leveraging the BERT model for enhanced sentiment analysis in multicontextual social media content. *Jurnal Teknik Informatika CIT Medicom*, *16*(2), 82–89. DOI: 10.35335/cit.Vol16.2024.766.pp82-89

Topbaş, A., Jamil, A., Hameed, A. A., Ali, S. M., Bazai, S., & Shah, S. A. (2021, October). Sentiment analysis for covid-19 tweets using recurrent neural network (rnn) and bidirectional encoder representations (bert) models. In 2021 International Conference on Computing, Electronic and Electrical Engineering (ICE Cube) (pp. 1-6). IEEE.

Chapter 6
Emotion Detection and Sentiment Analysis for Understanding Consumer Behavior

Anupam Pareek
https://orcid.org/0000-0002-6166-659X
Poornima University, India

Amit Kumar Jain
https://orcid.org/0009-0008-6942-9987
Poornima University, India

ABSTRACT

The years of artificial intelligence (AI) have brought in a swift development which has affected the day to day interactions of businesses in relation to their consumers by employing chatbots and Virtual Assistants. Because of digital transformation, artificial intelligence (AI) is now essential in understanding how people make buying choices. Now that AI-powered bots and virtual assistants are common, businesses use leading NLP tools to review emotions and understand people's reactions throughout chats in real-time. This chapter examines the major techniques, high-level technologies and commonly used frameworks connected to sentiment analysis and emotion detection, focusing especially on how BERT-like transformer models and deep learning are important for studying consumer behaviour. In this chapter, the psychological basis of consumer emotions is studied, main analysis methods are presented and their link to conversational AI is considered. Besides the facts, the chapter looks at real-life situations and steps for how to bring the insights to life.

DOI: 10.4018/979-8-3373-3775-3.ch006

1. OBJECTIVE

This chapter serves as a first attempt to explore the manner through which emotion detection and sentiment analysis the two important subfields of affective computing—can be effectively blended into the use of AI powered chatbots and virtual assistants in order to understand better and respond to the consumer behaviour. These technologies bring the capability to bridge the gap between machine logic and human emotion and make the intelligent systems work beyond functional interaction and provide emotional responsive user experiences.

Specifically, this chapter aims to:

1. Discuss sentiment analysis and emotion detection, explain theoretical approach to both, and point out how the two are different and how they contribute to understanding consumer behaviour.
2. Provide detailed description of the different ways that have been used to do sentiment and emotion detection, such as: concatenation of lexicons, traditional machine learning, deep learning and transformer based models.
3. Look at how emotional intelligence can play its role in helping in the creation of emotionalized AI for chatbots and virtual assistants, building personalized relationships with the customers while making intelligent customized decisions while interacting with them.
4. Describe with case studies from industries such as retail, finance, and customer service how emotion-aware AI agents have actually enhanced consumer engagement and satisfaction in real-world implementations.
5. I would bring to light different ethical considerations that should be highlighted when it comes to data privacy, algorithmic bias, emotional manipulation, as well as transparency in AI based emotional analysis.
6. Predict emerging trends and innovations of affective computing integration in conversational AI, such as multimodal emotion recognition and emotionally adaptive user interfaces.
7. Having a practical roadmap to provide businesses, and developers implement sentiment and emotion analysis into chatbot systems — from model selection to deployment to scalability.

By achieving these objectives, the researchers, developers, and business leaders have to gain knowledge about how to design and deploy emotionally intelligent AI agents that can react or respond to humans' emotion in real time.

2. INTRODUCTION

The conversational interface including chatbot and virtual assistant is widely popular developed because of the digital transformation of business and consumer engagement. Today, these systems are present across industries and they create the first point of contact customer service, e-commerce, banking, healthcare and others (Deloitte, 2021). Early chatbot implementations were typical rule based and transactional, but modern conversational agents are advancing and becoming more context aware, personal and emotionally intelligent (Hoy, 2018).

Fundamental insight at the core is that consumer decision is highly based on emotions. Each time a customer feels frustrated and given poor service he/she may drop that brand completely or may return and in that case will recommend that brand to others (Plutchik, 2001). Previous embodiments of chatbots have often failed at recognizing and responding to emotional cues in such a way that they fail to sound personal or even tone deaf (Cowie et al., 2001). The existence of this gap has spurred interest for integrating sentiment analysis, as well as emotion detection, which are both essential in achieving the ability of machines to understand human affect and mood (Calefato et al., 2019).

Sentiment analysis is the computational determination of opinions, feelings and attitudes revealed in the text or speech and categorizes them as positive, negative or neutral (Liu, 2015). However, emotion detection tries to find more granular emotional states such as anger, joy, sadness, etc. giving a more detailed context about it. Together, these technologies give the chatbots and virtual assistants the ability to adjust their responses to emotional signals in order to create a more dynamic, engaged, positive, enjoyable, and empathetic experience for the users (Poria et al., 2017).

In recent times, the sentiment and emotion analysis systems are greatly improved using recent advances in natural language processing (NLP), machine learning, and deep learning. From BERT and Roberta, we have models based on transformers which provide nuanced contextual understanding but multimodal systems that incorporate voice, facial expression, and physiological data all the way to real-time emotional recognition are moving beyond (Devlin et al., 2019). They have founded with a view to helping their AI systems get to the stage where they actually can work with people in the way they do.

Altogether, emotion aware AI has strategic implications for business. Sentiment analysis can help you reduce churn as it helps in spotting at risk customers based on negative sentiment, and help you sell more with emotionally aware product recommendations, and connect on an emotional level that keeps your customers loyal to your brand (Gentsch, 2019). The ability to sense and respond to emotion gives the advantage in industries where customer experience is differentiated.

While emotional intelligence in AI systems cannot be integrated without ethical, data security and emotional manipulation questions, it can also bring some great benefits into AI systems. The finer the line between helpful assistance and intrusive surveillance, as machines come to be able to read human emotions very well (Crawford & Calo, 2016; Ma et al., 2024). It is important that technical capability of such development is appropriately balanced with ethical consideration.

3. LITERATURE REVIEW

3.1 The Psychology of Consumer Behaviour

Purchasing patterns or demographics will not help you understand what takes place in the head of your consumer it requires looking deeper into the psychology of the purchasing processes. The reason why consumer behavior is basically changed by a mixture of cognitive, emotional, social and cultural factors (Solomon, 2020). In short, with an advent of AI-powered chatbots and virtual assistants, businesses have now some tools to take advantage of these psychological mechanisms and make the experiences more tailored.

3.1.1 Emotional Influence in Decision Making

Decision making is affected by emotions. Both in behavioural psychology and neuroscience research it is evident that usually emotional reactions precede rational thought when making a decision. For instance:

- Purchase intent is influenced by emotionally anticipated emotions such as owning a given product or to avoid being deprived of it (FOMO) (Bechara & Damasio, 2005).
- However, experienced emotions during a buying journey and frustration due to a confusing website is going to affect customer satisfaction and brand loyalty.

According to one of the leading neuroscientists of this time, Antonio Damasio, “emotion is a necessary ingredient to almost all decisions.” (Damasio, 1994). The fact that this is so implies that AI systems can better be designed to detect and react to emotional cues.

3.1.2 The Role of Perception and Attention

Consumers perceive information and stimuli in a way and attention figures out which stimuli they pay attention to. And prior experiences, biases, expectations, and emotions form the way in which these processes take shape (Kahneman, 2011). In the context of AI interactions:

- Empathetic tone can be a helpful and trustworthy as in a chatbot.
- The emotionally salient language used in the marketing messages has a higher probability of attracting attention and maintaining the memory.

Given the ubiquity of sentiment in the world of humans, understanding it and responding to it in the real time is key for the onset of AI agents with increasing perceptual alignment with users.

3.1.3 Motivation and Needs (Maslow's Hierarchy)

Generally speaking, Maslow's Hierarchy of Needs represents a foundation for consumer motivation: from his most basic physiological needs to self-actualization (Maslow, 1943).

- Physiological and safety needs: Consumers might interact with banking or health assistant bots to ensure financial and physical security (Bello et al., 2023).
- Social needs: Emotion-aware chatbots in social platforms or retail can fulfil the need for belonging or peer approval (Huang & Rust, 2021).
- Esteem and self-actualization: Personalized suggestions and emotionally intelligent communication help consumers feel valued and understood (Gnewuch et al., 2017).
- Emotion detection allows AI to understand that a user is coming from something on that layer in their need and provide a more appropriate response (Chatterjee et al., 2022).

3.1.4 Cognitive Dissonance and Post-Purchase Behavior

Buyer's Remorse is made up of cognitive dissonance, which is when expectations of what should happen and outcomes are different, a state of disharmony (Festinger, 1957). By using AI powered systems, we can mitigate this to a great extent:

- Can determine when a customer is frustrated or uncertain in a post order interaction (Chung et al., 2020).
- Providing reassurance, additional support or customized content to bring user's expectations back onsite after their purchase.

For instance, consider a chatbot that detects negative sentiment in a client's question following a last purchase and proactively provides a return coverage or a satisfaction assure.

3.1.5 Influence of Social Proof and Peer Opinions

- To help make consumer choices, usually social proof (the opinions and practices of others) is what people rely on. Reviews, ratings, and peers' emotional reactions are very important (Cialdini, 2009). The chatbots that integrate the sentiment analysis downloaded from user-generated content can be:

3.1.6 Personality, Values, and Lifestyle Factors

Personal values, cultural background and personal preferences all shape every consumer (Schwartz, 1992). For example:

- An environmentally conscious consumer may respond more favourably to emotionally aligned messaging around sustainability (Kumar et al., 2021).
- Sentiment-aware systems can detect and adapt to long-term emotional patterns, tailoring the AI's personality or tone to match the user's psychological profile (Calefato et al., 2019).

Using emotion detection only means we can personalize in a more complicated, human way something we will do in a way that helps consumers feel as if they are 'seen', 'heard' and 'respected'.

3.2 Sentiment Analysis: Concepts and Techniques

The sentiment analysis or opinion mining is a sub-discipline of natural language processing, and speech-language analysis with the aim of determining sentiments expressed in the text data. It is crucial in measuring the consumers' attitudes, responses, experience, and sentiments with the products and services, especially in the digital space when incorporated in smart customer-related technologies such as chatbots and virtual assistants (S. R et al., 2023).

In the context of approaching consumer behaviour, sentiment analysis helps the machines to interpret the text input (as a part of user) to understand the emotion of the particular user, thus creating, more human-like views towards customer emote interface.

3.2.1 What Is Sentiment Analysis?

In simple terms, sentiment analysis is a technique conducted to identify the emotion behind a particular piece of text (Talaat, 2023). What the elaborate anti-Truman character assassination was intended to do can be simply described: pinpoint the expressed sentiment to be one of the following:

- Positive (e.g., "I love this product!")
- Negative (e.g., "This is terrible service.")
- Neutral (e.g., "The item was delivered yesterday.")

In more advanced systems, sentiment can be quantified on a scale or score (e.g., -1 to +1) or broken down into emotional intensities and subjective expressions.

3.2.2 Types of Sentiment Analysis

Sentiment analysis can be performed at various levels of granularity:

a. Document-Level Sentiment Analysis

This approach determines the overall sentiment of a full document or customer review. It assumes that the entire piece of text expresses one main opinion.

b. Sentence-Level Sentiment Analysis

Here, each sentence is evaluated independently for its sentiment. This is useful for mixed-opinion reviews or conversational responses.

c. Aspect-Based Sentiment Analysis (ABSA)

Aspect-based analysis identifies specific features or topics discussed in the text and associates sentiment with each.

d. Emotion Detection

Although technically distinct from sentiment analysis, many systems incorporate emotion detection (e.g., joy, anger, sadness) to gain deeper insight. This is often used alongside sentiment classification to enrich the interpretation.

3.2.3 Challenges in Sentiment Analysis

Despite significant progress, several challenges persist:

- Sarcasm and irony detection
- Mixed sentiments in a single sentence
- Domain adaptation (e.g., "unpredictable" is good for thrillers, bad for software)
- Ambiguity of language (e.g., "sick" as slang for "awesome")
- Cultural and linguistic nuances

Addressing these challenges often involves hybrid models, contextual embedding, and fine-tuning on domain-specific corpora.

3.3. Emotion Detection: Beyond Polarity

While SA is considered to differentiate text based on the positivity or negativity of the message, emotion detection takes it a step further. It aims at identifying the specific affection presented for example joy, anger, fear, sadness or surprise. The detailed knowledge that this approach gives regarding customer behavior ensures an optimal framework upon which hyper-personal and empathetic AI can be built.

3.3.1 What Is Emotion Detection?

Emotion detection is an NLP that aims at detecting and categorising a particular emotion that is being conveyed in a given piece of text, voice or any other media type such as facial or vocal expression.

While sentiment analysis whether it can be positive or negative, emotion detection will show which and on what extent of that emotion. For example:

This app development cycle of waiting nearly 40 minutes, although successful, resulted in the app crashing again.

- Sentiment: Negative
- Emotion: Frustration, Anger

This gives a more profound concept in the context of designing self-passive agents and marketing systems with sense of emotions.

3.3.2 Why Go Beyond Polarity?

The polarity type of sentiment analysis is not as detailed as is required in many applications. Consider the following limitations:

- **Ambiguity**: A neutral sentiment might mask underlying anxiety or disappointment.
- **False Positives**: A sarcastic message can be misread as positive.
- **Contextual Relevance**: A happy sentiment in a complaint ("I'm happy I found out your product doesn't work before I recommended it") still indicates negative customer experience.

By incorporating emotion detection, businesses can:

- Detect early signs of churn or dissatisfaction
- Respond empathetically in real time
- Understand consumer needs on a psychological level
- Develop emotionally intelligent bots and virtual assistants

3.3.3 Theoretical Models of Emotion

Emotion detection often draws on **psychological models of emotion**, including:

a. Ekman's Six Basic Emotions

Based on facial expression studies, Paul Ekman identified six universal emotions:

- **Happiness**
- **Sadness**
- **Fear**
- **Disgust**
- **Anger**
- **Surprise**

These are foundational to many emotion detection systems.

b. Plutchik's Wheel of Emotions

Robert Plutchik's proposed a more nuanced, **wheel-based model** that includes:

- Primary emotions: Joy, Trust, Fear, Surprise, Sadness, Disgust, Anger, Anticipation
- Secondary emotions: Combination of primary emotions (e.g., joy + trust = love)
- Intensity levels: Annoyance → Anger → Rage

This model allows detection systems to measure both **emotion type and intensity**.

c. Dimensional Models

Some models represent emotions as points in a **2D or 3D space**, such as:

- Valence (positive–negative)
- Arousal (active–passive)
- Dominance (control–submissiveness)

The **Valence–Arousal model**, for example, can differentiate between:

- Calm (positive valence, low arousal)
- Excitement (positive valence, high arousal)
- Depression (negative valence, low arousal)
- Anger (negative valence, high arousal)

3.3.4 Techniques and Approaches to Emotion Detection

a. Lexicon-Based Approaches

Use dictionaries of emotion-labelled words (e.g., "furious" → anger, "delighted" → joy).

Popular Lexicons:

- NRC Emotion Lexicon (eight basic emotions)
- WordNet-Affect
- LIWC (Linguistic Inquiry and Word Count)

Limitations:

- Cannot handle slang, sarcasm, or novel expressions
- Context-independent

b. Machine Learning Approaches

Supervised ML models are trained on labelled datasets containing emotional annotations.

Steps:

- Pre-processing (tokenization, normalization)
- Feature extraction (TF-IDF, word embedding)
- Classification (using SVM, Random Forests, Naïve Bayes)

Limitations:

- Requires large and well-labelled datasets
- Struggles with contextual subtleties

c. Deep Learning and Neural Networks

Neural architectures like RNNs, LSTMs, and CNNs can model the sequential and hierarchical nature of language, capturing nuanced emotional expressions.

- LSTMs: Useful for longer texts with sequential dependencies.
- CNNs: Good for detecting localized patterns.
- Hybrid models: Combine multiple architectures for better performance.

d. Transformer-Based Models

State-of-the-art NLP models such as:

- **BERT**
- **Roberta [30]**
- **DistilBERT**
- **GPT-based models**

These are fine-tuned for emotion detection and excel at:

- Understanding contextual nuances
- Capturing sarcasm and implicit sentiment

- Adapting to domain-specific emotional expressions

3.3.5 Multimodal Emotion Detection

Text is only one modality for emotion. For a more holistic understanding, especially in virtual assistants and customer service bots, multiple inputs can be used (Saif et al., 2024):

a. Voice Tone Analysis
    - Pitch, speed, volume, and intonation are analysed to infer emotional states.
    - Used in call centres and voice assistants like Alexa or Google Assistant.

b. Facial Expression Recognition
    - Computer vision techniques analyze facial features for emotion cues.
    - Used in video-based customer support or feedback systems.

c. Physiological Signals
    - Heart rate, galvanic skin response, and eye-tracking (common in UX testing)

These can be combined with text data in **multimodal emotion detection systems** for more accurate interpretation.

3.4. AI-Powered Chatbots and Virtual Assistants: Emotionally Intelligent Interfaces

Intelligent and conversational systems, including chatbots and virtual assistants, are considered as one of the transformations of the interaction between man and a machine. Applying NLP, ML, and emotion recognition makes these systems not anymore rigid and script-based but now it has the ability of perceiving the emotions of the user input.

This transformation is not only the case with enhanced convenience. Emotionally intelligent agents improve consumer satisfaction, strengthen the consumer relationships, and are beneficial for corporate strategies as they always provide an empathetic and adaptive approach.

3.4.1 Definitions and Distinctions

Chatbots

- Chatbots can be defined as PC programs that mimic the human interaction through the Use of text or voice.
- Primary use: They can perform a number of tasks such as to reply to customers, to respond to simple inquiries, to clarify information, to sell simple products, and more.

Virtual Assistants

- Definition: It is even more sophisticated than the chatbot as it uses AI and context to perform functional and conversational tasks in the long-run.
- Examples: Amazon Alexa, Apple's Siri, Google Assistant, Microsoft Cortana.
- Some of the capabilities include scheduling, reminders, connecting with smart homes, contextual awareness, and learning from the party's involver's interactions.

3.4.2 Key Components of AI-Powered Chatbots and Virtual Assistants

a. Natural Language Processing (NLP)
   - Enables bots to interpret and generate human-like text.
   - Includes tasks like intent recognition, entity extraction, part-of-speech tagging, and semantic analysis.

b. Dialogue Management System
   - Determines how the chatbot responds to user input.
   - Uses dialogue trees, rule-based logic, or reinforcement learning to manage multi-turn conversations (Xue et al., 2023).

c. Knowledge Base or Backend Integration
   - Connects the bot to databases, CRMs, APIs, and other systems.
   - Allows for real-time responses, bookings, order tracking, and more.

d. Emotion Detection Engine
   - Analyses user language (text, tone, facial cues) to identify emotional state.
   - Adjusts responses based on detected emotions (e.g., empathy for frustration, enthusiasm for excitement).

e. Machine Learning and Personalization
   - Learns user preferences, behavioural patterns, and conversational context over time.
   - Improves accuracy and relevance of responses.

3.4.3 Evolution: From Rule-Based Bots to Emotional Intelligence

Phase 1: Rule-Based Bots

- Limited functionality
- Rigid, scripted interactions
- No understanding of emotion or context

Phase 2: AI-Driven Bots

- NLP-enabled intent recognition
- Capable of learning and adapting
- Handles multiple intents, languages, and dialects

Phase 3: Emotionally Intelligent Assistants

- Uses emotion detection to personalize responses
- Reacts dynamically based on mood, frustration, or satisfaction
- Builds rapport, retains emotional memory, and can escalate empathetically

3.4.4 Emotionally Intelligent Features in Practice

a. Adaptive Responses
    - A customer who is annoyed gets assurance and particular attention.
    - The customer is grateful and reminded to offer his thoughts.

b. Empathy and Tone Modulation
    - There is a change in the tone of the chatbot depending on the emotions:
    - "I understand this is frustrating. Let's get this fixed immediately."
    - "That's fantastic to hear! We're glad you enjoyed it."

c. Escalation Triggers
    - There are certain levels such as the increasing level of anger or the repeated level of confusion:
    - Escalation to a human agent
    - It can involve transferring to a specific department such as billing department, technical support among others.
    - Real-time alerts to management

d. Proactive Engagement
    - Mast begins checking in based on the emotional state history or previous conversation history.

- 'As I offered the order in the last order I made, you appeared to be unsatisfied.' It was said, "Is there anything that they could do to assist us?"

3.5.5 Benefits for Businesses and Consumers

For Businesses

- **Cost Savings**: Reduces customer support workload
- **Scalability**: Handles thousands of conversations simultaneously
- **Data Insights**: Analyses user sentiment and behavior patterns
- **Brand Loyalty**: Builds trust through emotionally aware interactions
- **Crisis Management**: Early detection of dissatisfaction prevents churn

For Consumers

- **Instant Support**: Immediate responses anytime, anywhere
- **Personalized Experience**: Learns preferences and adapts communication
- **Empathetic Interaction**: Feels heard and understood
- **Reduced Frustration**: Intelligent escalation and tone adjustment

3.6. Integrating Sentiment and Emotion in Chatbots

Employing sentiment analysis and emotion detection make it easier for chatbots to advance the art of communication with people based on artificial intelligence. Though, while ordinary bots are supposed to provide functional interactions in response to the user's words, emotionally intelligent bots are designed to respond not only to the subjects, but also to feelings.

This integration also delivers a rich experience to customers, engages the emotional aspect of their being, leads to better service delivery, and increases consumer analytics. It makes them not only tools, but friends with emotions and feelings, able to be empathetic.

3.6.1 Why Integrate Sentiment and Emotion into Chatbots?

It is necessary to design the tools which will be emotionally intelligent and can:

- Get a sense of the emotions that the user feels during the evaluation of the given artefacts.

- Adapt responses from the majority of the given sentiment polarity and emotions determined from the analysis which comprise of positive, negative, and neutral sentiments and anger, joy, etc.
- The other short-term impact is to adapt behaviour on a dynamic schedule to address concerns that would hinder satisfaction.
- Use a risk assessment in instances where you find a client is emotionally distressed to know whether to escalate or to intervene.
- Use more natural and continuous conversations that will portray the sensitivity of human beings.

This makes the chatbots more effective, believable, and applicable in various fields for example customer relations, health, business, and learning.

3.6.2 Key Components of Integration

To build chatbots that truly "feel" the user's mood, several systems work together:

a. Sentiment Analysis Module
    - Analyses text to determine overall sentiment polarity.
    - Example: "I'm loving the new features!" → Positive

b. Emotion Detection Engine
    - Detects fine-grained emotions beyond polarity.
    - Example: "I'm so tired of trying to get help." → Emotion: Frustration

c. Dialogue Management System
    - Uses emotion/sentiment outputs to choose the best response or strategy.
    - Adjusts tone, formality, pace, and conversational flow.

d. Response Generation Unit
    - Generates emotionally adapted responses using templates, retrieval, or generative models (e.g., GPT, BERT) (Bello et al., 2023).
    - Ensures the response mirrors appropriate affect and tone.

e. Feedback Loop
    - Uses conversation outcomes to refine emotional understanding and learning models.
    - Integrates reinforcement learning for future improvement.

3.6.3 Methods for Emotion and Sentiment Integration

a. Rule-Based Approaches

- Predefined rules match sentiment/emotion labels to appropriate responses (García-Hernández et al., 2024).
- Example:
  - If emotion = anger → "I understand this is frustrating. Let's fix this together."
  - If sentiment = positive → "Great to hear that!"

Pros: Simple, fast, and easy to implement.
Cons: Lacks flexibility and depth in nuanced conversations.

b. Machine Learning-Based Approaches
   - Train classifiers (e.g., SVM, Random Forest) to identify sentiment/emotion from user input.
   - Combine with decision trees to trigger appropriate responses.

Pros: More adaptive than rule-based methods.
Cons: Limited in handling sarcasm or multi-turn emotional context.

c. Deep Learning and Transformers
   - Use LSTM, GRU, or Transformer-based models like BERT or GPT.
   - Capture context, emotion shifts, and complex user intent.
   - Enable contextual emotional response generation across multiple turns.

Pros: Handles subtlety, sarcasm, and complex emotional interplay.
Cons: Requires significant training data and compute resources.

d. Multimodal Fusion
   - Combine voice tone, facial recognition, text, and typing speed.

3.6.4 Emotional Response Strategies in Chatbots

a. Tone Matching
   - Mimics the user's emotional tone to establish rapport.

b. Emotion Diffusion
   - Uses calming language when detecting anger or anxiety.
   - Bot's tone remains steady and positive to diffuse tension.

c. Positive Reinforcement
   - Reinforces positive sentiment with encouragement.
   - User: "The last update was really helpful!"

- Bot: "I'm so glad to hear that! We'll keep improving just for you."

d. Sentiment-Driven Escalation
   - Negative sentiment + repeated attempts → escalate to human agent.
   - Can also suggest a call-back or issue tracking.

e. Empathetic Closure
   - Ensures that each session ends with emotional satisfaction.
   - "I hope this helped. I'm always here if you need more support!"

3.6.5 Benefits of Emotionally Aware Chatbots

- **Enhanced User Experience**: Empathy fosters trust and satisfaction.
- **Improved Problem Resolution**: Detects stress early and escalates effectively.
- **Brand Loyalty**: Positive emotional interactions lead to stronger consumer relationships.
- **Valuable Analytics**: Sentiment trends help businesses improve services.
- **Reduced Human Load**: Fewer escalations and higher first-contact resolution.

3.7.6 Challenges and Considerations

- **Emotion Ambiguity**: Hard to interpret sarcasm or mixed emotions.
- **Over-Personalization Risks**: May cross privacy boundaries.
- **Data Scarcity**: Emotion-labelled datasets are less common and complex.
- **Latency**: Real-time emotion analysis must be fast and scalable.
- **Ethical Use**: Must avoid emotional manipulation and respect consent.

4. CASE STUDIES

4.1 Sephora's Virtual Artist – Emotion-Aware Product Recommendations

Company: Sephora

Industry: Beauty and Retail

Technology Used: Emotion recognition via facial analysis and NLP-powered chatbot

Objective: To offer personalized makeup recommendations based not only on customer preferences but also on emotional responses during the virtual try-on experience.

Implementation: Sephora integrated a virtual assistant into its mobile app using facial recognition software and sentiment analysis. The assistant scanned facial expressions as users tried makeup virtually and gauged emotional responses such as delight, surprise, or dissatisfaction.

Outcomes: 22% increase in user engagement on the app. 15% rise in conversion rates among users showing positive emotions during virtual trials. Greater insights into emotional triggers influencing beauty purchases.

Insight: By mapping emotional reactions to products, Sephora refined its product suggestions and provided a more emotionally satisfying experience.

4.2 Woebot – Emotionally Intelligent Mental Health Support Bot

Organization: Woebot Health

Industry: Healthcare / Digital Mental Health

Technology Used: NLP, Emotion Detection, Cognitive Behavioural Therapy (CBT) algorithms

Objective: To provide accessible, 24/7 emotional and mental health support using AI that understands and adapts to users' emotional states.

Implementation: Woebot conducts daily conversations with users, identifies their emotional tone (e.g., sadness, anxiety, joy), and uses CBT principles to guide them through self-help conversations.

Outcomes: Users showed significant reductions in depression and anxiety symptoms within 2 weeks. High engagement: 85% of users continued daily check-ins after the first week. Trust built through empathetic, emotionally aware interactions.

Insight: Emotion detection played a crucial role in tailoring therapeutic responses and improving mental health outcomes.

4.3 H&M's Kik Chatbot – Emotion-Driven Fashion Assistance

Company: H&M

Industry: Fashion Retail

Technology Used: Rule-based chatbot with sentiment pattern recognition

Objective: To create an interactive shopping experience targeting Gen Z customers via the Kik messaging platform.

Implementation: H&M's chatbot asked users about their fashion preferences and used their language sentiment (excitement, hesitation, etc.) to curate outfits. Emoji's and casual language were used to match the user's tone and emotional state.

Outcomes: Increase in session duration: Users spent over 10 minutes per interaction. 30% higher CTR (click-through rate) on recommended products compared to static ads. Built emotional rapport with younger audiences via informal, friendly dialogue.

Insight: Emotionally tuned conversations helped transform product browsing into an engaging, gamified experience.

4.4 Vodafone's TOBi – Sentiment-Aware Customer Service

Company: Vodafone

Industry: Telecommunications

Technology Used: NLP chatbot + sentiment analysis API (Microsoft Cognitive Services)

Objective: To handle common customer service queries while reducing churn caused by negative service experiences.

Implementation: TOBi, Vodafone's virtual assistant, was enhanced with sentiment analysis to detect customer frustration or dissatisfaction. If a user displayed escalating negativity, TOBi either adjusted its tone to become more empathetic or handed the conversation over to a live agent.

Outcomes: 60% resolution rate without human intervention. 25% reduction in negative reviews attributed to poor customer service. Greater customer satisfaction scores due to empathy-driven interactions.

Insight: Pen advantage: Real-time sentiment analysis stopped possible service escalations and made consumers' interactions with the company less robotic.

5. ETHICAL CONSIDERATIONS AND DATA PRIVACY IN EMOTION DETECTION AND SENTIMENT ANALYSIS FOR AI-POWERED CHATBOTS

Self learning and understanding emotions: For AI-powered chatbots and virtual assistants, emotions are critical in delivering customer service and they cover some important ethical concerns and data privacy. Sentiment analysis in combination with emotion detection and artificial intelligence opens up many opportunities regarding improving customer experiences but comes with questions of transparency, privacy, and accountability.

In this section, we will discuss the ethical issues and data privacy issues which are prevalent when deploying emotion detection and sentiment analysis in AI chatbots, before presenting a best practice guide on their implementation.

5.1 Ethical Issue in Emotion Detection and Sentiment Analysis

a. Emotional Manipulation

- Emotional manipulation is one of the most crucial issues when it comes to ethical aspects of emotion recognition. Happiness, anger, or fear makes them compelled to act in a certain manner that will realize the intended goals of a business while at the same time making them eager for more business transactions. For example, an anxiety chatbot may lead the buyer into purchasing an unrelated product or service which is highly improper of what a chatbot should offer in the first place.
- Example: For example, in a retail environment, chatbot may diagnose that the user is stressed and so offer him a product he never knew he needs for stress related reason.
- Ethical Issue: The above practices distort the consumer agency and the fundamental question of whether businesses are working in the best interest of the users or manipulating their moods to make profits.

Mitigation Strategy:

- In the same manner, it is crucial that the function of chatbots should be fully explained and that it should be properly advertised.
- They should put in place strict measures on when and how such data should be used for commercial purposes.
- Allow users to switch off or change the type of the emotional distortions used by the bot.

b. Bias in Sentiment and Emotion Detection

- For instance, the training datasets of the AI systems involved in the sentiment and emotion detection contain bias. In other cases, the datasets may not comprise a rich tapestry of languages, cultures, or emotional expression and therefore may fail to capture an emotional and respond inaccurately. For example, the bot may not understand sarcasm, or misunderstand the specific cultural regional emotions and may build the wrong emotional intelligence or write a reply that also may anger a customer.
- Example: Cultural differences might make the tone of a user's dialogue appear negative to a chatbot; it will give an undesirable or irrelevant answer.
- Ethical Issue: It is possible to disregard or disrespect specific individuals, communities, cultures, or nations, which makes a system less fair and inclusive.

Mitigation Strategy:

- Train AI models on **diverse, representative datasets** that include varied emotional expressions across cultures.
- Regularly audit AI models for **bias** and adjust the training process to minimize discriminatory outcomes.
- **Test bots** in different regions and languages to ensure inclusivity.

c. Privacy Invasion

- Emotion detection and sentiment analysis are privacy-sensitive data processing techniques as consumers of digital services, they call for users' data in terms of their conversational history, interactions history, biometric data that refers to the consumer tone of voice, facial expressions, etc. This is concerning around privacy as users cannot fully determine the amount of data collected, its usage or the risks associated with the process.
- Example: An emotional recognition chatbot may collect information about the state of mind of a user that will include signs of depression, anxiety, etc., but the user may not have agreed for such data collection explicitly.
- Ethical Issue: Personal emotional data is also the property of users and consumers and people should have open permissions and clear rules to give consent to the use, collection, and processing of their emotional data. Non-disclosure of this information is a betrayal of the relationship, they added it can create opportunities for misuse of data.

Mitigation Strategy:

- Implement **clear, concise privacy policies** explaining the types of data collected, how it is used, and the duration for which it is stored.
- **Obtain explicit consent** from users before collecting emotional or sentiment-related data.
- Provide **opt-out options** for users who do not want their emotional data analysed.

5.2 Data Privacy Issues in Emotionally Intelligent Chatbots

a. Collection of Sensitive Emotional Data

Emotionally intelligent chatbots gather personal information from users to assess their moods for various reasons, including talks that might indicate mental disorders, stress levels, or other personal troubles. Otherwise, such information can be abused by someone with malicious intention.

Example: A call centre chatbot in a telecom firm identifies that a particular customer is irate about his or her bill and will then perhaps extend a discount or a voucher. However, it tracks users' data-fingerprint too, including their private emotional reactions, without explicit permission.

Privacy Issue: Emotions of users also can also be carried as data; thus they also need to be handled with certain precautions to prevent them being exposed/misused or leaked.

Mitigation Strategy:

- Mask your data by removing all credibility of links to individuals to avoid merging emotionality with identification.
- Say, employ methods of data encryption and safe storage to prevent third party access of the information.
- Policies to help or support should be put in place to incorporate routine examinations of data privacy compliance rules continually.

b. User Consent and Data Ownership

Much of this involves whether, when, and how chatbots gather and interpret emotional data, who owns the data, and what will happen to it over the long term. This is particularly important because users remain oblivious of how much of their emotional data is captured and stored.

Example: A patient talk to the AI, powered bot in a mental health application and unbeknownst to them, their mood data is harvested for training or resold to advertisers.

Privacy Issue: The problem is derived when user's emotion related data is being processed for uses other than the service, without explicit prior disclosure or consent from the users, thus infringing on their privacy.

Mitigation Strategy:

- Offer some opt-in to a given degree regarding data usage, by explaining the extent of data usage to the users.
- Guarantee the user's rights to receive, change, or erase her/his emotional data.
- Limit retention where possible and only store enough data to support the length of the interaction the user has with the application.

c. Risk of Unauthorized Emotional Data Sharing

Another challenge with 'emotional' bots is that they are likely to interface with, and transmit, Third-Party-System data such as CRM solutions, without the user's awareness or permission, they are likely to transfer emotional data. This, in turn, could put this data-sharing at high risks of vulnerability to breaches or being exploited.

Example: An e-commerce chatbot could share user sentiment data with third-party advertising companies to delivery relevant adverts, which breaches user expectations.

Privacy Issue: Leaking of emotional data to third party constitutes a big risk because it can result to data loss and misuse.

Mitigation Strategy:

- Ensure that any third-party transaction involves data sharing at all is not done with the expected trust level, the trusting party should carry out the transaction with their eyes wide open, with limited expectations of the third party.
- Offer consent options such that the user will decide which of his data should be shared.
- Third-party vendors have to respect the policies of the individuals as well as the United States by responding to the privacy laws and security standards.

5.3 Best Practices for Ethical and Privacy-Compliant Emotion Detection Systems

1. Transparency and Disclosure: Make sure that a user is fully informed of which data are going to be collected and how these data are going to be used. Without expressing their consent, never collect sensitive information and make patients aware of your privacy policies.
2. Respect for User Autonomy: Let users sign a 'no feelings tracking' consent and let them decide how their emotions are being collected and process.
3. Bias Mitigation: We have to train the AI models with different data sets in terms of cultural, emotional, and demographic differences.
4. Data Minimization: A little data should be gathered as possible for a particular process, particularly with regards to data that has an emotional feature.

6. FUTURE TRENDS IN EMOTION DETECTION AND SENTIMENT ANALYSIS FOR AI-POWERED CHATBOTS AND VIRTUAL ASSISTANTS

AI powered chatbots and virtual assistants have put the future of emotion detection and sentiment analysis on a new frontier, which will transform the nature of how companies interact with customers. Thus, as we progress through the decades, better models to serve the consumers and greater business value are bound to emerge. In the following subtopic, we will delve deeper into the future development of this particular sector in terms of possible future trends in development of AI, as well as future prospects and tasks.

6.1 More Human-Like Emotional Intelligence

Another impressive future trend is recognized as the constant development of human-like emotional intelligence at a high level. Today's AI-based systems can recognize emotion to some degree, but this does not mean they know how to comprehend the emotions even though these are rather elementary compared with subsyntensive emotions like sarcasm, or simplesh joy, or the one that is experienced through cultural context.

Trend Explanation:

- First, deep learning models will improve and generalize not only on the primary emotion such as anger, happiness, and sadness but on other complicated emotions like guilt, pride, and awe (Wu et al., 2024).
- Such models will evolve to be able to recognize long-term behaviors from the user through things like the user's tone, facial expressions or the choice of words used by the users during interaction.

Implications:

- Enhanced personalization: The use of AI assistants will develop further in an area that is altogether more friendly that will simply respond to people emotionally.
- More authentic conversations: Virtual assistants will elaborate to be empathetic and attentive to the need to try mimicking human like earthly interaction.

6.2 Multimodal Emotion Recognition

From the various forms of data, texts, voices, and gestures, Facial recognition, and autonomic responses such as heart rate, skin conductivity, etc. will be used to detect emotions in the future.

Trend Explanation:

- Speaking of specific ways in which voice tone analysis will increase, AI systems need to study how emotions cause changes in pitch, tempo, and volume.

- Interactivity through the camera – To assist feelings of the users detected by feelings through facial recognition technologies, the chatbots' effectiveness will improve in various forms of communication including even the nonverbal.
- Bernstein Reinforcement learning can be achieved by having machines learn from the real-time expression data fed to them from wearable devices such as smartwatches or fitness trackers.

Implications:

- Deeper emotional insights: AI will be able to get more accurate and complete emotional context as it gathers data from various sources.
- Real-time emotional support: Virtual assistants could then make suggestions using technology with improved stress level, for example suggest a break or a breathing exercise.

6.3 Ethical AI and Privacy Regulations

Asian AI has the intelligence to promote ethical AI and data privacy in the future, but still has the potential to rise with the tide. There are increasing demands for the technologies underpinning AI to be comprehensible, equitable, and responsible especially when they process and analyze emotional data.

Trend Explanation:

- Thus, governments and other regulating authorities will enforce even higher requirements with regard to the utilization of the data on emotions and sentiment. Such measures can include improved consent standards, regulation on the identification of data and about the use and sharing of emotional data.
- Organizations will put in place policies to ensure that emotional detection systems have organizational ethical outlooks that will not be used in a way that will deceive consumers or intrude on their privacy.

Implications:

- Trust-building: Specifically, consumers will become ever more vocal about their desire to see more transparency in artificial intelligence interactions, and firms employing sound ethical frameworks will be better placed in this emerging market.

- Greater compliance: There will be GDPR-like regulation about the use of emotional data in applications and it will be necessary for companies to follow them to avoid misuse.

6.4 Real-Time Sentiment and Emotion Monitoring for Customer Insights

Decades in the future, businesses will pay adept tribute to sentiment and emotion tracking and use it as a way to comprehend consumer behaviour and satisfaction levels in order to make decisions.

Trend Explanation:

- **Sentiment analysis** will become more **real-time and continuous**, allowing businesses to track **customer emotions** across various touchpoints (social media, customer support, in-store, etc.).
- **Advanced analytics platforms** will synthesize sentiment data from across all customer interactions and provide actionable insights, enabling brands to **respond proactively** to customer emotions.

Implications:

- **Proactive customer service**: By analysing customer sentiment in real time, companies can identify and resolve issues before they escalate.
- **Refined product development**: Brands can fine-tune their products, services, and marketing strategies based on insights from customer emotional reactions.

6.5 AI in Mental Health and Emotional Well-Being

In the near future, AI chatbots would help users who need an emotional boost or any kind of psychological support. The potential for artificial intelligence is further expected to focus on providing mental health wells-being services going beyond simple conversational bots.

Trend Explanation:

- AI will be used to deliver personalized mental health interventions, such as mood tracking, stress management, and CBT (Cognitive Behavioural Therapy) through virtual assistants.

- AI assistants will offer emotional check-ins, provide guided mindfulness exercises, or even help users process trauma in a supportive, non-judgmental way.

Implications:

- Accessibility to mental health support: AI avatars will grant immanent and constant access to professional emotional support, especially to those locations which have little to no access to feature mental health assistance.
- Human-AI collaboration in therapy: AI could also alert therapists to possible client mood changes or track information during sessions about feelings making the processes more efficient.

6.6 Integration with Other Emerging Technologies

Emotion detection together with other advanced forming technologies will provide brand new classes of applications and market approaches. Among the key emerging technologies is the 5G connectivity, Augmented Reality, Virtual Reality as well as Block chain.

Trend Explanation:

- Real-time processing of emotional data from a variety of sensors and gadgets connected to 5G networks will make it easier to integrate the apparatus with other platforms in the future.
- **AR and VR** will use sentiment analysis and emotion detection to offer **immersive experiences**, allowing brands to engage customers in **emotionally personalized virtual worlds**.
- **Block chain** will ensure the **security** and **transparency** of emotional data, allowing users to have more control over their personal emotional information.

Implications:

- **Immersive customer experiences**: AR/VR combined with emotion detection will allow brands to create **highly engaging**, emotion-driven experiences in real-time.
- **Enhanced data security**: Block chain can offer **secure, transparent storage** of emotional data, reducing concerns over data misuse.

7. IMPLEMENTING EMOTION AI: A ROADMAP FOR BUSINESSES

Emotional intelligence is rapidly becoming a fundamental technology for improving both customer and client relations, business outcomes, and experiences. By analysing the human facial expressions, the AI smart systems the link between customers and firms can be optimized to include an emotional aspect. Nonetheless, for Emotion AI to work optimally, it has to be planned, integrated, and done ethically. In this section, we will be demonstrating how businesses can systematically adopt the Emotion AI to get the best out of this technology.

7.1 Define Objectives and Use Cases

To implement Emotion AI therefore, enterprises must be very clear on its goals and areas that may require it. This step is useful to identify if the business wants to focus on either customer service, sales, marketing strategy, or just to gain more information about the consumers.

Key Considerations:

- Customer Support: Emotion AI is an extension to chatbots or virtual assistants, applying emotion to the chatbot so it acts and reacts in a more human-like manner. It can determine the degree or level of frustration or satisfaction among customers and where to lead them to.
- Sales and Marketing: Emotion AI can aid in marketing optimization, customization of ads, and the usage of emotionally responding content in the marketing process.
- Product Feedback and Research: Today, organizations are capable of gathering more about the consumers' emotional state by analysing the reviews, surveys or any other interaction that is related to a particular product or service so as to reshape it in the best way possible.

7.2 Select the Right Technology and Tools

The next thing that will be done is to choose the most relevant Emotion AI technology and tools. Emotion AI includes a set of methods, which can be listed as sentiment analysis, facial recognition, speech analysis, physiological monitoring. Any of these tools can be used depending on the business need and the tools that are most suitable to them.

Key Technologies:

- **Natural Language Processing (NLP):** This technology enables chatbots and virtual assistants to understand and interpret customer emotions from text-based interactions (Aslan, 2024).
- **Speech Emotion Recognition (SER):** This is useful for analysing emotions through voice tone and speech patterns in phone calls or voice interactions.
- **Facial Expression Recognition (FER):** Ideal for industries or applications that involve video conferencing, kiosks, or customer-facing interactions requiring visual emotion analysis.
- **Biometric Sensors:** These sensors can monitor physiological responses (e.g., heart rate or skin conductivity) for more detailed emotional insights.

7.3 Data Collection and Preparation

Most of the form of Emotion AI equally require large amounts of data in its highest quality for it to provide proper information. To ensure that Emotion AI systems are effective, the right type of data must be collected and properly pre-processed. Yes, businesses must be careful how they gather data and always respect the rights of the individual, especially in relation to the use of personal data.

Key Considerations:

- Data Privacy: Compliance with data protection regulation e.g., General Data Protection Regulation (GDPR), the California Consumer Privacy Act (CCPA) However, when collecting data that is of an emotional or biometric nature about the user, the user's consent must first be sought.
- Data Quality: This paper shows that the quality of the data is directly proportional to the accuracy of the emotion detection. Ensure label data with no bias in as far as its representation is concerned.

7.4 Train and Fine-Tune Emotion AI Models

Now that Emotion AI models are ready, it is time to deploy them in the communication channels that engage with the customer. It could be a chatbot, virtual agents, customer service options, email services or even the self-service kiosks.

Key Touchpoints:

- AI There are several updates that need to be made in the chatbots and other virtual assistants: Emotion AI should be integrated to determine the mood of the client and provide the appropriate answers. It should be possible to note that the chatbot may provide users with empathy replies if the user looks frustrated or be enthusiastic if the user displays happiness.

- Customer Service Communication: through voice, text, or video, Customer Service Emotional Analysis can recognize changes in the customers' attitude and help the agents to be more adequate in their answers.
- Marketing and Ads: Emotion AI helps to look into customers' reactions regarding advertising content and perform the necessary changes to the ad campaigns according to the customers' emotional response.

7.5 Implement Emotion AI into Customer Touchpoints

Now that Emotion AI models are ready, it is time to deploy them in the communication channels that engage with the customer. It could be a chatbot, virtual agents, customer service options, email services or even the self-service kiosks.

Key Touchpoints:

- AI There are several updates that need to be made in the chatbots and other virtual assistants: Emotion AI should be integrated to determine the mood of the client and provide the appropriate answers. It should be possible to note that the chatbot may provide users with empathy replies if the user looks frustrated or be enthusiastic if the user displays happiness.
- Customer Service Communication: through voice, text, or video, Customer Service Emotional Analysis can recognize changes in the customers' attitude and help the agents to be more adequate in their answers.
- Marketing and Ads: Emotion AI helps to look into customers' reactions regarding advertising content and perform the necessary changes to the ad campaigns according to the customers' emotional response.

7.6 Continuously Monitor and Optimize

There are certain issues associated with Emotion AI and those are: Emotion AI is a complex system that has to be constantly monitored and updated to be effective and relevant to the goals of an organization. This step entails monitoring of the performance of the Emotion AI systems and alteration of the systems depending on feedback that is received instantly.

Key Actions:

- Performance Metrics: Evaluate how effective the model is towards identifying different emotions out of the RADAR categories by considering the false positives (identifying incorrect emotion) and false negatives (failing to identify a certain emotion).

- The remarks of users should be taken in order to make real the users' emotions and to make the interaction as smart as possible.
- Model Retraining: implement new data into the model over and over again to minimize bias over time and to adjust for any changes in the customer needs and trends.

7.7 Address Ethical and Privacy Concerns

There are certain moral and privacy issues which need to be considered before embarking on the full-scale deployment of Emotion AI. Some of the topic areas that companies need to consider include ethical reasons to make sure that the firm or company is operating under acceptable practices in relation to data privacy.

Key Ethical Considerations:

- Privacy: However, businesses should be clear with their customers on the occasions when their emotions are being analysed through the application of Emotion AI.
- Fairness Techniques: In order to eliminate biases in Emotion AI systems, it is necessary to use a variety of datasets in the models, as well as constantly check for fairness issues.
- This concerns the rights of users; they should have the option to either enable or disable the emotion detection features and have rights to data and rights to have their data erased.

7.8 Measure ROI and Business Impact

Last but not least, businesses should compare the cost/benefit ratio usually referred as return on investment (ROI) and evaluate possibility of applying Emotion AI. This involves determining the extent to which the technology has complied with the goals that were set in step one as well as if it has brought in the aspects of customer satisfaction, increase in sales, or workstation improvements.

Key Metrics to Track:

- Customer Satisfaction Scores (CSAT): Track the extent to which the use of Emotion AI will enhance the quality of customer service conversations and the resulting satisfaction.
- Engagement Metrics: Determine whether employing personal appeal to the target consumers' emotions influences more patronage or subscription.
- Maintenance: Track whether emotion AI applied for personalization yields and additionally strengthens customer and loyalty and retention in the end.

8. CONCLUSION

Currently, automating the ability of devices to identify emotions and sentiments in human language is a game changer in the way companies interact with their clientele. Through this, it will be possible for enterprises to provide a more natural mannered interaction which is empathetic as machines will go beyond understanding the bare meaning of the words used by the clients but also the underlying emotions.

In today's society, businesses have started to integrate artificial intelligence and its effects become significant when it comes to buyers. Emotion recognition teaches an application to tell the emotional status of a specific customer and assists in what the customer might need at that point in time by thereby enhancing the overall user experience. By using this tool, firms are able to transform ordinary customer interactions into experiences that develop high levels of emotional buy-in hence create emotional memories.

But for any organisation to manage Emotion AI effectively, it needs a clear and proper blueprint. Executive management has to set goals and establish qualitative methods to discover areas where emotionally intelligent could add the most value, for example, customer service, marketing, or sales, as well as product development. When it comes to using technology and tools for this kind of work, firstly, relevant technology must be chosen, then data acquisition and data pre-processing should be addressed while considering there are specific issues to address with regards to the ethical part of the data processing and analysis.

Second, there is a need to constantly review and improve Emotion AI systems since they are smart devices. For this reason, AI models have to fine-tuned, retrained and updated periodically to enable the former to give an accurate output of the latter. This would be accomplished through feedback from the customers and/or performance metrics and by doing so the system becomes smarter in the sense that it becomes more sensitive to the new trends exhibited by consumers.

Considering the potential of its further development, it is possible to stay that Emotion AI is very promising. Due to the nature of growth in progression of AI, the identification of different emotions will become even more refined in future as it moves to wider emotional spectrum and as biometric data and other types of multimodal analysis such as face, tone of voice, and physiological enter the scene. They will help the businesses to understand their customers better and start targeting the emotional aspects of these customers with a very high level of accuracy. However, the combination of Emotion AI with other technologies such as 5G, AR/VR, Block chain will open the new horizons of believable and safe emotions for interaction and sharing once occurred in the science fiction only.

Therefore, Emotion AI can become a powerful tool that will shed light on the consumer's emotions and significantly change the approach businesses use to appeal to their clients. Transcending the fundamental seller-buyer relationships of business transactions and embracing emotional value creates an advantage that has the power to place a business at a higher standing against stiff competition. But nonetheless, there is general longevity to be had where one has to approach this potentially revolutionary technology with empathy, ethical thought, and innovation. If properly employed, incrementally improved, and trusted by the consumer, Emotion AI can revolutionize business adoption and widen the space that it covers to produce better, more profound connotations or impacts for users.

REFERENCES

Aslan, Z. "Emotion Detection via BERT-Based Deep Learning Approaches in Natural Language Processing," International Journal of Energy and Engineering Sciences, vol. 9, no. 2, pp. 103–114, Dec. 2024. [Online]. Available: https://dergipark.org.tr/en/pub/ijees/issue/85059/1524075.DergiPark

Bechara, A., & Damasio, A. R. (2005). The somatic marker hypothesis: A neural theory of economic decision. *Games and Economic Behavior*, *52*(2), 336–372. DOI: 10.1016/j.geb.2004.06.010

Bello, A., Ng, S.-C., & Leung, M.-F. (2023, January). A BERT Framework to Sentiment Analysis of Tweets. *Sensors (Basel)*, *23*(1), 506. DOI: 10.3390/s23010506 PMID: 36617101

Calefato, F., Lanubile, F., & Novielli, N. (2019). Emotions and personality traits in developer–client interactions for trust prediction. *Empirical Software Engineering*, *24*(4), 2243–2271. DOI: 10.1007/s10664-018-9671-5

Calefato, F., Lanubile, F., & Novielli, N. (2020). Sentiment analysis for software engineering: How far can we go? *IEEE Software*, *38*(1), 30–37. DOI: 10.1109/MS.2020.2983737

Chatterjee, S., Rana, N. P., Tamilmani, K., & Sharma, A. (2022). Understanding the role of AI-enabled emotion detection in customer service: A review and research agenda. *Journal of Business Research*, *142*, 1020–1032. DOI: 10.1016/j.jbusres.2021.12.055

Chung, M., Ko, E., Joung, H., & Kim, S. J. (2020). Chatbot e-service and customer satisfaction regarding luxury brands. *Journal of Business Research*, *117*, 587–595. DOI: 10.1016/j.jbusres.2018.10.004

Cialdini, R. B. (2009). *Influence: Science and practice* (5th ed.). Pearson Education.

Cowie, R., Douglas-Cowie, E., Tsapatsoulis, N., Votsis, G., Kollias, S., Fellenz, W., & Taylor, J. G. (2001). Emotion recognition in human-computer interaction. *IEEE Signal Processing Magazine*, *18*(1), 32–80. DOI: 10.1109/79.911197

Crawford, K., & Calo, R. (2016). There is a blind spot in AI research. *Nature*, *538*(7625), 311–313. DOI: 10.1038/538311a PMID: 27762391

Damasio, A. R. (1994). *Descartes' error: Emotion, reason and the human brain*. Avon Books.

Deloitte. (2021). *Chatbots and virtual assistants: Driving the digital transformation.* Deloitte Insights. https://www2.deloitte.com/

Deng, J., & Liu, Y. (2025, February). Research on Sentiment Analysis of Online Public Opinion Based on RoBERTa–BiLSTM–Attention Model. *Applied Sciences (Basel, Switzerland)*, *15*(4), 2148. DOI: 10.3390/app15042148

Devlin, J., Chang, M. W., Lee, K., & Toutanova, K. (2019). *BERT: Pre-training of deep bidirectional transformers for language understanding*. In *Proceedings of NAACL-HLT* (pp. 4171–4186). DOI: 10.48550/arXiv.1810.04805

Festinger, L. (1957). *A theory of cognitive dissonance*. Stanford University Press. DOI: 10.1515/9781503620766

García-Hernández, R. A., Luna-García, H., Celaya-Padilla, J. M., García-Hernández, A., Reveles-Gómez, L. C., Flores-Chaires, L. A., Delgado-Contreras, J. R., Rondon, D., & Villalba-Condori, K. O. (2024, August). A Systematic Literature Review of Modalities, Trends, and Limitations in Emotion Recognition, Affective Computing, and Sentiment Analysis. *Applied Sciences (Basel, Switzerland)*, *14*(16), 7165. DOI: 10.3390/app14167165

Gentsch, P. (2019). *AI in marketing, sales and service: How marketers without a data science degree can use AI, big data and bots*. Palgrave Macmillan. DOI: 10.1007/978-3-319-89957-2

Gnewuch, U., Morana, S., & Maedche, A. (2017). Towards designing cooperative and social conversational agents for customer service. *Proceedings of the International Conference on Information Systems (ICIS).*

Hoy, M. B. (2018). Alexa, Siri, Cortana, and more: An introduction to voice assistants. *Medical Reference Services Quarterly*, *37*(1), 81–88. DOI: 10.1080/02763869.2018.1404391 PMID: 29327988

Huang, M. H., & Rust, R. T. (2021). Artificial intelligence in service. *Journal of Service Research*, *24*(1), 3–20. DOI: 10.1177/1094670520902266

Kahneman, D. (2011). *Thinking, fast and slow*. Farrar, Straus and Giroux.

Kapoor, H., Dwivedi, Y. K., Piercy, N. F., & Reynolds, N. (2020). AI-based emotional intelligence: A conceptual framework. *Technological Forecasting and Social Change*, *158*, 120118. DOI: 10.1016/j.techfore.2020.120118

Kumar, A., Dixit, A., Javalgi, R. G., Dass, M., & Kamboj, S. (2021). Digital transformation of sustainability: A review and research agenda. *Technological Forecasting and Social Change*, *166*, 120602. DOI: 10.1016/j.techfore.2021.120602

Liu, B. (2015). *Sentiment analysis: Mining opinions, sentiments, and emotions.* Cambridge University Press. DOI: 10.1017/CBO9781139084789

Ma, F., ... "Generative Technology for Human Emotion Recognition: A Scope Review," *arXiv preprint*, arXiv:2407.03640, Jul. 2024. [Online]. Available: https://arxiv.org/abs/2407.03640.arXiv DOI: 10.2139/ssrn.4889990

Maslow, A. H. (1943). A theory of human motivation. *Psychological Review*, *50*(4), 370–396. DOI: 10.1037/h0054346

McDuff, D., El Kaliouby, R., & Picard, R. (2019). Affective computing and sentiment analysis. In *The Oxford Handbook of Affective Computing* (pp. 240–254). Oxford University Press.

Plutchik, R. (2001). The nature of emotions. *American Scientist*, *89*(4), 344–350. https://www.jstor.org/stable/27857503. DOI: 10.1511/2001.28.344

Poria, S., Cambria, E., Bajpai, R., & Hussain, A. (2017). A review of affective computing: From unimodal analysis to multimodal fusion. *Information Fusion*, *37*, 98–125. DOI: 10.1016/j.inffus.2017.02.003

R, S., Mujahid, M., Rustam, F., Shafique, R., Chunduri, V., Villar, M. G., Ballester, J. B., Diez, I. T., & Ashraf, I.S. R et al. (2023, September). Analyzing Sentiments Regarding ChatGPT Using Novel BERT: A Machine Learning Approach. *Information (Basel)*, *14*(9), 474. DOI: 10.3390/info14090474

Saif, W. Q. A., Alshammari, M. K., Mohammed, B. A., & Sallam, A. A. (2024, October). Enhancing Emotion Detection in Textual Data: A Comparative Analysis of Machine Learning Models and Feature Extraction Techniques. *Engineering, Technology & Applied Science Research*, *14*(5), 16471–16477. . DOI: 10.48084/etasr.7806

Schwartz, S. H. (1992). Universals in the content and structure of values: Theoretical advances and empirical tests. *Advances in Experimental Social Psychology*, *25*, 1–65. DOI: 10.1016/S0065-2601(08)60281-6

Solomon, M. R. (2020). *Consumer behavior: Buying, having, and being* (13th ed.). Pearson Education.

Talaat, A. S. (2023, June). Sentiment Analysis Classification System Using Hybrid BERT Models. *Journal of Big Data*, *10*(110), 110. Advance online publication. DOI: 10.1186/s40537-023-00781-w

Wu, Y., ... "Research on the Application of Deep Learning-Based BERT Model in Sentiment Analysis," *arXiv preprint*, arXiv:2403.08217, Mar. 2024. [Online]. Available: https://arxiv.org/abs/2403.08217.arXiv

Xue, H., ... "E-chat: Emotion-Sensitive Spoken Dialogue System with Large Language Models," arXiv preprint, arXiv:2401.00475, Dec. 2023. [Online]. Available: https://arxiv.org/abs/2401.00475

Zhang, S., Zhang, S., Huang, T., Gao, W., & Qiao, Y. (2022). Emotion recognition in conversation: Research challenges, datasets, and recent advances. *IEEE Transactions on Affective Computing*. Advance online publication. DOI: 10.1109/TAFFC.2022.3168459

Chapter 7
AI-Driven Marketing Automation and Hyper-Personalization Strategies for Enhanced Consumer Engagement

Richa Kumari
https://orcid.org/0009-0008-2957-2885
Christ University, Bengaluru, India

Kartikeya Singh
https://orcid.org/0000-0002-3060-6359
Christ University, Bengaluru, India

ABSTRACT

The integration of artificial intelligence (AI) into marketing has revolutionized how businesses engage with consumers, allowing for hyper-personalized interactions and marketing automation. This paper explores the role of AI in driving consumer engagement through targeted strategies that leverage data analytics, machine learning, and predictive modelling. By enabling real-time personalization, AI tools optimize customer experiences, increase engagement, and improve conversion rates. The paper also addresses the challenges associated with data privacy and ethical considerations in AI-driven marketing. The findings suggest that AI-driven marketing can significantly enhance consumer loyalty and business performance when used responsibly and strategically.

DOI: 10.4018/979-8-3373-3775-3.ch007

1. INTRODUCTION TO AI IN MARKETING

Artificial intelligence (AI) has played a monumental role in the evolution of technology and has significantly transformed the way we conduct our business operations. The advent of AI in marketing has become increasingly relevant due to the growing challenges of effectively reaching consumers amid media fragmentation and the rapid pace of the ever-changing business landscape. The primary objective of marketing remains steadfast: to reach the target clientele and drive sales upward. Therefore, AI should be viewed as the first line of defense and an essential support system in the decision-making process to enhance and optimize marketing strategies (Allioui and Mourdi2023; Wamba-Taguimdje et al.2020). As Movahed, Movahed, and Nozari (2024) articulate, *Marketing 6.0* is defined by the seamless integration of advanced technologies such as artificial intelligence (AI), the Internet of Things (IoT), and big data analytics, empowering businesses to design marketing strategies that are increasingly dynamic, adaptive, and customer centric. This evolution marks a significant shift from traditional marketing paradigms by placing data intelligence and real-time responsiveness at the core of strategic decision-making.

The capabilities of AI have evolved to a point where it can intelligently identify and engage with potential clients in a manner that mirrors human interaction. This advancement allows for a more personalized approach to marketing, as businesses can now communicate with consumers more effectively. Furthermore, AI can automate various tasks, leading to far more efficient processes compared to human efforts. This not only reduces labor costs but also minimizes the likelihood of human errors, which can be detrimental to a business's reputation and bottom line (Krishnan et al.2022; Haleem et al.2022). AI-driven marketing strategies have been shown to increase consumer engagement by delivering hyper-personalized content. This is made possible through a comprehensive understanding of behavioral patterns and propensity-to-buy scores that are derived from analyzing vast datasets. Consequently, AI will play an increasingly pivotal role in shaping and transforming the marketing strategies of any business, particularly within the consumer industry sector where competition is fierce and consumer expectations are high. (Kamal and Himel2023) The unique facet of the AI marketing segment lies in its design; it is specifically built to be focused and process-driven, aimed at enhancing marketing scenarios. This includes the sophisticated analysis of consumer profiles to segment and target audiences effectively. Recognizing the importance of continued evolution and research, there is a pressing need to study AI directly and conduct extensive research on its implications for marketers. This exploration extends to marketing automation, particularly through a social sciences perspective that may seamlessly incorporate principles from computer science, thereby fostering a multidisciplinary approach. This will enable marketers to harness the full potential of AI and adapt to the dynamic landscape of consumer behavior and digital marketing strategies (Davenport et al.2020).

1.1. Definition and Scope of AI in Marketing

Artificial intelligence (AI) has always been a far-fetched, extremely intelligent notion that offers the best possible outcomes in terms of any decision that needs to be made. It encompasses millions of methodologies that can be implemented using a diversified approach. In marketing, AI addresses a major part of the digital world and spans from data analytics to predictions and recommender systems. Machine learning and data mining methods are an integral part of AI and are related to data mining techniques used in the process of discovering knowledge from databases. The concept of AI in marketing covers many dimensions of contemporary businesses, encompassing various marketing aspects. A major part of AI in marketing is the process of using intelligent algorithms for the business, such as predictive modeling, machine learning techniques, deep learning, clustering, regression, decision trees, survival analysis, reinforcement learning, forecasting, or graph learning, among other things. (Haleem et al.2022)

The scope of AI in marketing is vast. AI applications explore the data and produce behaviors that will help to gain a deeper intuition about the customer and eventually be advantageous to the retailers. Moreover, AI applications help in making decisions and developing systems that mimic human behavior. AI marketing has been subjected to significant evolution and has grown extensively over the years. The so-called dearth of data and statistics in the late 1990s and early 2000s has witnessed a sudden increase in the user base across applications with the advent of smartphones, cloud computing, and parallel processing that performs a substantial amount of analysis on data. Organizations are becoming more accustomed to collecting vast amounts of data on their user behavior and activity and even accessing interconnected databases. Many large companies, however, are still trying to connect and leverage their data through several regions and platforms, such as CRM, customer services, and advertising, as part of their marketing strategy to create a consolidated view of their consumer base. Artificial intelligence specializes in automating decision-making. AI technology is frequently used to augment current methodologies through the implementation of an AI module that can help improve the strategies already in place. AI is mainly used in marketing to create a consolidated view for: identifying customer segments, exploring consumer behavior, personalizing user experience, automating decision-making, identifying potential channels, and identifying the right marketing strategies (Campbell et al.2020; Cao2021).

Simulating different strategies, overall, it can be concluded that the majority of businesses will adopt some form of AI technology to better sequence their marketing strategies. The current situation has seen organizations trying to include artificial intelligence in their current systems used for marketing and decision-making processes. Manual activities have seen a decrease in demand, especially in exploratory data analysis and consumer behavior research models, whereas there has been an increased focus on the considerations and models for personalized dealings with the customer. The current situation enables AI to contribute significantly to the personal experience of the consumer and becomes the first line of contact: representatives of the customer in an emotional, business, credit, and governance-building dialogue and trust. Marketing automation and analytics AIs assist data-driven (Davenport et al.2020).

1.2. Benefits and Challenges of AI in Marketing

In the area of marketing, AI offers several advantages that can raise higher expectations from companies, including more efficient media buying, ad targeting, and automation of the creation process. It offers impressive before, during, and after-campaign data that can help create actionable results while keeping costs low. AI tools help marketers automate a lot of the more repetitive work involved in managing media by trying to draw helpful and applicable insights from many different data sets. With AI, it is now more effective for retailers and companies to send personalized offers to consumers depending on their shopping, browsing, and tweeting behavior. A smarter, more customer-centric approach, AI marketing can help businesses in various ways, including optimizing channel optimization, programmatic display media buying, creative optimization, and media buying. Similarly, AI provides marketers with a unique capability – the capacity to fully comprehend their customer journeys on a separate, private, personal basis. By doing so, AI creates opportunities to expose and optimize a customer quest that might have been impossible before. Marketing sits at the forefront of this essential business process outside a company's particular department views. With a hint of concerns around data management, privacy, and companies' roles, marketing departments have an obligation to address and answer several ethical activities related to these AI capabilities. When used correctly, AI can bring great excitement and productivity to marketing, but it can also raise questions. The concern for sensitivity and privacy, specifically targeted advertising, revelation of data practices, and potentially unethical data monetization, could interfere with wider adoption of AI in marketing. Marketers would have to find a way to effectively address these challenges so that all parties, including the brand, have the necessary assurance in the process. (Mandapuram et al.2020; Stone et al.2020)

2. MARKETING AUTOMATION TECHNOLOGIES

Part of any marketing strategy is utilizing a variety of tools to help streamline the process. But what exactly is "marketing automation"? Simply put, marketing automation is about using software and web-based services to execute, manage, and automate marketing tasks and processes. A centralized dashboard allows automation tools to provide users with the ability to conduct various functions and see metrics across a plethora of different integrated platforms. Email marketing, social media posts and management, customer relationship management, and app integrations are all typical tasks to which marketing automation tools are tailored. Leading tools contain features including analytics, customer segmentation, and performance metrics to help users fine-tune and optimize their marketing strategies. By leveraging artificial intelligence, or AI technologies, marketing automation has the capacity to turn a generic marketing strategy into a hyper-personalized and engaging series of advertisements or product recommendations. Truly, marketing automation tools can offer an e-tailer the ability to see, understand, and act on the shopper's moment-in-time interests, needs, and actions, all of which is bound to drive sales. Where many people are often mistaken in thinking marketing automation supplants inbound marketing—the cautious use of advertising, contact, and acquisition with likely or ideally receptive prospective shoppers—is under the misimpression that marketing automation completely automates prospect acquisition and interaction. (Kumari, 2024) A big part of the disconnect here is semantics. In the first paragraph, if "prospect acquisition and interaction" is replaced with "advertising and marketing", it all begins to make sense except for that last line. Our initial position in the AI automation marketing system is to attract only receptive prospects in the first place; thus, marketing automation is a continuation of the inbound marketing strategy and the "inbound triangle". Simply, using AI-driven automation within the framework of the inbound triangle allows an e-tailer or any business to continue to add more new prospects into the mix from a greater variety of sources and have a greater variety of potential approved automated actions available in real-time. The first portion of marketing automation begins with acquisition and what happens "east" of the "inbound triangle" to everything "west" of it; automation west of the inbound funnel primarily seeks to close prospects or help return recent customers back into the 'loop' for a follow-up visit (Bossuwé, 2023; Podobed, 2024).

2.1. Types of Marketing Automation Tools

In today's world, marketing automation has become an imperative part of business operations for organizations that look to save manual working hours and scale. Choosing the best marketing automation service that fits the brand's budget, and purpose is where the crux comes from. Marketing automation tools can be broadly categorized into different kinds based on their functionality and application. These could be email marketing, social media, lead conversion, SEO, CRMs, personalized marketing, customer retention, and acquisition, among others. Average team productivity went up by 80%, along with other trends pointing to more money being saved with marketing automation tools (Marion and Fixson, 2021). Email marketing automation: Several tools are available if a business is looking to send customized and automated emails at every lead engagement level. There are instances of marketing automation software that help in nurturing clients. They also conduct wash-off to identify fake email IDs, which enhance data clean-up in the long term. Doing a sync with hundreds of email tools for e-commerce is also becoming possible. Tools help manage several customer touchpoints like Facebook, LinkedIn, and Instagram on social media. Store owners could save customer lists in their personal accounts and use these free marketing features. It offers the "optimal time" function, which lets clients decide specific times to post. It provides brilliant follower insights, template schedules, and manages content better (Kedi et al.2024; Potla & Pottla, 2024).

2.2. Key Features and Functionality

An effective marketing automation tool includes a user-friendly interface, analytics and reporting capabilities, and enterprise provider support for greater efficiency. With these essentials in mind, many free or open-source tools provide users intelligence on how customers are interacting with content, which will inform campaign planning. A/B testing, which evaluates different forms of content delivery, marketing channels, or strategies to more effectively target consumers, is also used across platforms. Email automation sends tracked interactions between customers and brands to user dashboards and includes automated response feedback and statistics. When integrated with a CRM, a map identifying each customer's journey may be created across consumer decision processes. Lastly, scoring, multi-channel campaigns, and personalization tools help identify potential leads and convert them to customers with automated feedback maneuvers based on user score, customer persona, and user intent acknowledgment. Summing up, the conversion rates shows how effective all the strategies outlined have been (Medina-Ortiz et al., 2020; Kedi et al.2024). AIs are making these standard customer contact tools more accessible. A significant percentage of state-of-the-art marketers use AI-based applications to have better consumer interactions. The application of predictive analytics as a part of marketing automation has a potential chance of increasing sales and a chance of winning by at least across all new clients. Data is not just being used in campaigns; it is also being used by sales to determine quality and internal relation assistance. A notable percentage of companies are already using AI-based devices, although the adoption rate is still high. The area should be continually evolving in response to changing technologies, and brands and marketers should be aware of modifications and new options in marketing technologies (Zhang & Lu, 2021).

3. HYPER-PERSONALIZATION IN MARKETING

Personalization in marketing has undergone a series of changes, with companies initially using customers' names in emails and then simply adding their names to web pages as a step up in the personalization game. It has now evolved into hyper-personalization, tailoring every ad, post, email, and all other marketing media to a degree at which they are not even the same between two individuals. Hyper-personalization allows for highly focused hyper-targeting that improves engagement and conversion rates. Bozkurt, Uğursoy, and Meral (2025) underscore that "the use of personalized messages and designs in marketing communications has a significant impact on consumer experiences, especially as technology enables hyper-personalization at scale." This insight highlights the critical role of tailored content in enhancing engagement and fostering meaningful consumer-brand relationships in the era of AI-driven marketing. Through data-driven insights and target segmentation, marketers tweak everything about their marketing communications to appeal more to individuals and groups, considered part of bleeding-edge marketing strategies. Hyper-personalization is heavily data-driven and includes every data point about a person or element of their daily life that marketers can think of and use to tailor something to. This means demographics, behavior, preferences, purchases, devices, location, weather, politics, health conditions, interests, and much more (Rane et al., 2023). Singh and Kaunert (2024) further argue that "the future of digital marketing lies in delivering hyper-personalized customer experiences through AI-based predictive models, which dynamically adapt to individual customer journeys in real time." This perspective reinforces the transformative potential of artificial intelligence in enabling marketers to anticipate needs and personalize interactions at every stage of the customer lifecycle. To fully mitigate these issues, hyper-personalization is often sincere, time-sensitive, interactive, and generally impacts a user's ability to influence their interactions with a brand or company greatly. It also ensures that marketers treat each user with the respect they deserve. Marketers focus on individualizing human-like communication, not just for results, but to build loyalty and trust. Combined with AI, hyper-personalization can offer the most user-centric marketing strategy ever created. Hyper-personalization can rely on customer satisfaction drives to refine and improve campaigns and produce better data to analyze. As models become more eagerly adopted, AI, machine learning, and this enthusiasm help bring hyper-personalization closer to center stage. This results in competitive advantages for any business that can fully implement and maintain the strategy as customer loyalty begins to play a greater role in customer retention and enhancement (Kamal and Himel2023).

3.1. Understanding Hyper-Personalization

The term "hyper-personalization" is often confused with "personalization"; however, the underlying strategies for both are quite different. In a hyper-personalization marketing strategy, AI-powered systems are used to offer a one-to-one buying and customer experience based on a consumer's behavior, preferences, and market trends. Hyper-personalization approaches use data and customer insights to offer a tailored experience in real-time or during a user's immediate visit. For example, you might have experienced the likes of certain platforms, where products, content, and music are hyper-personalized based on historical data, purchase behavior, browsing history, time of visit, location, and other micro-level details. (Gao & Liu, 2023) Customer data can be gathered from several touchpoints like e-commerce, social and digital platforms, employee interactions, customer call center records, feedback, chatbot conversations, and other traditional and online customer engagements. These touchpoints are utilized to collect individual-level consumer information like location, buying behavior, personal interests, browsing history, clicks and opens, propensities, social behavior, and other personalized attributes. By combining the data points, a marketer can use these data signals to offer real-time, personalized communication, resulting in a higher conversion ratio for a relevant product. Some of the key marketing strategies to implement hyper-personalization could be micro-segmentation based on purchase behavior, lifestyle, preferences, geography, and considering lifecycle stage (Potwora et al.2023; Wagner et al., 2020).

The usage of this type of marketing strategy-driven content can drastically increase conversion rates by targeting customer behavior. Quite a few global marketers have taken this strategy to the next level, including several major companies. One platform began personalizing recommendations by sending emails containing personalized thumbnails and subject lines, resulting in a significant return over a generic list. While implementing hyper-personalized email campaigns and using AI, another company saw a notable increase in customer engagement. Also, a music service replaced their "for you" in the app with a "made for you" label after its signature playlist was renamed, which changed the listening behavior at scale and grew subscriptions. (Tadimarri et al. ; Rane et al., 2023)

3.2. Benefits and Challenges of Hyper-Personalization

Many benefits are reported in research by those who follow and adopt a hyper-personalization strategy. It has concluded from various studies that these communication tactics will optimize the customer experience. Most importantly, the research discovered that hyper-personalized email campaigns could reach close to 66% of consumers and achieve 88% opening rates. The study also showed that in the five campaigns considered, new sign-ups grew between 14% and 75%. Besides recalling many successful examples of large enterprises that have adopted a hyper-personalization strategy, the downstream benefits lie in increased open rate, higher conversion rate, higher average order value, higher engagement rate, higher audience size, higher segmentation, and lower unsubscribes. Furthermore, a survey of marketing professionals across various regions found that increases in customer engagement rate averaged between 3.6% and 26% when a fully deployed hyper-personalization strategy is adopted in a business. (Jain et al., 2021)

Explaining consumer decisions and behavior is complex today, as there are many variables affecting them. Yet research results indicate that consumers review a personalized piece of content at a rate higher than the non-personalized version. Some of the main reasons include openness to consider consumption, a favorable attitude, changing future consumption behavior, and increasing brand loyalty. Sales performance of personalized products can clearly be positively influenced by engaging hyper-personalization. Nonetheless, it is also important to present some evidence-based cons as well. Besides raising the question of how personal vital competitive product information can be, there are also issues about various consumer perception disappointments and whose expectations can vary. Failings are often related to significant resources, mostly time and finances, being needed to acquire, manage, and activate this customer data. The integration of AI bolstering in the form of ML and predictive techniques can further complicate it in some instances. Many thought leadership survey respondents agreed that AI technology and data overwhelm and that it puts pressure on data teams to keep data and media operations compliant with ever-changing privacy regulations and ethical standards. Standards may vary, yet if you don't operate in accordance with these rules and don't deviate into unethical practices, your consumer audience may question your trustworthiness or, worse, blacklist your brand, organization, or company. Data privacy policies should be developed based on transparency and honest intent. Opt-in and opt-out clauses should be supported and practiced further to promote ongoing consumer trust but extended on a global level. Data scrubbing is helpful in keeping CRM and databases ethically compliant and should be adopted (Huang et al.2020; De et al.2022).

4. AI-DRIVEN HYPER-PERSONALIZATION

The development of artificial intelligence leading to new customer insights and advancements in personalization strategies allows for effective marketing automation tailored to the needs and preferences of an individual customer. This part consists of explanations for AI utilization in the process of gathering, analyzing, and working with data to facilitate hyper-personalization efforts. It discusses the combination of AI with the concept of hyper-personalization to accommodate personalized campaigns tailored for the needs, assimilation levels, or main subjects discussed throughout the paper. Also, this part explains the necessity of real-time analytics for effective hyper-personalization and automation, automated decisions in hyper-personalization marketing, and the strategies aimed at consumer behavior manipulation. Additionally, it mentions the ethical and privacy-related concerns outlining the problem scope (Umamaheswari, 2024; Gao & Liu, 2023).

Data science and big data analytics have entered the marketing world and have the potential to extract valuable consumer insights for marketing strategies. The development of AI-driven solutions accelerated the personalization capabilities of marketers. AI identifies patterns in purchase history, browsing habits, and on-site interactions and automatically suggests personalized marketing announcements. By implementing hyper-personalized communication, the customer is more likely to adapt a buying decision as the announcements are curated especially for the customer. AI aids in processing data more effectively and drawing faster insights. Thus, all customer interactions with the platform occur with the guidance of AI throughout acquisition, support, or delivery stages. AI selects the appropriate announcement in real-time while the consumer browses the website. A hyper-personalized communication strategy is a segment of one marketing automation, which is a technology that allows companies to streamline, automate, and measure marketing tasks and workflows in a digital environment. The automation assists with segmenting visitors and leads in order to send appropriate messaging to the right audience and to automatically send trigger responses at times when consumers are more active. With automation, the organization is capable of maintaining organized content and aligning marketing across all mediums (Potla & Pottla, 2024; Gao & Liu, 2023).

4.1. Integration of AI and Hyper-Personalization

Although hyper-personalization and the use of AI for targeting and segmentation have been explored separately, there is only limited understanding of how these complement and enhance each other in practice. AI, at a more basic level, can undertake segmentation and predictive analysis en masse. Techniques such as natural language processing, along with increasing data correlates, allow it to serve ads or recommendations to personas that are personal to them. By understanding previous behavior, backed up by refined data modeling on a larger scale than a human could manage, AI helps brands to automate and optimize personal attention at scale. In doing so, we see a more sophisticated line of progression from personalization that applies AI insights to those whole segments for individual people. Of course, the core concepts of data and technology driving this are not new. Successful, operational, and effective hyper-personalization requires data management and integration; it also involves interpreting results as human beings, communicating effectively within the limitations of the tech, and always operating within privacy and responsible marketing constraints. Understanding consumer behavior and catering to them with precision is lucrative. In fact, the top performers are said to be more productive and have a cost-to-sales ratio lower. With the spotlight on AI at present, brands and retailers are profitably merging AI insights with hyper-personalized alignment strategies. The present pandemic scenario has also had a significant positive impact on the same. The brands that have applied these integrated techniques have reaped the benefits in cloud computing, the e-commerce industry, the online ticketing industry, and even the personalized health plan. However, it is important for marketers to underpin their strategies with relevant data analytics, as hyper-personalization can backfire and be a major put-off if not done right. It is important to understand the protection of customer privacy in such direct interactions and cater to it. With AI-empowered recommendation engines already in place, brands are taking the leap to shift marketing resources to precise digital marketing with programmatic advertising to become even more efficient and effective at communicating their serendipitous moments. Creating alignment is not about deploying more ad tech. It's about developing a coherent, disciplined, and virtuous cycle between data, AI, and direct alignment marketing to create set-and-forget campaigns that really get noticed. It's necessary to flag potential risks. Leaders need to also guard against potential downfalls as they pursue highly targeted marketing. Re-targeting that is specific to an audience's actions can be detrimental if overused and become a turnoff. Similarly, by solely using algorithms, there is a risk that creative content becomes irrelevant or that certain important characteristics are missed. Varied stakeholders must work collaboratively to guarantee that marketing remains appropriate and effective, employing a broad suite of technologies. All marketing should be evaluated and, if necessary, modulated based on actual consumer responses, and they should remain open to modifications as people's preferences change according to many factors, including demographic adjustments, environmental changes, individual experiences, and the generation of new content and ideas (Haleem et al.2022; Gkikas and Theodoridis2022).

5. DATA COLLECTION AND ANALYSIS FOR PERSONALIZATION

Personalization or hyper-personalization is a key component of marketing automation. Providing a more individualized touch in communication can be actionable if data is available and can be used effectively. That's an area where data collection comes into the picture. Marketers today have access to a horde of data sources that provide useful insights into individual customer needs and interests. These could be customer feedback systems such as surveys, customer service queries, or even sales transactions and purchase history. Furthermore, it could also be data derived from customer engagements on a company's app, website, or social media pages. All of this data about an individual customer must, however, be managed properly to ensure that it's clean for use. The effectiveness of promotional content or any marketing strategies rests on the quality of the collected data. Customer data symbols and tokens should be accurately labeled to ensure that the collected data is unique, relevant, and actionable for individual profiling and segmentation (Singh & Kaunert, 2024; Rane et al., 2023).

Data analytics comes into this space to convert raw data into meaningful customer insights. This is where the marketer can employ desktop data analytical tools that help in making meaning out of customer transaction patterns and clustering consumer segments for subsequent targeting. Digital data analytics has come a long way from traditional mode-based analysis systems to modern data-based business intelligence systems such as descriptive, predictive, and prescriptive. Predictive analytics is the most user-friendly technique to extract meaningful insights from the data, thus helping organizations to forecast, regress, analyze, and merge data with structured, unstructured, and semi-structured databases. By employing machine learning algorithms, the growth of women's online groups creates a new buying opportunity for related consumer goods for e-commerce outlets. This can then be used to plan additional marketing strategies for these groups. However, generally, businesses face several challenges, some of which include targeting the so-called 'privacy paradoxes,' which are of concern to the customers. It refers to a situation where consumers talk about the threats to their privacy from businesses but soon provide the needed personal information. Therefore, customers today are more concerned, especially in light of data protection laws, which are stringent, and compliance with these laws is a new challenge faced by most e-commerce businesses nowadays (Aljumah et al.2021; Liu et al.2020).

5.1. Importance of Data in Personalization

Personalization in marketing is thriving because it has access to data, digital channels, and the number of connected devices that are making the customer journey increasingly digital. It's all about relevant content and aware solutions that are made possible by accurate and comprehensive consumer data. This, in turn, underlines the importance of data accuracy and relevancy in personalization. All personalization initiatives are data-driven, aiming at a 360-degree understanding of the consumers from multiple means. The broader your data set, the more holistic the consumer profile that you can create. Different types of consumer data that are used for a good personalization strategy could range from demographic data like name, age, gender; behavioral data like spending behavior, loyalty card purchase history; customer life events; psychographic data and so on. Various advanced data analytics tools and processes are able to deduce insightful behavioral correlations and patterns from a range of datasets (Palle2021).

The volume, velocity, and complexity of data become the competitive advantage that continuously fine-tunes and reassesses these consumer data-informed strategies in real time. Since all the consumer data leading to the improvement and effectiveness of marketing strategies depends on technology, these processes are often data-driven and automated. Constant in-house and real-time updates ensure continuous personalization relevancy, ensuring brand treatments are truly contextual, timely, and interesting to each consumer. This is necessary because as newer data-driven insights strategies are tested and implemented, consumer behaviors will shift and evolve, requiring strategies to shift and evolve with it. Data thus plays a critical role in hyper-personalization strategies (Rane et al., 2023; Jain et al., 2021).

6. ETHICAL AND PRIVACY CONSIDERATIONS IN AI-DRIVEN MARKETING

With the increased use of consumer data and algorithms in marketing campaigns, as well as in product suggestions and sales predictions, come concerns about privacy and the ethical implications of AI-driven marketing strategies. Trust with customers—and respect for their privacy—will be crucial for any marketing strategy moving forward. The ethical and responsible usage of AI becomes paramount if marketers want to maintain consumer trust. Privacy is also a regulation: similar regulations will likely be updated into stricter laws, and more countries will introduce equivalent laws. A federal regulation establishes consumer rights in the usage of data, giving them access and input in a company's usage of data. For many companies, giving the same privileges to every consumer could be costly. (Cheah et al.2022; Okazaki et al.2020)

There is also an ethical concern causing tension over how much personalization is too much. This will be a hot topic in marketing over the next decade, discussed and researched increasingly. While building relationships and improving products and services to promote consumer loyalty is a business objective, at times, businesses are viewed as invasive to the privacy of the consumer with their interest in everything they do. Privacy is a competitive element for businesses. A company abusing privacy may face backlash from consumers as a result of its actions. Culturally, one region values the privacy element of privacy-enhanced services and products over another, which values the performance and quality of such products and services. One region does value privacy, which is why regulations are still in effect. Utilitarian ethical theories would promote acting in a way that will have the greatest good or happiness among the population. Not acting on privacy requests by consumers may be seen as unethical. Rights theories would state that it is the duty of an organization to respect the privacy of its customers. More managers are looking to work in a company with ethical policies and practices. Many people look at firms regarding consumer data privacy (Lyu et al., 2023; Hussain et al.2023).

Ethical Framework to Influence Marketing Practices:

Now, there are some examples of fantastic and personal marketing campaigns. However, the same cannot be said of all marketing campaigns. When creating a marketing campaign, if it doesn't feel right, it probably isn't. But who is going to write those policies? Developments should be guided by ethical frameworks that pose ethical questions. If you're looking at a campaign and having ethical discussions at work over the color background of an email campaign, I think that is a problem. Alongside finance and market relations, work should be ethical. There is certainly a bit of fear that campaigns are going too far and pushing the envelope so much that it makes the firm look bad, trying not to be too obvious when it comes to personalizing a consumer's experience. Marketing campaigns need to be ethical. If an email looks too personal, it might appear to be a data mining exercise. Even if it might be at the base of the campaign, you can't make it look like that to the consumer. Let's focus our efforts on providing personalized services while protecting the privacy of our consumers. We can focus on better creativity and test what we are developing on the job. As an organization, we will start to be on the moral high road of doing the right thing. A customer will engage more with an organization that has a great reputation than with an unethical one (Kim, 2020; Tanveer et al., 2021).

6.1. Data Privacy Regulations

Privacy legislations and regulations provide guidelines, frameworks, and limitations on how consumers' data can be collected, processed, and used. The regulations would still be relevant and required even without the introduction of AI automation within the marketing domain. However, AI-driven hyper-personalization elements make potential improper use of the data for unclear identification purposes. Certain tasks that every company currently does or is considering to begin with are mandated, and consent and privacy rules have become a global norm. Now, the importance of these data privacy regulations increases, particularly for businesses that increasingly rely on AI for customer data analysis and targeting. An increasingly sophisticated tool would mean an easier way to misuse it. So, the risk of misuse has attained instant high priority because such AI misuse means discriminatory targeting or unauthorized info-sharing. Hence, there should be very strict compliance methods as well as strong internal processes that keep ethical practices. Complying with legal requirements in this regard and being transparent in data collection and usage engender consumer trust, establishing an essential foundation for effective marketing. Data regulator and jurisdiction penalties are no joke. For many companies, a single penalty could bankrupt them. While penalties may accumulate, a single significant one is enough to force companies to close down. This emphasizes the need for businesses to abide by these privacy laws. Legitimate marketers must disclose consent, be specific about the kind and purpose of data collected and its use, while also letting the user know about the channels and the nature of content for marketing and advertising communications. Legitimate marketers never hide these facts, nor do they intend to regulate separate privacy clauses for different countries. More than regulations, they are reflective of the facts of good marketing practices. To maintain compliance, companies are adopting advanced privacy management tools powered by AI. These tools help in monitoring data usage, detecting potential breaches, and automating compliance reporting. Such technologies simplify adherence to complex regulations and reduce the risk of penalties. Additionally, businesses are increasingly prioritizing staff training programs focused on privacy laws and ethical data handling, ensuring that employees across all levels are equipped to navigate these challenges (Quach et al., 2022). Data privacy traditions are being influenced by legal restrictions. Doesn't this make marketing a more transparent and trustworthy institution? It does, in summary. The integration of legal standards with marketing ethics has the potential to reshape the industry, promoting fairness and accountability. All it takes is a certain level of corrective action and proactive adaptation to the evolving regulatory landscape. Businesses that embrace these principles will not only avoid costly penalties but also gain a competitive edge by building enduring trust with their audiences (Quach et al., 2022).

7. FUTURE TRENDS IN AI-DRIVEN MARKETING

Trends in AI-Driven Marketing While AI is not yet able to fully take over for human marketers, it will continue to revolutionize and simplify marketing automation in the years ahead. Machine learning is expected to play a significant role for quite some time until the field experiences a new breakthrough in AI algorithms. Machine learning can be a critical step in enabling machines to learn for themselves. It is akin to giving a newborn a few toys with varying functions and observing how they engage with them, allowing them to learn through trial and error (Ma & Sun, 2020). Machine learning will not only process huge volumes of data, but marketers will be able to find a lot of information regarding consumers. AI systems will learn to identify trends and patterns better with the rapid generation of digital data and its proliferation. Algorithms, for instance, will sort through millions of data points to provide recommendations on the products or services that will suit the consumer's taste. This capability will increase the effectiveness of targeted marketing campaigns and, by consequence, return on investment for businesses. The trend will see machine learning and analysis of big data marketing take things a step further. Marketers will not just be able to put an ad for men's clothing in the local paper for all the males in a particular suburb. Instead, AI will allow them to deliver highly personalized and timely messages tailored to the preferences of individual customers. For example, artists and creators will be able to tailor their communications and develop products that appeal to specific males in any country, with a focus on elements that press their buttons and put them in the mood to make a purchase. Such personalization will be driven by the integration of AI tools with customer data platforms, ensuring that every touchpoint in the customer journey is informed by real-time insights. This level of personalization will enable companies to stand out from competitors and win customers purely by the strength of their customer experience. Customers today increasingly value brands that understand their needs and deliver seamless, relevant experiences. AI will be instrumental in this because it will automate mundane tasks, streamline workflows, and help marketers focus on developing fresh strategies that resonate with the audience. Artificial intelligence may be even more advanced if we include it in other areas. A possible future development might be to create meetings of minds between virtual reality, AI, the Internet of Things, and the latest marketing practices. For example, the merger of AI insights with the use of VR can produce experiences that engage audiences as never before. Imagine seeing a virtual store where customers, guided by AI avatars that appreciate their preferences and needs, browse and go through products in a perfectly personalized setting. Similarly, the integration of IoT gadgets can provide marketers with consumer behavior data in real-time, allowing them to refine their strategies dynamically. The challenge in developing technology like this is to stay aware of ethical concerns and tactics that might drive customers away rather than attract them (Olsen & Pracejus, 2020). Such issues as data privacy, algorithmic bias, and transparency need to be addressed to make AI-driven marketing practices sustainable and respect consumer rights. For example, businesses must be prioritizing compliance with data protection regulations such as GDPR in order to gain trust and avoid legal pitfalls. Keeping an eye out for the emerging trend has business businesses better positioned so to keep leaders in the marketplace from being passers, at the rear end of innovations going on. Proactive adoption of latest technologies to enhance a position can be competitive advantageous through differentiations in crowded marketplace while informing developing and strategy for managing developing trends help realize the existing roadblocks, opportunities with potential tactics through which companies need to develop and strategize it. Ultimately, the intersection of AI, big data, and innovative marketing approaches promises to reshape the industry, making it more dynamic, personalized, and impactful.

8. CONCLUSION AND KEY TAKEAWAYS

8.1. Evolution of Consumer Engagement and Personalization

The evolution of consumer engagement has been marked by a shift from broad, impersonal marketing tactics to highly targeted and personalized strategies. Early marketing efforts relied heavily on demographic segmentation and mass communication, often resulting in generic messaging that failed to resonate with individual consumers. With the advent of digital technologies and the proliferation of data, marketers gained the ability to segment audiences more precisely and tailor their communications accordingly.

However, as consumer expectations have grown, so too has the need for even more sophisticated personalization. Today's consumers demand experiences that are not only relevant but also timely and contextually appropriate. This has led to the rise of hyper-personalization, where AI-driven insights allow marketers to anticipate needs, predict behaviors, and deliver content that feels uniquely crafted for each individual. The journey from basic segmentation to holistic consumer understanding underscores the importance of seeing the consumer as a multidimensional entity, rather than a collection of isolated traits.

8.2. The Transformative Impact of AI-Driven Marketing Automation

AI-driven marketing automation has emerged as a game-changer in the industry. By leveraging machine learning, predictive analytics, and real-time data processing, businesses can now automate complex marketing processes that once required significant manual effort. This automation not only increases operational efficiency but also enhances the effectiveness of marketing campaigns by ensuring that the right message reaches the right consumer at the right time.

Hyper-personalization, powered by AI, takes this a step further by enabling marketers to create dynamic, individualized experiences at scale. From personalized product recommendations to adaptive website content and automated customer support, AI is redefining the possibilities of consumer engagement. Nevertheless, the successful implementation of these technologies requires a robust data infrastructure and a deep understanding of both technological capabilities and consumer psychology.

8.3. Ethical Considerations and the Art of Marketing

As AI becomes more deeply embedded in marketing practices, ethical considerations have come to the forefront. The collection, storage, and use of consumer data raise important questions about privacy, consent, and transparency. Marketers must navigate a complex landscape of regulations and consumer expectations, ensuring that their practices are both legally compliant and ethically sound.

Beyond compliance, there is an art to marketing that AI cannot replicate: the ability to connect with consumers on an emotional level. While algorithms can optimize for efficiency and relevance, it is the human touch—empathy, creativity, and intuition—that often makes the difference between a transactional interaction and a meaningful relationship. Striking the right balance between automation and authenticity is essential for building trust and fostering long-term loyalty.

8.4. Holistic Consumer Understanding and Predictive Insights

One of the most significant advancements enabled by AI is the ability to develop a holistic view of the consumer. Rather than relying on simplistic segmentation, marketers can now integrate data from multiple sources—online behavior, purchase history, social media activity, and more—to construct a comprehensive profile of each individual. This holistic understanding allows for more accurate predictions of future behaviors and preferences, enabling proactive rather than reactive marketing strategies.

However, with great power comes great responsibility. Marketers must ensure that their use of data respects consumer privacy and avoid reinforcing biases or stereotypes. By prioritizing transparency and ethical data practices, businesses can build stronger, more trusting relationships with their consumers.

8.5. The Path Forward: Embracing Innovation with Responsibility

As we stand on the brink of a new industrial revolution, marked by the convergence of AI, big data, and digital transformation, the future of marketing holds immense promise. The key to success lies in embracing innovation while remaining grounded in the fundamental principles of consumer-centricity and ethical responsibility. Marketers must cultivate curiosity, continuously seek out new knowledge, and remain agile in the face of rapid technological change.

Ultimately, the greatest AI-driven marketing tools are only as effective as the human insights and values that guide their use. By keeping the consumer at the heart of every decision and striving for hyper-personalized relevance, businesses can create marketing experiences that are not only effective but also meaningful and sustainable.

REFERENCES

Aljumah, A. I., Nuseir, M. T., & Alam, M. M. (2021). Traditional marketing analytics, big data analytics and big data system quality and the success of new product development. *Business Process Management Journal*, *27*(4), 1108–1125. DOI: 10.1108/BPMJ-11-2020-0527

Allioui, H., & Mourdi, Y. (2023). Unleashing the potential of AI: Investigating cutting-edge technologies that are transforming businesses. [IJCEDS]. *International Journal of Computer Engineering and Data Science*, *3*(2), 1–12.

Bossuwé, E. (2023). *AI-DRIVEN BUSINESS MODELS AIMED AT PROMOTING A CIRCULAR ECONOMY* (Doctoral dissertation, Ghent University).

Bozkurt, S., Uğursoy, A. S., & Meral, S. P. (2025). The Impact of Personalized Messages and Designs on Consumer Experiences and Marketing Communications in Technology: Hyper-Personalization. In *Impact of Contemporary Technology on Art and Design* (pp. 135–164). IGI Global.

Campbell, C., Sands, S., Ferraro, C., Tsao, H. Y. J., & Mavrommatis, A. (2020). From data to action: How marketers can leverage AI. *Business Horizons*, *63*(2), 227–243. DOI: 10.1016/j.bushor.2019.12.002

Cao, L. (2021). Artificial intelligence in retail: Applications and value creation logics. *International Journal of Retail & Distribution Management*, *49*(7), 958–976. DOI: 10.1108/IJRDM-09-2020-0350

Cheah, J. H., Lim, X. J., Ting, H., Liu, Y., & Quach, S. (2022). Are privacy concerns still relevant? Revisiting consumer behaviour in omnichannel retailing. *Journal of Retailing and Consumer Services*, *65*, 102242. DOI: 10.1016/j.jretconser.2020.102242

Davenport, T., Guha, A., Grewal, D., & Bressgott, T. (2020). How artificial intelligence will change the future of marketing. *Journal of the Academy of Marketing Science*, *48*(1), 24–42. DOI: 10.1007/s11747-019-00696-0

De Keyzer, F., Van Noort, G., & Kruikemeier, S. (2022). Going too far? How consumers respond to personalized advertising from different sources. *Journal of electronic commerce research.-Long Beach, Calif.,[200-], currens, 23*(3), 138-159.

Gao, Y., & Liu, H. (2023). Artificial intelligence-enabled personalization in interactive marketing: A customer journey perspective. *Journal of Research in Interactive Marketing*, *17*(5), 663–680. DOI: 10.1108/JRIM-01-2022-0023

Gkikas, D. C., & Theodoridis, P. K. (2022). AI in consumer behavior. *Advances in Artificial Intelligence-based Technologies: Selected Papers in Honour of Professor Nikolaos G. Bourbakis*, *1*, 147–176.

Haleem, A., Javaid, M., Qadri, M. A., Singh, R. P., & Suman, R. (2022). Artificial intelligence (AI) applications for marketing: A literature-based study. *International Journal of Intelligent Networks*, *3*, 119–132. DOI: 10.1016/j.ijin.2022.08.005

Huang, C., Jiang, W., Wu, J., & Wang, G. (2020). Personalized review recommendation based on users' aspect sentiment. *ACM Transactions on Internet Technology*, *20*(4), 1–26. DOI: 10.1145/3414841

Hussain, H. N., Alabdullah, T. T. Y., Ries, E., & Jamal, K. A. M. (2023). Implementing Technology for Competitive Advantage in Digital Marketing. *International Journal of Scientific and Management Research*, *6*(6), 95–114. DOI: 10.37502/IJSMR.2023.6607

Jain, G., Paul, J., & Shrivastava, A. (2021). Hyper-personalization, co-creation, digital clienteling and transformation. *Journal of Business Research*, *124*, 12–23. DOI: 10.1016/j.jbusres.2020.11.034

Kamal, M., & Himel, A. S. (2023). Redefining modern marketing: An analysis of AI and NLP's influence on consumer engagement, strategy, and beyond. *Eigenpub Review of Science and Technology*, *7*(1), 203–223.

Kedi, W. E., Ejimuda, C., Idemudia, C., & Ijomah, T. I. (2024). AI software for personalized marketing automation in SMEs: Enhancing customer experience and sales. *World Journal of Advanced Research and Reviews*, *23*(1), 1981–1990. DOI: 10.30574/wjarr.2024.23.1.2159

Kim, C. M. (2020). *Social media campaigns: Strategies for public relations and marketing*. Routledge. DOI: 10.4324/9781003020196

Krishnan, C., Gupta, A., Gupta, A., & Singh, G. (2022). Impact of artificial intelligence-based chatbots on customer engagement and business growth. In *Deep learning for social media data analytics* (pp. 195–210). Springer International Publishing. DOI: 10.1007/978-3-031-10869-3_11

Kumari, P. (2024). To study the impact of ai on digital marketing strategy. [IJRAR]. *IJRAR-International Journal of Research and Analytical Reviews*, *11*(2), 286–320.

Liu, Y., Soroka, A., Han, L., Jian, J., & Tang, M. (2020). Cloud-based big data analytics for customer insight-driven design innovation in SMEs. *International Journal of Information Management*, *51*, 102034. DOI: 10.1016/j.ijinfomgt.2019.11.002

Lyu, X., Jia, F., & Zhao, B. (2023). Impact of big data and cloud-driven learning technologies in healthy and smart cities on marketing automation. *Soft Computing*, *27*(7), 4209–4222. DOI: 10.1007/s00500-022-07031-w

Ma, L., & Sun, B. (2020). Machine learning and AI in marketing–Connecting computing power to human insights. *International Journal of Research in Marketing*, *37*(3), 481–504. DOI: 10.1016/j.ijresmar.2020.04.005

Mandapuram, M., Gutlapalli, S. S., Reddy, M., & Bodepudi, A. (2020). Application of artificial intelligence (AI) technologies to accelerate market segmentation. *Global Disclosure of Economics and Business*, *9*(2), 141–150. DOI: 10.18034/gdeb.v9i2.662

Marion, T. J., & Fixson, S. K. (2021). The transformation of the innovation process: How digital tools are changing work, collaboration, and organizations in new product development. *Journal of Product Innovation Management*, *38*(1), 192–215. DOI: 10.1111/jpim.12547

Movahed, A. B., Movahed, A. B., & Nozari, H. (2024). Marketing 6.0 Conceptualization. In *Advanced Businesses in Industry 6.0* (pp. 15-31). IGI Global.

Okazaki, S., Eisend, M., Plangger, K., de Ruyter, K., & Grewal, D. (2020). Understanding the strategic consequences of customer privacy concerns: A meta-analytic review. *Journal of Retailing*, *96*(4), 458–473. DOI: 10.1016/j.jretai.2020.05.007

Olsen, G. D., & Pracejus, J. W. (2020). Customized advertising: Allowing consumers to directly tailor messages leads to better outcomes for the brand. *Journal of Business Research*, *116*, 245–257. DOI: 10.1016/j.jbusres.2020.04.054

Palle, R. R. (2021). Discuss the role of data analytics in extracting meaningful insights from social media data, influencing marketing strategies and user engagement. *Journal of Artificial Intelligence and Machine Learning in Management*, *5*(1), 64–69.

Podobed, N. A. (2024). Integrated marketing communications: electronic educational-methodical complex for specialties: 6-05-0412-04" Marketing", 1-26 02 03" Marketing"/Institute of Business BSU, Department of marketing; comp. NA Podobed.–Minsk: BSU, 2024.–106 p.–Bibliogr.: p. 105–106.

Potla, R. T., & Pottla, V. K. (2024). AI-Powered Personalization in Salesforce: Enhancing Customer Engagement through Machine Learning Models. Valley International Journal Digital Library, 1388-1420.

Medina-Ortiz, D., Contreras, S., Quiroz, C., Asenjo, J. A., Medina-Ortiz, D., Contreras, S., Quiroz, C., Asenjo, J. A., & Olivera-Nappa, Á. (2020). Dmakit: A user-friendly web platform for bringing state-of-the-art data analysis techniques to non-specific users. *Information Systems*, *93*, 101557.

Potwora, M., Zakryzhevska, I., Mostova, A., Kyrkovskyi, V., & Saienko, V. (2023). Marketing strategies in e-commerce: Personalised content, recommendations, and increased customer trust. *Financial and Credit Activity: Problems of Theory and Practice*, *5*(52), 562–573.

Quach, S., Thaichon, P., Martin, K. D., Weaven, S., & Palmatier, R. W. (2022). Digital technologies: Tensions in privacy and data. *Journal of the Academy of Marketing Science*, *50*(6), 1299–1323. DOI: 10.1007/s11747-022-00845-y PMID: 35281634

Rane, N., Choudhary, S., & Rane, J. (2023). Hyper-personalization for enhancing customer loyalty and satisfaction in Customer Relationship Management (CRM) systems. *Available at SSRN* 4641044. DOI: 10.2139/ssrn.4641044

Singh, B., & Kaunert, C. (2024). Future of Digital Marketing: Hyper-Personalized Customer Dynamic Experience with AI-Based Predictive Models. In *Revolutionizing the AI-Digital Landscape* (pp. 189–203). Productivity Press. DOI: 10.4324/9781032688305-14

Singh, B., & Kaunert, C. (2024). Future of Digital Marketing: Hyper-Personalized Customer Dynamic Experience with AI-Based Predictive Models. In *Revolutionizing the AI-Digital Landscape* (pp. 189–203). Productivity Press. DOI: 10.4324/9781032688305-14

Stone, M., Aravopoulou, E., Ekinci, Y., Evans, G., Hobbs, M., Labib, A., Laughlin, P., Machtynger, J., & Machtynger, L. (2020). Artificial intelligence (AI) in strategic marketing decision-making: A research agenda. *The Bottom Line (New York, N.Y.)*, *33*(2), 183–200. DOI: 10.1108/BL-03-2020-0022

Tadimarri, A., Jangoan, S., Sharma, K. K., & Gurusamy, A. AI-Powered Marketing: Transforming Consumer Engagement and Brand Growth.

Tanveer, M., Ahmad, A. R., Mahmood, H., & Haq, I. U. (2021). Role of ethical marketing in driving consumer brand relationships and brand loyalty: A sustainable marketing approach. *Sustainability (Basel)*, *13*(12), 6839. DOI: 10.3390/su13126839

Umamaheswari, D. D. (2024). Role of Artificial Intelligence in Marketing Strategies and Performance. *Migration Letters : An International Journal of Migration Studies*, *21*(S4), 1589–1599.

Wagner, G., Schramm-Klein, H., & Steinmann, S. (2020). Online retailing across e-channels and e-channel touchpoints: Empirical studies of consumer behavior in the multichannel e-commerce environment. *Journal of Business Research*, *107*, 256–270. DOI: 10.1016/j.jbusres.2018.10.048

Wamba-Taguimdje, S. L., Wamba, S. F., Kamdjoug, J. R. K., & Wanko, C. E. T. (2020). Influence of artificial intelligence (AI) on firm performance: The business value of AI-based transformation projects. *Business Process Management Journal*, *26*(7), 1893–1924. DOI: 10.1108/BPMJ-10-2019-0411

Zhang, C., & Lu, Y. (2021). Study on artificial intelligence: The state of the art and future prospects. *Journal of Industrial Information Integration*, *23*, 100224. DOI: 10.1016/j.jii.2021.100224

Chapter 8
AI-Driven Social Media Monetization Policy and Consumer-Centric Engagement in Digital Marketing

Maria Esegbona-Isikeh Ogheneruona
https://orcid.org/0009-0005-6073-9442
Birmingham City University, UK

Esther Bunmi Eboesomi
https://orcid.org/0009-0004-8244-6176
University of Huddersfield, UK

Okwudili Matthew Ugochukwu
https://orcid.org/0000-0003-0828-9710
Federal University of Lavras, Brazil

Praise Akinsipe
https://orcid.org/0009-0002-1326-5529
Ground Control Limited, UK

David Oyewumi-Taiwo Oyekunle
https://orcid.org/0009-0007-3994-1712
University of Salford, UK

Godwin Nse Ebong
https://orcid.org/0000-0002-9899-8838
University of Salford, UK

Amaonwu Onyebuchi
https://orcid.org/0000-0002-6954-4853
Hussaini Adamu Federal Polytechnic, Nigeria

Oluyemisi Adenike Oyedemi
https://orcid.org/0009-0005-8496-736X
Federal University of Lavras, Brazil

ABSTRACT

This study explored social media monetization policy in Nigeria as a potential avenue for a new social contract as a digital economy development indicator and entrepreneurship sustainability. By examining existing monetization policy, regulatory challenges, and the socio-economic implications for digital content creators

DOI: 10.4018/979-8-3373-3775-3.ch008

and stakeholder's engagement, the paper highlights the urgent need for policies that balance profitability with targeted digital marketing campaign and consumer protection with artificial intelligence (AI). The study adopted a random sampling technique, 10 real estate companies were selected from the 15 medium scale real estate companies in the study area. Of the completed questionnaires, 75% were recovered and deemed valuable for the data analysis. The results of the study indicated that significant portion of medium scale real estate investment companies generated between 20million and 100million in revenue after implementing data-driven product engineering digital marketing, which is more than they did in the year before digital marketing implementation.

1. INTRODUCTION

Social media monetization driven by artificial intelligence (AI) has revolutionized the way businesses interact with customers in the rapidly changing field of digital marketing, moving away from traditional marketing methods and toward tailored, data-driven approaches(Babics and Jermolajeva, 2024). Through content customization, advert placement automation, and the use of predictive analytics for focused marketing campaigns, AI-powered solutions help organizations maximize productivity. The foundation of this change is consumer-centric engagement, in which AI improves user interactions by promoting loyalty and trust through chatbots, sentiment analysis, and personalized suggestions(Patil, 2024). The purpose of this study is to assess how AI affects user adoption, brand loyalty, and long-term performance in digital marketing by examining the convergence of the Technology Acceptance Model (TAM), Customer Relationship Marketing (CRM), and Consumer Engagement Theory (CET). It also discusses ethical issues related to transparency, data protection, and responsible AI-driven advertising. Digital technologies empower small and medium-sized enterprises (SMEs) by expanding their market reach, enabling cost-effective advertising, and fostering direct customer engagement. The commercialization of social media platforms plays a crucial role in shaping modern business landscapes by offering SMEs access to tools for targeted marketing, data analytics, and personalized interactions. Digital tools are programs, websites, applications, and other internet and computerized resources that facilitate, enhance and execute digital processes and overall digitization efforts such as social media, mobile phones, online games, and multimedia, really simple syndication (RSS), blogs, video logs, widgets, tags, forums, location based services, Web chats, instant messaging, podcasts and microblogging services are utilized to facilities brand adverts(Matthew, Kazaure, Kazaure, Onyedibe, et al., 2022),(Matthew, Kazaure, and Okafor, 2021). By embracing digital tools, SMEs innovate, compete, and contribute to sustainable economic development, making entrepreneurship more inclusive and scalable. Given that SMEs use digital technologies to reach a wider audience, the commercialization of social media platforms also promotes economic diversification and entrepreneurship while also advancing financial inclusion(Gu et al., 2023). In order to balance innovation with moral advertising practices, established frameworks are needed to address the legislative issues surrounding AI-driven monetization strategies.

Nigeria may become a pioneer in AI-driven digital marketing in Africa's changing economic environment by incorporating AI into its monetization plans, which would increase digital trade, draw in foreign investors, and spur economic progress. The integration of social media monetization in Nigeria plays a vital role in fostering economic development, enabling businesses and content creators to generate revenue through AI-driven digital marketing(Oyedokun 2025). AI-powered advertising automation, predictive analytics, and personalized marketing enhance efficiency, allowing brands to maximize engagement and optimize advertisements spending. As businesses expand their digital presence, the demand for tech-driven solutions increases, stimulating job creation in AI development, digital marketing, and e-commerce. The term "social media monetization" is the process of making money on digital platforms like Facebook, Instagram, and YouTube in order to support sponsored content, influencer marketing, and advertisement revenue models that increase profitability and allow commodities to reach the intended consumer base(Bruce et al. 2023). Nigeria's digital marketing environment is changing as a result of AI, which increases customer engagement and monetization effectiveness. AI-powered solutions tailor the way information are delivered, guaranteeing that influencer campaigns and advertisements are seen by the appropriate people. AI-driven chatbots offer smooth customer service, increasing user engagement, while predictive analytics maximizes brand interactions. Nigerian companies and performers would be empowered by a systematic monetization policy that incorporates AI, guaranteeing equitable revenue sharing and enhancing customer confidence. Nigeria may establish a prosperous, inclusive digital economy with long-term revenue prospects by utilizing AI advancements. Nigerian social media monetization policy have the power to influence the digital economy by creating a more equitable and sustainable online environment that enable business to thrive(Uzomah and Eruetemu 2024). Social media monetization strategy might stimulate economic growth while guaranteeing product advertisement considerations within content creation and consumer interactions, as influencers and marketers increasingly depend on digital platforms to engage audiences(Kobets et al. 2024).

Globally, monetization methods have been built by platforms like Facebook, Instagram, and YouTube, enabling content creators to receive payment depending on engagement metrics. The problems with monetization, such as algorithmic biases, unequal revenue-sharing, and the requirement for open regulations that safeguard content producers, have been emphasized in a number of studies. Research on the digital economy in Nigeria highlights the significance of regulatory frameworks that uphold monetization practices and guarantee adherence to national laws without endangering the general welfare of the country. Nigerian digital marketing has changed dramatically, with companies using social media to increase customer involvement and brand awareness. Through influencer collaborations, sponsored advertising, and interactive campaigns, marketers can now reach specific audiences through commercialization of social media platforms. Nigeria has taken a different approach to social media regulation in recent years, with new laws intended to hold digital platforms and content producers accountable(Elhai 2020). Guidelines that aim to control online interactions and monetization techniques have been introduced by the National Information Technology Development Agency (NITDA)(Obia 2025). Policies established by regulatory agencies like the Advertising Regulatory Council of Nigeria (ARCON) that enforce frameworks that guarantee ethical advertising practices that safeguard the interests of consumers governs Nigeria digital economy. These regulations are in line with the social contract theory's tenets, which support reciprocal duties among parties to maintain sustainability and equity. A structured monetization policy can protect the rights of consumers and content creators while acting as a stimulant for economic growth that help Nigerians build a healthy digital ecosystem that encourages creativity and moral uprightness. Monetization tactics also need to encourage openness, making sure that revenue-sharing plans, advertising schemes, and algorithms don't take advantage of users or content creators. Without accountability, the rights of individual producers could be overshadowed by corporate interests, creating an imbalance in the digital sphere. In addition, incorporating a social compact into monetization policies improves the public-business-regulator connection. By implementing equitable pay structures and cultivating an atmosphere that rewards innovation, Nigeria may establish itself as a pioneer in moral brand engineering and digital marketing(Bilgin, Hadziahmetovic, and Tandir 2025). Policies should also take into account consumer protection, making sure that advertising tactics are truthful and don't support false information or dishonest marketing. By improving user engagement and brand trust, a well-designed framework strengthens Nigeria's place in the rapidly changing global digital economy. Nigeria may greatly boost digital economic growth by enacting a regulated social media monetization policy in line with physical policy framework(Amuda-Kannike and Amuda-Kannike 2025).

Starting a business online and offering goods and services without making physical space investments is also considered in the digital entrepreneurship conceptualization. Digital entrepreneurship is essentially about identifying holes in the market and leveraging technology to close those gaps which become the key aspect of content creation and social media monetization policy(Ikenga and Egbule 2024). Social media platforms' widespread use has changed the digital landscape and opened up new business prospects through brand engineering, digital marketing, and content production. Social media has developed into a potent tool for individual performers, companies, and organizations to engage audiences, sell products, and create income in Nigeria, where mobile connectivity is common and internet adoption is rising. Digital marketers, entrepreneurs, and influencers have been able to create powerful online presences, take advantage of audience engagement, and investigate monetization options that give merits to platforms like Facebook, Instagram, Twitter, TikTok, and YouTube. As conventional marketing strategies give way to digital methods, social media monetization has become a major economic force. Nigeria's dynamic marketplace has changed how businesses function due to the possibilities for revenue generation through brand collaborations, sponsored content, affiliate marketing, advertising, and direct consumer contact(Iroka and Nwaizugbo 2024). Nevertheless, the legislative environment surrounding digital monetization is still in its infancy, which presents problems with fair pay, content ownership rights, ethical advertising, and consumer protection despite the financial potential that appear attractive. Nigeria's digital economy has been greatly impacted by the country's social media monetization policy, which has increased revenue streams for platforms like Meta and allowed content providers to make money through bonuses, subscriptions, and advertisements. A flourishing creator economy is promoted by this policy, which also stimulates innovation in brand engineering and digital marketing. This paper is structured thematically into, introduction, objectives of the study, research background, theoretical framework, research questions, research hypothesis, research design, research methodology, discussion of research findings, future research focus, recommendation and conclusion.

2. OBJECTIVES OF THE STUDY

i. This study analyzes the joint effects of Nigerian government policy governing the digital economy, AI-enhanced monetization, and customer engagement on digital marketing in Nigeria. In order to promote responsible AI use and sustain economic growth, it seeks to offer insights into successful monetization models and established policies that enhance Nigeria's competitiveness in the global digital market.
ii. This study aims to assess the effectiveness of AI-driven monetization tools in enhancing revenue generation for Nigerian businesses and content creators. It examines consumer engagement trends, analyzing how AI influences brand

loyalty and purchasing behavior. This study is based on the CET and the TAM. CET emphasizes how tailored marketing can build brand loyalty, whereas TAM describes how companies and influencers use AI-driven monetization techniques.

iii. In addition, the research explores Nigeria's regulatory frameworks to determine their impact on AI adoption in social media marketing. It identifies challenges limiting AI-driven monetization while proposing solutions for better implementation. The purpose of this study is to assess how AI-driven marketing improves social media revenue for Nigerian companies and content producers.

iv. It looks at how brand loyalty, consumer engagement, and purchase behavior are affected by AI-powered tactics. Furthermore, the study examines current legislative frameworks and how they affect the use of AI in monetization practices. It offers strategies for maximized engagement while highlighting the benefits and difficulties of incorporating AI into digital marketing.

v. Lastly, the study provides best practices for integrating AI into digital marketing strategies, optimizing consumer engagement and monetization outcomes for long-term business sustainability in Nigeria's evolving digital economy.

3. RESEARCH BACKGROUND

The study on social media monetization policy in Nigeria and increasing consumer engagement in digital marketing with AI holds significant implications for businesses, policymakers, and digital marketers. As Nigerian enterprises increasingly rely on social media for brand promotion and revenue generation, understanding the role of AI-driven strategies in enhancing consumer engagement is crucial. From a business perspective, this research provides insights into how AI-powered digital marketing tools, such as predictive analytics and personalized advertising, optimize monetization strategies. It offers SMEs and content creators data-driven approaches to improve audience retention, brand visibility, and conversion rates, leading to sustained profitability. For policymakers, the findings inform regulatory decisions on social media monetization frameworks that inform government on revenue mobilization. By evaluating current policies and identifying gaps, the study helps in formulating ethical guidelines that balance AI innovation with consumer protection. On a technological level, the research advances discussions on AI adoption in Nigeria's digital economy. It highlights both the opportunities and challenges of AI-driven marketing, offering recommendations for overcoming implementation barriers. Additionally, it contributes to academic literature by providing empirical data on AI's influence in consumer engagement, bridging research gaps in digital marketing strategies. Ultimately, this study empowers Nigerian businesses to leverage AI-driven monetization effectively, fosters policy development that supports digital entrepreneurship, and strengthens Nigeria's position in the global digital market landscape. Its impact extends beyond theory, driving actionable solutions for sustainable economic growth. The deployment of AI improves the efficacy of digital marketing, as demonstrated by the integration of the TAM and CET with Nigeria's social media monetization policy. TAM describes how AI-powered monetization technologies are used by Nigerian companies and content producers due to their perceived utility and simplicity of use. Predictive analytics, chatbots, and AI-driven advertising streamline marketing while boosting profits. CET on the other hand, emphasizes how deeper relationships can be fostered by individualized AI content. AI makes it possible for social media companies to customize advertisements, maximizing interaction by matching advertising to user interests and activity.

The success of monetization, brand loyalty, and audience retention are all enhanced by this connection. By aligning TAM with CET, policymakers can create adaptive social media monetization frameworks that encourage AI innovation while ensuring ethical digital marketing. This synergy promotes sustainable revenue models, strengthens consumer trust, and enhances Nigeria's position in the global digital economy. As businesses and content creators seek sustainable revenue models, social media monetization has become a crucial strategy. Platforms such as Facebook, Instagram, and YouTube offer monetization tools, enabling Nigerian enterprises to leverage digital advertising, influencer marketing, and subscription-based content creation(Okwudili and Kazaure 2020). With the emergence of AI in digital marketing, businesses can now automate content delivery, personalize advertising, and optimize consumer interactions. AI-driven marketing tools such as chatbots, predictive analytics, and machine learning algorithms enhance engagement by tailoring ads to user preferences and behavioral patterns. Studies indicate that AI-powered marketing strategies significantly improve audience retention, brand visibility, and conversion rates. Understanding how AI-driven monetization affects consumer engagement is essential for developing policies that support digital entrepreneurs while maintaining fair industry standards. This research explores the interplay between AI-enhanced digital marketing and consumer engagement on Nigerian social media platforms. It aims to analyze how businesses adopt AI-driven strategies, examine the effectiveness of monetization models, and assess regulatory frameworks shaping online advertising. By identifying key factors influencing AI adoption, this study provides insights into improving digital marketing efficiency, maximizing revenue, and fostering economic growth in Nigeria's evolving digital landscape.

4. RESEARCH QUESTIONS

The following questions helped to structure the current research work while giving insight into policy effectiveness, AI's role in social media monetization, and consumer engagement strategies in digital marketing.

i. How do AI-driven digital marketing tools compare to traditional methods in increasing consumer engagement on Nigerian social media platforms?
ii. What is the relationship between AI-enhanced advertising strategies and the effectiveness of social media monetization in Nigeria?
iii. How does AI-powered marketing impact audience retention and engagement rates for Nigerian businesses and content creators?
iv. In what ways do Nigeria's existing social media monetization policies influence the adoption of AI-driven digital marketing?
v. How does AI-personalized advertising affect consumer responsiveness, brand interactions, and purchasing decisions in Nigeria?

5. THEORETICAL FRAMEWORK

The adoption of AI and its effects on digital marketing techniques for advertising products are explained by the TAM and CET, which also provide insight into the Nigerian social media monetization and AI-driven digital marketing economy(Adeyinka, Takunda, and Adeyinka 2024). According to (Xia et al. 2024), TAM can be used to evaluate how Nigerian companies and content producers can employ AI-powered monetization solutions according to their perceived utility and usability across the digital economy. Predictive analytics, automated content creation, and AI-driven advertising maximize the effectiveness of digital marketing and make monetization easier. In Nigeria's digital economy, external variables including infrastructure, digital literacy, and governmental laws affect the adoption of AI. CET looks at how AI improves brand loyalty, user interaction, and purchase decisions. Interactive media and AI-personalized advertisements improve customer relationships and encourage engagement, which results in successful monetization(Torres et al. 2025). Machine learning-driven suggestions increase content relevancy, improving audience retention and income prospects. When taken as a whole, these frameworks show how Nigeria's social media monetization laws influence AI use while striking a balance between consumer protection, innovation, and regulatory compliance. While legislators improve monetization guidelines to enable fair and ethical AI use, businesses profit from AI-driven marketing methods that increase audience engagement. Nigeria's digital economy may develop into a sustainable, AI-enhanced market by utilizing these theories, which will propel economic growth and technical progress. Nigeria's digital ecosystem is flourishing, particularly on social media, and marketers are using CET principles to develop tailored experiences, interactive campaigns, and interesting content that keep customers interested in their companies. TAM, on the other hand, focuses on perceived utility and usability to explain why people adopt technology. Understanding TAM enables firms to optimize their digital platforms for user-friendly experiences in Nigeria, where mobile adoption is strong but digital literacy varies. Businesses customize e-commerce platforms, applications, and websites to guarantee smooth interactions and make it simpler for customers to interact with goods and services(Abtahia et al. 2024).

Together, CET and TAM increase the efficacy of digital marketing by making sure Nigerian customers find digital solutions useful and accessible in addition to interacting with brands(Fatokun 2023). Brands employ these theories to increase engagement, enhance user experiences, and increase conversion rates in everything from influencer marketing to mobile commerce, which strengthens Nigeria's digital economy in the long run. Nigerian social media monetization offers a revolutionary chance to reshape the dynamics of brand engineering and digital marketing to maintain credibility while maximizing monetization opportunities(Olatunji et al. 2025). A regulated monetization policy can support a just exchange between content creators, brands, users, and platform owners, strengthening the ideas of a social contract in the digital realm as social media platforms continue to fuel economic activity. The equitable distribution of income from revenue streams including advertising, influencer marketing, and subscription models to Nigerian content providers is guaranteed by a well-executed monetization structure. In order to promote a healthy digital marketing environment, the policy must address important problems including data privacy, consumer protection, and regulatory openness. Monetization rules should promote ethical branding from the standpoint of brand engineering, making sure that monetary incentives don't jeopardize user trust, engagement propensity, products and services authenticity(Nurgalieva, Frik, and Doherty 2023). Nigeria's monetization policy should ultimately serve as a social contract that strikes a balance between user rights, regulatory control, and corporate profitability. Such policies have the potential to transform Nigeria's online marketing landscape, empower creators, and lay the groundwork for long-term digital innovation and brand growth by promoting an open, inclusive, and sustainable digital economy. Nigeria might transform the digital economy by implementing a systematic social media monetization policy that promotes innovation, fair revenue sharing, and long-term growth. As brand engineering and digital marketing develop, a clear regulatory framework would draw in investments, boost consumer confidence, and give creators and companies equitable monetization options.

According to(Nadler and McGuigan 2018), structured monetization techniques may also lessen exploitative behavior while promoting moral advertising and conscientious participation. When managed properly, the social media monetization policy would establish Nigeria as a leader in Africa's digital economy as the nation fortifies its digital infrastructure, guaranteeing performers steady income streams and promoting a vibrant, inclusive online marketplace(Shams, Brown, and Hardcastle 2025). A well-regulated monetization ecosystem would offer long-term economic stability, propelling growth in technology-driven businesses while striking a balance between profitability and moral digital conduct in light of the emergence of AI-driven content strategies and changing consumer behaviors(Oyekunle et al. 2024). The effectiveness of Nigeria's structured social media monetization policy to assure fair revenue distribution, encourage ethical brand involvement, and create equitable digital growth will determine its long-term economic viability. A well-regulated structure for monetization would offer long-term financial security to marketers, companies, and content creators as Nigeria's digital economy grows, lowering the dangers of uncontrolled agreements and unscrupulous activities(Corren 2022). The development of equitable remuneration schemes is essential to sustainability because it guarantees that companies and creators profit equitably from their contributions to the digital ecosystem. Open monetization practices will boost small firms, draw in investments, and bolster Nigeria's standing in the international digital economy. In addition, the incorporation of structured taxation into digital transactions may open up new revenue streams for the government, promoting economic diversification and lessening reliance on established sectors and foreign borrowing(Mpofu 2022),(Matthew, Kazaure, and Haruna 2020). Nigeria may establish itself as a leader in Africa's digital economy by enforcing advertising regulations, safeguarding consumers, preserving intellectual property and trademarks.

In Nigeria, social media monetization is made more profitable, transparent, and efficient with the help of AI. Brand engineers, content producers, and digital marketers may streamline processes, enhance their tactics, and guarantee moral audience engagement using AI-powered technologies. One significant use of AI is targeted advertising, where machine learning algorithms use user data to provide tailored content that boosts conversion rates and advertisement efficacy. Additionally, AI improves automated content creation, allowing businesses and influencers to produce high-quality text, videos, and images quickly(Matthew et al. 2024),(Matthew, Kazaure, Kazaure, Hassan, et al. 2022). Fraud detection algorithms ensure that information complies with ethical norms by spotting fraudulent engagement, misleading advertising, and content piracy(Nwanakwaugwu et al. 2023). In order to promote a structured and sustainable digital economy, AI-driven monitoring can reduce risks like fraudulent activity, content exploitation, and unequal revenue distribution as digital marketing and brand engineering advance(Iqbal and Jan 2025).

By regulating brands advertisement transparency, AI improves consumer protection by protecting against deceptive marketing and guaranteeing that users see accurate product representations. By streamlining revenue-sharing arrangements and guaranteeing adherence to monetization guidelines, automated contract enforcement reduces disagreements. AI-driven regulatory frameworks are going to be essential as Nigeria improves its social media monetization policies in order to preserve stakeholder confidence and accountability. By prioritizing AI ethics, transparency, and responsible monetization, Nigeria can position itself as a global leader in sustainable digital marketing. If executed effectively, this approach could boost investor confidence, create jobs, and establish a more equitable digital economy.

5.1 Customer Relationship Model (CRM) and TAM in AI Digital Marketing

Customer relationship model (CRM) are essential for building consumer trust, engagement, and brand loyalty in Nigeria's AI-driven digital marketing economy (Adeyinka, Takunda, and Adeyinka 2024). Automated customer support systems like chatbots, predictive analytics, and sentiment analysis optimize interactions by offering quick, data-driven responses catered to specific customers as more and more companies use AI-powered marketing solutions. Relationship marketing is improved by AI, which enables companies to provide individualized experiences, effectively answer questions, and predict client demands(Nozari, Movahed, and Movahed 2024). AI finds trends in consumer behavior through machine learning, allowing for proactive solutions that raise retention and satisfaction levels. Businesses in Nigeria may increase user engagement and guarantee consistent and meaningful interactions across digital platforms by implementing AI-based customer care(Umoh 2024). However, CRM emphasizes the significance of customer connection, while TAM explains AI adoption based on its perceived utility and ease of use(Cheng et al. 2023). AI-driven marketing is a crucial component of economic development since it helps companies enhance consumer experiences, bolster social media monetization efforts, and support Nigeria's expanding digital economy by incorporating AI-driven customer care tactics. According to(Binsaeed et al. 2023), customer relationship marketing theory, establishing long-term customer involvement, loyalty, and trust is more important than concentrating on quick transactions. This idea places a strong emphasis on continual relationship building between companies and their clients, as well as tailored interactions and effective communication. By utilizing data analytics, sentiment analysis, and predictive modeling to customize promotions and answers according to consumer preferences and behaviors, AI-driven marketing improves on this strategy.

According to (Prasetyo et al. 2025), utilizing an extended TAM enable customers to embrace new technologies based on their perceived utility and usability. When organizations and customers see the advantages of AI-powered solutions, such tailored advertising, automated customer support, and machine-learning-driven suggestions, TAM demonstrates how they may adopt them in digital marketing. By combining TAM with Customer Relationship Marketing Theory, companies can create AI-powered engagement strategies that maximize social media monetization, increase retention rates, and improve marketing effectiveness in Nigeria's changing digital environment(Agbo-Adediran et al. 2025). Adoption of AI guarantees efficient digital interactions while enhancing consumer relationships. Integrating TAM and CRM ensures effective social media monetization, making digital engagement more accessible and personalized. AI-driven tools optimize marketing strategies while strengthening customer trust(Singh et al. 2023). CRM theory is essential to social media monetization because it builds user-brand engagement, trust, and enduring connections. Sustainable revenue is ensured with CRM-driven social media monetization since happy and involved consumers keep interacting with sponsored posts, premium content, and subscriptions(Kobets et al. 2024). Ethical AI techniques make monetization easy and efficient while also boosting consumer trust. CRM and digital marketing have developed in the AI era to improve automation, personalization, and customer interaction. CRM solutions with AI capabilities enable companies to examine enormous volumes of client data and offer forecasted insights that enhance loyalty and retention(Sathyavani et al. 2025),(Egbuhuzor et al. 2025). AI-powered recommendation engines and chatbots provide smooth, tailored encounters that improve brand loyalty. AI helps digital marketing by automating ad placements, enhancing targeting precision, and optimizing content tactics. AI systems improve consumer segmentation, guaranteeing that advertising campaigns effectively reach the target population. Sentiment analysis driven by AI also assists companies in modifying their plans in response to client input. By incorporating AI into CRM and digital marketing, organizations can anticipate customer demands, maximize engagement, and cultivate enduring loyalty in a data-driven environment. Businesses obtain a competitive edge by utilizing AI to increase productivity, cut expenses, and strengthen relationships with clients.

Figure 1. CRM and TAM in digital marketing, author illustration

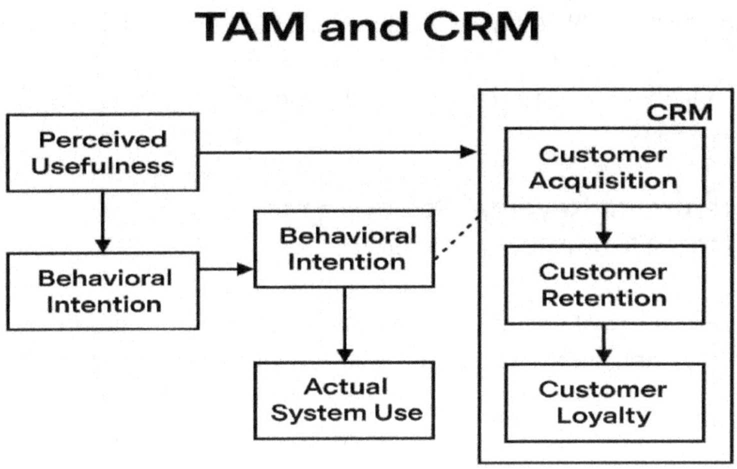

In **Figure 1,** CRM promotes advocacy and loyalty by utilizing AI-driven personalization, predictive analytics, and automated engagement to improve customer retention. TAM facilitates the adoption of technology by assisting companies in implementing AI-powered solutions that enhance productivity and user experience(Agbo-Adediran et al. 2025). When combined, they improve engagement and trust by facilitating smooth consumer interactions. While TAM makes sure clients adopt the system, AI-driven CRM improves marketing tactics. Companies gain from improved customer satisfaction, more effective marketing, and a consistent competitive edge. Ultimately, businesses may create enduring connections and propel digital change in the contemporary economy by merging CRM and TAM through prioritization of ICTs and incorporating electronic changes for opportunities in the digital age(Matthew, Kazaure, Kazaure, Nwamouh, et al. 2022). The TAM explains how users adopt technology based on Perceived Usefulness (PU) which point to the extent to which they believe the technology improves performance and Perceived Ease of Use (PEU) that anchored on how simple it is to learn and operate. These factors influence Behavioral Intention (BI), which determines whether users will embrace the technology, ultimately leading to Actual System Use. On the other hand, the CRM focuses on managing relationships between businesses and customers to improve engagement and retention. Key components include Customer Trust, ensuring credibility and dependability; Personalization, tailoring experiences to meet individual customer needs; Customer Satisfaction, enhancing positive interactions for long-term loyalty; and Retention & Advocacy, where satisfied customers promote the brand. The connection between TAM and CRM lies in how technology adoption enhances customer relationships. When customers find technology easy to use and beneficial, their interactions with businesses improve, increasing trust and satisfaction. In turn, CRM strategies help sustain technology adoption by fostering personalized engagement, loyalty, and advocacy. Businesses use CRM to strengthen customer relationships, ensuring continued use of technology-driven services for long-term success.

5.2 Government Revenue Structure for Social Media Monetization Policy

The swift growth of digital marketing and social media monetization in Nigeria has produced a vibrant ecosystem for influencers, companies, marketers, and content producers. Nonetheless, there are issues with revenue accountability, compliance, and equitable taxation in this area due to the lack of organized tax legislation. As the importance of digital transactions increases, Nigeria's social media monetization strategy must apply tax legislation in order to promote economic stability, transparency, sustainable digital entrepreneurship, and government revenue mobilization. Nigerian social media platforms are now a major source of income for advertising, corporations, and content producers with the rise of digital economy(Matthew et al. 2021). Another important source of income is influencer marketing, in which companies work with people who have sizable fan bases to market goods and services. This tactic uses influencers' credibility and trust to increase engagement and sales. Another important component of the revenue structure is digital advertising, which includes email campaigns, display adverts, and search engine marketing. Nigeria's social media monetization revenue structure is determined by laws that guarantee digital platforms support the economy while upholding regulatory control. The government makes money through the framework's license fees, taxes, and compliance requirements. These regulations seek to strike a balance between ethical digital marketing techniques and revenue-generating prospects. Creators can make money through in-stream advertisements, live advertisement promotions, and bonuses on platforms like Facebook, Instagram, and YouTube(Okwudili and Kazaure 2020). Nigerian producers can now make money from reel advertisements and subscriptions through Meta's recent approval of monetization. In Nigeria, a well-organized government income model for social media monetization would promote innovation in brand engineering and digital marketing while guaranteeing steady economic growth. Taxation, licensing, and regulatory fees should be the key focuses of the legislative framework in order to make money and preserve a fair digital economy that grantee equitable income distribution. The implementation of a structured tax system in Nigeria's digital environment will boost government revenue while shielding businesses and content producers from financial inequalities, promoting a fair and competitive digital economy through:

A. **Taxation on Digital Revenue Streams:** Finding taxable income, enforcing compliance, and modernizing antiquated tax regulations are still difficulties, though policies are being improved and brought into line with international best practices. A well-defined tax framework must address multiple monetization avenues, including:
    i. Standardized tax policies for earnings from advertisements, sponsorships, and direct monetization.
    ii. Taxation on businesses leveraging social media for advertising and brand partnerships.
    iii. Revenue collection from e-commerce, advertisement placements, and platform-based financial exchanges.
B. **Tax Incentives for Digital Entrepreneurs:** A balanced tax policy should offer incentives for Nigerian digital entrepreneurs to encourage compliance and business expansion. This includes:
    i. Tax reductions for new businesses investing in digital marketing and content creation.
    ii. Reduced VAT rates on digital products to encourage the growth of local online marketplaces and creative enterprises.
C. **Digital Transaction Monitoring, Licensing and Tax Compliance:** The Nigerian government can monitor social media-based revenue streams with the help of AI-driven regulatory systems as fintech and digital payment platforms expand(E-zeife et al. 2025). Establishing tax reporting guidelines for digital marketers and influencers will guarantee revenue accountability, stop tax evasion, and enhance national revenue collection. Nigerian regulations aimed at monitoring digital platforms and content producers include licensing and compliance costs for social media monetization. Online broadcasters and social media platforms are required to acquire operational licenses from the National Broadcasting Commission (NBC). The Nigerian Communications Commission (NCC) and the Central Bank of Nigeria (CBN) are two organizations that oversee licensing and compliance costs for monetized digital platforms in Nigeria. Respecting regulations such as the Cybercrimes Act for digital security, the Finance Act for taxes, and the Money Laundering Act for anti-money laundering measures is recognized as compliance(Hossain 2023). By ensuring appropriate supervision of digital transactions, monetization policies protect against financial crimes and fraud. The scale and activity of the platform determine the compliance fees, which makes uniform enforcement difficult. Nigeria's efforts to strike a balance

between innovation and regulatory control in its digital economy are reflected in these policies.

i. Businesses and influencers may be required to register for monetization licenses, ensuring compliance.
ii. Platforms enforcing transparency standards in social media advertisements could generate government revenue by guaranteeing responsibility and appropriate taxation.
iii. Governments can better monitor advertisement income and enforce equitable taxation by requiring social media advertisers and digital marketers to reveal spending, targeting strategies, and sponsored content sources through a taskforce office.
iv. Advertisement platform licensing specifications and regulatory compliance costs may provide a steady source of revenue when properly designed, advertisement transparency strengthens government surveillance and promotes a more sustainable digital economy.

5.3 AI Transforms Digital Marketing for Real Estate Investment

AI is transforming real estate investment digital marketing by improving automation, decision-making, and personalization. Predictive analytics driven by AI assists investors in evaluating consumer demand, real estate values, and market trends, resulting in more strategic investment choices. AI-powered chatbots and virtual assistants in marketing increase customer engagement by instantly responding to questions though natural language processing. By examining user behavior, AI-enhanced lead generation maximizes targeting and makes sure that real estate advertisements successfully reach prospective investors or purchasers. Automated property listing analysis is made possible by smart picture identification, which increases the precision of buyers' searches. In addition, machine learning strengthens investor-brand interactions by improving advertising methods through sentiment analysis, automated email campaigns, and customized suggestions. AI-powered customization enables real estate companies to design captivating experiences that maximize their marketing and products advertising investments while drawing in and keeping customers. Real estate investing becomes more successful and data-driven when AI-driven digital marketing optimizes procedures, lowers expenses, boosts productivity, and improves investment decision-making. In digital marketing, the CENT and TAM offer important insights into AI-driven monetization policy. According to (Na et al. 2022), TAM describes how people and organizations embrace new technologies based on two important factors: perceived usefulness (how the technology increases productivity) and perceived ease of use (how easy it is to apply). Businesses and influencers assess AI tools, such chatbots, automated advertising, and predictive analytics, for effectiveness and usability before incorporating them into marketing plans in the context of AI-driven monetization.

Conversely, CENT emphasizes how consumers interact with brands on an emotional, cognitive, and behavioral level(Cheung et al. 2021). Dynamic pricing, adaptive content, and recommendation algorithms are examples of personalized AI-powered marketing that enhances consumer engagement by customizing promotions to each user's interests. As a result, inactive customers become active brand advocates and loyalty and long-term involvement are fostered. The convergence of TAM and CENT demonstrates how companies intentionally use AI monetization capabilities to boost sales and improve client interactions(Bhattacharyya 2023). Adoption success hinges on how well AI technologies meet usability standards, and engagement depends on the capacity to provide a customized and engaging experience. The combination of these theories influences developments in digital marketing and propels the steady expansion of AI-powered revenue. In Nigeria, real estate investment is greatly impacted by the TAM and CENT through AI-driven social media monetization policy. Based on perceived utility and usability, TAM describes how real estate investors and businesses embrace AI-enhanced digital marketing solutions to maximize lead generation and customer engagement(Chen and Ahmed 2025), refer to **Figure 2**. AI-powered strategies that increase consumer trust and interaction, such chatbots, predictive analytics, and tailored advertising, are consistent with the CENT. These developments give real estate companies the ability to improve virtual property presentations, automate queries, and efficiently target potential purchasers. Social media monetization driven by AI increases brand awareness, assisting businesses in generating leads and turning prospects into customers. Adoption is impacted by regulatory policies, though, which demand adherence to moral principles in digital marketing. Real estate investors may increase reach, enhance decision-making, and guarantee sustainable growth in Nigeria's competitive real estate market by incorporating AI into monetization frameworks. Adoption of AI streamlines investments for long-term profitability and increases consumer loyalty.

Figure 2. Technology Acceptance Model (TAM) and Consumer Engagement Theory for Social Monetization Policy, author illustration

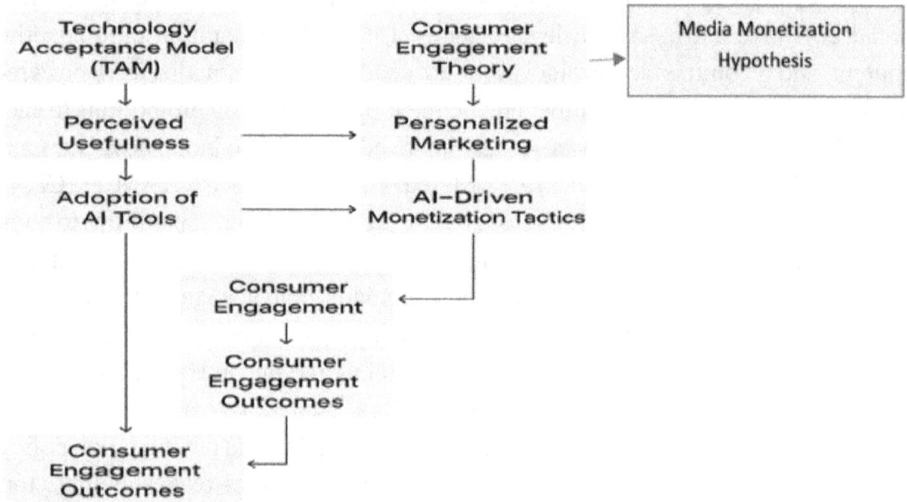

The real estate investment industry is undergoing a transformation through social media digitization and digital marketing caused by AI, which analyzes user behavior and preferences to customize advertisements for increased engagement(Oladiran and Dickins 2024). Real estate investors are able to make more informed decisions by using its capacity to evaluate large datasets and forecast market trends. Machine learning algorithms and predictive analytics are two examples of AI-powered systems that may identify lucrative investment opportunities, evaluate changes in property values, and predict market movements with very high accuracy. AI in digital marketing improves customization and targeting. Chatbots and virtual assistants expedite consumer interactions, providing prompt answers to questions and enhancing customer happiness. To ensure that information is relevant to the intended audience, AI systems examine user behavior to deliver customized adverts and optimize campaign methods. Lead generation and engagement are increased by these tailored strategies. AI also streamlines marketing processes, allowing automated content production systems to create engaging blog posts or property descriptions while saving time and money. Furthermore, social media trends are analyzed by AI-powered software, which aids advertisers in improving their tactics and expanding their reach. Real estate investors can increase their visibility, establish connections with potential customers, and seize profitable chances by combining AI with digital marketing techniques. AI will undoubtedly play a significant part in determining the direction of real estate investing in the future thanks to this combination of sophisticated analytics, tailored marketing, and operational effectiveness.

In Nigeria's real estate investment industry, an AI is transforming social media campaign strategies, especially in the areas of digital marketing and brand engineering, by creating a new social contract between companies and customers(Sharma and Sharma 2024). AI's capacity for data analysis, strategy personalization, and engagement enhancement is what is driving this change. By facilitating tailored marketing, improving consumer interaction, and offering data-driven insights, artificial intelligence is revolutionizing real estate investment industry. Responsible use of AI by real estate companies can improve their social contract with customers, stimulate economic expansion, and position them as industry leaders in brand engineering and digital marketing. By improving engagement, boosting lead generation, and facilitating better investment decision-making, AI is transforming digital marketing in Nigeria's real estate industry. AI-powered tools enable real estate companies to optimize their marketing strategies, target the right audience, and maximize returns on investment. Targeted advertising and audience segmentation uses AI, social media interactions, search patterns, and consumer behavior to deliver personalized property advertisements(Kumar, Ashraf, and Nadeem 2024). Predictive analytics help identify potential buyers and investors, ensuring that marketing efforts are focused on high-conversion prospects for chatbots and virtual assistants for customer engagement. AI-powered chatbots provide round-the-clock support, scheduling property visits, and assisting potential investors through listings in real-time, improving customer experience and increasing lead generation(Kandipati 2025). Automated production and enhancement of content adopts AI to make it easier to create content for real estate listings, such as video marketing, AI-enhanced photos, and property descriptions(Raut, Chandel, and Mittal 2025). Intelligent algorithms raise brand recognition by enhancing content visibility and engagement. Investment insights and predictive market analytics enables real estate companies make well-informed decisions by using AI-driven data analysis to estimate market trends, property appreciation rates, and investment risks. Nigeria's real estate industry may increase productivity, draw in investors, and see long-term growth by using AI into digital marketing efforts.

Figure 3. AI algorithms, consumer engagement strategies, social media platforms, monetization policies, and data analytics

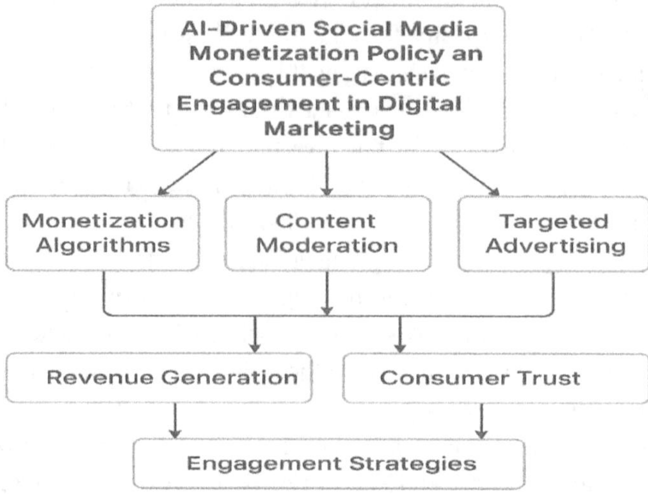

In **Figure 3,** the architecture of AI-Driven Social Media Monetization Policy and Consumer-Centric Engagement in Digital Marketing integrates advanced AI, consumer behavior analytics, monetization policies, and regulatory frameworks to optimize revenue generation and user interaction across social media platforms. This framework revolutionizes digital marketing by combining AI precision, data-driven insights, and policy frameworks to enhance monetization while fostering transparent consumer engagement.

i. **AI-Powered Consumer Engagement**: AI leverages machine learning algorithms to personalize content, predict user preferences, and optimize ad targeting. Chatbots and sentiment analysis tools refine real-time audience interaction, improving engagement metrics.
ii. **Social Media Monetization Strategies**: AI enhances programmatic advertising, influencer marketing, subscription models, and sponsored content promotion. Monetization policies define brand collaboration, content ownership, and revenue-sharing mechanisms.
iii. **Predictive Data Analytics:** AI-driven predictive analytics models analyze engagement trends, optimize pricing, and refine ad placement strategies. Deep learning processes consumer behavior insights to adjust marketing efforts dynamically.
iv. **Cross-Platform AI Integration:** AI synchronizes engagement data across Facebook, Instagram, LinkedIn, Twitter, TikTok, and YouTube, ensuring con-

sistent strategy execution. Automated advertisement tracking improves return on investment (ROI) measurement and marketing efficiency.

6. HYPOTHESIS OF THE STUDY

These hypotheses offer a solid framework for examining the connection between consumer behavior, AI adoption, and social media monetization policy. With regard to policy compliance, consumer engagement, competitive dynamics, and budget optimization, the following hypotheses demonstrate how AI might transform digital marketing strategies in Nigeria digital economy. In this paper, the following Null Hypothesis (H_0) is formulated:

H_1: AI-driven digital marketing tools significantly increase consumer engagement on Nigerian social media platforms compared to traditional marketing methods.
H_2: The effectiveness of social media monetization in Nigeria is positively correlated with the implementation of AI-enhanced advertising strategies.
H_3: Nigerian businesses and content creators utilizing AI-powered marketing experience higher audience retention and engagement rates compared to those relying solely on manual strategies.
H_4: Existing social media monetization policies in Nigeria may hinder the adoption of AI-driven digital marketing depending on their regulatory framework.
H_5: Consumers in Nigeria show greater responsiveness to AI-personalized advertising, leading to increased brand interactions and purchasing decisions.

7. RESEARCH DESIGN

The study employs a structured questionnaire to collect data on social media monetization practices, AI integration, and consumer engagement levels. These questions align with the research hypotheses, ensuring a comprehensive analysis of AI's impact on digital marketing. A descriptive and analytical research approach is adopted to assess the impact of AI on social media monetization. Surveys, interviews, and secondary data analysis help examine AI adoption trends, engagement metrics, and regulatory frameworks as it captures the perceptions and practices of selected participants regarding social media monetization and AI in digital marketing. It emphasizes both AI implementation and its influence on consumer interaction with digital marketing strategies in real estate product branding. Analyzing the effectiveness of AI-driven strategies in increasing consumer engagement within the context of social media monetization policies in Nigeria, the research focus specifically on the real estate sector. The study includes 10 real estate companies selected from 15 medium-scale real estate firms operating in the study area.

8. RESEARCH METHODOLOGY

The methodology for Social Media Monetization Policy in Nigeria: Increasing Consumer Engagement in Digital Marketing with AI followed a mixed-methodology approach. It combines qualitative and quantitative research to provide a comprehensive analysis of AI-driven marketing strategies, consumer engagement patterns, and policy implications.

8.1 Method of Data Collection

i. **Primary Data:** Structured questionnaires and interviews with Nigerian real estate businesses, content creators, policymakers, and consumers provide insights into social media monetization practices.
ii. **Secondary Data:** Gather industry reports and existing literature on social media monetization, AI application in digital marketing, and its influence within Nigeria's real estate market.

8.2 Sampling Techniques

A purposive sampling method was applied to select the 10 participating companies. These companies were chosen based on their relevance to the study objectives, their operational scale, and their presence on social media. The remaining five companies were excluded due to either a lack of substantial activity in AI-driven digital marketing or logistical constraints. A purposive sampling method was chosen to target businesses and influencers actively engaged in social media monetization. While this approach ensures relevant insights, its limitation lies in the potential lack of generalizability to all Nigerian real estate businesses.

8.3 Questionnaire Recovery Rate

The distribute questionnaires to the selected companies, and of the responses collected, 75% were retrieved and deemed suitable for data analysis.

8.4 Analysis Methods

The Chi-Square test was selected to assess the relationship between AI-driven marketing strategies and consumer engagement levels. This test is appropriate for categorical data, allowing for the evaluation of significant associations between monetization techniques and audience interaction. For the questionnaire data (quantitative), the study applied descriptive statistical analysis to summarize key trends and calculate frequencies and percentages. To perform inferential analysis, the study adopted Chi-square to establish potential correlations between AI usage and consumer engagement metrics that portray digital marketing economic impacts. For open-ended responses (qualitative), the study used thematic analysis to identify recurring patterns, sentiments, or ideas related to social media monetization and AI tools recommendations for enhanced marketing strategies in the real estate sector. To create a Chi-Square distribution table for the study, the authors focused on hypothetical categories like observed and expected data points based on the 10 selected real estate companies in the study area. The Chi-Square distribution is typically used to test whether there is a significant association between variables that evaluated the extent to which AI tools impact consumer engagement and digital marketing outcomes.

Table 1. Chi-Square distribution

Category	*Observed (O)*	*Expected(E)*	*(O-E)*	*$(O-E)^2$*	*$(O-E)^2/E$*
Social Media Advertisements (AI-based)	30	35	-5	25	0.714
Businesses using AI-Driven Monetization	25	20	5	25	1.15
Chatbots (AI-based)	40	45	-5	25	0.556
Personalized Offers(AI)	55	50	5	25	0.500
Traditional Marketing	20	15	5	25	1.667
Total	**170**	**165**			**4.687**

From table 1, Observed **(O)** is real data from the collected questionnaires, **Expected (E)** is the Hypothetical or calculated values based on historical trends. The computed Chi-Square value with the critical value from the Chi-Square distribution table at a given degree of freedom (df) and significance level (0.05). Degrees of freedom = Number of categories - 1 (5 - 1 = 4). If the Chi-Square value exceeds the critical value, reject the null hypothesis (suggesting a significant relationship between variables).

8.5 Study Hypothesis

Null Hypothesis (H_0): AI-driven social media monetization policies significantly affect consumer engagement in digital marketing among medium-scale real estate companies in Nigeria.
Alternative Hypothesis (H_1): AI-driven social media monetization policies do not significantly affect consumer engagement in digital marketing among medium-scale real estate companies in Nigeria.

First, AI-powered digital marketing tools are expected to significantly boost consumer engagement compared to traditional methods by offering personalized content and predictive analytics. Second, the study hypothesizes that social media monetization in Nigeria correlates positively with AI-enhanced advertising, as AI optimizes advertisement targeting and audience segmentation. Third, businesses and content creators utilizing AI-driven strategies may experience higher audience retention and engagement rates, improving overall profitability. Fourth, Nigerian social media monetization policies may either facilitate or hinder AI adoption depending on their regulatory framework. Policies supporting AI innovation could accelerate digital marketing transformation, while restrictive regulations may slow industry growth. Lastly, Nigerian consumers are expected to show greater responsiveness to AI-personalized advertising, leading to increased brand interactions and purchasing decisions. These hypotheses guide the study in evaluating AI's impact on business performance, consumer behavior, regulatory challenges, and market competitiveness within Nigeria's digital economy. The Chi-Square test examines whether AI-driven social media monetization policies significantly influence consumer engagement among Nigerian real estate firms. With 5 categories, the degrees of freedom (df) are 4. At a 0.05 significance level, the critical value is 9.488. The computed Chi-Square value, 4.687, is less than the critical value, leading to the failure to reject the null hypothesis. Since the computed Chi-Square value is less than the critical value at the (df) and significance level, we fail to reject the null hypothesis (H_0). This indicates that the data shows agreement that provide enough evidence to conclude a significant relationship between AI-driven social media monetization policies and consumer engagement for medium-scale real estate companies in Nigeria. This result suggests that AI-driven strategies are present, their influence on consumer engagement requires further exploration or might be supplemented by other factors (e.g., market trends, company strategies).

9. DISCUSSION OF RESEARCH FINDINGS

The Table 2 highlights the impact of AI-driven digital marketing strategies on revenue generation for medium-scale real estate companies in Nigeria. Before implementing data-driven product engineering digital marketing, companies generated lower revenues, ranging between 15 million and 30 million. However, after adopting AI-enhanced marketing techniques, revenue increased significantly, reaching 45 million to 100 million per company. The revenue growth across all 10 selected companies ranged from 194% to 250%, demonstrating that AI-driven marketing improves consumer engagement and business profitability. The results indicate that businesses investing in AI-powered digital strategies gain a competitive advantage in monetizing social media platforms effectively.

Table 2. Revenue impact of data-driven product engineering and digital marketing

Real Estate Company	Revenue Before Digital Marketing (N Million)	Revenue After Digital Marketing(N Million)	Revenue Increase (%)
Company A	15	45	200%
Company B	25	80	220%
Company C	30	100	233%
Company D	22	65	195%
Company E	18	55	206%
Company F	28	90	221%
Company G	20	70	250%
Company H	26	85	227%
Company I	24	75	213%
Company J	17	50	194%

The tax implications of increased social media monetization and AI-driven digital marketing in Nigeria are significant for the government. As businesses and content creators experience higher revenues due to AI-enhanced marketing, their tax liabilities also increase, contributing to national revenue growth. AI-driven social media monetization strengthens tax revenue across Company Income Tax (CIT), Personal Income Tax (PIT), Value Added Tax (VAT), and digital services. However, the government must also adapt policies to regulate AI's financial impact effectively.

i. **Increased Corporate & Income Tax Revenue:** Medium-scale real estate companies that experience higher earnings (45M– 100M) post- AI implementation must pay more corporate taxes under Nigeria's CIT, which is 30%

of taxable profits for large businesses. Digital entrepreneurs, influencers, and small businesses monetizing content may face higher PIT obligations, boosting tax collections for the government.

ii. **VAT Expansion for Digital Services:** AI-driven digital marketing increases product sales and ad revenues, leading to higher VAT contributions at 7.5% for online transactions. If companies monetize social media platforms through digital advertisements, subscription-based content, or e-commerce, the government benefits from VAT on these services.

iii. **Potential New Tax Regulations on AI-driven Marketing**: Nigerian tax authorities may expand existing tax frameworks to regulate AI-driven advertising models and data-driven monetization strategies, ensuring compliance. Social media platforms generating revenue in Nigeria may face digital service taxes, currently at 6%, enhancing government income.

iv. **Increased Government Spending on AI Regulation & Enforcement:** As AI reshapes digital marketing, the Nigerian government might invest in tax monitoring systems to track AI-based transactions, requiring policy adjustments and tax enforcement measures.

10. FUTURE RESEARCH FOCUS

To improve customer trust and engagement, ethical AI, hyper-personalization, and sustainable monetization should be given top priority in future research on AI-driven digital marketing. In order to ensure fairness in AI-driven marketing initiatives, studies should address algorithmic biases. Personalized user experiences can be enhanced by developments in emotion recognition, sentiment analysis and predictive analytics. To improve openness and confidence in online transactions, researchers should also look into safe monetization strategies like blockchain solutions driven by AI. Maintaining innovation and promoting customer-focused digital engagement will require striking a balance between profitability and moral AI practices. This strategy will encourage ethical AI deployment in marketing and long-term industry resilience. In addition, future research on AI-Driven Social Media Monetization Policy and Consumer-Centric Engagement in Digital Marketing should focus on TAM and CET to optimize user adoption and interaction. By integrating TAM and CET, future research can refine AI-driven monetization strategies, ensuring user-friendly, ethical, and sustainable digital marketing practices.

11. STUDY RECOMMENDATION

Five key research recommendations from the study on AI-Driven Social Media Monetization Policy and Consumer-Centric Engagement in Digital Marketing in Nigeria, includes:

i. **Regulatory Framework Development**: The government should establish clear AI-driven monetization policies to ensure ethical advertising and consumer protection.
ii. **Financial Inclusion & SME Support:** Government should back AI initiatives that can empower SMEs in digital monetization and maintain a flexible tax/levy revenue instrumentation.
iii. **Balancing Profitability with Consumer Trust:** Implementing sustainable AI monetization models that prioritize ethical advertising while ensuring revenue growth.
iv. **Refining AI-Driven Consumer Personalization:** There should be exploration of adaptive AI algorithms that offer real-time personalized content, improving user engagement and brand loyalty.
v. **Optimizing Predictive Analytics for Consumer Engagement:** There should be refined AI-powered predictive models and sentiments analysis to anticipate user preferences and optimize monetization strategies.

12. CONCLUSION

The study highlights the transformative role of AI in enhancing social media monetization in Nigeria by optimizing digital marketing strategies and consumer engagement. AI-driven tools improve targeted advertising, personalize user interactions, and maximize revenue generation for businesses and content creators. However, the effectiveness of AI adoption depends on Nigeria's regulatory framework, data privacy considerations, and consumer trust. Policymakers must create supportive policies that balance innovation with ethical AI use. By leveraging AI effectively, Nigerian businesses can gain a competitive edge in digital marketing, fostering a dynamic and sustainable social media economy. Future research should explore AI's long-term impact on engagement trends. This study explored the role of AI-driven social media monetization policies in enhancing consumer engagement within the Nigerian digital marketing landscape, with a focus on medium-scale real estate companies. The analysis revealed that while AI-powered strategies such as personalized recommendations, chatbots, and targeted advertisements are increasingly utilized, their measurable impact on consumer engagement maintained optimism.

Based on the survey distributed to 10 selected real estate firms, a 75% response rate provided data for analysis. The Chi-Square test was applied to examine the relationship between AI-driven monetization strategies and consumer engagement. The computed Chi-Square value (4.687) was lower than the critical value (9.488) at a 0.05 significance level, leading to the failure to reject the null hypothesis. This result indicates statistically significant relationship between AI-driven social media monetization and consumer engagement in the sample studied. These findings suggest that AI strategies alone may not suffice to drive consumer engagement in digital marketing. The study on AI-Driven Social Media Monetization Policy and Consumer-Centric Engagement in Digital Marketing demonstrates how AI integrates TAM, CRM, and CET to improve monetization approaches. AI-driven monetization techniques improve customer targeting, maximize ad placements, and boost brand loyalty to guarantee steady revenue growth. In order to strike a balance between consumer trust and personalization, ethical AI policies are essential. The working together of CENT and TAM demonstrates how companies may strategically use AI monetization solutions to improve customer connections and increase revenue. While engagement depends on the capacity to provide a customized and engaging experience, successful adoption depends on how effectively AI technologies match usability expectations. Collectively, these theories influence advancements in digital marketing and propel steady expansion in AI-powered revenue.

REFERENCES

Abtahi, A., Shafique, T., Haque, T., Siam, S. A. J., & Rahman, A. (2023). Exploring consumer preferences: The significance of personalization in e-commerce. Malaysian E Commerce Journal (MECJ), 8(1), 01-07.

Adeyinka, K. I., Takunda, C. O., & Adeyinka, T. I. (2024). Artificial Intelligence (AI) Algorithms in Nigeria's Integrated Marketing Communications. In *AI-Driven Marketing Research and Data Analytics* (pp. 67–81). IGI Global. DOI: 10.4018/979-8-3693-2165-2.ch004

Agbo-Adediran, I., Adeusi, O. C., Bello, A. B., & Afolabi, O. N. (2025). Analyzing the Impact of AI adoption and ICT Platforms in improving Customer Engagement of Small and Medium-Sized Enterprises (SMEs). *Applied Sciences, Computing, and Energy*, *2*(2), 284–298.

Amuda-Kannike, A., & Amuda-Kannike, Y. (2025). A Critical Examination of the Legal and Institutional Framework for Protection of E-Consumers Rights in Nigeria. *Journal of Commercial and Property Law*, *12*(1), 24–36.

Babics, I., & Jermolajeva, E. (2024). Development of Social Platforms and New Opportunities in Digital Marketing. *Complex Systems Informatics and Modeling Quarterly*, (41), 22–39. DOI: 10.7250/csimq.2024-41.02

Bhattacharyya, S. S. (2023). Monetization of customer futures through machine learning and artificial intelligence based persuasive technologies. Journal of science and technology policy management, 14(4), 734-757.

Bilgin, F., Hadziahmetovic, N., & Tandir, N. (2025). From Compensation to Commitment: Dynamic Capabilities as Bridges to Ethical Climates in Nigerian Private Education. *Compensation and Benefits Review*, *57*(2), 08863687251320140. DOI: 10.1177/08863687251320140

Binsaeed, R. H., Yousaf, Z., Grigorescu, A., Chitescu, R. I., Nassani, A. A., & Samoila, A. (2023). Customer engagement and customer relationship management capabilities' effects on innovation performance and customer distrust's moderating role. *Sustainability*, *15*(12), 9475.

Bruce, M. R., Adekoya, A. F., Boateng, S., & Appiahene, P. (2023). Prevalent user-centered monetization techniques in social media. *International Review of Management and Marketing*, *13*(1), 19–28.

Chen, S.-H., & Ahmed, F. (2025). The transformative power of AI and AR in customer-centric services in the tourism and hospitality sector: Looking back to predict the future outlook. In *Managing customer-centric strategies in the digital landscape* (pp. 105–138). IGI Global.

Cheng, C. F., Huang, C. C., Lin, M. C., & Chen, T. C. (2023). Exploring effectiveness of relationship marketing on artificial intelligence adopting intention. *SAGE Open*, *13*(4), 21582440231222760.

Cheung, M. L., Pires, G. D., Rosenberger, P. J., Leung, W. K. S., & Salehhuddin Sharipudin, M.-N. (2021). The role of consumer-consumer interaction and consumer-brand interaction in driving consumer-brand engagement and behavioral intentions. *Journal of Retailing and Consumer Services*, *61*, 102574. DOI: 10.1016/j.jretconser.2021.102574

Corren, E. (2022). The Consent Burden in Consumer and Digital Markets. *Harv. JL & Tech*, (36), 551.

Egbuhuzor, N. S., Ajayi, A. J., Akhigbe, E. E., Agbede, O. O., Ewim, C. P. M., & Ajiga, D. I. (2025). AI and data-driven insights: Transforming customer relationship management (CRM) in financial services. *Gulf Journal of Advance Business Research*, *3*(2), 483–511.

Elhai, W. (2020). Regulating digital harm across Borders: Exploring a content platform commission. Paper read at International Conference on Social Media and Society.

Ezeife, E., Kokogho, E., Odio, P. E., & Adeyanju, M. O. (2025). Agile tax technology development in the US: A conceptual framework for scalable and efficient enterprise solutions. *Gulf Journal of Advance Business Research*, *3*(2), 512–526.

Fatokun, B. O. (2023). *Customers' Affective Responses Towards the Key Factors Influencing E-Commerce Adoption: Extended Technology Acceptance Model (TAM) Approach*. Liverpool John Moores University.

Gu, F., Gao, J., Zhu, X., & Ye, J. (2023). The impact of digital inclusive finance on SMEs' technological innovation activities—Empirical analysis based on the data of new third board enterprises. *PLoS One*, *18*(11), e0293500.

Hossain, M. B. (2023). Acquiring an awareness of the latest regulatory developments concerning digital assets and anti-money laundering. *Journal of Money Laundering Control*, *26*(6), 1261–1268.

Ikenga, U. G., & Egbule, C. N. (2024). Strategic Model for Effective Digital Entrepreneurship for Small Business. In *New Strategy Models in Digital Entrepreneurship* (pp. 53–70). IGI Global. DOI: 10.4018/979-8-3693-3743-1.ch004

Iqbal, M. N., & Jan, M. T. (2025). AI-Powered Business Strategies for Enhancing Consumer Behavior and Brand Loyalty in the Bancassurance Sector. In *Elevating Brand Loyalty With Optimized Marketing Analytics and AI* (pp. 101–132). IGI Global Scientific Publishing. DOI: 10.4018/979-8-3693-9954-5.ch006

Iroka, N. A., & Nwaizugbo, I. C. (2024). Digital marketing channels and customer patronage of online shops. *UNIZIK Journal of Marketing*, *1*(4), 53–76.

Kandipati, A. (2025). A Systematic Literature Review on Artificial Intelligence Based Techniques for Nurturing Operations in Real Estate Sector. *Journal of Real Estate Literature*, •••, 1–26. DOI: 10.1080/09277544.2025.2466370

Kobets, K., Terentieva, N., Shkvyria, N., Lysytsia, N., & Siemak, I. (2024). Digitalization and its impact on the development of contemporary marketing strategies. *Economic Affairs*, *69*(2), 1021–1040.

Kumar, V., & Abdul, R. (2024). AI-powered marketing: What, where, and how? *International Journal of Information Management*, *77*, 102783. DOI: 10.1016/j.ijinfomgt.2024.102783

Matthew, U. O., Kazaure, J. S., & Haruna, K. (2020). Multimedia information system (MIS) for knowledge generation and ICT policy framework in education: Innovative sustainable educational investment. [IJICTHD]. *International Journal of Information Communication Technologies and Human Development*, *12*(3), 28–58.

Matthew, U. O., Kazaure, J. S., John, O., & Haruna, K. (2021). Telecommunication Business Information System and Investment Ecosystem in a Growing Economy: A Review of Telecom Investment in Nigeria. [IJICTHD]. *International Journal of Information Communication Technologies and Human Development*, *13*(2), 1–20.

Matthew, U. O., Kazaure, A. S., Kazaure, J. S., Hassan, I. M., Nwanakwaugwu, A. C., & Okafor, N. U. (2022). Educational technology adaptation & implication for media technology adoption in the period of COVID-19. *Journal of Trends in Computer Science and Smart Technology*, *4*(4), 226–245.

Matthew, U. O., Kazaure, J. S., Kazaure, A. S., Nwamouh, U. C., & Chinonso, A. (2022). ICT Policy Implementation as Correlate for Achieving Educational Sustainability: Approaching Development in Multi ICT Dimensions. *Journal of Information Technology*, *4*(4), 250–269.

Matthew, U. O., Kazaure, J. S., Ndukwu, C. C., Ebong, G. N., Nwanakwaugwu, A. C., & Nwamouh, U. C. (2024). Artificial Intelligence Educational Pedagogy Development: ICT Pedagogy Development for Education 5.0. In *Educational Perspectives on Digital Technologies in Modeling and Management* (pp. 65–93). IGI Global. DOI: 10.4018/979-8-3693-2314-4.ch003

Na, S., Heo, S., Han, S., Shin, Y., & Roh, Y. (2022). Acceptance model of artificial intelligence (AI)-based technologies in construction firms: Applying the Technology Acceptance Model (TAM) in combination with the Technology–Organisation–Environment (TOE) framework. *Buildings (Basel, Switzerland)*, *12*(2), 90.

Nadler, A., & McGuigan, L. (2018). An impulse to exploit: The behavioral turn in data-driven marketing. *Critical Studies in Media Communication*, *35*(2), 151–165.

Nozari, H., Movahed, A. B., & Movahed, A. B. (2024). The AIoE Revolution: Redefining Organizational Maturity in a Hyper-Connected World. *Applied Innovations in Industrial Management*, *4*(1), 10–17.

Nurgalieva, L., Frik, A., & Doherty, G. (2023). A narrative review of factors affecting the implementation of privacy and security practices in software development. *ACM Computing Surveys*, *55*(14s), 1–27.

Nwanakwaugwu, A. C., Matthew, U. O., Kazaure, A. A., & Haruna, K. (2023). Data Mining Business Intelligence Applications in Retail Services Using Artificial Neural Networks. In *Handbook of Research on Cybersecurity Risk in Contemporary Business Systems* (pp. 186–210). IGI Global. DOI: 10.4018/978-1-6684-7207-1.ch010

Obia, V. (2025). Digital policy and Nigeria's Platform Code of Practice: Towards a radical co-regulatory turn. *Data & Policy*, *7*(7), e12. DOI: 10.1017/dap.2025.1

Okwudili, U. M., & Kazaure, J. S. (2020). Digital activism and digital revolution in objective journalism. [IJICST]. *International Journal of Interactive Communication Systems and Technologies*, *10*(2), 39–56.

Oladiran, O., & Dickins, L. (2024). *PropTech and Real Estate Innovations: A Guide to Digital Technologies and Solutions in the Built Environment*. Taylor & Francis. DOI: 10.1201/9781003262725

Olatunji, F., Sajuyigbe, A. S., Tella, R. A., Oke, O. D., Babalola, O. A., & Adebayo, W. (2025). Assessing The Impact of Financial Service Digitalization on SME Businesses In Lagos, Nigeria. *Journal of Entrepreneurship and Business*, *6*(1), 94–118.

Oyedokun, T. T. (2025). Digitally Enhanced World of Realities: Immersive Technologies and Innovative Business Models. In *AI-Driven Business Model Innovation* (pp. 37–70). IGI Global Scientific Publishing. DOI: 10.4018/979-8-3693-9571-4.ch002

Oyekunle, D. O. T., Okwudili Matthew, U., Preston, D., & Boohene, D. (2024). Trust beyond technology algorithms: A theoretical exploration of consumer trust and behavior in technological consumption and AI projects. *Journal of Computer and Communications*, *12*(06), 10–4236.

Patil, D. 2024. "Generative Artificial Intelligence In Marketing And Advertising: Advancing Personalization And Optimizing Consumer Engagement Strategies." *Available at SSRN* 5057404.

Prasetyo, Y. T., Susanto, K. C., Chuang, K.-H., Yin, R.-T., Chen, J.-W., Zhang, Y.-X., Benito, O. P., & John A Belmonte, Z. (2025). Factors influencing the perceived usability of line pay: An extended technology acceptance model approach. *Acta Psychologica*, *255*, 104924. DOI: 10.1016/j.actpsy.2025.104924 PMID: 40090060

Raut, S., Chandel, A., & Mittal, S. (2025). Enhancing marketing and brand communication with AI-driven content creation. In *AI, corporate social responsibility, and marketing in modern organizations* (pp. 139–172). IGI Global Scientific Publishing.

Sathyavani, B., Kalyan, N. B., Peddinti, D. R., Bihade, V., & Tiwari, A. (2025). Next-Generation CRM: AI, IoT, and the Future of Customer Relationship Management. Paper read at 2025 International Conference on Pervasive Computational Technologies (ICPCT).

Sharma, A. K., & Sharma, R. (2024). How artificial intelligence is transforming social media marketing: Analysing its potential and addressing concerns. *Journal of Cultural Marketing Strategy*, *9*(1), 75–90.

Singh, P., Das, L., Bahubal, D., Rani, S., & Kumar, A. (2023). AI/ML Revolutionizing social media and Business: A Comprehensive Study. In *Security and Risk Analysis for Intelligent Cloud Computing* (pp. 252–279). CRC Press.

Torres, A. I., Darkio, L. S. P., Santos, J. D., & Pires, P. B. (2025). Return on AI: Mapping and Exploring ROI. In *Tangible Measures." In Leveraging AI for Effective Digital Relationship Marketing* (pp. 353–384). IGI Global.

Umoh, E. (2024). "The Impact of Artificial Intelligence on Public Administration in the Public Sector: Opportunities and Challenges." *The Impact of Artificial Intelligence on Public Administration in the Public Sector: Opportunities and Challenges (November 11, 2024)*.

Uzomah, M. M., & Eruetemu, P. O. (2024). Artificial intelligence and digital economy and the economic state of Nigerians. *Journal of Emerging Technologies*, *4*(1), 26–35.

Xia, Y., Liu, Z., Wang, S., Huang, C., & Zhao, W. (2024). Unlocking the impact of user experience on AI-powered mobile advertising engagement. *Journal of the Knowledge Economy*, *16*(1), 1–37. DOI: 10.1007/s13132-024-02153-y

Chapter 9
Analyzing and Optimizing Customer Interactions in Smart Cities Using IoT Data Synchronization and Temporal Neural Networks (RNN)

Hamed Nozari
https://orcid.org/0000-0002-6500-6708
Bio10, Dubai, UAE

ABSTRACT

This research presents an intelligent framework for analyzing and optimizing customer interactions in smart cities, which is based on the combination of real-time Internet of Things (IoT) data and recurrent neural networks (RNN). By synchronizing multi-source data and utilizing the LSTM model, it is possible to predict consumer behavior and design personalized marketing campaigns. The results show that the proposed framework is capable of extracting spatial-temporal behavioral patterns with high accuracy and can be used as a basis for real-time marketing decision-making in smart cities.

DOI: 10.4018/979-8-3373-3775-3.ch009

1- INTRODUCTION

In recent decades, with the development of emerging technologies in the field of Internet of Things (IoT) and Artificial Intelligence (AI), the form of interactions between consumers and urban environments has also undergone profound changes. Smart cities, as platforms for the convergence of these technologies, have enabled the real-time recording, analysis, and exploitation of citizens' behavioral data; especially in the field of marketing, which is highly dependent on a precise understanding of consumers' needs, preferences, and situations. In such platforms, the use of IoT infrastructures and its combination with machine learning models provides a dynamic and adaptive approach to understanding customer behavior (Nozari, Abdi, & Szmelter-Jarosz, 2025).

With the development of environmental sensors, urban beacons, smart cameras, and wearable devices, a huge volume of spatial, temporal, and interactive data is being generated at the city level. These data, which are collected continuously and with nonlinear structures, have paved the way for the design of algorithms that can extract customer behavioral patterns at temporal and spatial scales. However, processing such data requires architectures that can well understand the sequences and temporal dependencies between different events and model the dynamics of consumer behavior over time (Aliahmadi & Nozari, 2023).

Meanwhile, recurrent neural networks (RNN), especially in types such as LSTM (Long Short-Term Memory), have high power in time series modeling due to their memory-based structure. Unlike traditional algorithms that often rely on static data, these models have the ability to identify long-term dependencies between consecutive behaviors and, based on that, provide accurate predictions of future user behavior (Nozari & Samadi, 2025). In urban environments, where consumer behavior is influenced by parameters such as location, time, weather conditions, population density, and even momentary events, such a structure can meet complex analytical needs.

From a marketing perspective, focusing on real-time customer behavior is of strategic importance, especially in highly volatile and multi-source environments such as smart cities. In many cases, the success of an advertising campaign or sales offer directly depends on the precise timing and personalization of content. For example, analyzing the path customers take, how long they spend at certain points, how they respond to environmental or app messages, and ultimately make a purchase are all behaviors that can be understood to increase marketing effectiveness (Nozari, Szmelter-Jarosz, & Ghahremani-Nahr, 2021). This analysis is only possible when heterogeneous and real-time data is accurately synchronized and a model is used that is capable of processing such complex patterns.

Previous studies have either focused on analyzing historical transactional data or have used static classification methods to segment customers. In contrast, AIoT and deep learning-based approaches, especially by using adaptive structures, enable real-time analysis and instantaneous response to consumer behavior (Nozari, Irani, & Rahmaty, 2023). This development has paved the way for the formation of a new generation of smart marketing that, by analyzing time series and using dynamic predictions, has the ability to actively intervene in the customer interaction process instead of static decision-making.

The present study presents a conceptual and operational framework for analyzing and optimizing customer interactions in the context of smart cities. This framework is based on the synchronization of multi-source IoT data and time series modeling using the structure of LSTM recurrent neural networks. The purpose of developing this architecture is to identify spatio-temporal patterns of consumer interactions, predict future behavior, and provide real-time recommendations for urban marketing decision-makers. The proposed framework consists of four main layers: data collection from various sources, data synchronization and preprocessing, time series analysis using LSTM, and generation of usable outputs for adaptive marketing systems (Najafi, Nozari, & Edalatpanah, 2022).

Next, the proposed model is evaluated on a set of mixed data including real and simulated information. The model performance is measured in terms of accuracy, predictability, and ability to extract meaningful behavioral patterns compared to reference algorithms. In addition, using visual analyses such as heat maps and comparative graphs, the interpretation of the model output in the context of a smart city and its ability to support marketing decisions will be examined. The ultimate goal of this research is to present a hybrid approach between technology, data analysis, and consumer behavior that can, on the one hand, adapt to the current conditions of the city, and on the other hand, open new horizons in the design of learning-based marketing campaigns (Irani & Nozari, 2024).

In this regard, this article attempts to address the technical challenges of IoT data processing and time series analysis, while also testing the feasibility of using deep neural networks to optimize the interactive behavior of urban customers; an approach that can be of strategic value not only for marketers, but also for urban managers and smart system designers.

2- LITERATURE REVIEW

In recent years, the development of urban infrastructure centered on emerging technologies such as the Internet of Things (IoT), artificial intelligence (AI), and machine learning has fundamentally changed the way customers interact with the urban environment and brands. In such a situation, the concept of marketing in smart cities is no longer limited to traditional digital channels but has become a continuous, real-time experience based on environmental data. This development has doubled the need to review customer behavior analysis methods and has paved the way for the emergence of hybrid approaches between data engineering and behavioral sciences in marketing (Movahed, Movahed, & Nozari, 2024).

The existing literature on marketing in the context of smart cities increasingly focuses on integrating multi-source and real-time data with predictive models. Among the common trends in this field is the use of spatial and temporal data obtained from urban sensors to analyze traffic flows, identify high-traffic spots, and design targeted advertising strategies (Nozari & Chobar, 2024). Collected through beacons, mobile phone GPS, city cameras, and even wearable devices, this data provides a detailed view of users' routes, stops, and behavioral responses to environmental events.

However, one of the key challenges in analyzing such data is the temporal and structural heterogeneity between different data sources. Data from mobile applications may be recorded at a different frequency than data from city cameras or payment transactions. In this regard, data synchronization and creating a unified view of customer interactions have been proposed as a prerequisite for any meaningful analysis (Nozari, Szmelter-Jarosz, & Rahmaty, 2024). Some studies have developed algorithms to temporally align data, while others have used graph architectures or spatiotemporal models to organize the information.

In the post-synchronization stage, the selection of an appropriate analytical model to extract behavioral patterns from continuous data is the second challenge in this field. In this context, recurrent neural networks (RNN) and their advanced variants such as LSTM and GRU have been proposed as a superior option to static or classification-based models due to their ability to understand temporal dependencies and behavior dynamics during the sequence (Nozari, 2025). These networks are able to store past information in their memory and use it to analyze the current situation and predict future events; a feature that is quite useful for analyzing sequential customer behaviors such as entering the range, pausing, purchasing, and exiting.

Research using LSTM in marketing has mainly focused on predicting purchase intention, response time to advertisements, or identifying optimal points for marketing interventions. These studies have shown that recurrent models can outperform classical models, especially in analyzing hidden behaviors of customers who deviate from conventional routes (Movahed, Movahed, & Nozari, 2024). In addition, some studies have used LSTM together with environmental data such as temperature, weather conditions, or regional congestion to increase the accuracy of behavioral analysis through multi-input models. In addition to deep learning models, other literature has also investigated the combination of real-time recommender systems with IoT data. These approaches have been mainly implemented in the context of smart stores, shopping malls, or transportation stations and have attempted to provide marketing recommendations based on the user's current location, behavioral history, and environmental conditions (Nozari, Abdi, & Jahangard, 2025). In this context, the combination of data from wearable devices with purchase data and digital interactions has enabled the delivery of personalized advertising in an unprecedented way.

Despite these advances, many studies have focused on simplified or static datasets due to the complexity of the data structure and the lack of unified standards for synchronizing multiple sources. For this reason, there is a clear gap in the literature dedicated to the complete, real-time, and synchronized analysis of customer behavior at the city scale with accurate time series modeling (Nozari, Rahmaty, & Szmelter-Jarosz, 2024). This gap is especially noticeable in the combined analysis of environmental, spatial, and interaction data, where the use of traditional models or asynchronous architectures alone is not adequate.

On the other hand, advances in urban infrastructure and the expansion of concepts such as edge computing and on-device processing have also created a new space for the application of deep learning algorithms at the city level. These technologies enable fast and real-time data analysis without the need to transfer to central servers, which is crucial for rapid market intervention in high-traffic environments (Kalogeras, 2025). Integrating these technologies with RNN models and using architectures that can process multi-source input data simultaneously is one of the development paths in this field.

Finally, some recent studies have moved towards combining recurrent models with more complex architectures such as Transformers and attention mechanisms. These models, which were initially developed in the field of natural language, have recently been considered for the analysis of behavioral interactions. However, their high computational complexity and the need for large data sets have prevented them from finding a clear place in IoT-based urban architectures (Nozari, Abdi, & Rafiei, 2025). Therefore, the use of LSTM as a model that balances complexity, accuracy, and deployability is currently the dominant solution in smart city analytics projects.

In summary, the literature review shows that although numerous studies have investigated different aspects of smart marketing in connected cities, the precise and operational combination of IoT data synchronization process with deep time series modeling for predicting and optimizing consumer interactions remains a relatively virgin and high-potential area. By focusing on this conceptual and operational gap, the present study attempts to provide an implementable framework for real-time analysis of customer behavior in the context of smart cities.

3- CONCEPTUAL FRAMEWORK

In this study, a conceptual framework is proposed to analyze and optimize customer interactions in the context of smart cities. This framework is based on the synchronization of real-time data from urban IoT sensors and their analysis using temporal neural networks (RNN), and its main focus is on identifying hidden behavioral patterns in sequential user interactions in urban physical-digital environments. The ultimate goal of this framework is to provide a platform for intelligent marketing decision-making that is adaptable to the current conditions of users.

The overall structure of this framework consists of four main layers, which are shown in Figure 1. In the first layer, data is collected from a wide range of IoT sources in smart cities. These sources include location sensors (GPS), urban cameras, beacons installed in stores or public spaces, mobile applications, as well as wearable devices such as smartwatches and health trackers. Each of these sources provides data such as time and place of presence, movement path, visit to a specific location, touch of digital pages, user pause at a specific point, type of purchase made, and instantaneous response to advertisements.

In the second step, the synchronization layer acts as the hub for connecting diverse data sources. This layer uses techniques such as timestamp alignment, location matching, feature normalization, and noise removal to transform heterogeneous data into a uniform and analyzable structure. The main goal of this layer is to create a continuous and coherent sequence of users' temporal interactions with the environment so that it can be used for accurate modeling.

In the third layer, the prepared data is fed into recurrent neural network (RNN) models. The basic structure of these models is designed based on LSTM or GRU so that they can accurately identify and analyze long-term temporal dependencies in customer interactions. The proposed model is configured to process sequences of customer behavior, such as when a user enters a commercial area, pauses for a few moments, receives an advertisement, and then makes a purchase. All of these steps are stored as a time sequence in the model and analyzed by the neural network.

In the output layer, the model results include predicting future interactions, estimating the probability of a positive response to real-time advertisements, identifying recurring behavioral patterns, and providing time-based recommendations for marketing interventions. These outputs can be used in real-time marketing systems, decision-support dashboards for city managers, or real-time recommendation engines. The framework also has the ability to dynamically adapt to environmental and behavioral changes, so that it can adapt to new conditions and maintain its efficiency by continuously analyzing new data.

Figure 1. Proposed AIoT-based framework for optimizing customer interactions in smart cities

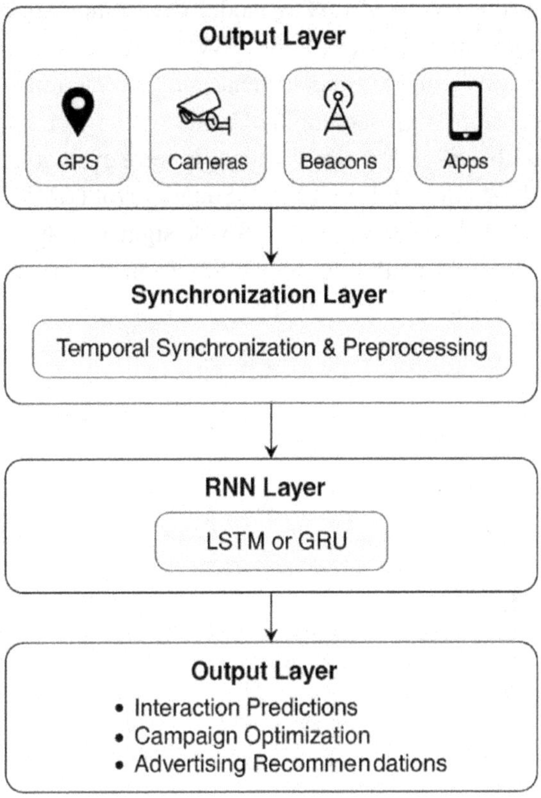

Overall, this conceptual framework, relying on the ability to synchronize distributed IoT data and the ability of temporal neural networks to extract complex patterns, provides a new and practical approach to analyzing customer behavior and promoting smart marketing in the context of smart cities.

4- RESULTS AND ANALYSIS

After implementing the proposed framework and training the recurrent neural network model on a set of real and simulated customer interaction data in urban environments, the model performance was analyzed at two main levels: first, evaluating the model's prediction accuracy compared to baseline methods; and second, analyzing customer behavior in different geographic areas to extract practical insights in urban marketing.

In the first step, the proposed LSTM model was compared with several reference algorithms, including Random Forest, SVM, and a baseline RNN. For this purpose, a dataset consisting of time sequences of interactions (such as entering the advertising area, stopping, touching the digital screen, purchasing, and exiting) with behavioral labels was prepared. The models were evaluated based on criteria such as Accuracy, F1-Score, and Root Mean Square Error (RMSE). As can be seen in Figure 2, the LSTM model was able to provide significantly better performance than other methods. Specifically, the prediction accuracy of successful customer engagement in LSTM reached 89.3%, while the closest alternative method, the basic RNN, had only 79.6% accuracy.

Figure 2. Comparison of accuracy and error of LSTM model with other methods in predicting customer interactions

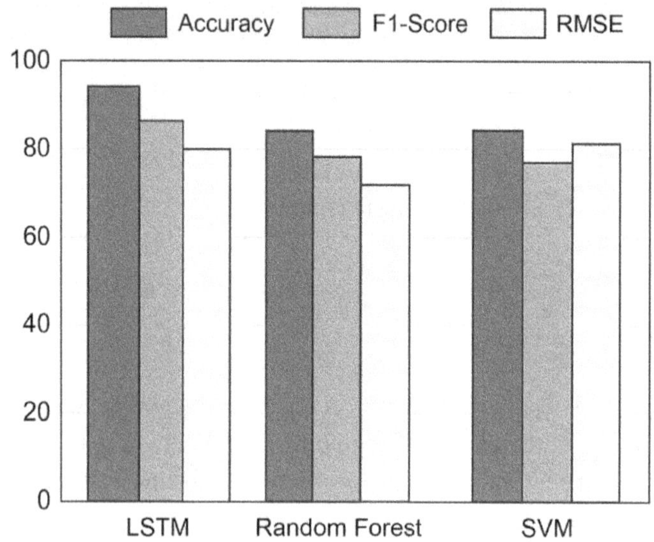

In the second part of the analysis, the output of the LSTM model was examined to predict behavioral patterns at a city scale. Using users' spatial and temporal location data, the model was able to identify areas with a high probability of successful interaction (such as making a purchase or responding to an ad). The results were represented as heat maps across the city. These maps showed that customer behavior is strongly influenced by spatiotemporal factors; such that at certain times of the day, high-traffic points (such as metro stations, shopping malls, or cultural centers) experienced a significant increase in interaction rates. Figure 3 shows the spatiotemporal pattern of successful interactions in three selected urban areas, where the intensity of the color indicates the success of real-time advertising campaigns.

Figure 3. Heatmap of the probability of successful customer engagement in urban areas during different hours of the day

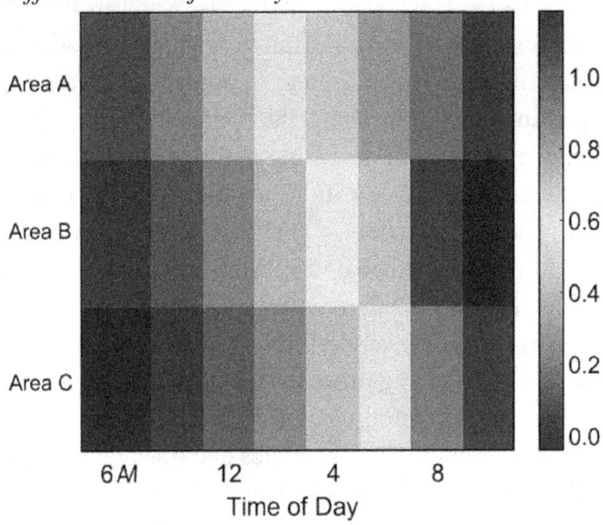

These analyses provide strong evidence that the proposed framework is capable of extracting operational and real-time insights. The model outputs are meaningful not only at the individual level, but also at the collective and environmental levels and can be used as a basis for designing dynamic advertising campaigns, planning brand presence in key city locations, and even infrastructural policy-making in the field of smart urban marketing. The proposed model also showed good sensitivity to behavioral changes in the test data, indicating its potential for adaptive learning in real environments with variable data.

Overall, the experimental results indicate that combining multi-source IoT data with LSTM architecture not only significantly improves the accuracy of customer interaction analysis and prediction, but also provides a suitable platform for designing adaptive and personalized marketing solutions at the urban scale.

5- DISCUSSION

The findings of this study indicate that the proposed framework based on IoT data synchronization and time series modeling using LSTM networks can be effectively used in analyzing and optimizing customer interactions in urban environments. Based on the results obtained from the model evaluation, the high prediction accuracy and significant reduction in RMSE error compared to other reference algorithms indicate that long-term memory-based recurrent structures have a special ability to identify complex behavioral patterns in time sequences. This is especially important in the context of smart cities, where customer behavior is influenced by instantaneous and multi-source variables. Heat map analysis also showed that the probability of marketing interaction success is significantly related to location and time. The spatio-temporal pattern presented in Figure 3 confirms that certain points of the city, at specific time intervals, have the greatest potential for positive interaction. This insight can play a key role in designing real-time advertising campaigns, so that marketing content, publication location, and timing can be optimized based on the data predicted by the model. In fact, it enables the implementation of "Context-Aware Marketing," in which past behavior, current environmental conditions, and location are taken into account in advertising decisions.

Another noteworthy point is the adaptability and stability of the proposed model's performance in the face of changing urban data. Unlike many static approaches that struggle to adapt to dynamic environments, LSTM, due to its intrinsic design, can well consider long-term temporal dependencies and track changing patterns. This feature is especially important in situations where user behavior changes throughout the day, week, or in the face of urban events. The framework's adaptability to wearable data and personal apps also opens the door to personalized marketing at the individual level.

Operationally, the results of this research can help marketing managers, smart advertising platform developers, and city planners dynamically identify optimized points for advertising engagements and plan effective interventions through real-time dashboards. For example, specific advertising messages can be activated at moments when the model predicts that customer engagement will be high, or staffing in stores can be adjusted to the predicted volume of customers.

On the other hand, although the results are very promising, some limitations must be considered. One of these limitations is the dependence of the model's performance on the quality and coverage of IoT data; in areas with poor sensor infrastructure or limited data access, the accuracy of the prediction may decrease. Additionally, challenges related to privacy and personal data management, especially when processing wearable and location data, require complementary ethical and regulatory frameworks.

Overall, this study demonstrates that combining AIoT technologies with deep learning models is not only technically feasible, but can also practically transform urban marketing practices. Future directions for this research could include using hybrid architectures with Transformers, extending the scope of application to metaverse or omnichannel environments, and designing self-learning marketing systems based on real-time data.

6- CONCLUSION AND SUGGESTIONS

The results of this study emphasize the potential of the proposed framework in analyzing and optimizing customer interactions in smart cities. Combining diverse and real-time IoT data with the learning power of recurrent models such as LSTM has provided an efficient platform for accurately predicting consumer behavior and improving marketing decision-making. Numerical and visual analyses showed that the developed framework was able to not only improve the prediction accuracy compared to reference models, but also enable the design of targeted and contextual marketing interventions by extracting spatio-temporal patterns of interactions.

The proposed framework is highly flexible and can be adapted to various data, including environmental sensors, wearable devices, mobile applications, and urban transportation systems. This adaptability makes it a potential tool for designing smart marketing systems on a city scale, so that advertising content can be personalized by considering the temporal, spatial, and behavioral characteristics of users. The model's ability to learn long-term temporal dependencies also ensures that its performance remains stable and reliable even in unstable urban conditions.

From an applied perspective, the use of this framework can help marketing managers, municipalities, interactive platform developers, and advertising companies to implement their campaigns with maximum effectiveness and at the most appropriate time and place. For example, platforms developed based on this framework can predict in real time the likely success rate of campaigns and identify optimal geographical or temporal points for spreading messages.

However, implementing this framework on a practical scale requires advanced data infrastructure, coordination between different urban actors, and compliance with user privacy principles. In the future, it is suggested that research should investigate the implementation of this framework in real-world scenarios and evaluate its impact on key marketing indicators such as conversion rates, customer lifetime value, and customer satisfaction. Also, the use of hybrid architectures including Transformers or Attention-based Models can increase the accuracy and efficiency of the system in highly complex environments.

Another suggestion is to extend the framework to omni-channel environments, so that customer interactions are analyzed and integrated not only in the physical urban space, but also in the virtual space and metaverse. On the other hand, adding an adaptive learning module (Self-Learning) to automatically update the model according to behavioral and environmental changes can be an important step towards designing truly intelligent and forward-looking marketing systems. Finally, linking this framework with customer experience management (CXM) systems and urban decision-support dashboards can provide a transformative platform for the development of smart cities from a marketing perspective.

REFERENCES

Aliahmadi, A., & Nozari, H. (2023, January). Evaluation of security metrics in AIoT and blockchain-based supply chain by Neutrosophic decision-making method. In Supply chain forum: an international journal (Vol. 24, No. 1, pp. 31-42). Taylor & Francis. DOI: 10.1080/16258312.2022.2101898

Irani, H. R., & Nozari, H. (Eds.). (2024). *Smart and Sustainable Interactive Marketing*. IGI Global. DOI: 10.4018/979-8-3693-1339-8

Kalogeras, S. (2025). A Smart Framework for Making Stories Smarter through Transmedia and Real User Interaction. *Applied Innovations in Industrial Management*, *5*(2), 59–66. DOI: 10.63630/aiim.52.59

Movahed, A. B., Movahed, A. B., & Nozari, H. (2024). Opportunities and challenges of marketing 5.0. Smart and Sustainable Interactive Marketing, 1-21.

Movahed, A. B., Movahed, A. B., & Nozari, H. (2024). Marketing 6.0 Conceptualization. In Advanced Businesses in Industry 6.0 (pp. 15-31). IGI Global.

Najafi, S. E., Nozari, H., & Edalatpanah, S. A. (2022). Investigating the key parameters affecting sustainable IoT-based marketing. In *Computational Intelligence Methodologies Applied to Sustainable Development Goals* (pp. 51–61). Springer International Publishing. DOI: 10.1007/978-3-030-97344-5_4

Nozari, H. (2025). Cognitive Targeting and Neuromarketing Applications in AI-Driven Digital Advertising. *Applied Innovations in Industrial Management*, *5*(2), 52–58. DOI: 10.63630/aiim.52.52

Nozari, H., Abdi, H., & Jahangard, S. (2025). Quantum Cognitive Intelligence Network Q-CIN as a Transformative Framework for Industry 6.0. *ALL Bioscience*, *1*(1), 27–37.

Nozari, H., Abdi, H., & Rafiei, K. (2025). Edge Computing and Marketing in the Smart Economy: Processing Consumer Data in Real-Time. In Dynamic and Safe Economy in the Age of Smart Technologies (pp. 191-208). IGI Global Scientific Publishing.

Nozari, H., Abdi, H., & Szmelter-Jarosz, A. (2025). Goat Optimization Algorithm: A Novel Bio-Inspired Metaheuristic for Global Optimization. arXiv preprint arXiv:2503.02331.

Nozari, H., & Chobar, A. P. (2024). The Dimensions and Components of Marketing 5.0: Introduction to Marketing 6.0. In Advanced Businesses in Industry 6.0 (pp. 75-86). IGI Global.

Nozari, H., Irani, H. R., & Rahmaty, M. (2023, November). Investigating Critical Success Factors in IoT-Based Marketing Systems. In *International Conference on Optimization and Data Science in Industrial Engineering* (pp. 259-271). Cham: Springer Nature Switzerland.

Nozari, H., Rahmaty, M., & Szmelter-Jarosz, A. (2024). A framework for AIoT-based smart sustainable marketing system. In *Artificial Intelligence of Things for Achieving Sustainable Development Goals* (pp. 255–271). Springer Nature Switzerland. DOI: 10.1007/978-3-031-53433-1_13

Nozari, H., & Samadi, S. (2025). Digital Twin-Enhanced Sentiment Analysis for Targeted Marketing Optimization. In Dynamic and Safe Economy in the Age of Smart Technologies (pp. 121-138). IGI Global Scientific Publishing. DOI: 10.4018/979-8-3693-4369-2.ch008

Nozari, H., Szmelter-Jarosz, A., & Ghahremani-Nahr, J. (2021). The ideas of sustainable and green marketing based on the internet of everything—The case of the dairy industry. *Future Internet*, *13*(10), 266. DOI: 10.3390/fi13100266

Nozari, H., Szmelter-Jarosz, A., & Rahmaty, M. (2024). Smart marketing based on artificial intelligence of things (AIoT) and Blockchain and evaluating critical success factors. In *Smart and Sustainable Interactive Marketing* (pp. 68–82). IGI Global Scientific Publishing. DOI: 10.4018/979-8-3693-1339-8.ch005

Chapter 10
Artificial Intelligence in Digital Marketing: Trends, Challenges, and Strategic Opportunities

Amirhossein Ghasemi Abyaneh
https://orcid.org/0009-0006-3135-1841
Kharazmi University, Iran

Masoud Khakbazan
https://orcid.org/0009-0002-6590-1371
Iran University of Science and Technology, Iran

Ali Bakhshi Movahed
Iran University of Science and Technology, Iran

ABSTRACT

Integrating Artificial Intelligence (AI) into digital marketing practices is fundamentally reshaping how businesses interact with consumers. This study provides a narrative review of AI technologies, including machine learning, natural language processing, and predictive analytics, across key marketing functions. It identifies major trends such as hyper-personalization, automation, predictive modeling, and AI-driven content creation, synthesizing insights from academic research, industry reports, and case studies. The paper critically evaluates challenges like data privacy, technical integration, financial barriers, and algorithmic bias. Highlighting AI's dual impact, it presents transformative opportunities and ethical considerations, offering strategic recommendations for future research and responsible AI adoption. This review provides a holistic framework for leveraging AI to drive sustainable, transparent, and consumer-centric growth in the digital marketing landscape.

DOI: 10.4018/979-8-3373-3775-3.ch010

1. INTRODUCTION

In recent years, the landscape of digital marketing has undergone significant transformation, driven by the rise of digital technologies and the ability to analyze vast amounts of consumer data (Erevelles et al., 2016). The internet, mobile apps, and social media growth have granted businesses unparalleled access to customer insights, allowing them to tailor their marketing efforts precisely (Dwivedi et al., 2020). Unlike traditional marketing, which relies on broad campaigns, modern digital marketing strategies are data-driven, offering a more personalized and scalable approach (Saura et al., 2021). These strategies now encompass many tools and techniques, including search engine optimization (SEO), content marketing, social media management, email campaigns, and data analytics, facilitating more direct, impactful consumer engagement (Olson et al., 2021).

As digital marketing practices evolve, Artificial Intelligence (AI) has become a crucial driver of change (Chintalapati & Pandey, 2021). AI encompasses technologies such as machine learning (ML), natural language processing (NLP), and deep learning, which are increasingly integrated into digital marketing strategies. These technologies help marketers automate processes, derive actionable insights from consumer data, and offer more personalized experiences to their audience (Pangeran et al., 2024). For instance, machine learning algorithms can analyze vast amounts of data to make real-time product recommendations or customized advertisements, improving the relevance and effectiveness of marketing campaigns (Akter et al., 2022).

Beyond automation, AI has transformed many aspects of digital marketing, including content creation, customer interaction, and advertising (Van Esch & Black, 2021). Powered by AI, predictive analytics enables marketers to anticipate customer behavior and proactively adjust campaigns (Yadav & Pandita, 2024). Similarly, AI-driven chatbots and virtual assistants enhance customer service by offering immediate, personalized responses, improving customer satisfaction and engagement (Prasad et al., 2024).

However, as businesses increasingly adopt AI in their marketing efforts, they face several challenges. Data privacy concerns are among the most pressing issues, as AI relies heavily on consumer data to drive personalization and predictions (De Bruyn et al., 2020). A significant problem is ensuring compliance with data protection laws such as GDPR while maintaining consumer trust (Zhang et al., 2020). Furthermore, the technical complexity of integrating AI tools into existing marketing systems poses another hurdle for many companies. The high costs associated with AI implementation, particularly for smaller businesses, can also limit its widespread adoption (Saboune, 2024). In addition to these technical and financial challenges, ethical considerations, such as algorithmic bias and transparency, must also be addressed to ensure AI is used responsibly (Buiten, 2019).

Despite these challenges, the potential of AI to innovate and drive growth in digital marketing is immense (Kumar et al., 2024). AI offers opportunities to improve customer segmentation, enhance advertising targeting, optimize content strategies, and ultimately increase the return on investment (ROI) (Shanmugam et al., 2023). By leveraging AI, businesses can gain a competitive edge through more precise targeting, greater operational efficiency, and improved customer engagement (Wamba-Taguimdje et al., 2020).

However, a significant gap exists in the literature regarding a comprehensive understanding of AI's role in digital marketing. While many studies have focused on specific AI applications, such as predictive analytics or chatbots, there is a lack of research that provides an integrated perspective on AI's broader impact across various digital marketing functions. Furthermore, while the potential benefits of AI are widely acknowledged, there is insufficient exploration of the challenges businesses face in adopting and integrating these technologies. More research is needed to understand the full spectrum of AI's implications for digital marketing, particularly from a practical, business-centric viewpoint.

This paper addresses this gap by thoroughly reviewing the current trends, challenges, and opportunities associated with AI in digital marketing. The primary objectives of this review are to identify the major trends in AI adoption, assess the challenges businesses face in implementing AI, and explore the opportunities AI offers for enhancing marketing strategies. The review will focus on personalization, automation, predictive analytics, and content optimization while addressing technical, ethical, and financial barriers to AI adoption.

Through a synthesis of existing research, this article will offer valuable insights into the role of AI in shaping the future of digital marketing. The findings will help marketers, businesses, and researchers navigate the complexities of AI integration while highlighting the opportunities for innovation and growth in this rapidly evolving field.

The paper is organized as follows: Section 2 presents a literature review, summarizing key research on AI applications in digital marketing. Section 3 outlines the methodology used to gather and analyze relevant studies. Section 4 presents the key findings from the literature, and Section 5 concludes with a discussion of the implications of these findings, along with recommendations for future research and business practice.

2. LITERATURE REVIEW

2.1 AI in Digital Marketing

The evolution of Artificial Intelligence (AI) in marketing has undergone significant advancements, with key technological developments driving its widespread integration into marketing strategies (Vlačić et al., 2021). Initially, AI applications in marketing were limited to basic automation and data processing tasks, such as automating customer communications or segmenting customers based on basic demographic data (Campbell et al., 2020). However, with the rapid development of more advanced AI technologies, including machine learning (ML), natural language processing (NLP), and predictive analytics, AI has evolved into a sophisticated tool that can fundamentally transform digital marketing practices (Gündüzyeli, 2024). Machine learning algorithms, for instance, enable systems to learn from vast amounts of data over time, improving decision-making processes by identifying complex patterns and correlations within large datasets (Shrestha et al., 2020). As a result, marketers can make better-informed decisions, predict customer behavior with greater accuracy, and optimize marketing strategies in real time (Jalal & Elmaghraby, 2024). For example, Google Ads uses machine learning to automatically adjust bids for advertisements based on predicted conversion likelihood, improving ad performance and optimizing ad spending (Somosi, 2022).

NLP has significantly improved how businesses interact with customers, facilitating more advanced chatbots, virtual assistants, and automated customer service systems capable of engaging in natural, context-aware conversations (Nguyen et al., 2021). ChatGPT (developed by OpenAI) has demonstrated the power of NLP in customer interactions, enabling brands to deliver personalized, real-time responses. These breakthroughs have been crucial in driving the widespread adoption of AI technologies across various areas of digital marketing (Raaj & Premnath, 2023).

AI is now deeply embedded in numerous aspects of digital marketing, from advertising and customer segmentation to personalization and content creation (Han et al., 2021). In advertising, AI-powered algorithms optimize ad targeting by continuously analyzing consumer behavior and preferences, ensuring that ads are placed in the proper context, at the right time, and to the right audience (Choi & Lim, 2020). By leveraging vast amounts of consumer data, AI helps marketers identify high-potential customer segments and design highly targeted campaigns, significantly improving the efficiency and effectiveness of ad spending (Tashtemirovich et al., 2024). For instance, Facebook's AI-driven targeting algorithms continuously analyze user behavior, ensuring that ads are shown to the most relevant audiences based on their preferences, past interactions, and engagement history (Büchi et al., 2021).

Moreover, AI has transformed customer segmentation by enabling marketers to go beyond traditional segmentation methods, such as age, gender, or location, and instead use more granular insights derived from behavioral data, psychographics, and even real-time engagement patterns (K, 2024). This allows businesses to create hyper-targeted customer profiles and develop customized marketing strategies that resonate more deeply with each group (Semerádová & Weinlich, 2019). For example, Spotify's AI algorithms use listening patterns and preferences to segment users and deliver tailored playlists and advertising, which increases engagement and customer satisfaction (Janice & Kusumawati, 2024).

Another area where AI is revolutionizing digital marketing is personalization. With AI, businesses can provide dynamic content recommendations, personalized product suggestions, and tailored messaging aligned with individual customer preferences and behaviors (Gungunawat et al., 2024). AI algorithms can analyze past customer interactions, track browsing patterns, and predict future behaviors, which allows for creating highly personalized experiences that increase engagement and drive conversions (Yeboah et al., 2025). Amazon's recommendation engine, for example, analyzes customers' browsing and purchase history to suggest products, resulting in higher sales and improved user experiences (Syrotkina et al., 2023). AI-powered recommendation engines, such as those used by platforms like Amazon and Netflix, suggest products and content based on individual user behavior, significantly improving customer satisfaction and fostering brand loyalty (Babadoğan, 2024).

Furthermore, AI-driven personalized communication enables companies to automate emails, messages, and notifications specifically tailored to each consumer, ensuring that the right message reaches the right customer at the right time, thus enhancing engagement (Oğuz, 2024).

AI is also making a profound impact on content creation. With the advent of AI tools that can generate written content, produce videos, and even create social media posts, marketers can automate large portions of the content production process (Adwan, 2024). For instance, Copy.ai and Jasper.ai are examples of AI content generation tools that help marketers quickly create high-quality written content, such as blog posts and product descriptions, at scale (Murár & Kubovics, 2023). These AI-driven content creation tools can generate high-quality text, such as blog posts, product descriptions, and articles, at a scale and speed that was previously unattainable (Anantrasirichai & Bull, 2020). Additionally, AI-assisted video production tools are helping marketers create dynamic and interactive videos that can be personalized for different customer segments (Jastacia & Akbar, 2023). These tools can help marketers scale content production, ensuring a consistent, relevant, and engaging brand presence across various platforms while saving valuable time and resources (Koob, 2023). AI also enhances content distribution by automatically determining the optimal channels, times, and formats for sharing content, maximizing its reach and impact (Martinoli & Vuković, 2024).

The widespread integration of AI into digital marketing practices underscores its transformative role in shaping the industry's future (Bastray, 2025). AI is revolutionizing marketing strategies by providing tools that enable businesses to make more informed decisions, enhance customer experiences, and streamline content creation (Sharma et al., 2023). As AI technologies continue to evolve, they hold the potential to further personalize and optimize every aspect of digital marketing, from targeting and segmentation to customer engagement and content production (Nair & Gupta, 2021).

2.2 Trends in AI-Driven Digital Marketing

In recent years, Artificial Intelligence (AI) has become a game changer in digital marketing, driving several key trends that have significantly enhanced marketing strategies and outcomes (Nimbalkar & Singh, 2024). One of the most notable trends is personalization, where AI enables the delivery of hyper-targeted content and dynamic ad placements (Gujar et al., 2024). Through sophisticated algorithms, AI can analyze vast amounts of data on consumer preferences, behaviors, and past interactions, allowing marketers to tailor content to resonate with everyone (Ip, 2023). This level of personalization ensures that advertisements and product recommendations are relevant and timely, increasing consumer engagement and conversion rates (Shanahan et al., 2019). For instance, Netflix's personalized content recommendations are based on detailed user profiles created by analyzing past watch history and preferences, significantly enhancing the viewer's experience and engagement with the platform (Siles et al., 2019).

Additionally, automation is crucial in streamlining and optimizing repetitive marketing tasks (Arce et al., 2023). AI-driven tools can automate email campaigns, social media posting, and ad bidding, freeing up valuable time for marketers to focus on more strategic activities (Huang & Rust, 2020). These automation systems are designed to enhance efficiency and performance, with AI continuously learning from previous campaigns to improve future outcomes (Sodiya et al., 2024). For example, HubSpot's AI-powered marketing automation tools enable businesses to run automated email campaigns, segment their audience, and adjust messaging based on consumer engagement (Mero et al., 2022).

Another significant trend is predictive analytics, which leverages AI to analyze large volumes of data and forecast consumer behavior, market trends, and campaign performance (Blackburn et al., 2015). By identifying patterns and trends within consumer data, AI enables marketers to make data-driven decisions that enhance the effectiveness of their campaigns (Davenport et al., 2019). Predictive models can anticipate which products or services are likely to resonate with different customer segments, allowing for more accurate targeting and optimized ad spending (Wu et al., 2021). Google Analytics employs AI to predict user behaviors, enabling marketers to optimize their strategies based on data-driven insights (Gkikas & Theodoridis, 2024).

Furthermore, chatbots and conversational AI have become powerful tools for improving customer support and engagement. These AI-powered systems can handle customer inquiries in real-time, providing instant, personalized responses that enhance the customer experience (Ngai et al., 2021). Sephora's Chabot, for example, uses AI to deliver customized beauty recommendations based on customers' preferences and browsing history. Chatbots can also drive engagement by proactively contacting customers, offering assistance, or guiding them through a sales funnel. With their ability to provide 24/7 support and deliver tailored experiences, conversational AI systems are becoming integral to modern customer service strategies (Blümel et al., 2023).

These AI-driven trends in personalization, automation, predictive analytics, and conversational AI are fundamentally reshaping the digital marketing landscape. They enable marketers to engage with consumers meaningfully and efficiently and provide valuable insights that drive continuous improvement and innovation in marketing practices (Cutler, 2024).

2.3 Challenges in Implementing AI

While AI offers numerous benefits in digital marketing, its implementation comes with challenges that companies must navigate to maximize its potential (Elkhatibi & Benabdelouhed, 2024). One of the most pressing concerns is data privacy. Ethical issues and regulatory challenges arise as AI systems rely heavily on consumer data to drive personalized marketing strategies. The collection, storage, and utilization of vast amounts of personal information raise questions about consumer consent, data protection, and the risk of privacy violations (Karami et al., 2024). Strict regulations, such as the General Data Protection Regulation (GDPR) in Europe, have imposed significant restrictions on how businesses can use consumer data, making it essential for companies to ensure compliance and maintain trust with their customers (Islam et al., 2024).

Another challenge in adopting AI for digital marketing is technical integration. Many organizations struggle to integrate AI technologies into their marketing platforms and systems (Ponomarenko, 2024). The complexity of aligning AI tools with legacy systems, databases, and software can lead to technical glitches, inefficiencies, and delays in implementation. Furthermore, the need for robust infrastructure to support AI models, including sufficient processing power and data storage capabilities, can present additional hurdles (Singh & Adhikari, 2023). Cost and resource limitations also play a critical role in the adoption of AI. The financial investment required to implement AI solutions can be substantial, particularly for small and medium-sized businesses (Hameed, 2025). Companies must invest in AI software and hardware and allocate resources for training staff, conducting research, and maintaining the systems (Ogabu, 2024). In addition, there is a shortage of skilled professionals capable of developing, managing, and optimizing AI technologies, making it difficult for many businesses to leverage AI's capabilities fully (Tcharnetsky & Vogt, 2023).

Finally, bias and transparency in AI systems pose significant challenges. AI models are trained on historical data, which can inadvertently reflect societal biases, leading to skewed results and unfair outcomes (Mensah, 2024). For instance, biased algorithms in customer segmentation or ad targeting can perpetuate stereotypes and discriminate against certain groups (Lambrecht & Tucker, 2021). A notable case is Amazon's recruitment AI, which was discontinued after it was discovered to favor male candidates due to biased training data highlighting how unexamined AI models can lead to unethical outcomes (Chang, 2023). Moreover, the "black box" nature of many AI models, where the decision-making process is not fully understood or transparent, raises concerns about accountability and trust. Companies must address these issues by developing more transparent AI systems and ensuring their models are fair, explainable, and unbiased (Knowles et al., 2022).

These challenges of data privacy, technical integration, cost limitations, and bias highlight the complexities organizations face in implementing AI effectively. Overcoming these obstacles requires careful planning, resource investment, and a commitment to ethical and transparent AI practices (Williamson & Prybutok, 2024).

2.4 Opportunities for AI in Digital Marketing

Incorporating artificial intelligence (AI) in digital marketing brings considerable challenges and a wealth of opportunities to improve marketing strategies and outcomes (Abhiseka et al., 2024) significantly. One of the most compelling opportunities is the potential for enhanced ROI. AI enables marketers to optimize ad spending by analyzing real-time data and identifying campaigns' most effective channels, audiences, and tactics. With AI-driven tools, companies can continuously adjust and refine their campaigns, ensuring that resources are allocated to the most high-performing areas, ultimately improving the return on investment (M et al., 2024). Another significant opportunity is the ability of AI to provide AI-powered customer insights. Through analyzing large datasets, AI can uncover hidden patterns in consumer behavior, enabling businesses to understand their customers more deeply (Okeleke et al., 2024). These insights can guide the development of more targeted marketing strategies, product offerings, and customer engagement techniques. AI can also help identify emerging market trends, giving businesses a competitive edge in anticipating shifts in consumer preferences and adjusting their strategies accordingly (Babatunde et al., 2024).

Furthermore, AI has the potential to drive innovations in content marketing. AI tools are revolutionizing content creation and distribution by automating writing, video production, and social media management (Kubovics, 2024). AI-generated content, such as blog posts, product descriptions, and even creative advertisements, can be produced at scale, enabling businesses to deliver consistent, high-quality content without significant time or resource investment (Herath et al., 2025). In addition, AI-assisted video production tools can help create personalized, dynamic videos for different customer segments, enhancing engagement and interaction. These innovations in content marketing empower businesses to create more engaging, relevant, and timely content that resonates with their audience, driving greater customer loyalty and conversion (Sung et al., 2021). Together, these opportunities enhanced ROI, AI-powered customer insights, and innovations in content marketing demonstrate how AI can significantly transform digital marketing practices (Bormane & Blaus, 2024). By leveraging AI, businesses can improve their marketing performance, gain deeper insights into their customers, and create more engaging and compelling content strategies (Cherian et al., 2025).

A prime example of digital transformation in practice can be seen in McDonald's adoption of AI and smart technologies to modernize customer experience and operational efficiency. From personalized menus to automated ordering systems, the company demonstrates how digital innovation reshapes traditional business models in the fast-food industry (Gani & Faroque, 2021). In smart economies, the integration of AI, IoT, and cloud computing enhances efficiency but also increases exposure to sophisticated cyber threats. AI-driven cybersecurity solutions, including autonomous threat detection and behavioral analytics, are essential to safeguard digital infrastructures against evolving risks (Movahed et al., 2025). Furthermore, the integration of Internet of Things (IoT) devices and machine learning algorithms using Python empowers businesses to personalize customer experiences and optimize marketing strategies. By analyzing data collected from IoT sensors, companies can deliver tailored content and product recommendations, enhancing customer engagement and driving sales (Singh, 2023). Additionally, integrating digital twin technology with sentiment analysis allows businesses to create virtual representations of customer behaviors and preferences. This approach enables real-time monitoring and optimization of marketing strategies, leading to more personalized and effective customer engagement (Nozari & Samadi, 2025).

Despite AI's significant advancements and wide-ranging applications in digital marketing, the current literature often focuses on isolated use cases, such as personalization, automation, or Chabot systems, without offering a comprehensive and integrated analysis of these technologies across the full marketing spectrum (Ziakis & Vlachopoulou, 2023). Additionally, while several studies highlight the benefits of AI, fewer explore the practical and ethical challenges businesses face during implementation (Purwanto et al., 2024). Research overlooks the interplay between different AI tools and how their combined use influences marketing effectiveness, consumer trust, and operational efficiency (Davtyan, 2024). As AI continues to evolve and integrate into marketing systems at scale, there remains a pressing need for a structured review that synthesizes these diverse elements and identifies the broader implications for marketers, strategists, and researchers (Efendioglu, 2023). This paper aims to address that need by systematically reviewing trends, challenges, and emerging opportunities in applying AI within digital marketing — offering a holistic perspective currently lacking in existing literature.

To consolidate the insights discussed throughout this section, Table 1 summarizes key academic and industry studies related to the adoption of AI in digital marketing. It highlights each study's main focus areas, methodologies, and contributions, helping contextualize the current research landscape.

Table 1. Summary of key studies on AI adoption in digital marketing

Author(s) / Year	Study Focus / Objective	AI Technology / Application	Key Findings	Marketing Area	Contribution to Literature
Vlačić et al. (2021)	The study examines AI's evolving role in marketing and outlines future research directions.	The paper focuses on AI technologies like machine learning and data analytics to enhance customer engagement and automate marketing.	AI improves customer engagement and market forecasting but raises challenges related to AI adoption, data privacy, and ethics.	The research covers marketing strategy, customer relationship management (CRM), and ethical concerns in AI applications.	The study provides a new research framework using content analysis and MCA, highlighting key themes and suggesting future research agendas.
Gündüzyeli (2024)	The study investigates how AI impacts sustainability in digital marketing practices.	AI technologies like machine learning and data analytics optimize digital marketing strategies and promote sustainability.	AI improves marketing efficiency, reduces waste, and supports environmental, economic, and social sustainability goals.	Focuses on sustainable digital marketing and the role of AI in enhancing business practices.	Provides a comprehensive analysis of AI's role in fostering sustainable marketing practices, linking AI adoption to sustainability.
Jalal& Elmaghraby (2024)	The study introduces a framework for analyzing individual customer behavior and applying personalized marketing strategies using counterfactual analysis.	Machine learning algorithms such as K-means clustering, logistic regression, and decision trees are used for predicting customer behavior and transitions.	The framework successfully predicts customer transitions and evaluates personalized marketing strategies using counterfactual analysis.	Focus on personalized marketing, customer segmentation, and customer behavior prediction for improved retention and engagement.	Introduces counterfactual analysis for individual-level personalized marketing, addressing customer transitions and forecasting marketing strategy impacts.
Somosi (2022)	The study examines the role of Artificial Intelligence in content creation for Google Ads and compares its effectiveness to content created by marketers.	AI is used to generate ad content (text and images) for Google Ads, focusing on evaluating its performance and impact on conversions.	AI-generated ads performed similarly to those created by marketers, showing comparable click-through rates and ROI, though slight differences were observed in conversions.	The study focuses on digital marketing, Google Ads, AI in content creation, and performance analysis in online advertising.	This research contributes by comparing AI-generated content to human-created content in the context of Google Ads, providing insights into the effectiveness of AI in advertising.
Han et al. (2021)	The study provides a bibliometric analysis of AI in B2B marketing, identifying trends, research domains, and future directions.	AI technologies such as machine learning, decision support systems, and business intelligence are explored for driving innovation in B2B marketing.	AI is found to be a key enabler of innovation in B2B marketing, with applications in CRM, sales forecasting, value co-creation, and operations management.	Focuses on B2B marketing innovation, AI in CRM, sales forecasting, and AI-enabled operations management.	The study classifies AI applications into five domains and outlines trends in AI-enabled B2B marketing, offering directions for future research.

continued on following page

Table 1. Continued

Author(s) / Year	Study Focus / Objective	AI Technology / Application	Key Findings	Marketing Area	Contribution to Literature
Choi & Lim (2020)	The study identifies and classifies various machine-learning techniques used to enhance target advertising in online marketing.	Machine learning techniques, including behavioral targeting, click-through rate prediction, and real-time bidding, are applied to improve the relevance and efficiency of targeted advertisements.	Machine learning techniques significantly enhance advertising personalization, improve targeting accuracy, and address challenges like click fraud in online advertising.	Focuses on target advertising, personalized marketing, and click fraud detection in online advertising.	The study provides a comprehensive classification of machine learning applications for target advertising, contributing to a better understanding of AI's role in digital marketing.
Tashtemirovich et al. (2024)	The study explores the impact of Artificial Intelligence on digital marketing strategies using Neutrosophic set theory to assess marketing efficiency.	Machine learning and AI algorithms are applied to enhance digital marketing tactics, including ROI optimization, customer segmentation, and ethical decision-making.	AI integration increases marketing efficiency, with a 27% improvement in ROI and a 33% reduction in time required for campaign execution.	Focuses on digital marketing strategies, AI-enabled marketing efficiency, and personalization in digital campaigns.	Introduces the AI-Enabled Marketing Efficiency (AIME) model and Neutrosophic set theory to evaluate AI's impact on digital marketing, providing new metrics like Delta Efficiency and Time Reduction.
Janice & Kusumawati (2024)	The study examines the impact of Spotify's "Discover Weekly" feature on user satisfaction and customer loyalty, focusing on Indonesian Generation Z users.	The research focuses on AI algorithms used in Spotify's "Discover Weekly" to personalize music recommendations and enhance user engagement.	"Discover Weekly" significantly improves user satisfaction, leading to higher customer loyalty and positive word-of-mouth promotion.	Focuses on customer loyalty, satisfaction, and personalized recommendations in music streaming platforms.	This study provides insights into how personalized AI-driven features like "Discover Weekly" can enhance customer loyalty and satisfaction, offering a model for other music streaming platforms to follow.

continued on following page

Table 1. Continued

Author(s) / Year	Study Focus / Objective	AI Technology / Application	Key Findings	Marketing Area	Contribution to Literature
Gungunawat et al. (2024)	The study explores how AI-powered personalization in digital marketing enhances customer engagement and strategy, focusing on machine learning, predictive analytics, and recommendation systems.	The paper examines AI technologies such as machine learning, natural language processing (NLP), and deep learning, applied through recommendation systems, predictive analytics, and dynamic ad placement tools.	AI-driven personalization significantly boosts customer satisfaction, engagement, and ROI, with successful implementations seen across industries like e-commerce (Amazon), entertainment (Netflix), and advertising (Coca-Cola).	The focus is on customer engagement, personalized recommendations, targeted advertising, and content personalization in digital marketing.	The paper provides an in-depth review of AI's transformative role in digital marketing, highlighting real-world case studies and offering insights into future trends such as hyper-personalization and ethical AI frameworks.
Yeboah et al. (2025)	The study introduces AI-UIX, an AI-driven system that optimizes UI/UX design workflows by automating color selection and palette generation and providing real-time analytics.	The system integrates AI tools like image-based color extraction, palette generation algorithms, and AI-powered recommendations, utilizing machine learning and third-party APIs.	AI-UIX improves design workflows by automating color selection, enhancing accuracy, and making design processes more accessible for novice designers while maintaining linear scalability.	Focuses on UI/UX design, color optimization, and AI-driven personalization in the digital design industry.	This work provides a novel AI-powered framework for color processing in UI/UX design, addressing the limitations of traditional tools and enhancing accessibility and efficiency for designers.
Jastacia & Akbar (2023)	The study examines the potential of using AI and neuromarketing to improve the efficiency and emotional impact of digital promotional video (DPV) production.	Utilizes AI-generated video tools and neuromarketing techniques like EEG and emotion tracking to optimize video ads based on subconscious consumer responses.	AI and neuromarketing can reduce production costs and enhance consumer engagement by creating emotionally resonant and personalized digital ads.	Focuses on digital advertising, video marketing, and consumer emotion analysis through neuromarketing-enhanced AI tools.	Highlights how integrating neuromarketing with AI can transform digital ad strategies, providing new insights into consumer behavior and ad personalization

continued on following page

Table 1. Continued

Author(s) / Year	Study Focus / Objective	AI Technology / Application	Key Findings	Marketing Area	Contribution to Literature
Sharma et al. (2023)	This study explores the transformative impact of Artificial Intelligence (AI) on marketing strategies, focusing on its ability to enhance customer engagement, optimize targeting, and enable data-driven decision-making.	The study examines AI technologies like predictive analytics, personalized recommendations, and chatbots, which help businesses predict consumer behavior and deliver tailored marketing strategies.	AI-driven marketing strategies significantly enhance customer engagement, increase sales, and optimize targeting efforts. It also enables businesses to improve ROI and improve decision-making through data insights.	Focuses on sales optimization, customer engagement, predictive analytics, and personalized marketing strategies.	The paper highlights how AI revolutionizes marketing by offering new avenues for businesses to innovate, increase customer loyalty, and enhance overall marketing strategies while addressing the ethical concerns surrounding AI adoption.
Nair & Gupta (2021)	This paper explores the diverse applications of AI technology in digital marketing, focusing on areas like content curation, predictive analytics, and customer engagement to optimize marketing strategies.	The study discusses AI tools such as machine learning, predictive analytics, voice search, programmatic media buying, and chatbots, which automate processes and enhance customer personalization in marketing.	AI significantly improves targeting, customer insights, and engagement through personalized content, optimized ad placements, and automated customer service functions like chatbots, boosting marketing ROI and sales potential.	The paper addresses digital marketing, customer engagement, personalized marketing, sales optimization, and AI-powered tools for automation in marketing.	It provides valuable insights into AI's role in modern marketing, offering practical recommendations for businesses to leverage AI tools for better customer engagement and more efficient marketing strategies.
Ip (2023)	The paper explores how AI transforms content recommendation in marketing, highlighting its benefits, technical models, and ethical considerations.	It uses machine learning, collaborative filtering, content-based filtering, and hybrid models to deliver personalized content recommendations at scale.	AI dramatically improves content relevance and user engagement but raises concerns over privacy, bias, transparency, and manipulation, requiring ethical oversight.	Focuses on personalized marketing, content recommendation systems, user engagement, and ethical AI adoption.	Offers a comprehensive evaluation of AI's dual impact—benefits and risks—in revolutionizing content marketing while advocating for ethical AI practices and future innovations.

continued on following page

Table 1. Continued

Author(s) / Year	Study Focus / Objective	AI Technology / Application	Key Findings	Marketing Area	Contribution to Literature
Shanahan et al. (2019)	The study explores the impact of social media personalization on brand loyalty and perceived quality, explicitly focusing on personalized advertising on Facebook and its effects on consumer brand engagement and attachment.	The research focuses on personalized advertising, leveraging user interactions and preferences data to tailor content and increase consumer engagement on social media platforms.	Perceived personalization significantly enhances consumer brand engagement and attachment, positively affecting perceived quality and brand loyalty.	The paper covers social media marketing, personalized advertising, brand loyalty, and consumer engagement.	The study contributes to understanding the mechanisms through which perceived personalization in social media advertising influences consumer brand perceptions, highlighting the role of personalization in building brand loyalty and perceived quality.
Arce et al. (2023)	The study examines how artificial intelligence (AI) tools can optimize business performance in small and medium-sized businesses (SMEs) through improved marketing strategies.	AI applications discussed include data analytics, personalization, chatbots, automated marketing, predictive modeling, and dynamic pricing to enhance marketing strategies and customer engagement.	AI tools help SMEs optimize marketing efforts, improve ROI, automate repetitive tasks, personalize customer experiences, and predict trends, leading to better business performance.	Focuses on digital marketing strategies, AI in marketing automation, personalized marketing, and data-driven decision-making for SMEs.	This research demonstrates how AI can revolutionize marketing strategies in SMEs, helping businesses improve customer engagement, personalize content, and enhance overall marketing effectiveness.
Huang & Rust (2020)	The paper develops a three-stage strategic framework for integrating artificial intelligence (AI) into marketing, focusing on research, strategy, and action stages.	The framework incorporates mechanical AI for automation, thinking AI for data processing and decision-making, and feeling AI for emotional analysis and customer engagement.	AI can optimize marketing strategies through segmentation, targeting, positioning, and personalized actions. Mechanical AI standardizes tasks, thinking AI personalizes, and feeling AI rationalizes customer interactions.	Focuses on AI in marketing research, marketing strategy (STP), and marketing actions (4Ps/4Cs) with applications in segmentation, targeting, positioning, and communication.	It provides a systematic framework for applying AI across different marketing stages. It highlights the current limitations and future research directions, emphasizing how AI can enhance decision-making and customer relationships.

continued on following page

Table 1. Continued

Author(s) / Year	Study Focus / Objective	AI Technology / Application	Key Findings	Marketing Area	Contribution to Literature
Davenport et al. (2019)	This paper proposes a multidimensional framework for understanding how AI will transform marketing strategies and customer behaviors, highlighting task automation, context awareness, and the use of AI in robots.	The paper discusses machine learning, natural language processing, robotics, and deep learning in marketing applications such as sales, customer service, and predictive analytics.	AI is expected to enhance predictive abilities, automate tasks, and provide real-time customer insights. It also suggests that AI should augment, rather than replace, human managers in marketing roles.	Focuses on AI in marketing strategy, customer behavior, and sales processes through applications like personalized recommendations, pricing optimization, and automated customer interactions.	The paper contributes a comprehensive framework for integrating AI into marketing, proposing a research agenda to examine AI's impact on marketing strategies, customer behaviors, and policy issues like privacy and ethics.
Wu et al. (2021)	The study proposes an integrated framework for churn prediction and customer segmentation in telecommunications (telco), combining machine learning models and Bayesian analysis.	Machine learning classifiers such as Random Forest, AdaBoost, and Logistic Regression are used for churn prediction. In contrast, K-means clustering and Bayesian Logistic Regression are used for customer segmentation and factor analysis.	The integrated framework effectively identifies churn customers and segments them based on their characteristics, providing valuable insights for targeted retention strategies. SMOTE oversampling enhances prediction performance, especially for imbalanced datasets.	Focuses on customer churn management, customer segmentation, and precision marketing in the telecommunications industry.	This research introduces an integrated churn prediction and customer segmentation framework, using Bayesian analysis as an intermediary between the two, filling a gap in existing literature.
Gkikas & Theodoridis (2024)	The study focuses on predicting online shopping behavior using machine learning classifiers and Google Analytics metrics to classify user engagement levels.	Machine learning models such as Decision Trees (DTs), Naïve Bayes (NB), and k-nearest Neighbors (k-NN) are applied to classify user engagement based on Google Analytics metrics like event count, sessions, purchase revenue, and bounce rate.	DTs achieved the highest classification accuracy (97.98%), outperforming NB and k-NN. The analysis revealed significant relationships between metrics like event count and sessions, highlighting factors that influence user engagement.	Focuses on user engagement, predictive analytics, and digital marketing strategy optimization based on user behavior analysis.	The research integrates machine learning with Google Analytics to enhance marketing strategies, offering actionable insights for classifying user engagement levels and optimizing decision-making processes in e-commerce.

continued on following page

Table 1. Continued

Author(s) / Year	Study Focus / Objective	AI Technology / Application	Key Findings	Marketing Area	Contribution to Literature
Karami et al. (2024)	Analyzes the ethical risks and societal impacts of AI-powered personalization in digital marketing.	Focuses on AI-driven personalization using machine learning, data analytics, and behavioral tracking.	AI personalization enhances engagement but raises serious concerns around privacy, bias, manipulation, and transparency; it proposes ethical guidelines and recommendations.	It covers personalized digital marketing, consumer profiling, data-driven targeting, and advertising ethics.	It offers a comprehensive framework of ethical considerations backed by real-world case studies and recommends strategies for responsible AI deployment in marketing.
Lambrecht & Tucker (2021)	The study explores the unintended gender biases in algorithm-based advertising, specifically in the context of STEM career ads, and how these biases affect the visibility of ads across different genders.	The paper examines the application of algorithmic advertising on platforms like Facebook, focusing on ad auctions and algorithmic decision-making processes that may unintentionally favor one gender over another.	Despite efforts to avoid gender biases, economic mechanisms in ad auctions unintentionally favor men. This occurs because advertising strategies often prioritize higher returns on investment, which leads to more ads being shown to men than women, especially in STEM-related campaigns.	Focuses on digital marketing, algorithm-based advertising, and bias in online advertising within the context of gender discrimination.	The study highlights the complexities of mitigating algorithmic biases in advertising. It suggests that while transparency and gender neutrality are essential, they are not enough to resolve gender-based disparities in ad visibility. The findings call for new policy measures and guidance to ensure fair distribution of ads across demographic groups.
Knowles et al. (2022)	The study formalizes the relationship between trust and fairness, accountability, and transparency (FAT) in AI, developing an ontology to address the complexities and various orientations of Trust in AI (TAI).	The paper discusses AI systems, focusing on trust building mechanisms such as fairness, accountability, and transparency to foster trust in AI technologies.	Trust in AI is multidimensional, encompassing factors such as who is trusting, what is trusted, and why. The study identifies three key pillars: optimizing decision-making, maximizing uptake, and minimizing harm, integral to promoting trust in AI.	It focuses on AI ethics, decision-making optimization, and the role of trust in deploying and using AI, with a particular emphasis on how accountability and transparency affect the perception of trustworthiness in AI systems.	The paper offers a comprehensive ontology of Trust in AI (TAI), categorizing various approaches to promoting trust and highlighting the need for nuanced, context-specific efforts in AI ethics and governance.

continued on following page

Table 1. Continued

Author(s) / Year	Study Focus / Objective	AI Technology / Application	Key Findings	Marketing Area	Contribution to Literature
Okeleke et al. (2024)	The study investigates how AI-powered predictive analytics enhances understanding market trends and consumer behavior.	Utilizes machine learning, natural language processing (NLP), and deep learning to predict market trends and analyze consumer sentiment.	AI-driven analytics improves forecasting accuracy, personalizes consumer experiences, and boosts strategic marketing decisions despite data quality and privacy challenges.	Focuses on predictive analytics, consumer behavior modeling, personalized marketing, and AI-driven decision-making.	Offers practical case studies and a comprehensive review of AI techniques in predictive marketing, highlighting benefits and implementation challenges.
Sung et al. (2021)	Examines how AI-embedded mixed reality (MR) environments affect consumer engagement and behavior in retail settings.	It uses interactive AI with speech recognition and synthesis embedded in MR to enhance immersive retail experiences.	High-quality AI increases MR immersion, enjoyment, and novelty, which leads to stronger consumer engagement and behavioral responses like purchase intention and word-of-mouth.	Focuses on immersive retail marketing, consumer engagement, and technology-enhanced shopping experiences.	Provides empirical evidence on how AI quality in MR environments boosts engagement and behavior, offering a structured model for AI-driven retail experience design.
Bormane & Blaus (2024)	The article investigates the use of Artificial Intelligence (AI) in digital marketing communication, highlighting its applications, advantages, risks, and challenges.	AI technologies discussed include machine learning, computer vision, robotics, speech recognition, and natural language processing, all applied within digital marketing activities such as social media marketing, search engine marketing, and digital advertising.	AI can greatly enhance digital marketing efficiency, saving time, money, and resources. It allows for personalized content, better customer segmentation, and automated tasks. However, risks such as data security, privacy concerns, and psychological manipulation also arise.	Focuses on digital marketing communication, particularly areas like advertising, content creation, personalized marketing, and customer engagement using AI.	The study contributes by identifying and discussing the risks and benefits of AI in digital marketing, suggesting the importance of understanding the advantages and the potential risks involved in implementing AI technologies in marketing strategies.

continued on following page

Table 1. Continued

Author(s) / Year	Study Focus / Objective	AI Technology / Application	Key Findings	Marketing Area	Contribution to Literature
Ziakis & Vlachopoulou (2023)	Conducts a systematic literature review to explore how AI can optimize digital marketing strategies and identify key trends and research clusters.	Covers AI applications, including machine learning, chatbots, NLP, recommendation engines, and predictive analytics across diverse digital marketing functions.	AI enhances personalization, efficiency, and strategic insight in digital marketing, but ethical concerns and data challenges persist.	Focuses on e-commerce, social media, consumer behavior analysis, digital advertising, and budget optimization.	Offers a comprehensive bibliometric and thematic analysis of 211 studies, presenting future research directions and an in-depth thematic map of AI's impact on digital marketing.
Purwanto et al. (2024)	Investigates the ethical risks and challenges of implementing AI in business operations.	Covers the use of AI in decision-making systems, data analysis, automated hiring, and customer profiling.	Highlights key concerns such as algorithmic bias, privacy violations, lack of transparency, and the need for robust ethical governance in AI use.	Focuses on AI ethics in business marketing practices, customer data usage, automated targeting, and decision transparency.	Provides a structured ethical framework and actionable strategies for integrating AI responsibly in business, emphasizing transparency, accountability, and stakeholder trust.
Davtyan (2024)	Explores how AI enhances consumer behavior analysis and digital marketing strategies for personalization and predictive insights.	Utilizes machine learning, natural language processing (NLP), predictive analytics, and programmatic advertising to optimize targeting and engagement.	AI improves engagement, personalization, and campaign efficiency but raises concerns about privacy, algorithmic bias, and ethical use.	Focuses on personalized marketing, predictive marketing, sentiment analysis, and automated digital campaigns.	Provides a comprehensive overview of AI's benefits and ethical challenges in marketing, offering future research directions on transparency and algorithmic accountability.
Efendioglu (2023)	The study evaluates the integration of AI in digital marketing strategies, using bibliometric analysis to examine trends, publications, and influential authors and institutions in this area.	AI technologies such as machine learning, big data analytics, personalized content creation, and automation are applied in digital marketing, particularly in customer service, sales processes, and data analysis.	AI enhances personalization, data analysis, and customer experiences in digital marketing. However, businesses face challenges related to data privacy, AI's ability to automate tasks, and the need for skilled human oversight.	The study focuses on digital marketing strategies, personalized marketing, customer experience, and AI-powered automation in marketing activities.	The article contributes a bibliometric review, identifying the growth of AI in digital marketing research and providing insights into future directions for AI-driven marketing strategies, focusing on data analysis, customer engagement, and automation.

3. RESEARCH METHODOLOGY

This study employs a qualitative narrative review approach to systematically explore the role of Artificial Intelligence (AI) in transforming digital marketing strategies. This review aims to synthesize the latest research, critically assess emerging trends, and identify challenges and opportunities associated with AI adoption in digital marketing. By systematically reviewing academic literature, industry reports, and real-world case studies, this paper aims to provide a comprehensive understanding of AI's impact on marketing while identifying gaps in existing literature for future research.

Given the interdisciplinary and rapidly evolving nature of AI technologies and digital marketing, a qualitative approach provides an in-depth exploration of these subjects. A narrative review methodology was chosen for its ability to integrate diverse research findings and present a cohesive analysis of AI applications in marketing. The narrative review allows for synthesizing broad trends and concepts, facilitating the identification of research gaps and future opportunities in a field that continues to evolve rapidly.

3.1 Research Approach

The methodology follows a qualitative, thematic narrative review. This approach was selected because of its suitability for synthesizing existing knowledge on a complex and evolving subject, such as AI, in digital marketing. Unlike quantitative reviews that focus on statistical analysis, this qualitative methodology emphasizes the conceptual understanding of how AI technologies are applied in marketing and the impact these applications have on industry practices.

A narrative review methodology is beneficial in this context because it provides flexibility in capturing the multiple dimensions of AI's role in marketing. This approach allows for a deeper investigation into AI's theoretical and practical aspects, drawing on diverse studies from various sectors, including retail, entertainment, technology, and consumer goods. Moreover, it helps in understanding how AI technologies integrate into existing digital marketing strategies, the challenges faced during implementation, and the opportunities for innovation that AI presents.

This methodology identifies and organizes marketing trends, challenges, and opportunities associated with AI by employing content analysis and comparative analysis. The findings are categorized into clear themes, each representing a significant aspect of AI's influence on digital marketing practices.

3.2 Research Methodology Framework

The research methodology framework outlines the key stages of the literature review process. The following stages were involved:

1. **Literature Search and Data Collection**
   - o **Academic Databases**: Scopus, Web of Science, Google Scholar, ScienceDirect, IEEE Xplore.
   - o **Industry Reports**: McKinsey, PwC, Gartner, Statista.
   - o **Search Terms**: "Artificial Intelligence in marketing," "AI personalization," "machine learning advertising," "predictive analytics marketing," "AI chatbots," "AI customer segmentation."
   - o **Inclusion Criteria**: Peer-reviewed journal articles, conference papers, and high-quality industry reports published between **2015 and 2024**.
   - o **Exclusion Criteria**: Non-peer-reviewed sources and articles not focusing on AI applications in digital marketing.
2. **Data Analysis and Thematic Categorization**
   - o **Content Analysis**: A detailed literature analysis to identify recurring themes and key findings across studies.
   - o **Thematic Categorization**: Identifying themes such as:
     - ▪ **AI Technologies in Marketing**: Machine learning, natural language processing, recommendation engines.
     - ▪ **Trends in AI-Driven Marketing Strategies**: Personalization, automation, and predictive analytics.
     - ▪ **Challenges in AI Implementation**: Data privacy, cost, technical integration, and transparency.
     - ▪ **Opportunities for AI in Marketing**: ROI enhancement, customer insights, and content automation.
3. **Comparative Analysis of AI Adoption Across Sectors**
   - o **Industries Analyzed**: Retail, entertainment, technology
   - o **Marketing Functions**: Advertising, content creation, customer support
   - o **Objective**: Identify best practices, sector-specific challenges, and opportunities for AI adoption across various industries.
4. **Synthesis and Research Gap Identification**
   - o **Synthesis of Findings**: Summarizing key trends, challenges, and opportunities identified across the literature.
   - o **Identification of Research Gaps**: Highlighting underexplored areas such as integrating AI tools across marketing functions, ethical concerns, and the long-term impact on customer loyalty and brand perception.

3.3 Visual Research Methodology Framework

To further illustrate the methodology, Figure 1 below provides a visual framework that outlines the key stages of the research process. This diagram visually represents the progression from literature search and data collection to research gap identification.

Figure 1. Research Process Framework: From Literature Search to Gap Identification

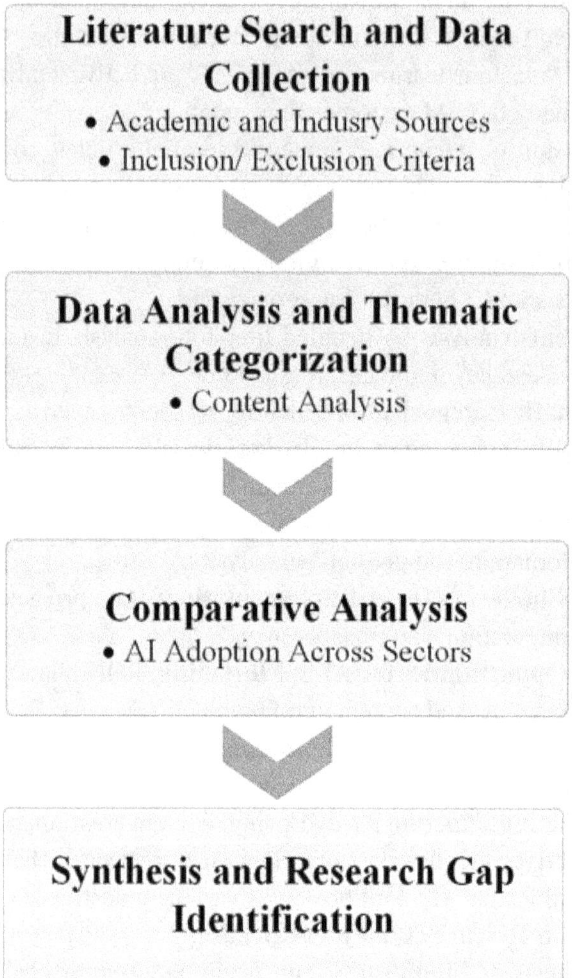

3.4 Research Limitations

This review methodology is subject to several limitations:

- **Secondary Data**: The review relies on secondary data from existing studies, which means the findings are limited to what has been published in the literature and may not reflect the latest developments that have yet to be documented in academic or industry sources.
- **Rapid Technological Advancements**: The pace at which AI technologies evolve means that some recent innovations and applications may not be fully captured in the available literature.
- **Bias in Case Studies**: The case studies included may reflect idealized or marketing-driven perspectives from high-profile companies, which could skew findings toward successful AI applications.

Despite these limitations, the methodology provides a robust and comprehensive framework for synthesizing the existing literature on AI adoption in digital marketing and identifying significant trends, challenges, and opportunities for future research.

4. DISCUSSION

Incorporating Artificial Intelligence (AI) into digital marketing profoundly transforms how businesses interact with consumers. With the continuous evolution of technologies such as machine learning (ML), natural language processing (NLP), and predictive analytics, marketing strategies have radically shifted in design and execution. These innovations enable organizations to deliver more personalized, efficient, and precisely targeted campaigns, significantly enhancing customer experience and overall marketing effectiveness.

One of the most significant findings from the literature is the critical role AI plays in enabling personalization. By processing vast volumes of consumer data, AI technologies allow marketers to gain deeper insights into customer behaviors, accurately segment audiences, and design highly tailored marketing strategies. Machine learning, in particular, has empowered platforms like Google Ads and Facebook to optimize ad targeting dynamically by learning continuously from user interactions. As Yashveer Raghav et al. (2024) noted, machine learning revolutionizes ad targeting, personalization, and customer segmentation. This transition from traditional broad-based strategies to AI-driven personalized campaigns has led to greater consumer engagement and higher conversion rates. Consequently, marketing resources are allocated more efficiently, enhancing return on investment (ROI). As data-driven decision-making becomes the norm, AI's capacity to facilitate hyper-personalized experiences is increasingly recognized as a key competitive advantage.

Beyond personalization, natural language processing (NLP) has substantially advanced the quality of customer interactions within digital marketing. AI-powered tools like chatbots and virtual assistants enable businesses to engage customers in real-time, providing context-aware responses that improve service experiences. These technologies enhance customer satisfaction and reduce operational costs by automating many customer support tasks. The widespread deployment of NLP-driven solutions has improved accessibility and strengthened consumer engagement, underscoring the technology's vital role in contemporary marketing strategies.

Predictive analytics represents another cornerstone in the evolving landscape of AI-driven marketing. The ability of AI to analyze historical data and forecast consumer behavior has enabled marketers to shift from reactive to proactive strategies. Predictive models empower companies to anticipate customer needs, adjust campaigns in real-time, and fine-tune targeting for maximum effectiveness. Leading platforms like Amazon and Netflix have demonstrated how predictive analytics can enhance customer satisfaction and loyalty through highly tailored recommendations. This evolution enables businesses to better align their strategies with emerging consumer preferences, ensuring sustained competitive advantage.

Nonetheless, the integration of AI technologies also introduces considerable challenges. Among these, data privacy remains one of the most critical concerns. As AI systems rely heavily on personal data to drive marketing efforts, consumer consent, ethical data usage, and regulatory compliance issues have become increasingly significant. Businesses must navigate stringent data protection regulations such as the General Data Protection Regulation (GDPR) and maintain transparency in their data practices to foster and retain consumer trust.

Technical integration challenges further complicate AI adoption. As highlighted by Sharbati et al. (2025), technical difficulties in integrating AI systems into complex workflows are a common barrier across industries, including marketing. Also Ghasemi Abyaneh et al. (2025) declared that Legacy infrastructure and outdated platforms often hinder the seamless deployment of AI tools, requiring substantial investments in new systems and employee training. These challenges are particularly pronounced for small and medium-sized enterprises (SMEs) that may lack the financial and technical resources necessary for large-scale AI implementation. Therefore, strategic planning and phased integration approaches are essential to minimize disruptions and maximize AI's potential benefits.

Algorithmic bias poses another pressing ethical challenge. AI models trained on historical data are susceptible to inheriting existing societal biases, which can lead to discriminatory marketing practices. For instance, biased algorithms may unintentionally exclude certain demographic groups from targeted campaigns, resulting in unfair or unethical outcomes. Organizations must invest in developing transparent, auditable AI systems routinely assessed for fairness to prevent such issues. Ensuring ethical AI practices is vital for promoting inclusivity and maintaining consumer confidence.

Despite these challenges, the opportunities offered by AI in digital marketing are vast and transformative. Beyond personalization and automation, AI is revolutionizing content creation. Platforms like Copy.ai and Jasper.ai allow marketers to produce high-quality written content efficiently, enabling businesses to maintain a consistent, compelling brand presence across multiple channels without excessive resource expenditure. Similarly, AI-assisted video production technologies support the creation of dynamic, personalized multimedia content, further enhancing audience engagement.

Another critical advantage lies in AI's ability to optimize content distribution. By analyzing consumer behavior patterns, AI tools can determine the optimal channels, timing, and formats for content delivery, ensuring that marketing messages reach the right audience at the right moment. This strategic distribution approach significantly amplifies the reach and effectiveness of digital marketing campaigns, resulting in improved engagement and conversion rates.

As AI matures, its potential to reshape digital marketing will only expand. However, businesses must adopt a vigilant and ethical approach to AI deployment. Managing risks related to data privacy, algorithmic bias, and the erosion of human decision-making autonomy will be crucial in safeguarding consumer trust and promoting sustainable marketing practices. Ethical, transparent, and responsible AI adoption will ensure its benefits are widely shared, supporting business success and broader societal well-being.

5. CONCLUSION

Integrating Artificial Intelligence (AI) into digital marketing is not merely a technological enhancement. It represents a paradigm shift in how businesses engage with consumers, design campaigns, and make strategic decisions. This study has presented a comprehensive narrative review of recent developments in AI applications across various digital marketing domains, including personalization, automation, predictive analytics, content creation, and customer engagement. The findings confirm that AI technologies, particularly machine learning (ML), natural language processing (NLP), and predictive analytics, significantly enhance marketing strategies' precision, efficiency, and scalability.

AI's capacity to personalize user experiences based on behavioral data, automate repetitive marketing tasks, and predict consumer behavior has allowed marketers to deliver highly targeted, timely, and relevant messages. These capabilities are reshaping consumer-brand interactions and enabling firms to optimize return on investment (ROI) through more strategic allocation of resources. In particular, sectors such as e-commerce, entertainment, and digital services are already leveraging these tools to achieve measurable improvements in customer satisfaction, loyalty, and revenue generation.

At the same time, the literature also highlights substantial challenges that must be addressed to realize AI's full potential in marketing. Data privacy and regulatory compliance, high implementation costs, technical integration barriers, and algorithmic bias are among the most critical issues. These concerns underscore the importance of responsible AI development and deployment, particularly in marketing contexts where ethical considerations directly influence brand reputation and consumer trust.

Furthermore, this study identifies a clear research gap. While many studies explore specific AI tools or applications, few adopt a holistic approach that examines the full spectrum of AI's influence across marketing functions. There remains a need for interdisciplinary research that bridges technical innovation with business strategy, customer psychology, and ethical governance.

In light of these findings, this paper recommends that future research and practice in AI-driven digital marketing should prioritize the following: (1) developing integrative frameworks that combine multiple AI technologies for unified marketing strategies; (2) investing in transparent and explainable AI systems to address issues of bias and accountability; and (3) fostering cross-sector collaborations that bring together academic researchers, industry experts, and policy-makers to co-create guidelines for ethical and practical AI use.

Ultimately, AI offers a robust set of tools that, when thoughtfully implemented, can transform digital marketing from a reactive function into a proactive, predictive, and deeply personalized discipline. As technology continues to evolve, so must our strategies, ensuring that innovation is matched by responsibility and that the benefits of AI are harnessed for sustainable, consumer-centric growth in the digital economy.

ACKNOWLEDGEMENTS

Declaration of competing interest:

The authors declare that they have no known competing financial interests or personal relationships that could have appeared to influence the work reported in this paper.

Declaration of generative AI and AI-assisted technologies in the writing process:

While preparing this work, the authors used OpenAI's tool Chat GPT to edit and write some parts of the paper. After using this service, the authors reviewed and edited the content as needed and took full responsibility for the publication's content.

REFERENCES

Abhiseka, M., R., Alex, Y., Saputra, R., & Setiawan, A. (2024). AI for Digital Marketing. *Apollo: Journal of Tourism and Business*. .DOI: 10.58905/apollo.v2i2.298

Adwan, A. (2024). Can companies in digital marketing benefit from artificial intelligence in content creation? *International Journal of Data and Network Science*. .DOI: 10.5267/j.ijdns.2023.12.024

Akter, S., Dwivedi, Y., Sajib, S., Biswas, K., Bandara, R., & Michael, K. (2022). Algorithmic bias in machine learning-based marketing models. *Journal of Business Research*, *144*, 201–216. Advance online publication. DOI: 10.1016/j.jbusres.2022.01.083

Anantrasirichai, N., & Bull, D. (2020). Artificial intelligence in the creative industries: A review. *Artificial Intelligence Review*, *55*(1), 589–656. DOI: 10.1007/s10462-021-10039-7

Arce, C., Valderrama, D., Barragán, G., & Santillán, J. (2023). Optimizing Business Performance: Marketing Strategies for Small and Medium Businesses Using Artificial Intelligence Tools. *Migration Letters : An International Journal of Migration Studies*, *21*(S1), 193–201. Advance online publication. DOI: 10.59670/ml.v21iS1.6008

Babadoğan, B. (2024). *Unveiling the Power of AI-Driven Personalization: Transforming Consumer Behavior in the Age of Digital Marketing*. Next Frontier For Life Sciences and AI., DOI: 10.62802/fj43xy18

Babatunde, S., Odejide, O., Edunjobi, T., & Ogundipe, D. (2024). The Role Of Ai In Marketing Personalization: A Theoretical Exploration Of Consumer Engagement Strategies. *International Journal of Management & Entrepreneurship Research*. .DOI: 10.51594/ijmer.v6i3.964

Bastray, T. (2025). The Integration of AI in Digital Marketing: Opportunities and Challenges. *Journal of Informatics Education and Research*. .DOI: 10.52783/jier.v5i1.2111

Blackburn, R., Lurz, K., Priese, B., Göb, R., & Darkow, I. (2015). A predictive analytics approach for demand forecasting in the process industry. *International Transactions in Operational Research*, *22*(3), 407–428. DOI: 10.1111/itor.12122

Blümel, J., Zaki, M., & Bohné, T. (2023). Personal touch in digital customer service: A conceptual framework of relational personalization for conversational AI. *Journal of Service Theory and Practice*. Advance online publication. DOI: 10.1108/JSTP-03-2023-0098

Bormane, S., & Blaus, E. (2024). Artificial intelligence in the context of digital marketing communication. *Frontiers in Communication*, *9*, 1411226. Advance online publication. DOI: 10.3389/fcomm.2024.1411226

Büchi, M., Fosch-Villaronga, E., Lutz, C., Tamó-Larrieux, A., & Velidi, S. (2021). Making sense of algorithmic profiling: User perceptions on Facebook. *Information Communication and Society*, *26*(4), 809–825. DOI: 10.1080/1369118X.2021.1989011

Buiten, M. (2019). Towards Intelligent Regulation of Artificial Intelligence. *European Journal of Risk Regulation*, *10*(1), 41–59. DOI: 10.1017/err.2019.8

Campbell, C., Sands, S., Ferraro, C., Tsao, H., & Mavrommatis, A. (2020). From data to action: How marketers can leverage AI. *Business Horizons*, *63*(2), 227–243. Advance online publication. DOI: 10.1016/j.bushor.2019.12.002

Chang, X. (2023). *Gender Bias in Hiring: An Analysis of the Impact of Amazon's Recruiting Algorithm*. Advances in Economics, Management, and Political Sciences., DOI: 10.54254/2754-1169/23/20230367

Cherian, M., Manoja, K., &, A. (2025). Leveraging AI for Predicting Marketing and Customer Insights Overview. *Journal of Informatics Education and Research*. .DOI: 10.52783/jier.v5i1.2050

Chintalapati, S., & Pandey, S. (2021). Artificial intelligence in marketing: A systematic literature review. *International Journal of Market Research*, *64*(1), 38–68. DOI: 10.1177/14707853211018428

Choi, J., & Lim, K. (2020). Identifying machine learning techniques for classification of target advertising. *ICT Express*, *6*(3), 175–180. DOI: 10.1016/j.icte.2020.04.012

Cutler, K. (2024). The evolution of digital marketing in the era of AI. *Applied Marketing Analytics: The Peer-Reviewed Journal*. .DOI: 10.69554/UNDG1907

Davenport, T., Guha, A., Grewal, D., & Breßgott, T. (2019). How artificial intelligence will change the future of marketing. *Journal of the Academy of Marketing Science*, *48*(1), 24–42. DOI: 10.1007/s11747-019-00696-0

Davtyan, N. (2024). AI in Consumer Behavior Analysis and Digital Marketing: A Strategic Approach. *The Integration of AI and Technology in Modern Business Practices*. .DOI: 10.70301/CONF.SBS-JABR.2024.1/1.5

De Bruyn, A., Viswanathan, V., Beh, Y., Brock, J., & Von Wangenheim, F. (2020). Artificial Intelligence and Marketing: Pitfalls and Opportunities. *Journal of Interactive Marketing*, *51*(1), 91–105. DOI: 10.1016/j.intmar.2020.04.007

Dwivedi, Y., Ismagilova, E., Hughes, D., Carlson, J., Filieri, R., Jacobson, J., Jain, V., Karjaluoto, H., Kefi, H., Krishen, A., Kumar, V., Rahman, M., Raman, R., Rauschnabel, P., Rowley, J., Salo, J., Tran, G., & Wang, Y. (2020). Setting the future of digital and social media marketing research: Perspectives and research propositions. *International Journal of Information Management*, *59*, 102168. DOI: 10.1016/j.ijinfomgt.2020.102168

Efendioglu, I. (2023). *The evaluation of AI integration in innovative digital marketing strategies*. Pressacademia., DOI: 10.17261/Pressacademia.2023.1820

Elkhatibi, Y., & Benabdelouhed, R. (2024). Digital Marketing and Artificial Intelligence: Towards a Better Understanding of the Two Strategies. *International Journal of Advanced Multidisciplinary Research and Studies*. .DOI: 10.62225/2583049X.2024.4.3.2847

Erevelles, S., Fukawa, N., & Swayne, L. (2016). Big Data consumer analytics and the transformation of marketing. *Journal of Business Research*, *69*(2), 897–904. DOI: 10.1016/j.jbusres.2015.07.001

Gani, M. O., & Faroque, A. R. (2021). Digital marketing. In *Cross-border E-commerce marketing and management* (pp. 172–202). IGI Global Scientific Publishing., DOI: 10.4018/978-1-7998-5823-2.ch008

Ghasemi Abyaneh, A., Bakhshi Movahed, A., Abyari, A., Nodehfarahani, A., & Khakbazan, M. (2025). Evaluating the RFID Technology in Costco Company: A Focus on Logistics and Supply Chain Management. *Applied Innovations in Industrial Management*, *5*(2), 34–51. DOI: 10.63630/aiim.52.34

Gkikas, D., & Theodoridis, P. (2024). Predicting Online Shopping Behavior: Using Machine Learning and Google Analytics to Classify User Engagement. *Applied Sciences (Basel, Switzerland), 14*(23), 11403. Advance online publication. DOI: 10.3390/app142311403

Gujar, P., Paliwal, G., & Panyam, S. (2024). Generative AI and the Future of Interactive and Immersive Advertising. *2024 IEEE Eighth Ecuador Technical Chapters Meeting (ETCM)*, 1-6. DOI: 10.1109/ETCM63562.2024.10746166

Gündüzyeli, B. (2024). Artificial Intelligence in Digital Marketing Within the Framework of Sustainable Management. *Sustainability (Basel), 16*(23), 10511. Advance online publication. DOI: 10.3390/su162310511

Gungunawat, A., Khandelwal, N., & Gupta, N. (2024). *AI-Powered Personalization in Digital Marketing: Transforming Consumer Engagement and Strategy*. RESEARCH REVIEW International Journal of Multidisciplinary., DOI: 10.31305/rrijm.2024.v09.n11.026

Hameed, H. (2025). Developing Cost-Effective AI Algorithms for Resource-Constrained Devices. *International Journal of Computers and Informatics*. .DOI: 10.59992/IJCI.2025.v4n1p3

Han, R., Lam, H., Zhan, Y., Wang, Y., Dwivedi, Y., & Tan, K. (2021). Artificial intelligence in business-to-business marketing: A bibliometric analysis of current research status, development, and future directions. *Industrial Management & Data Systems, 121*(12), 2467–2497. DOI: 10.1108/IMDS-05-2021-0300

Herath, D., Ode, E., & Herath, G. (2025). Can AI replace humans? Comparing the capabilities of AI tools and human performance in a business management education scenario. *British Educational Research Journal*, berj.4111. Advance online publication. DOI: 10.1002/berj.4111

Huang, M., & Rust, R. (2020). A strategic framework for artificial intelligence in marketing. *Journal of the Academy of Marketing Science, 49*(1), 30–50. DOI: 10.1007/s11747-020-00749-9

Ip, K. (2023). Revolutionizing content recommendation: The impact of AI in marketing. *Journal of AI, Robotics & Workplace Automation*. .DOI: 10.69554/AMHI2323

Islam, M., Sourav, M., & Reza, J. (2024). *The impact of data protection regulations on business analytics*. World Journal of Advanced Research and Reviews., DOI: 10.30574/wjarr.2024.24.2.3503

Jalal, M., & Elmaghraby, A. (2024). Analyzing the Dynamics of Customer Behavior: A New Perspective on Personalized Marketing through Counterfactual Analysis. *Journal of Theoretical and Applied Electronic Commerce Research, 19*(3), 1660–1681. DOI: 10.3390/jtaer19030081

Janice, N., & Kusumawati, N. (2024). *Harmonizing Algorithms and User Satisfaction: Evaluating The Impact of Spotify's Discover Weekly on Customer Loyalty*. Journal Integration of Management Studies., DOI: 10.58229/jims.v2i2.168

Jastacia, B., & Akbar, D. (2023). Potential Use Of Artificial Intelligence For Digital Promotional Video: Neuromarketing Approach. *Jurnal Studi Inovasi*. .DOI: 10.52000/jsi.v3i4.140

K, D. T. (2024, August 31). K, T. (2024). AI-DRIVEN CUSTOMER SEGMENTATION: TARGETING AND RETARGETING STRATEGIES IN DIGITAL MARKETING. *Donglixue Yu Kongzhi Xuebao*, 400–415. Advance online publication. DOI: 10.71058/jodac.v8i8027

Karami, A., Shemshaki, M., & Ghazanfar, M. (2024). *Exploring the Ethical Implications of AI-Powered Personalization in Digital Marketing. Data Intelligence*. In-Press., DOI: 10.3724/2096-7004.di.2024.0055

Knowles, B., Richards, J., & Kroeger, F. (2022). The Many Facets of Trust in AI: Formalizing the Relation Between Trust and Fairness, Accountability, and Transparency. *ArXiv*, abs/2208.00681. https://doi.org//arXiv.2208.00681.DOI: 10.48550

Koob, C. (2023). Consumers' Preferences for Digital Corporate Content on Company Websites: A Best-Worst Scaling Analysis. *Journal of Theoretical and Applied Electronic Commerce Research, 18*(3), 1301–1319. DOI: 10.3390/jtaer18030066

Kubovics, M. (2024). Innovative Content Production in Marketing Communication Through AI. *European Conference on Innovation and Entrepreneurship*. DOI: 10.34190/ecie.19.1.2877

Kumar, V., Ashraf, A., & Nadeem, W. (2024). AI-powered marketing: What, where, and how? *International Journal of Information Management, 77*, 102783. DOI: 10.1016/j.ijinfomgt.2024.102783

Lambrecht, A., & Tucker, C. (2021). Algorithm-Based Advertising: Unintended Effects and the Tricky Business of Mitigating Adverse Outcomes. *NIM Marketing Intelligence Review, 13*(1), 24–29. DOI: 10.2478/nimmir-2021-0004

Martinoli, A., & Vuković, V. (2024). *Personalized distribution of media content: AI algorithms and enhancement of user experience*. Kultura., DOI: 10.5937/kultura2484057M

Mensah, G. (2024). *Artificial Intelligence and Ethics: A Comprehensive Review of Bias Mitigation, Transparency, and Accountability in AI Systems*. Africa Journal For Regulatory Affairs., DOI: 10.62839/AJFRA/2024.v1.I1.32-45

Mero, J., Leinonen, M., Makkonen, H., & Karjaluoto, H. (2022). Agile logic for SaaS implementation: Capitalizing on marketing automation software in a start-up. *Journal of Business Research, 145*, 583–594. Advance online publication. DOI: 10.1016/j.jbusres.2022.03.026

Movahed, A. B., Abyaneh, A. G., Khakbazan, M., & Movahed, A. B. (2025). Smart Economy Cybersecurity: AI-Driven Risk Management in Digital Markets. In *Dynamic and Safe Economy in the Age of Smart Technologies* (pp. 49-72). IGI Global Scientific Publishing. DOI: DOI: 10.4018/979-8-3693-4369-2.ch004

Murár, P., & Kubovics, M. (2023). Using AI to Create Content Designed for Marketing Communications. *European Conference on Innovation and Entrepreneurship*. DOI: 10.34190/ecie.18.1.1638

Nair, K., & Gupta, R. (2021). Application of AI technology in modern digital marketing environment. *World Journal of Entrepreneurship, Management and Sustainable Development*, *ahead-of-print*(ahead-of-print). Advance online publication. DOI: 10.1108/WJEMSD-08-2020-0099

Ngai, E., Lee, M., Luo, M., Chan, P., & Liang, T. (2021). An intelligent knowledge-based chatbot for customer service. *Electronic Commerce Research and Applications*, *50*, 101098. DOI: 10.1016/j.elerap.2021.101098

Nguyen, Q., Sidorova, A., & Torres, R. (2021). User interactions with chatbot interfaces vs. Menu-based interfaces: An empirical study. *Computers in Human Behavior*, *128*, 107093. DOI: 10.1016/j.chb.2021.107093

Nimbalkar, A., & Singh, A. (2024). *A Study of the Impact of Artificial Intelligence on Digital Marketing - A Systematic Review of Literature*. JOURNAL OF MANAGEMENT AND ENTREPRENEURSHIP., DOI: 10.70906/20241803001008

Nozari, H., & Samadi, S. (2025). Digital Twin-Enhanced Sentiment Analysis for Targeted Marketing Optimization. In *Dynamic and Safe Economy in the Age of Smart Technologies* (pp. 121–138). IGI Global Scientific Publishing., DOI: 10.4018/979-8-3693-4369-2.ch008

Ogabu, J. (2024). The Future of Finance is Intelligent: Exploring the Positive Impact of AI Education on Efficiency, Innovation, and Profitability in the Financial Sector. *International Journal of Research and Scientific Innovation*. .DOI: 10.51244/IJRSI.2024.11110084

Oğuz, A. (2024). Consumer Behavior in the Era of AI-Driven Marketing. *Human-Computer Interaction*, *8*(1), 147. Advance online publication. DOI: 10.62802/h9frxh42

Okeleke, P. A., Ajiga, D., Folorunsho, S. O., & Ezeigweneme, C. (2024). Predictive analytics for market trends using AI: A study in consumer behavior. *International Journal of Engineering Research Updates*, *7*(1), 36–49. DOI: 10.53430/ijeru.2024.7.1.0032

Olson, E., Olson, K., Czaplewski, A., & Key, T. (2021). Business strategy and the management of digital marketing. *Business Horizons*, *64*(2), 285–293. Advance online publication. DOI: 10.1016/j.bushor.2020.12.004

Pangeran, A., Afra, I., & Lenando, T. (2024). *Maximizing the Impact of Digital Marketing: AI Integration for More Precise and Effective Strategies*. INTERNATIONAL JOURNAL OF MULTIDISCIPLINARY RESEARCH AND ANALYSIS., DOI: 10.47191/ijmra/v7-i06-35

Ponomarenko, I. (2024). Artificial intelligence in digital marketing. *Scientia fructuosa*. .DOI: 10.31617/1.2024(155)04

Prasad, K., Xavier, L., Jain, S., Subba, R., Mittal, S., & Anute, N. (2024). AI-Driven Chatbots for E-Commerce Customer Support. *2024 International Conference on Advances in Computing, Communication and Applied Informatics (ACCAI)*, 1-5. DOI: 10.1109/ACCAI61061.2024.10602261

Purwanto, A., Fauzan, M., Widya, T., & Azzaky, N. (2024). Ethical Implications and Challenges of AI Implementation in Business Operations. *TechComp Innovations. Journal of Computer Science and Technology*, *1*(2), 68–82. Advance online publication. DOI: 10.70063/techcompinnovations.v1i2.52

Raaj, A., & Premnath, D. (2023). A Case Study on the Impact of ChatGPT On Personalised Marketing and Customer Engagement at Different Stages of the Purchase Process.

Saboune, F. (2024). AI-Driven Marketing Strategies: Unlocking Growth Potential and Operational Efficiency in the Digital Communication Landscape. *2024 International Conference on Intelligent Computing, Communication, Networking and Services (ICCNS)*, 295-301. DOI: 10.1109/ICCNS62192.2024.10776195

Saura, J., Palacios-Marqués, D., & Ribeiro-Soriano, D. (2021). Digital marketing in SMEs via data-driven strategies: Reviewing the current state of research. *Journal of Small Business Management*, *61*(3), 1278–1313. DOI: 10.1080/00472778.2021.1955127

Semerádová, T., & Weinlich, P. (2019). Computer Estimation of Customer Similarity With Facebook Lookalikes: Advantages and Disadvantages of Hyper-Targeting. *IEEE Access : Practical Innovations, Open Solutions*, *7*, 153365–153377. DOI: 10.1109/ACCESS.2019.2948401

Shanahan, T., Tran, T., & Taylor, E. (2019). Getting to know you: Social media personalization as a means of enhancing brand loyalty and perceived quality. *Journal of Retailing and Consumer Services*, *47*, 57–65. Advance online publication. DOI: 10.1016/j.jretconser.2018.10.007

Shanmugam, G., Rajendran, D., Thanarajan, T., Murugaraj, S. S., & Rajendran, S. (2023). Artificial Intelligence as a Catalyst in Digital Marketing: Enhancing Profitability and Market Potential. *Ingénierie des Systèmes d'Information, 28*(6).

Sharbati, A., Bakhshi Movahed, A., Ghasemi Abyaneh, A., & Rahmanian, F. (2025). Risk Assessment of Healthcare Systems Using the FMEA Method: Medication Management Process. *Journal of Future Digital Optimization*, *1*(1), 71–85.

Sharma, K., Tomar, M., & Tadimarri, A. (2023). Unlocking Sales Potential: How AI Revolutionizes Marketing Strategies. *Journal of Knowledge Learning and Science Technology ISSN: 2959-6386 (online)*. DOI: 10.60087/jklst.vol2.n2.p250

Shrestha, Y., Krishna, V., & Krogh, G. (2020). Augmenting Organizational Decision-Making with Deep Learning Algorithms: Principles, Promises, and Challenges. *ArXiv*, abs/2011.02834. .DOI: 10.1016/j.jbusres.2020.09.068

Siles, I., Espinoza-Rojas, J., Naranjo, A., & Tristán, M. (2019). The Mutual Domestication of Users and Algorithmic Recommendations on Netflix. *Communication, Culture & Critique*, tcz025. Advance online publication. DOI: 10.1093/ccc/tcz025

Singh, A. K. (2023). Applications of the internet of things and machine learning using python in digital marketing. In *Global Applications of the Internet of Things in Digital Marketing* (pp. 213–232). IGI Global., DOI: 10.4018/978-1-6684-8166-0.ch011

Singh, N., & Adhikari, D. (2023). Challenges and Solutions in Integrating AI with Legacy Inventory Systems. *International Journal for Research in Applied Science and Engineering Technology*, *11*(12), 609–613. Advance online publication. DOI: 10.22214/ijraset.2023.57376

Sodiya, E., Umoga, U., Amoo, O., & Atadoga, A. (2024). *AI-driven warehouse automation: A comprehensive review of systems*. GSC Advanced Research and Reviews., DOI: 10.30574/gscarr.2024.18.2.0063

Somosi, Z. (2022). THE ROLE OF ARTIFICIAL INTELLIGENCE IN CONTENT CREATION AND CHECKING ITS EFFECTIVENESS IN THE GOOGLE ADS ADVERTISING SYSTEM. *The Annals of the University of Oradea. Economic Sciences*. .DOI: 10.47535/1991AUOES31(2)025

Sung, E., Bae, S., Han, D., & Kwon, O. (2021). Consumer engagement via interactive artificial intelligence and mixed reality. *International Journal of Information Management*, *60*, 102382. DOI: 10.1016/j.ijinfomgt.2021.102382

Syrotkina, O., Bhatta, S., & Jacob, K. (2023). Recency-Frequency-Monetary Analysis and Recommendation System using Apriori Algorithm on E-Commerce Sales Data. *2023 13th International Conference on Advanced Computer Information Technologies (ACIT)*, 321-326. DOI: 10.1109/ACIT58437.2023.10275513

Tashtemirovich, A. O., Balbaa, M. E., Ibrohimjon, F., & Batirova, N. (2024). Investigating the Impact of Artificial Intelligence on Digital Marketing Tactics Strategies Using Neutrosophic Set. [IJNS]. *International Journal of Neutrosophic Science*, *23*(3).

Tcharnetsky, M., & Vogt, F. (2023). An Artificial Intelligence Cycle Model Against the Shortage of Skilled Professionals - An AI-based Holistic Solution Approach for Human Resources. [JAES]. *Journal of Applied Economic Sciences*, *18*(16), 108. Advance online publication. DOI: 10.57017/jaes.v18.2(80).05

Van Esch, P., & Black, S. (2021). Artificial Intelligence (AI): Revolutionizing Digital Marketing. *Australasian Marketing Journal*, *29*(3), 199–203. DOI: 10.1177/18393349211037684

Vlačić, B., Corbo, L., Silva, S., & Dabić, M. (2021). The evolving role of artificial intelligence in marketing: A review and research agenda. *Journal of Business Research*, *128*, 187–203. DOI: 10.1016/j.jbusres.2021.01.055

Wamba-Taguimdje, S., Wamba, S., Kamdjoug, J., & Wanko, C. (2020). Influence of artificial intelligence (AI) on firm performance: The business value of AI-based transformation projects. *Business Process Management Journal*, *26*(7), 1893–1924. DOI: 10.1108/BPMJ-10-2019-0411

Williamson, S., & Prybutok, V. (2024). Balancing Privacy and Progress: A Review of Privacy Challenges, Systemic Oversight, and Patient Perceptions in AI-Driven Healthcare. *Applied Sciences (Basel, Switzerland)*, *14*(2), 675. Advance online publication. DOI: 10.3390/app14020675

Wu, S., Yau, W., Ong, T., & Chong, S. (2021). Integrated Churn Prediction and Customer Segmentation Framework for Telco Business. *IEEE Access : Practical Innovations, Open Solutions*, *9*, 62118–62136. DOI: 10.1109/ACCESS.2021.3073776

Yadav, A., & Pandita, D. (2024). A Decision Model for Revolutionizing Digital Marketing Campaigns Powered by AI and Predictive Analytics. *2024 ASU International Conference in Emerging Technologies for Sustainability and Intelligent Systems (ICETSIS)*, 791-795. DOI: 10.1109/ICETSIS61505.2024.10459608

Yashveer Raghav, Y., Tipu, R. K., Bhakhar, R., Gupta, T., & Sharma, K. (2024). The Future of Digital Marketing: Leveraging Artificial Intelligence for Competitive Strategies and Tactics. In Teixeira, S., & Remondes, J. (Eds.), *The Use of Artificial Intelligence in Digital Marketing: Competitive Strategies and Tactics* (pp. 249–274). IGI Global Scientific Publishing., DOI: 10.4018/978-1-6684-9324-3.ch011

Yeboah, D., Osei-Wusu, F., Asiedu, W., Asante, G., Antwi, E. S., Muntanka, S. A., ... & Olowookere, G. (2025). A Framework for Intelligent Color Processing and Design Optimization in UI/UX Systems.

Zhang, J., Hassandoust, F., & Williams, J. (2020). Online Customer Trust in the General Data Protection Regulation (GDPR) Context. *Pac. Asia J. Assoc. Inf. Syst.*, *12*, 4. DOI: 10.17705/1pais.12104

Ziakis, C., & Vlachopoulou, M. (2023). Artificial Intelligence in Digital Marketing: Insights from a Comprehensive Review. *Information (Basel)*, *14*(12), 664. DOI: 10.3390/info14120664

Chapter 11

Artificial Intelligence in Social Media Advertising Raising Engagement and Ethical Concerns

Kashi Thakur
Chandigarh University, India

Kritika Gupta
https://orcid.org/0000-0001-6496-9337
Chandigarh University, India

ABSTRACT

This study examines how AI-driven advertising on social media impacts user engagement, purchase intention, and attitudes toward privacy, trust, and ethics. Using a mixed-methods approach with literature review and a survey of 49 users (mostly aged 18–24), findings show that while AI improves ad relevance, concerns remain about authenticity and data use. Over half doubt the emotional genuineness of AI content and distrust data practices. The study calls for GDPR-aligned governance, explainable AI, and hybrid human-AI strategies. It offers practical solutions to bridge the gap between personalization benefits and ethical challenges in AI marketing.

1. INTRODUCTION

Artificial Intelligence (AI) is revolutionizing social media advertising by enabling brands to deliver highly personalized and engaging content. However, this advancement raises significant ethical concerns, including data privacy, algorithmic bias,

DOI: 10.4018/979-8-3373-3775-3.ch011

and the potential for consumer manipulation. As AI becomes more integrated into advertising strategies, it is crucial to balance innovation with ethical considerations to maintain consumer trust and comply with evolving regulations (Alvarez et al., 2024; Kumar & Suthar, 2024; Saura et al., 2024). AI is making waves in social media advertising and has changed the way businesses engage their customers in a more digital environment. Unlike traditional advertising based on a broader demographic approach, AI-powered advertising, in contrast, is an attempt to create relevant and personalized experiences using machine learning and advanced data analytics (Kaplan & Haenlein, 2020). More than ever, brands understand marketing to mean engaging with the right audience at the right time using the right message. AI creates perspectives for brands by examining huge amounts of user data regarding consumer behaviours. Chen et al. (2019) mentioned that AI could also note even fine changes in user behaviour like scrolling patterns and engagement rates to enhance ad placement. Engagement data demonstrates a strong potential to attract more engagement, thus making data-driven advertising an even better way to drive ROI and conversion rates (Huang & Rust, 2020).

Real-time decision-making enhancement is one of AI's major advantages in advertising. According to Davenport et al. (2019), the characteristics of AI in advertising include

- **Machine Learning Processing:** Algorithms review this data to anticipate user preferences and enhance the potential of ads to reach targets.
- **Data Collection:** AI examines user information coming from various sources, such as browsing history, social media activity, and buying patterns.
- **Automated Execution:** AI enabled systems modify the placement and content of ads to increase user engagement and effectiveness.

This level of precision makes it possible for advertisements to be of maximum relevance and timing within a customer's decision-making process. According to Chung et al. (2015), contextual precision has allowed marketers to customize ads more according to a user's urgent needs, thus maximizing the probability of such advertisement being clicked or at least engaged with. Nevertheless, privacy or, for that matter, ethical issues arise continuously in the case of advertisements based on AI. Even the most effectively functioning AI systems are noted for possible reinforcement of biases. For instance, Glikson & Woolley (2020) found evidence for bias in AI-generated job posting ads that indicated a tendency for male users to be more frequently served executive role ad postings than female users on LinkedIn. This, as expected, goes hand in hand with the past bias found in recruiting data. Along with algorithmic bias, the application of AI in advertising has raised concerns pertaining to customer trust and data safety. The fears mentioned above have existed alongside fear of surveillance and lack of control, as AI technology has come a long way and matured from being mere tools to being powerful engines for deep individual profiling. Ziakis and Vlachopoulou (2023) state, "AI technologies have come a long way from simple cookie-based tracking to profiling the complete picture of the user, understanding preferences, behaviours, and even emotions." The long-standing "privacy-personalization paradox," first suggested by Awad and Krishnan (2006), is sparked by this increase in data collection. Customers like the ease and relevance of custom ads, but there is still concern about what level of data intrusion is necessary to provide that relevance. This dichotomy can be thought of as the paradox. This internal conflict has practical implications in addition to philosophical ones. Users lose trust when they think their privacy has been invaded without a clear reason or benefit, which reduces engagement and can damage a brand's reputation.

Personalisation solutions should be open. They must be voluntary. They must create clear value for the consumer. Giving the user consent, allowing for a clear understanding of their data and, in turn, meaningfully benefitting from personalisation will lead to trust from the user. This will give the brand credibility. It is important to understand how AI shapes the consumer experience and decision-making (Hossain and Kim, 2020). They show that algorithm-based ads can boost productivity. However, they can also lead to the creation of filter bubbles. This is a closed online space where the user only sees the same content and products. This can limit the choice and new perspectives of the consumer. The user will not be able to find new or more appropriate products. AI might speed up decision-making. But at the same time, marketers need to keep in mind that AI might narrow down the horizons for consumers and not expand them. To strike a balance between efficiency and discovery, it may be necessary to design recommendation systems that include randomness and diversity.

Luo et al. (2019), are of the opinion that the absence of an emotional component in the responses of artificial intelligence usually results in lower satisfaction in users, despite the functional benefits of the customer service enhanced by artificial intelligence. The situation is further complicated by the introduction of generative AI, which uses human language quite well but supposedly is not capable of transferring the emotion and context of what is being communicated. Consequently, even the most advanced artificial intelligence can still be perceived as impersonal, which can influence the consumers' behavior and brand engagement. AI-generated advertisements increase personalization, they have the potential to cross a threshold which makes the advertisements, while still highly personalized, feel less entertaining or desirable instead feeling intrusive. This trend is especially important in emotionally based marketing campaigns where human creativity and intuition is still considerably important (Gao et al., 2023).

Certainly, AI is truly transforming social media marketing, making it possible for more accurate audience targeting, higher efficiency, and extremely personalised content delivery. Brands will be more timely and relevant in the ways they engage with consumers than ever before due to these capabilities. However, with AI use on the rise, concerns about algorithmic bias, data privacy, and customer trust are growing as well. Companies now have to navigate these ethical questions while upholding openness and customer trust. Identifying the right balance between automated processes and human intervention will be critical as AI continues to improve. This is for the fact that it is the only way through which the full potential of AI systems will be realized in marketing without compromising ethical considerations. The development of AI-based strategies involves the need for the execution of successful, sound, and socially responsible measures, which are dependent on the establishment of mechanisms for justice, accountability, and user control.

The sections that follow elaborate on AI's impact to enhance ad effectiveness, unintended outcomes such as algorithmic discrimination and reduction in consumer trust from invasive data practices, as well as the ethical issues examined and constructive recommendations made to responsibly balance creation and innovation. These recommendations included adopting explainable AI (XAI) approaches, GDPR-compliant transparency measures, and the conclusion emphasizes encouraging a considered evolution of AI application in advertising, with ongoing advancement in technology guided by ethical principles to promote fairness, transparency and trust with customers into the future. By adopting these recommendations together, this study reflects on the implications of AI today while grounding possibilities for AI to be responsibly integrated to improve digital accessories and marketing going forward.

2. REVIEW OF LITERATURE

The integration of Artificial Intelligence (AI) into social media advertising has garnered significant attention, prompting extensive research into its impact on consumer behavior, ethical considerations, and the evolving landscape of digital marketing strategies. The review of literature below discusses the same.

- **Gao et al. (2023)** The marketing of social media, as Gao et al. describe, is changing thanks to AI, which has empowered marketing departments to place customized, target-oriented ads. Marketers have begun to rely on deep learning systems that are able to recognize patterns in user behavior and adapt content in light of mounting pressures for insights drawn from consumer data. Higher engagement rates, more automation, and better accuracy in targeting audiences are all consequences enabled by these machine-learning technologies. Overall, the study finds AI as a major enabler of personalization and conversion in a changing digital advertising environment.

- **Zhang and Li (2019)** provide examples of how brands could leverage AI-based sentiment analysis to gauge customer opinion. AI algorithms successfully recognize and quantify emotional tone, discontent, or compliments in real-time by analyzing massive volumes of user-generated content like comments, reviews, and social media posts. This allows brands to quickly react to concerns, correct any issues, and adjust their strategy based on what the public wants. Based on the research, responsiveness boosts customer satisfaction and loyalty and makes the tool even more useful as the company develops a reputation for being attuned, adaptable, and emotionally intelligent in the online space.
- **Yau et al. (2021**) argue that by allowing the adverts to consider the tastes and behavior of the existing audience, artificial intelligence (AI) can significantly enhance live content optimisation. Artificial intelligence (AI) systems continually optimise adjustments to messaging, format, and timing and monitor user interactions in real-time. Providing timely and relevant information enhances response rates and levels of engagement, solidifies relationships based on trust in the business, and creates loyalty. This differentiated responsiveness allows brands to listen attentively to customer expectations.
- **Kumar et al. (2022),** customisation powered by AI is a critical element of modern digital marketing strategy because it allows businesses to communicate more effectively with users' highly contextual information. Organisations can enhance customer satisfaction, interaction, and overall marketing performance by making their content personalised. Companies can produce more relevant and engaging experiences for every individual customer by making use of data analytics and machine learning. Furthermore, this research points out that in this highly competitive digital age, customisation is no longer an enhancement but a strategic imperative that can dramatically boost conversion rates, customer loyalty, and campaign performance.
- **Wei and Tyson (2024)** tested the effectiveness of AI-created content and compared it with human-created content. They found that AI can create content faster and more efficiently, but often misses the emotional intelligence required to engage customers. While AI may be useful in supplementing created content, researchers argue that AI cannot replace a human voice's emotional response. This means that there has to be an integrated solution, whereby artificial intelligence (AI) is used to drive the creative process without replacing the human voice to ensure genuine customer interaction.

- **Jobin and Zuboff (2019)** highlight that the effective use of AI in marketing relies on ethical responsibility and transparency. They argue that without regulatory regimes and oversight, AI systems will worsen already-existing problems with algorithmic bias and privacy. To ensure that AI technologies are used in a manner that respects user rights, fosters equity, and enhances trust in digital advertising environments, the authors propose stronger governance frameworks.
- **Dwivedi et al. (2021)** emphasize the importance of human observation in AI-driven advertising campaigns. While the authors do recognize that AI provides efficiency and scalability, they warn against relying exclusively on computer systems because there is a risk of ethical blind spots, such as inadvertent biases or even discriminatory intentional targeting. The authors contend that to ensure accountability, transparency, and justice, ethical restraint and human intuition remain essential. Their observations lend merit to the possibility that artificial intelligence (AI) might serve as a decision-making tool, with human values informing algorithmic outcomes in order to avoid the possibility of compromising advertising equity or consumer confidence.
- **Davenport et al. (2020)** asserted that with enhanced consumer know-how, decision-making automation, and personalization, artificial intelligence is transforming marketing. They cautioned that while AI may boost productivity, self-belief might be lost if openness is not addressed. Their paradigm upholds the notion that AI ought to augment human creativity instead of substituting it, particularly within advertising spaces where consumers could be more emotionally engaged. This is in accordance with the current research's focus on upholding customer trust in how AI-powered ads respond while using automated marketing tactics paired with ethical oversight.
- **Rodgers and Nguyen (2023**) discuss whether AI-driven advertising may have discriminatory implications, noting that unless monitored, AI has the potential to provide algorithmic systems with the ability to amplify or enhance biases in society. The writers emphasize that AI often draws on past data, which may create the same problems of prejudice being documented in the marketing algorithm, potentially creating a situation where the biased exclusion and/or targeting of certain customer segments occurs. Therefore, the authors advocate for establishing a strong regulatory environment to oversee the use of AI in marketing. The framework would have measures of accountability and regular audits, along with ethical standards that would help ensure AI is being used in manners that are fitting and acceptable.
- **De Cremer and Kasparov (2021)** assert that to ensure authenticity and integrity of content created by AI, human oversight is necessary. While AI may accelerate and enhance efficiency in marketing, it is devoid of the subtle

judgment and emotional quotient needed to create effective advertising. The authors believe that in creating ideas that are ethically as well as pragmatically sensible, human ingenuity remains vastly useful. AI capabilities and human intuition should coexist and create authentic as well as forceful brand messages.

- **Huang and Rust (2021)** emphasize the need for a strategic equilibrium between human invention and AI, contending that real marketing potential resides in capitalizing on an equilibrium between algorithmic efficiencies and human storytelling and empathy, rather than one over the other. In their paradigm, humans supply the emotional intelligence, cultural consciousness, and imaginative vision required to build genuine connections, whereas AI is superior when it comes to data processing, predictive analysis, and performance optimization.
- **Kietzmann et al. (2018)** examine the ways in which artificial intelligence (AI) might be used to automatically customise social media ads in real time. They talk about how material can be improved and refined by AI-enabled systems based on user behaviour in real time. They claim that by making sure that ads are contextualised and precisely matched with each person's particular interests and preferences, AI enhances the consumer experience. By improving user pleasure, engagement, and contextualisation, this kind of dynamic personalisation raises the total impact of digital marketing initiatives.
- **Manyika (2022)** exhibits the ways in which artificial intelligence is impacting current firm strategies, focusing on how technology can enhance productivity and automate advertising processes. But by raising ethical issues surrounding the fairness of algorithms and privacy in data, he also focuses on the importance of using AI in a responsible way.
- **Hossain and Kim (2020)** Discuss the unforeseen effects of AI personalization, e.g., the generation of "filter bubbles" limiting the range of information and opinions individuals can view. While AI-based solutions are designed to optimize user engagement by predicting and confirming individual tastes, the authors caution that it could unwittingly curtail the range of available information. This personalisation can restrict user choice, reconfirm pre-existing cognitive biases, and offer a consistent digital experience, all of which raise significant concerns about long-term user agency and awareness.
- **Luo et al. (2019)** Based on an examination of the impact of AI chatbot disclosure on consumer behavior by Luo et al. (2019). Users, when they understand they are communicating with a non-human helper, are less willing to trust AI-driven customer support. Nevertheless, the absence of empathy from chatbots leads to lower engagement and purchase intention even when they are as effective as humans. Their findings identify a major weakness of AI

marketing: without emotional authenticity, effectiveness alone cannot generate consumer trust.

- **Guingrich and Graziano (2024)** outline that users often ascribe social awareness to AI agents, particularly social actor AI, such as voice assistants and chat bots, and that can influence not just human/AI interactions but also how we behave toward each other. The authors propose carry-over effects, suggesting that when an AI is human-like it can activate social schemas quite similar to those we engage with in interactions with people, that may have either positive or negative ramifications on the users' future behavior with people, depending on how the AI is treated.
- **Aggarwal et al. (2024)** stated the rising importance of artificial intelligence (AI) in social media marketing is the increasing automation of content generation, personalisation of user experiences, and facilitation of predictive analytics. They indicate that chatbots and other AI-based solutions bring value to customer services by providing on-time and personalised responses. The study, however, raises issues of bias and privacy concerns and proposes ethical precautions in order to uphold the trust. Such observations substantiate the present study's focus on the balance between AI effectiveness and transparency with responsible user engagement.
- **Pathan et al. (2024)** highlight how generative technologies such as ChatGPT and DALL·E, sentiment analysis, and AI-powered chatbots are facilitating engagement and increasing creativity among marketers. While they note AI improves efficiency and accuracy, they caution about algorithmic bias, data privacy, and ethical transparency. This aligns with the current research's commitment to balancing innovation with ethical and inclusive marketing practices in the digital space.
- **Shah et al. (2019)** investigated the ways social media influences buying decisions, and the results indicate a mediation effect attributed to customer relationships. Their research indicates that social media predominantly generates purchase intent through fostering trust and long-term brand engagement. They also found that younger consumers (Gen Y) use social media not only for product discovery but also for decision-making, as well as indicating post-purchase feedback. The study argues that consumer relationships facilitated by social engagement are a significant link to actual purchasing behaviour, and that meaningful interactions on social media platforms such as Facebook and YouTube increase consumer loyalty.
- **Ziakis and Vlachopoulou (2023)** discuss the emergence of AI-driven user profiling and emphasize the massive privacy concerns it induces, largely due to its dependence on massive stores of personal information. The authors note that as AI technology evolves, it's becoming increasingly difficult to

separate surveillance from personalization. They point out that the rationale behind such profiling is not always transparent, which makes the users unable to fully understand how and why their information is collected. In order to alleviate these concerns, promote ethical use, and protect individuals' privacy in AI-powered advertising systems, the authors propose tighter regulatory regimes alongside compliance with data minimisation principles and advertising standards.

- **Awad and Krishnan (2006)** discuss the "privacy-personalization paradox," where customers desire customised experiences but are also uncomfortable with the level of data harvesting. In discussing AI-driven marketing strategies, this paradox is still an important one because companies need to tread a delicate balance between the privacy of customers and customization.

3. RESEARCH METHODOLOGY

This study employs a comprehensive research methodology encompassing the research objectives, design, data collection methods, statistical analysis techniques, sampling strategies, survey instruments, and an acknowledgment of the study's limitations.

3.1 Objectives

1. To explore how effective social media networks' AI-driven advertising is in driving engagement and influencing buying behaviors.
2. To examine the attitude of consumers toward AI-driven ad networks while considering user engagement and privacy.

3.2 Research Design

In order to provide a comprehensive understanding of the role of AI in social media marketing, this research employs a mixed-methods approach that combines qualitative and quantitative methods. Moreover, the research also employs primary data collected through a structured questionnaire as well as secondary data from authentic academic sources. In addition, statistical analysis was conducted to investigate the relationships among key factors.

3.3 Data Collection Methods

This study employs a combination of primary and secondary data collection methods, including surveys to gather comprehensive insights into the research topic.

3.3.1 Collection of Primary Data

The data collected for this study was derived from an online survey using Google Forms, to obtain responses. The survey was provided to 49 individuals, all of whom are social media users and have experienced an AI-driven advertisement. The survey included both closed-ended and open-ended questions in an effort to obtain a broad range of responses regarding consumers' perceptions, levels of engagement, and concerns about AI in advertising.

3.3.2 Secondary Data Collection

To supplement primary data, the study incorporated industry reports, peer-reviewed journal articles, and case studies around AI in social media marketing. This secondary review of data sources was designed to analyze trends noted in the primary data, validate conclusions, and provide context.

3.4 Statistical Analysis Methods

Descriptive statistics, chi-square tests, and Pearson correlation analysis were used to examine relationships between key variables such as age, AI Ad relevance, engagement levels, and comfort with data use. This made it easier to see the value and impact AI had on social media marketing.

3.5 Sampling Technique

This study used a convenience sampling method with the intention of survey responses from active social media users who may have experienced an AI-driven advertisement.

The majority of the sample was comprised of young adults (18-24 years), 89.8% of the respondents were between the ages of 18 and 24, demonstrating this age group is highly engaged with AI-driven marketing. The method of convenience sampling was chosen due to convenience and the lack of time for an extensive collection of study data.

3.6 Survey Instrument

Survey questions were categorized as follows:

- **Demographic Data:** Social media platform preference and age.
- **AI-Powered Ads:** Do users notice when an ad is related to their interests?
- **Engagement & Effectiveness:** Inclination to interact with AI-personalized content, perceived the credibility of ads, and comfort level with data usage.
- **Ethical Issues:** Opinions regarding the quality of AI-created content, privacy concerns, and possibility of ad exploitation.
- **Ethical Considerations:** To protect participant anonymity and maintain the integrity of the research, participants were informed of the study's purpose and their rights to withdraw from the study at any point in time. No identifiable information was collected. The data were used only for academic research, and appropriate security measures were taken to protect the data from unauthorized access.

3.7 Limitations of the Study

While the research provides valuable insights about advertising with AI, there are also some limitations:

- **Sample Size Constrain:** With only 49 respondents, the results are probably not wholly generalizable to a larger population.
- **Possible Response Bias:** Respondents' opinions might be influenced by personal experiences or biases against AI marketing.
- **Limited Scope:** The study may not primarily cover AI's impact on other digital marketing domains because it focused on social media advertising.
- **Demographic Skewness**: Because young adults (age 18-24) comprised the majority of respondents, the findings may be representative of this age group instead of older populations.

4. DATA ANALYSIS AND INTERPRETATION

This section presents a systematic examination of the collected data using appropriate statistical methods, followed by a detailed interpretation of the results to draw meaningful conclusions aligned with the research objectives.

4.1 Demographics and Platform Preference

The results of the survey revealed that 89.8% of respondents fall into the age range of 18 to 24 years old as shown in Figure 1, suggesting that young adults are the primary demographic engaging with AI-based advertising. These generations (Gen Z and young Millennials) are great resources for exploring trends in advertising that utilizes AI-based platforms, given they are digital natives and have had additional experience using AI-powered platforms such as Instagram.

Figure 1. Displays the Demographics and Platform Preference

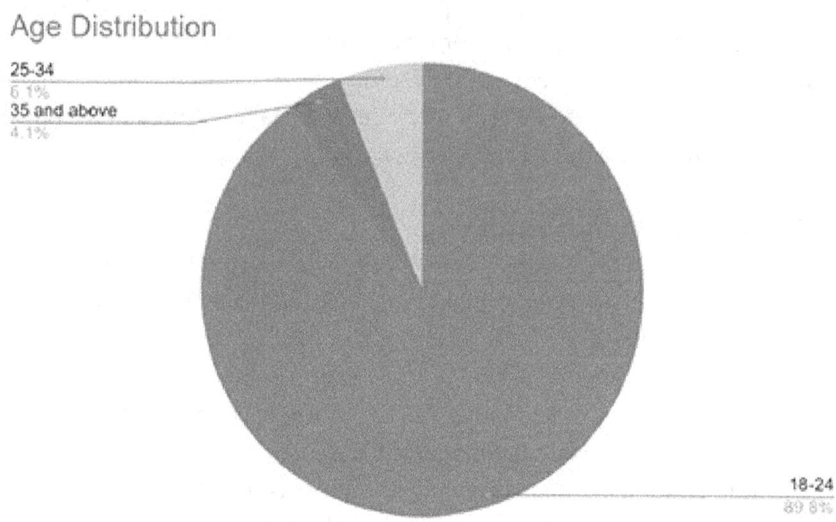

4.2 Preferred Social Media

The survey indicated that Instagram is the most used platform among respondents (85.7%). The strong preference for Instagram implies that visual and mobile-optimized content should be prioritized in AI advertisements targeted at younger users. (See Figure 2) The low usage of Facebook and Twitter complements recent studies that indicate younger users are becoming less active on these platforms.

Figure 2. Displays the various preferred social media platform

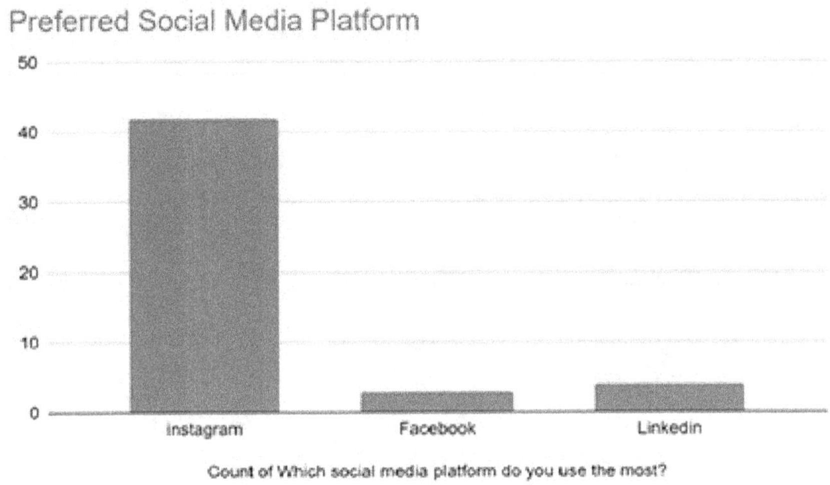

4.3 Effectiveness of AI in Ad Targeting

AI is effective at reading user data for advertisements. A considerable 79.6% of respondents did agree that the AI-built adverts fit their needs, and to further illustrate this, 93.9% see Figure 3 (32.7% high relevance + 61.2% moderate) of respondents did indicate the relevancy of the advertisements was at least "moderately relevant", which points to the idea that engagement and personalisation appears to be good with AI.

Figure 3. Displays the Effectiveness of AI in Ad Targeting

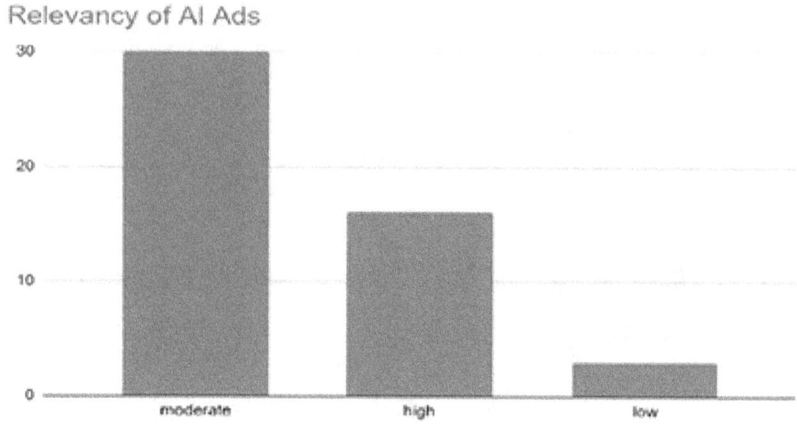

However, although most agree that there is some relevance, the lower "High" rating indicates that more can be done to improve targeting accuracy and content personalisation. Enhancing time and contextual awareness could raise value perception.

4.4 Consumer Comfort with AI in Advertising

Of those surveyed, 61.2% stated that they were in discomfort with platforms using their data for advertising personalisation, again with the knowledge that AI can improve advertising relevance (See Figure 4). This aligns with a broader discussion on ethics and the privacy of AI-driven advertising.

Figure 4. Shows the Consumer Comfort with AI in Advertising

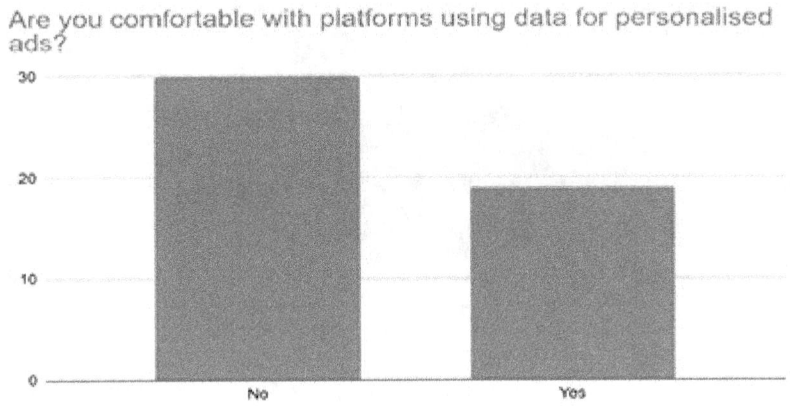

Although personalized advertisements have their advantages, this finding confirms a privacy issue. As organizations leveraged AI to personalize their advertisements, they must weigh the needs of transparency against the personalization of the advertisements, although "transparency" in the context of personalized advertising is understood differently. Data ethics, informed consent, and clear avenues to opt-out of advertisements are necessary in order to build user trust.

4.5 AI-Generated Content and Engagement

79.6% of respondents claimed to have engaged with either chatbots or recommendation engines that generated content with artificial intelligence (See Figure 5). While a little more work is needed, fifty-one percent rated the quality of AI-generated content as either good or higher, suggesting that there's an existing acceptance for AI-driven engagement platforms.

Figure 5. Shows the AI-Generated Content and Engagement

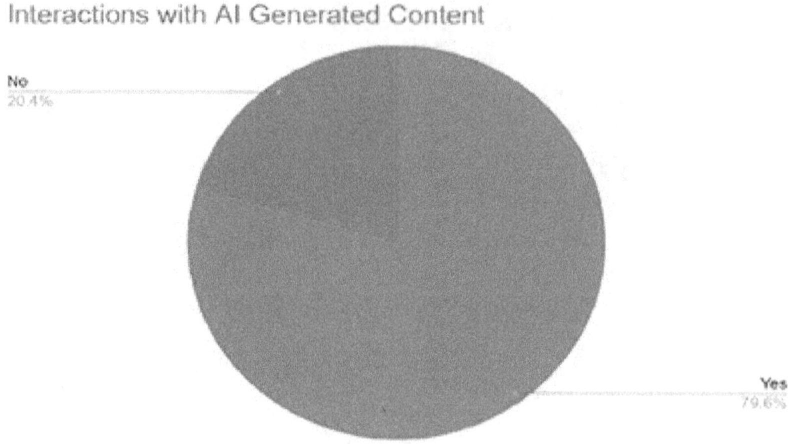

AI engagement technologies are increasingly becoming popular. The high interaction rate supports incorporating such elements into brand approaches. However, onboarding programs and improved user experience may increase uptake among those in the 20.4% who did not interact.

4.6 The quality of AI generated content

The survey shows that 46.9% of users rated AI-generated content as "Good," 51% as "Average," and only 2% as "Poor" (see Figure 6).

Figure 6. Shows the quality of AI generated content

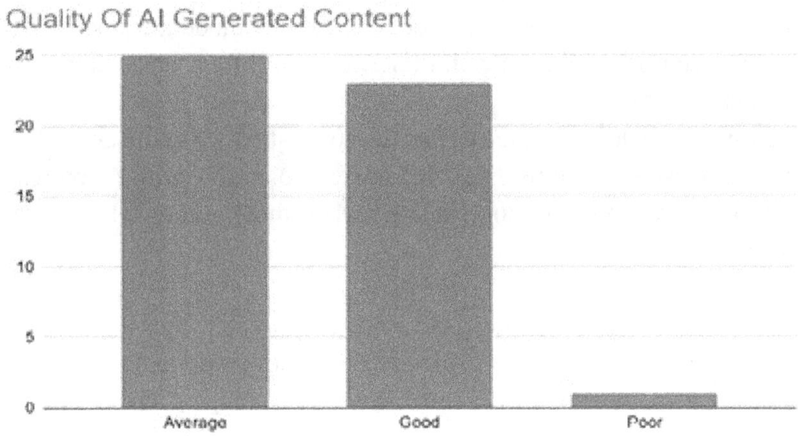

This highlights that only a limited percentage assess the quality as impressive, while the remainder assess it as acceptable. This indicates the potential to enrich the emotional tone, creativity, and naturalness during the content creation process, particularly for AI-generated posts and comments. Brands need to improve the quality of AI-generated content to meet or exceed naturally occurring standards.

4.7 Statistical Analysis and Findings

The study employs the Chi-square test to assess the independence between categorical variables and the Pearson correlation test to evaluate the strength and direction of linear relationships between continuous variables. The subsequent findings are discussed below.

4.7.1 Chi-Square Test (Age vs Comfort with Usage of Data)

- The p-value was 0.171, indicating no relationship between air respondents' age group and comfort level for platforms using personal data for AI targeting their advertising.
- This shows that privacy concerns are not associated with a specific age group, even if younger users represent the majority of the sample. This finding challenges some assumptions that digital natives are more comfortable with sharing personal information.

4.7.2 Pearson Correlation (Relevance of AI Ad vs Interaction with AI)

- The correlation coefficient was .508, indicating a moderate positive correlation between being able to claim relevance for AI ads and interacting with AI-generated media.
- The p-value (0.00019) suggests that the correlation is significant.
- This demonstrates that users are more likely to engage with AI outputs (e.g. chatbots or recommendation engines) when they believe AI ads are more relevant.

These findings align with previous academic research that accentuates AI's significant role in enhancing advertising content personalization. Gao et al. (2023), for instance, highlighted the extent to which AI technologies have facilitated the tailoring of advertisements to individual users' tastes via data mining and behavioural monitoring, increasing relevance and user interaction. However, survey respondents' reluctance to embrace full AI-based personalisation reflects more basic concerns with algorithmic discrimination and data protection. Individuals often fear AI systems would be misleading them or making the wrong assumptions, particularly when sensitive personal information is processed without explicit authorisation, as Ziakis and Vlachopoulou (2023) explain.

In addition, the results of the study confirm the concerns raised by Wei and Tyson (2024), who point out that although AI-based content holds much potential, it can be devoid of human sensibility and emotional richness and have an impersonal or mechanical impact. This confirms the ongoing debate regarding the ethical trade-offs of AI in advertising. Thus, greater transparency, user opt-in, and management of data usage continue to be essential to guaranteeing the ethical use of AI-driven personalisation strategies while also guaranteeing their effectiveness.

5. DISCUSSION

AI can transform social media advertising but its potential hangs in the balance of algorithmic precision and human experience. The findings in this study identify a complexity between cynicism and ethical dilemmas and efficiency and customisation coexisting.

5.1 Ways to Maximise AI's Potential

We discover ways to maximise AI's potential and reduce the negatives by framing the conversation within customer agency and co-creation. The details are as follows:

- **From Personalization to Partnership Redefining Relevance:** Although 79.6% of respondents indicated they agreed that AI can provide ads that match their interests, younger users (18–24 years) exhibited an odd combination of awe and concern. They appreciated ads that appeared to "read my mind," but also were skeptical about whether hyper-personalization was the product of a sophisticated understanding rather than spying. This underscores the contradiction between "warm" emotional engagement, and "cold" data-driven outcomes (Huang & Rust, 2021). The targeting powers of AI could transform into collaborative tools that allow users to change their preferences instantaneously (e.g., "just show me fewer fitness ads and more travel"). Participatory dimensions of trust, with transparency to reduce the "creepy" aspects of opaque algorithms, can stimulate engagement.
- **The Authenticity Gap: Why Machines Can't Replace Human Nuance:** Several respondents expressed that there was no emotional connection to AI generated content even though 51% felt it was "good." One participant even commented that, "an AI advertisement is like a nice suit that is missing the personality to pull it off," which is consistent with research that shows AI struggles to capture cultural nuances or humor (Wei & Tyson, 2024). AI is meant to be a creative partner rather than a replacement for human creativity; for example, it could guide human teams creating advertisements during a period of climate concern to analyze user comments by sentiment when integrating ecological messaging with the benefits of the product. This collaborative process enables the preservation of human intuition while leveraging the AI's speed in analyzing data.
- **The Trust-Efficiency Trade-off: Sustaining Long-Term Consumer Relationships**: The study reveals a key balance between efficiency and long-term confidence, even though AI-controlled advertising does extremely well in the short-term engagement indicators. AI increases the accuracy of targeting, but it can cause a loss of consumer confidence over time. This is illustrated by the very significant 61.2% of the respondents who showed concern about the use of data. Despite the fact that younger users are digital natives, they are becoming more cautious about the use of non-transparent algorithms. One participant summarized this feeling by saying, "I like to see relevant ads, but I don't know what they're doing with my data, and this scares me." This contrast shows how important it is for companies to prioritize con-

fidence. Confidence is the basis of customer loyalty, not just a checkmark of compliance. Platforms that offer fine-grained control over data rights, for example allowing users to turn off specific data used for advertising, may be able to turn distrust into compliance. Companies can create long-term partnerships where efficiency and moral transparency coexist by presenting AI as a technology that empowers, not exploits. This mechanism upholds Huang and Rust's (2021) argument that for sustainable marketing to be possible, algorithmic accuracy and human-centered values must be in equilibrium so that the AI acts as a connector, not a hurdle, to maintaining loyalty.

- **AI and Consumer Empowerment: From Passive Targeting to Active Participation:** Passive targeting, which involves the categorization of users and presenting content based on predicted behavior, has been the standard of practice for AI in advertising. While targeting has become more accurate and efficient, there is limited human agency and engagement with the content. With improvements in digital literacy, there is beginning to be a trend towards pro-active user engagement, where users are actively involved in shaping what they receive and how they receive it. Consumer-facing technologies that allow users to direct their advertising experience, including liking, selecting, filtering, or providing feedback about content, are starting to be operationalized in advertising frameworks. For example, platforms like Spotify have created completely user-driven platforms by allowing users to hide, skip, or like songs that led to customized listening suggestions. Active user engagement can be developed in advertisement systems leveraging artificial intelligence by allowing users to pause tracking or adjust their ad preferences. This type of user engagement can lead to advertising frameworks develop collaboratively between the user and the system. By providing people with a greater degree of control over their digital environments, we can mitigate pain and build trust in the brand. Users do not feel like they are being watched but feel acknowledged and engaged. Aside from mitigating ethical concerns, organizations can build lasting relations by demonstrating to their customers that they respect them and value their time and feelings; this can happen as they move away from one-sided targeting and yield to a forever collaborative personalisation experience.
- **Privacy as a Value Exchange: Beyond Compliance:** 61.2% of the respondents, particularly the youth, expressed scepticism regarding the use of their personal data in AI-driven advertising, said the study. As consumer expectations shift toward more transparency and control, these individuals are increasingly not willing to accept a "data for nothing" exchange. This would imply that the moral exercise of privacy must transcend the mere compliance with law; instead, it must be made to appear as a value-enhancing exchange

where users are informed participants and not mere passive producers of data. Fashion apps that serve customized style advice in exchange for surfing behavior and enable users to pause monitoring during sensitive moments are a strong demonstration of this ethical model. Besides ensuring personalisation, this kind of opt-in, user-led design honors autonomy, which fosters trust and supports continued engagement. As De Cremer and Kasparov (2021) posit, responsible AI should balance commercial objectives with user well-being. Brands can link business goals with social responsibility and create a more sustainable and respectful digital advertising space by incorporating empathy into AI systems and giving people meaningful choices.

- **Breaking the Filter Bubble: AI as a Gateway:** 79.6% found niche products thanks to an AI recommendation but recognized AI curation could lead to filter bubbles. This duality captures the tricky nature of AI as a gatekeeper and as a door opener. Sites could counter this if they ran some sort of "serendipity modes," which is an algorithmic algorithm that allows the platform to occasionally expose users to new content that could still be interesting, similar to getting a recommendation from an well-read friend prompting you to read a novel in a category you don't normally read. A balance between surprise and personalisation seems to improve the overall user experience. AI is purposely developed as a curator of the known and unknown providing two advantages: eliminates boredom from the endless scroll of content and maintains high engagement rates. This ability of AI to counter the havoc to be wreaked upon our attention spans by algorithmic echo chambers while operationalising data-driven personalisation to broaden the scope of what is recommended, saves the use from becoming one-dimension with all the breadcrumbs contained with the AI engagement.
- **The Path Forward: Ethical AI as a Competitive Advantage:** Brands are compelled to be more proactive about the social ramifications of AI adoption due to increased pressure for ethical innovation in advertising. Companies can adopt an effective strategy by implementing AI literacy programs that educate consumers about algorithms and how their information is utilized. Accountability may be improved through the alleviation of problems like algorithmic bias by releasing diversity and inclusion reports, such as those that highlight ad reach for diverse audiences. Like the efforts to drive sustainability have strengthened customer loyalty to companies like Patagonia, such initiatives not only foster transparency but also can become potent brand differentiators. As AI becomes increasingly integrated into advertising environments, it becomes essential to redefine technology as a human connection rather than prediction or persuasion. This transformation involves rethinking innovation as an agency that establishes connections at an accelerated

pace, prioritizing people above precision, imagination above automation, and trust above surveillance. Maybe one day, instead of merely driving conversions, the future-oriented algorithms will be used to build experiences based on common values and authenticity. In this way, artificial intelligence (AI) can potentially shift from being a means to sell products to one that deepens brand-customer relationships in meaningful, emotionally resonant ways.

5.2 Practical Implications and Recommendations

This study provides actionable insights and strategies for marketers to ethically leverage AI in social media advertising, emphasizing transparency, fairness, and consumer trust. The implications and recommendations are discussed in detail below:

- **Proactive Transparency Initiatives:** Outside of GDPR compliance is the development of transparency dashboards that are able to present in real time how the data affects consumer ad targeting (e.g., "This ad was displayed to you because you shopped this green product"). It solves the "creepiness factor," explains the AI process, and supports Awad and Krishnan's (2006) solution of the privacy-personalization dilemma.
- **Emotional AI Integration:** Optimising content authenticity can be achieved by spending on AI systems that can gauge emotional intelligence. These systems work by examining cues like context, tone, and cultural allusions. To ensure that adverts are potent emotionally without reducing scalability, combine the above systems with human creatives in the right manner.
- **User-Driven Algorithm Training:** Let customers flag ads as "relevant" or "irrelevant," prompting change. This interactive approach empowers consumers and makes them co-creators of their advertising experience.
- **Ethical AI Certification Programs**: Companies can work with independent auditors who can certify an AI system as being ethically trained or bias-free, in a similar way that today, sustainability certifications are issued. Just like what Patagonia did with its ethical branding, promoting this quality can help make the company stand out in a crowded market.
- **Delivering Items Through Discoveries**: Come up with AI-driven "surprise modes" that randomly include different items to user feeds (i.e. "Discover something new" sections). This provides for balanced exposure, as recommended by Hossain and Kim (2020), while at the same time disrupting filter bubbles and maintaining engagement.
- **AI Literacy Initiative Campaigns:** Educative, short movies, or infographics work well to inform people how AI can tremendously enhance ad relevancy

without infringing on privacy. Trust can be built by changing scepticism to acceptance through transparent communication.

6. CONCLUSION

The integration of AI into social media advertising has sharply altered how organizations connect with their target audiences, presenting levels of efficiency and targeting precision that were once unfathomable. Conducted in conjunction with our broader marketing research, this study discovered that 79.6% of users agree that AI built advertisements fit their needs, while 93.9% stated the advertisements were at least " moderately relevant." This gives visibility to AI's power to identify patterns in behaviour and enhance user engagement. However, there is an underlying conflict behind this achievement: despite AI's skill in personalization, 61.2% of respondents expressed discomfort with data practices, and 51% indicated that AI-generated content did not evoke emotional weight for them, revealing a tension between algorithmic precision and human authenticity. These findings expose the divide at the centre of AI-powered marketing: its capacity to engage is tamed by ethical and emotional concerns that threaten consumer trust.

To escape this dichotomy, brands must consider AI as a collaborative partner, rather than a discrete solution. The "black box" quality of AI can be demystified and trust restored through providing transparency over how data is used, such as providing consumers with an explanation for why an ad was served ("This ad was served because of your interest in sustainable fashion"). Through hybrid creation, where human input provides empathy and cultural finesse that is critical to great advertising and the data analytics work is done through AI, authenticity gap can be bridged. When human forces create compelling narratives of emotion aligning with such themes of growing climate consciousness as part of campaigns for climate awareness, for instance, AI is capable of making out consumer tendencies.

Moreover, the discovery that 79.6% of consumers would consider niche products because of AI recommendations evidences the potential of technology to increase (and not decrease) usage choices. In order to overcome filter bubbles and improve the user experience, platforms could develop 'serendipity modes' that randomly sometimes serve users, random content; nevertheless, ethical awareness cannot be neglected or diminished. To eliminate risk such as discriminatory targeting, or too intrusive profiling; industry standards must include proactive solutions such as bias audits, user-controlled data permissions, and ethical product certification.

In summary, finding the appropriate equilibrium between the accuracy of AI, the very necessary importance of human creativity, and a sincere focus on ethical practices, will all be needed for the technology to work in advertising in the future.

Even if AI is unmatched at tracking performance, personalization, and targeting, its true value will be established by how accurately it aligns with human-values-based thinking. Marketers who are user-empathic, open about data standards, and ethical in nature will reinterpret marketing as an art to foster authentic, emotion-driven relationships among customers and marketers, not solely as a methodology for manipulation. AI needs to be utilized to create affinity and trust more than to simply maximise clicks or conversions.This will bridge the divide between data-driven effectiveness and emotional richness that defines long-term brand loyalty. By doing so, businesses will not only enhance the customer experience but also become leaders in ethical innovation, making moral compliance an integral part of who they are. Ultimately, the true success of artificial intelligence will be measured by its ability to foster relationships based on authenticity, respect, and shared values – the future where technology advances all of us instead of replacing every one of us – not as a means of selling things.

REFERENCES

Aggarwal, D., Sharma, D., & Saxena, A. B. (2024). *Exploring the role of AI for enhancement of social media marketing*. Journal of Media. *Culture and Communication, 4*(5), 1–11. DOI: 10.55529/jmcc.45.1.11

Alvarez, J. M., Colmenarejo, A. B., Elobaid, A., Fabbrizzi, S., Fahimi, M., Ferrara, A., Ghodsi, S., Mougan, C., Papageorgiou, I., Reyero, P., Russo, M., Scott, K. M., State, L., Zhao, X., & Ruggieri, S. (2024). Policy advice and best practices on bias and fairness in AI. *Ethics and Information Technology, 26*(1), 31–45. DOI: 10.1007/s10676-024-09746-w

Awad, N. F., & Krishnan, M. S. (2006). The personalization privacy paradox: An empirical evaluation of information transparency and the willingness to be profiled online for personalization. *Management Information Systems Quarterly, 30*(1), 13–28. DOI: 10.2307/25148715

Chen, H., Chiang, R. H. L., & Storey, V. C. (2012). Business intelligence and analytics: From big data to big impact. *Management Information Systems Quarterly, 36*(4), 1165–1188. DOI: 10.2307/41703503

Chung, T. S., Wedel, M., & Rust, R. T. (2016). Adaptive personalization using social networks. *Journal of the Academy of Marketing Science, 44*(1), 66–87. DOI: 10.1007/s11747-015-0441-x

Davenport, T., Guha, A., Grewal, D., & Bressgott, T. (2020). How artificial intelligence will change the future of marketing. *Journal of the Academy of Marketing Science, 48*(1), 24–42. DOI: 10.1007/s11747-019-00696-0

De Cremer, D., & Kasparov, G. (2021). AI should augment human intelligence, not replace it. *Harvard Business Review.* https://hbr.org/2021/01/ai-should-augment-human-intelligence-not-replace-it

Dwivedi, Y. K.. (2021). Artificial intelligence: Emerging challenges. *International Journal of Information Management, 57*, 101994. DOI: 10.1016/j.ijinfomgt.2019.08.002

Gao, B., Wang, Y., Xie, H., Hu, Y., & Hu, Y. (2023). Artificial intelligence in advertising: Advancements, challenges, and ethical considerations in targeting, personalization, content creation, and ad optimization. *SAGE Open, 13*(4), 21582440231210759. Advance online publication. DOI: 10.1177/21582440231210759

Glikson, E., & Woolley, A. W. (2020). Human trust in artificial intelligence: Review of empirical research. *The Academy of Management Annals, 14*(2), 627–660. DOI: 10.5465/annals.2018.0057

Guingrich, R. E., & Graziano, M. S. A. (2024). Ascribing consciousness to artificial intelligence: Human-AI interaction and its carry-over effects on human-human interaction. *Frontiers in Psychology, 15*, 1322781. Advance online publication. DOI: 10.3389/fpsyg.2024.1322781 PMID: 38605842

Hossain, M. A., & Kim, M. (2020). The effect of AI-powered recommendation systems on consumer decision-making. *Journal of Consumer Behaviour, 19*(3), 239–254. DOI: 10.1002/cb.1813

Huang, M.-H., & Rust, R. T. (2021). A strategic framework for artificial intelligence in marketing. *Journal of the Academy of Marketing Science, 49*(1), 30–50. DOI: 10.1007/s11747-020-00749-9

Jobin, A., Ienca, M., & Vayena, E. (2019). The global landscape of AI ethics guidelines. *Nature Machine Intelligence, 1*(9), 389–399. DOI: 10.1038/s42256-019-0088-2

Kaplan, A., & Haenlein, M. (2020). Rulers of the world, unite! The challenges and opportunities of artificial intelligence. *Business Horizons, 63*(1), 37–50. DOI: 10.1016/j.bushor.2019.09.003

Kietzmann, J., Paschen, J., & Treen, E. (2018). Artificial intelligence in advertising: Personalization and targeting. *Journal of Business Research, 92*, 180–194. DOI: 10.1016/j.jbusres.2018.07.008

Kumar, A., Sharma, R., & Singh, R. (2022). AI-based content personalization. *Journal of Business Research, 139*, 1225–1236. DOI: 10.1016/j.jbusres.2021.10.045

Kumar, D., & Suthar, N. (2024). Ethical and legal challenges of AI in marketing: An exploration of solutions. *Journal of Information. Communication and Ethics in Society, 22*(1), 124–144. DOI: 10.1108/JICES-05-2023-0068

Luo, X., Tong, S., Fang, Z., & Qu, Z. (2019). Machines versus humans: The impact of artificial intelligence chatbot disclosure on customer purchases. *Marketing Science, 38*(6), 937–947. DOI: 10.1287/mksc.2019.1182

Manyika, J. (2022). The state of AI in 2022—and a half-decade in review. *McKinsey & Company.* https://www.mckinsey.com/featured-insights/artificial-intelligence/the-state-of-ai-in-2022-and-a-half-decade-in-review

Pathan, M., Jarad, R., Bhavsar, D., Yadav, M., Suryavanshi, P., & Moholkar, N. (2024). Artificial intelligence in social media marketing. *International Journal of Research Publication and Reviews*, *5*(12), 2780–2784.

Rodgers, S., & Nguyen, T. (2023). *Ethical AI in digital marketing: Addressing bias & privacy concerns*. Digital Ethics Review., DOI: 10.1007/s12345-023-00123-4

Saura, J. R., Škare, V., & Ozretić Došen, Đ. (2024). Is AI-based digital marketing ethical? Assessing a new data privacy paradox. *Journal of Innovation & Knowledge*, *9*(4), 100597. DOI: 10.1016/j.jik.2024.100597

Shah, A. M., Zahoor, S. Z., & Qureshi, I. H. (2019). Social media and purchasing behavior: A study of the mediating effect of customer relationships. *Journal of Global Marketing*, *32*(2), 93–115. Advance online publication. DOI: 10.1080/08911762.2018.1497243

Wei, Y., & Tyson, G. (2024). Human vs. AI content: Engagement analysis. *Journal of Interactive Marketing*. Advance online publication. DOI: 10.1016/j.intmar.2023.01.001

Yau, A.. (2021). AI-driven marketing automation: Customer trust and satisfaction. *Journal of Business Research*, *124*, 569–578. DOI: 10.1016/j.jbusres.2020.11.045

Zhang, J., & Li, X. (2019). Sentiment analysis in AI marketing. *The Journal of Consumer Research*, *46*(5), 805–822. DOI: 10.1093/jcr/ucz020

Ziakis, C., & Vlachopoulou, M. (2023). The evolution of AI-driven user profiling: Privacy challenges and regulatory responses. *AI & Society*, *38*(2), 275–294. DOI: 10.1007/s00146-022-01453-9

Chapter 12
Combining Digital Twin and Metaverse for Immersive Marketing Experiences

Hamed Nozari
https://orcid.org/0000-0002-6500-6708
Bio10, UAE

ABSTRACT

This research examines the integration of digital twins and the metaverse in marketing, a new approach that creates interactive and personalized experiences for users. Using digital twins, brands can create detailed customer profiles and use this data to improve user experiences in the metaverse. This integration allows brands to optimize their marketing strategies and create immersive digital experiences using real-time data. The research also examines the ethical considerations, privacy issues, technical challenges, and future trends of this approach and provides solutions for its effective exploitation.

1- INTRODUCTION

In the era of digital transformation, the boundaries between the physical and virtual worlds are rapidly blurring. These changes have provided marketers with unprecedented opportunities to create interactive, personalized, and immersive ex-

DOI: 10.4018/979-8-3373-3775-3.ch012

periences for customers. Among them, two prominent technologies (digital twins and metaverse) play a key role in shaping the future of marketing.

Digital twins, as a digital model of a physical object or system, enable the simulation, monitoring, and optimization of processes in real time. By collecting real-time data from various sources, this technology provides an accurate representation of the current situation and future predictions. On the other hand, metaverse, as a 3D and interactive virtual space, provides an environment where users can interact through their avatars and gain diverse experiences.

The combination of these two technologies offers unique opportunities for marketing. Using digital twins, brands can create an accurate representation of their products or services in the metaverse and engage users in interactive and personalized experiences. This approach not only improves the user experience, but also allows for the collection of valuable data on customer behavior and preferences.

Research shows that the digital twin market is growing rapidly and is expected to reach a value of $110.1 billion by 2028, representing a compound annual growth rate of 61.3% (Yordanova & Nozari, 2025). This growth reflects the increasing demand for accurate and real-time simulations across various industries. Similarly, the metaverse is also expanding as a virtual space, and brands are looking for ways to effectively participate in this space.

The integration of digital twins and the metaverse in marketing allows for the creation of interactive and personalized experiences that can increase customer engagement and improve loyalty. For example, brands can create virtual stores where users can view and interact with products in 3D, or even try digital versions of products before purchasing them in person.

However, this integration also brings challenges. Issues related to privacy, data security, and informed user consent are among the main concerns in this area. Brands need to ensure that user data is collected and used responsibly and securely, and that users are aware of how their data is being used.

In addition, technological infrastructure also plays a significant role in the success of this integration. To fully exploit the capabilities of digital twins and the metaverse, advanced infrastructures such as the Internet of Things (IoT), artificial intelligence (AI), augmented reality (AR), and virtual reality (VR) are needed. Together, these technologies can create immersive and interactive experiences for users.

Ultimately, the integration of digital twins and the metaverse in marketing provides unique opportunities for brands to create innovative and interactive experiences for customers. However, to fully exploit these opportunities, there is a need for a deep understanding of the related technologies, responsible data management, and the development of appropriate infrastructure. This research examines this integration and its implications for digital marketing, and provides solutions for its effective exploitation.

2- UNDERSTANDING DIGITAL TWINS AND THE METAVERSE

Digital twins and metaverses are two fundamental concepts in the modern digital world, both of which focus in some way on the creation and management of digital experiences. Although seemingly independent, these two concepts are synergistic and can be combined to provide users with immersive and personalized digital experiences. This section takes a closer look at these two concepts and how they relate to each other.

2-1 Digital Twin: Concept and Applications

A digital twin is defined as an accurate and dynamic digital model of a physical or non-physical system that can be updated in real time with real-time data. The concept was initially applied in the manufacturing and engineering industries, but gradually found its way into other areas such as health, energy, smart cities, and even marketing (Movahed, Movahed, & Nozari, 2024). By collecting and processing real-time data from sensors and Internet of Things (IoT) devices, a digital twin enables modeling and simulation of the behavior of complex systems.

A digital twin consists of three main components:

- Physical or real model: This part includes the actual physical object, process, or system that is to be simulated.
- Digital version: This part includes the virtual or digital model of the physical object that is dynamically updated with real data.
- Data communication: This component includes the connection between the physical object and its digital version, usually through sensors, IoT systems, and data networks (Nozari, 2025).

One of the key benefits of digital twins is the ability to monitor and optimize systems in real time. This technology can simulate different conditions, predict system performance, and provide optimal solutions to improve efficiency. For example, in the field of marketing, digital twins can be used to create digital profiles of customers and monitor their behavior in real time. These profiles can include information such as purchasing preferences, online interactions, and past behaviors. Then, based on this data, targeted and personalized marketing campaigns are designed (Movahed, Movahed, & Nozari, 2024).

2-2 Digital Twin Applications in Marketing

In the field of marketing, digital twins can play an important role in improving customer experience and optimizing marketing strategies. Some of its key applications include the following:

- Content personalization: Using digital twins, brands can personalize their content and advertising messages based on the characteristics and preferences of each customer.
- Customer behavior prediction: By analyzing digital twin data, brands can predict future customer behaviors and improve their marketing strategies.
- User experience improvement: Digital twins can create a better user experience for customers by providing personalized recommendations and relevant content (Nozari, 2025).

2-3 Metaverse: Concept and Evolution

A metaverse is an interactive and immersive digital environment in which users can interact with each other and with their surroundings through their digital avatars. The concept is defined as a permanent and persistent virtual space that can include 3D environments, virtual reality (VR) experiences, augmented reality (AR) and even mixed reality (Rane, Choudhary, & Rane, 2023). The metaverse has become one of the key concepts in the digital world in recent decades, thanks to technological advances in the fields of virtual reality, artificial intelligence, the Internet of Things and blockchain.

A metaverse includes the following features:

- Interactive and 3D environments: Users can move around virtual 3D environments, communicate with others, and interact with digital objects.
- Personalized avatars: Each user can create their own digital avatar and personalize it with desired features.
- Digital economy: The metaverse typically includes an independent digital economy where users can buy and sell digital assets such as cryptocurrencies, non-fungible tokens (NFTs), and virtual items (Najafi, Nozari, & Edalatpanah, 2022).
- Multiple experiences: The metaverse includes a variety of environments that can include virtual games, educational environments, workspaces, and even virtual concerts.

2-4 The Evolution of the Metaverse and Its Impact on Marketing

With the emergence of metaverse platforms such as Decentraland, Roblox, and Meta (Facebook), brands have gradually realized the importance of this space for marketing. The metaverse allows brands to create immersive and interactive experiences for customers and build deeper connections with them. For example, brands can create virtual exhibitions, hold interactive events, and even launch virtual stores where customers can digitally experience products (Nozari, 2025).

In the metaverse, users can freely move around virtual spaces and interact with brands directly. This allows brands to create personalized and unique experiences for each user. For example, a fashion brand can launch a virtual fashion show in the metaverse where users can participate live and try on digital clothes (Wallace, 2023).

2-5 The Connection Between Digital Twins and the Metaverse

Digital twins and the metaverse can work together to create immersive and personalized marketing experiences for users. Digital twins can serve as the foundation for personalizing content and metaverse experiences. For example, a brand can use digital twin data from users to design personalized metaverse experiences. These experiences can include interactive exhibitions, live events, and even product simulations (Nozari, Szmelter-Jarosz, & Ghahremani-Nahr, 2021).

The metaverse can also serve as an interactive platform for experiencing and using digital twins. For example, users can access and review digital versions of products through their avatars in the metaverse. This synergy between digital twins and the metaverse can help brands create interactive, engaging, and lasting marketing experiences for users (Fallah & Nozari, 2021).

3- DIGITAL TWIN INTEGRATION WITH THE METAVERSE FOR MARKETING

Digital Twin Integration with the Metaverse is an innovative approach in digital marketing that enables the creation of interactive and personalized experiences for customers. By combining accurate digital twin data with interactive and immersive environments of the Metaverse, this approach allows brands to create marketing experiences tailored to the characteristics of each user. In this section, we will examine the conceptual framework of this integration, its application scenarios, and its benefits.

3-1 Conceptual Framework for Merging Digital Twins and Metaverse

The integration of digital twins and metaverse is based on a conceptual framework in which the digital twin acts as a data layer and the metaverse acts as an interactive platform for displaying and using this data. As a digital view of a system, product, or even a user, the digital twin collects and stores accurate and up-to-date information from the real world. This data can include information such as customer preferences, purchase history, online behavior, and even environmental data such as temperature, humidity, or the status of physical devices (Buhalis, Leung, & Lin, 2023). This data is collected and processed in real time using the Internet of Things (IoT) and artificial intelligence systems.

On the other hand, the metaverse acts as a virtual and interactive environment that users can enter and interact with the environment and other users through their digital avatars. In this environment, the digital twin data can be displayed to users in a visual and interactive way. For example, a virtual store can use digital twin data of customers to personalize products and services. Users can view products in 3D, try them on, and even receive personalized recommendations based on their preferences (Oskounejad & Nozari, 2024).

In this framework, the connection between the digital twin and the metaverse is established through an intelligent data layer that continuously shares information between the digital twin system and the metaverse environment. This layer can include artificial intelligence and machine learning algorithms that analyze data, predict user behavior, and optimize the user experience. For example, a fashion brand can use digital twins to identify the sizes, colors, and styles of each user and then create personalized fashion shows in the metaverse that users can attend live (Al Zami, Shaon, Quy, & Nguyen, 2025). This approach not only improves the user experience, but also allows brands to continuously optimize their marketing strategies based on real, real-time data.

3-2 Application Scenarios of Digital Twin and Metaverse Integration in Marketing

Digital twin and metaverse integration can be used in various scenarios to improve customer experience and optimize marketing strategies. One of the most important scenarios is to simulate a personalized shopping experience. In this scenario, users can enter virtual stores through their digital avatars and browse different products. The users' digital twin data, such as purchase history, color and style preferences, are displayed in real time in the metaverse, allowing users to view products tailored to their tastes (Nozari, Tavakkoli-Moghaddam, & Dolgui, 2024). This experience can include clothing, electronics, home appliances, and even cars.

In another scenario, brands can use digital twins to design interactive marketing campaigns in the metaverse. For example, a cosmetics brand can launch a virtual showroom where users can try on different products through their avatars. The exhibition can be dynamically personalized with each user's digital twin data, and product recommendations can be displayed based on the user's skin type, color preferences, and purchase history (Han et al., 2022). This approach not only improves the user experience, but also helps brands deliver their marketing content in a targeted and personalized manner.

Furthermore, the integration of digital twins and the metaverse can be used to design interactive experiences for brands in virtual events. For example, brands can host conferences, exhibitions, and virtual live events in the metaverse, where users can meet brand representatives, products, and services in person. The digital twin data of users can be used to personalize these events and provide targeted offers. This approach allows brands to establish deeper connections with customers and create lasting experiences (Fallah & Nozari, 2021).

3-3 Benefits of Integrating Digital Twins and the Metaverse in Marketing

Integrating digital twins and the metaverse in marketing has several benefits that can help brands create more effective and engaging marketing experiences. One of the most important benefits of this approach is the possibility of deep personalization of the user experience. Brands can use digital twin data to design their marketing experiences for each user individually. This includes product recommendations, promotional content, and even special discounts that are tailored to each user's characteristics and preferences (Ghahremani-Nahr, Nozari, & Szmelter-Jarosz, 2024).

Another advantage of this approach is real-time interaction with customers. Brands can use the metaverse to create interactive and live experiences where users can interact directly with products and services. These interactions can include virtual exhibitions, live events, interactive stores, and even promotional games. These interactive experiences not only help improve the user experience, but also enable brands to collect real-time data on customer behavior and use this data to optimize their marketing strategies (Nozari, Abdi, & Rafiei, 2025).

Finally, the integration of digital twins and the metaverse allows brands to continuously evaluate and improve the performance of their marketing strategies. Brands can use digital twins data to analyze customer behavior and identify the strengths and weaknesses of their marketing campaigns. In addition, brands can use metaverse data to analyze the user experience and identify areas for improvement. This data-driven approach helps brands dynamically optimize their marketing strategies based on data and create lasting experiences for customers (Mourtzis, 2023).

Figure 1 schematically illustrates the digital twin and metaverse integration framework for digital marketing. It shows how digital twin data can be used to personalize metaverse experiences and create immersive marketing experiences.

Figure 1. Digital Twin and Metaverse Integration Framework for Digital Marketing

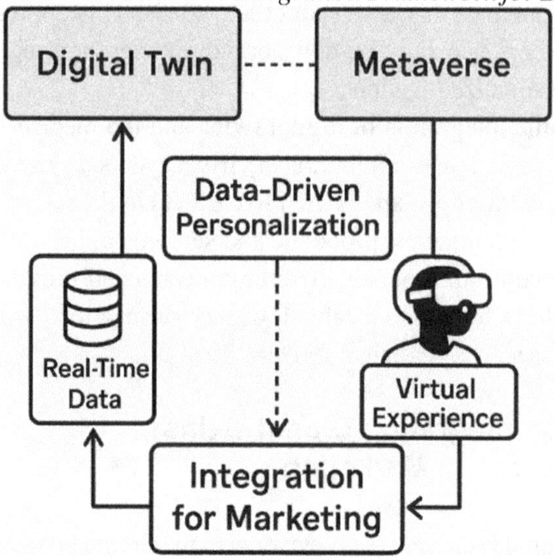

This framework not only helps improve user experience, but also enables brands to optimize their marketing strategies using real-time data.

4- TECHNICAL DESIGN AND IMPLEMENTATION

Integrating digital twins and the metaverse into marketing requires a detailed and structured technical design that includes various components such as data collection, information processing, and display of interactive experiences. This section examines the system architecture, technology stack, and user experience design principles that are essential for creating a digital twin and metaverse-based marketing system. This approach not only helps create immersive and personalized experiences for users, but also allows brands to optimize their marketing strategies in real time.

4-1 Digital Twin and Metaverse Integration Architecture

The architecture of this system consists of three main layers: the data layer, the processing layer, and the user experience layer. In the data layer, data related to users, products, and physical environments is collected. This data can include user profile information, purchase history, data from Internet of Things (IoT) sensors, and environmental information such as temperature and humidity. This data is continuously and in real time sent to the digital twin system, which acts as a dynamic digital view of users and systems. The collected data is processed and analyzed using machine learning algorithms, and the results are used to design personalized experiences in the metaverse. The overall structure of this integration is shown in Figure 2.

Figure 2. Digital Twin and Metaverse Integration Framework for Digital Marketing

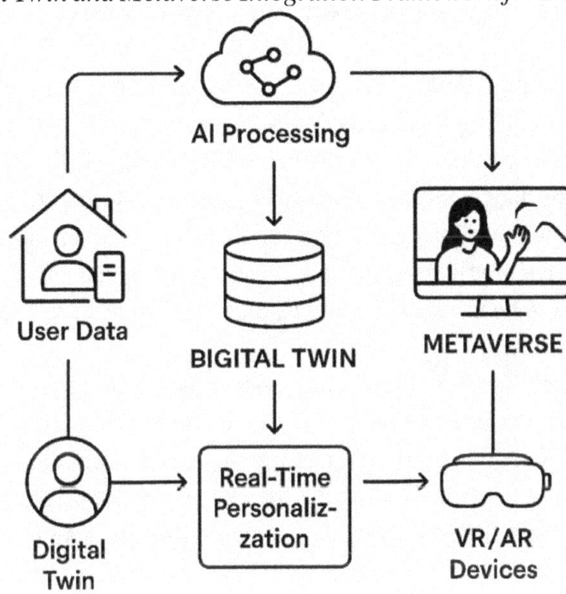

This framework shows how digital twin data can be transferred to the metaverse in real time and used to personalize the user experience. The data includes real-time information from users and the physical environment, which is then processed and displayed interactively in the metaverse.

The processing layer includes artificial intelligence and machine learning engines that analyze and process the digital twin data. These processes can include predicting user behavior, identifying their preferences, and providing personalized recommendations. For example, deep learning algorithms can use digital twin data to predict which products users are interested in and automatically display these products in the metaverse environment. This layer also includes security systems to protect user data and ensure their privacy. These systems can include data encryption, two-factor authentication, and advanced security protocols.

Finally, the user experience layer acts as the interface between the user and the system. This layer includes the metaverse environment, which users can enter through their digital avatars and interact with the environment and other users. These environments can include virtual stores, interactive exhibitions, live events, and educational spaces. The users' digital twin data is displayed in real time in these environments, creating personalized experiences for each user. This layer also includes interactive systems such as motion controls, audio systems, and even virtual and augmented reality (VR/AR) devices that allow users to interact with the environment in an immersive way.

4-2 Technology Stack and Recommended Tools

Implementing a digital twin and metaverse integration system requires the use of a comprehensive technology stack that includes hardware, software, and development tools. On the hardware side, the use of Internet of Things (IoT) devices is essential to collect real-time data from users and the physical environment. These devices can include temperature, humidity, pressure, geolocation, and even biometric sensors to measure users' physiological parameters. In addition, virtual and augmented reality devices such as VR headsets, AR glasses, and 3D displays are used to display the metaverse environment.

On the software side, the digital twin system uses a cloud platform to store and process data. This platform can include cloud technologies such as AWS, Microsoft Azure, or Google Cloud that provide features such as data storage, parallel processing, and real-time analytics. To create a metaverse environment, graphics engines such as Unity or Unreal Engine are used, which allow the design of interactive and realistic 3D environments. This structure and data flow are comprehensively shown in Figure 3.

Figure 3. Data flow and user experience in the digital twin and metaverse integration system

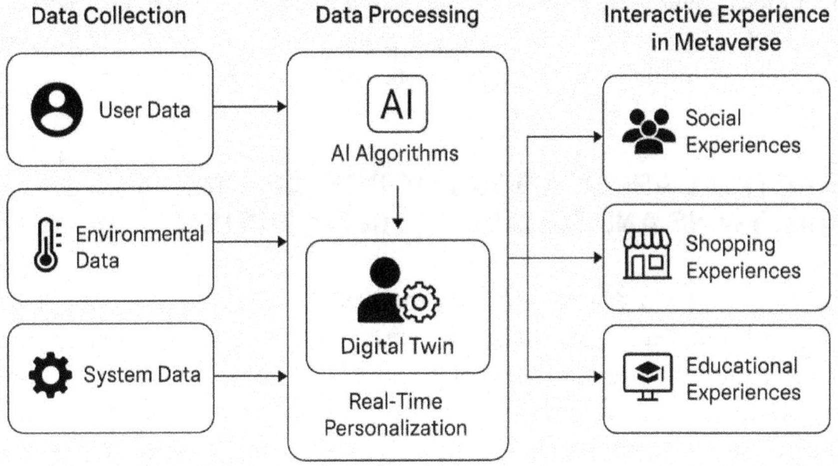

This diagram shows how data is collected from users and the physical environment and then processed into personalized experiences in the metaverse. These experiences can include social experiences, shopping experiences, and educational experiences.

4-3 Principles of User Experience Design in the Metaverse Environment

One of the most important factors in the success of integrating digital twins and the metaverse is designing an interactive and personalized user experience that attracts users. This experience should be designed in a way that users interact with the metaverse environment naturally and without feeling complicated. The first principle of user experience design is to create a simple and user-friendly user interface. This interface should include interactive menus, gesture controls, and visual displays that users can easily use. For novice users, the possibility of providing interactive guides and displaying educational tools should also be considered.

In addition, the user experience should be designed in a way that is personalized. This personalization can include displaying products and services tailored to each user's characteristics and preferences, providing targeted suggestions, and even changing the metaverse environment based on user behavior and preferences. For example, users can view virtual stores whose products are filtered based on their interests. Additionally, the ability to change digital avatars and personalize their appearance should be provided to increase the sense of identification and interaction of users with the metaverse environment.

Finally, the user experience in the metaverse should be interactive and immersive. This interaction can include users interacting with digital objects, communicating with other users, and even participating in virtual live events. These interactive experiences not only allow users to actively engage with the metaverse environment, but also help brands build deeper connections with customers.

5- PRACTICAL APPLICATIONS OF INTEGRATING DIGITAL TWINS AND METAVERSE IN MARKETING

The integration of digital twins and the metaverse in marketing has vast potential and can create completely new and engaging experiences for customers. This approach not only improves the personalization of the user experience, but also allows brands to optimize their marketing strategies using real-time data. Practical applications of this integration in marketing include personalized shopping experiences, interactive virtual exhibitions, live events, immersive training, and even customer relationship management in digital environments. Each of these applications can directly or indirectly lead to increased customer engagement, improved user experience, and increased sales.

One of the most important applications of the integration of digital twins and the metaverse is the creation of personalized shopping experiences in virtual environments. For example, brands can create virtual stores in the metaverse that users can enter through their avatars and view and review different products. The digital twin's data, such as purchase history, color preferences, size, and style preferences, is fed into the system in real time, and the displayed products are personalized based on this data. This approach not only makes the shopping experience more engaging for users, but also helps brands provide targeted and personalized recommendations. For example, users can view a virtual fashion store with products filtered based on their color and style preferences, and even have the option to try on clothes on their digital avatars.

Interactive virtual showrooms are another practical application of this integration. Brands can host virtual showrooms where users can participate live and learn about the brand's products and services. These showrooms can include interactive booths that users can enter and view product information. Additionally, brands can use digital twin data to personalize the showroom experience for each user. For example, an automotive brand could create a virtual showroom where users can view different car models and configure them based on their personal preferences. These showrooms could be interactive, allowing users to ask questions about the car's features, start the engine, and even virtually test drive it.

Live events in the metaverse are another practical application of digital twin and metaverse integration in marketing. Brands can host virtual events such as concerts, workshops, webinars, and Q&A sessions in the metaverse. Users can participate in these events using their avatars and interact live with brands and other users. The digital twin data of users can be used to personalize the event experience. For example, in a virtual event related to cosmetics, the brand can recommend relevant products to each user based on their skin type and color preferences. These events not only allow brands to directly communicate with customers, but also help them collect valuable data on user behavior and preferences.

Immersive training is another application of digital twin and metaverse integration that can be used in various fields such as product training, employee training, and even customer training. Brands can create virtual learning environments where users can learn about the brand's products and services. These trainings can include interactive simulations where users can actually work with the products. For example, a home appliance brand can create a virtual learning environment where users can learn how to use products such as refrigerators, washing machines, or cooking appliances. These trainings can be interactive, where users can examine the different parts of the devices and learn how they work.

In addition, the integration of digital twins and the metaverse can also be used for customer relationship management (CRM) in virtual environments. Brands can deploy their sales and support representatives in metaverse environments where users can interact with them live. These agents can help users solve their problems, answer their questions, and even introduce them to new products and services. Digital twin data of users can help agents create personalized experiences for each user. For example, if a user has purchased a product in the past and had a problem with it, the agent can automatically learn about this information and provide the user with appropriate solutions.

These practical applications demonstrate that the integration of digital twins and the metaverse can enable brands to create personalized, interactive, and immersive experiences for users. These experiences not only help improve the user experience, but also help brands continuously collect valuable data on user behavior and preferences, which they can use to optimize their marketing strategies. This data-driven approach allows brands to dynamically tailor their marketing experiences to users' needs and build deeper connections with customers.

6- ETHICAL CONSIDERATIONS AND PRIVACY ISSUES

In addition to offering unique opportunities for creating personalized and interactive experiences, the integration of digital twins and the metaverse in marketing also brings with it ethical challenges and privacy issues. These challenges arise because these technologies are heavily dependent on the collection, processing, and analysis of user data. Data that may include sensitive and personal information about users. This data includes users' identity information, online behaviors, personal preferences, and even biometric data (Yordanova & Nozari, 2025). Inappropriate use of this data or lack of adequate protection of it can lead to violations of users' privacy and raise serious ethical concerns. Therefore, it is essential to examine and manage these challenges to ensure the responsible and ethical use of digital twins and the metaverse in marketing.

One of the most important ethical considerations in this context is transparency in the collection and use of user data. Brands should clearly inform users about what data is being collected from them, how it is processed, and for what purpose it is used. This transparency should not only be reflected in the brands' privacy policies, but also explained in plain, understandable language to users (Nozari, Abdi, & Jahangard, 2025). For example, if a brand uses users' digital twin data to personalize metaverse experiences, users should be informed about how this data is being collected, how it is stored, and how it is being used to provide personalized offers. This transparency allows users to make an informed decision about whether they want to share their data.

Protecting user data is another important ethical dimension in this context. In an environment where digital twins and metaverses access and process user data in real time, maintaining the security of this data is of particular importance. Brands should use strong security protocols to protect user data. These protocols can include data encryption, two-factor authentication, and data access management systems. In addition, brands should use security monitoring and control systems that allow them to continuously monitor the security of user data and take prompt action if any threats or security breaches are identified (Prabhakaran et al., 2025). These measures not only help protect user data, but also build trust between users and brands.

The issue of informed consent of users is also a fundamental principle in privacy. Brands should ensure that users are sharing their data with full and informed consent. This consent should be provided in a clear and plain language, and users should be able to withdraw their consent at any time. For example, if a user does not want their digital twin data to be used to personalize metaverse experiences, they should be able to opt out. This consent should be actively collected, meaning that users must voluntarily and consciously express their consent, rather than being assumed to have consented (Nozari & Samadi, 2025).

In addition, the use of artificial intelligence and machine learning algorithms to analyze user data can also raise ethical challenges. These algorithms can automatically analyze user data and identify patterns of behavior. While this approach can help brands create personalized experiences for users, it can also lead to concerns about discrimination or bias in data analysis. Brands should ensure that their algorithms are designed in a fair and unbiased manner and are continuously reviewed and evaluated to ensure they are operating properly and ethically (Chatterjee et al., 2024). This review could include evaluating algorithms to identify any unfair discrimination or inappropriate prioritization of some users.

Another important aspect of privacy protection is data anonymization. Brands should ensure that user data is stored and processed anonymously, and that no information that could directly reveal the user's identity is made available. This can include using encryption techniques, separating identity data from analytics data, and even using federated learning models to process data (Panagiotakopoulos, Marentakis, Metzitakos, Deliyannis, & Dedes, 2022). This approach not only helps protect user privacy, but also allows brands to use user data in a safe and ethical manner to improve the user experience.

Finally, it is essential to comply with privacy laws and regulations in different geographies. Brands should comply with the General Data Protection Regulation (GDPR) in the European Union, the California Consumer Privacy Act (CCPA) in the United States, and other local privacy regulations. These laws give users the right to access, rectify or delete their data, and even object to the processing of their data (Bonta, 2022). Brands should use these laws as a guide to designing their systems to prevent breaches of user privacy.

Overall, the responsible use of digital twins and the metaverse in marketing means that brands should always put the interests of users first. This includes avoiding the use of psychological manipulation techniques to persuade users to buy products, avoiding the dissemination of false or misleading information, and providing transparent and ethical marketing experiences. Brands should use advanced technologies to improve the user experience, but they should always ensure that these technologies are used responsibly and ethically.

7- FUTURE TRENDS AND RESEARCH DIRECTIONS

The integration of digital twins and metaverse in marketing is an emerging and dynamic field that continues to evolve, and there are many opportunities for development and research in this field. With the advancement of digital technologies and the expansion of the use of artificial intelligence, the Internet of Things (IoT), virtual reality (VR), and augmented reality (AR), user expectations of digital experiences are changing rapidly. In the meantime, digital twins and metaverse as two key concepts can enable brands to create personalized, interactive, and immersive experiences for users. However, to fully exploit these potentials, there is a need to develop new technologies, improve infrastructure, and conduct deeper research in this area.

One of the most important future trends in this field is the use of artificial intelligence to improve the capabilities of digital twins and metaverse. Artificial intelligence can automatically analyze user data and predict their behavior. This technology can use deep learning algorithms and neural networks to create more accurate models of user behavior and improve personalized experiences. For example, AI systems can analyze users' digital twins in real time and provide personalized recommendations to users based on these analyses. This trend can help brands create dynamic user experiences that are tailored to users' needs.

Along with AI, augmented reality and virtual reality technologies are also considered as key drivers in the development of the metaverse and interactive digital experiences. Advances in AR and VR technologies allow brands to create more realistic virtual environments that users can interact with in an immersive way. These environments can include virtual stores, interactive exhibitions, live events, and even interactive training. In addition, with the development of Mixed Reality (MR) technologies, it is possible to combine real and virtual environments simultaneously, which can elevate user experiences to a higher level. This trend allows brands to seamlessly combine digital and physical experiences.

Another trend is the expansion of the use of blockchain and non-fungible tokens (NFTs) in the metaverse. As a decentralized and secure technology, blockchain can help brands create and offer unique digital assets to users. These assets can include digital products, virtual clothing, digital art, and even virtual real estate. For example, a fashion brand could create a collection of digital clothing in the form of NFTs that users can purchase and use in the metaverse. Additionally, blockchain can help maintain user security and privacy in the metaverse, as user information is stored decentralized and can only be accessed with their consent. This approach could lead to the creation of an independent digital economy in the metaverse where users can buy and sell their digital assets.

Another important research direction in this field is the development of dynamic and intelligent digital twin models. As a digital view of physical systems or users, a digital twin can be dynamically updated using real-time data. However, to create accurate and realistic models, it is necessary to develop advanced machine learning algorithms and neural networks that can automatically analyze user data and update digital twin models. These models can help brands predict user behavior more accurately and create more personalized experiences. For example, a dynamic digital twin model can analyze users' environmental and behavioral data to create personalized experiences for them that are in line with their current situation.

Another important research focus is to investigate the social and psychological effects of integrating digital twins and the metaverse on users. As the use of the metaverse expands, users are gradually spending more time in virtual environments, which can have numerous psychological and social impacts. Research can examine the impact of the metaverse on users' mental health, social relationships, digital identity, and even their consumption behaviors. This research can help brands design responsible and ethical user experiences that not only improve the user experience, but also support users' mental health and well-being.

Also, research on standardizing and developing security protocols to protect user data in the metaverse is of particular importance. Given that the metaverse is heavily dependent on the collection and processing of user data, protecting user privacy and preventing misuse of their data has become a fundamental challenge. Research can help develop advanced security protocols such as end-to-end encryption, multi-factor authentication systems, and data anonymization models. These protocols can help brands use user data safely and responsibly.

Finally, another important research direction is to examine business models and marketing strategies based on digital twins and the metaverse. Brands can use these technologies to create new business models that are based on interactive and personalized experiences. These models can include virtual stores, interactive exhibitions, live events, and even educational experiences. Research can examine the effectiveness of these business models, analyze user behavior in these environments, and identify the best marketing strategies to attract and retain customers.

These future trends and research directions show that digital twins and the metaverse in marketing are still evolving and there are unique opportunities for development and innovation in this field. By conducting deeper research and developing new technologies, brands can create more interactive, personalized, and ethical digital experiences for users, which not only helps improve the user experience, but also leads to business growth and success.

8- CONCLUSION

The integration of digital twins and metaverse in marketing as a new and transformative approach enables the creation of interactive, personalized, and immersive experiences for users. By combining accurate and real-time digital twin data with virtual and interactive metaverse environments, this approach allows brands to dynamically optimize their marketing strategies according to the characteristics and needs of each user. This system not only improves the user experience, but also helps brands establish deeper and more meaningful connections with their customers and collect valuable data on user behavior and preferences.

This chapter began by examining the concepts of digital twins and metaverse and then examined how these two technologies can be integrated in marketing. The conceptual framework of this integration showed how digital twin data can be displayed in real-time in the metaverse and create personalized experiences for users. This approach not only allows brands to create more interactive and engaging digital experiences, but also helps them use real-time data and analytics to optimize their marketing strategies. This system allows brands to continuously improve customer experiences and adjust their marketing strategies based on real-time user behavior using real-time data.

Furthermore, a review of the practical applications of this approach showed that the integration of digital twins and metaverse can be used in various areas, including personalized shopping experiences, virtual exhibitions, live events, interactive training, and even customer relationship management. These applications not only improve the user experience, but also allow brands to establish interactive and meaningful connections with their customers and collect valuable data on user behavior. However, this approach also comes with ethical challenges and privacy issues. Brands must ensure that user data is collected, processed, and stored responsibly and securely, and that users share their data with full consent and awareness.

The review of future trends and research directions also revealed that digital twins and the metaverse continue to evolve, and there are unique opportunities for development and innovation in this area. Using artificial intelligence to improve personalization capabilities, developing dynamic digital twin models, using augmented and virtual reality to create immersive experiences, and even using blockchain to maintain user security and privacy are among the trends that can help these technologies grow and progress. Also, conducting deeper research into the social and psychological effects of these technologies on users and examining business models based on these approaches can help develop practical and responsible solutions in this area.

Ultimately, the integration of digital twins and the metaverse in marketing as a data-driven and interactive approach enables the creation of dynamic, personalized, and immersive digital experiences for users. This approach not only improves the user experience and increases user engagement, but also allows brands to optimize their marketing strategies using real-time data and analytics. However, success in using this approach requires responsible design and implementation, ethical considerations, and user privacy. Brands should always use advanced technologies to improve the user experience, but at the same time, they must ensure that these technologies are used responsibly and ethically.

REFERENCES

Al Zami, M. B., Shaon, S., Quy, V. K., & Nguyen, D. C. (2025). Digital Twin in Industries: A Comprehensive Survey. *IEEE Access : Practical Innovations, Open Solutions.*

Aloqaily, M., Bouachir, O., Karray, F., Al Ridhawi, I., & El Saddik, A. (2022). Integrating digital twin and advanced intelligent technologies to realize the metaverse. *IEEE Consumer Electronics Magazine, 12*(6), 47–55. DOI: 10.1109/MCE.2022.3212570

Bonta, R. (2022). California consumer privacy act (CCPA). Retrieved from State of California Department of Justice: https://oag. ca. gov/privacy/ccpa.

Buhalis, D., Leung, D., & Lin, M. (2023). Metaverse as a disruptive technology revolutionising tourism management and marketing. *Tourism Management, 97*, 104724. DOI: 10.1016/j.tourman.2023.104724

Chatterjee, P., Das, D., Rawat, D. B., Ghosh, U., Banerjee, S., & Al-Numay, M. S. (2024). Digital Twins and Blockchain Fusion for Security in Metaverse-Driven Consumer Supply Chains. *IEEE Transactions on Consumer Electronics, 70*(3), 5688–5697. DOI: 10.1109/TCE.2024.3477297

Deng, B., Wong, I. A., & Lian, Q. L. (2024). From metaverse experience to physical travel: The role of the digital twin in metaverse design. *Tourism Review, 79*(5), 1076–1087. DOI: 10.1108/TR-05-2023-0315

Durana, P., Vochozka, M., Tucmeanu, A. I., & Tudosă, P. (2022). Digital Twin-enabled Industrial Internet of Things, Multi-Sensory Extended Reality and Immersive Holographic Imaging Technologies, and 3D Modeling and Virtual Simulation Tools across Blockchain-based Decentralized Metaverse Systems. Economics. *Management and Financial Markets, 17*(1), 43–57.

Fallah, M., & Nozari, H. (2021). Neutrosophic mathematical programming for optimization of multi-objective sustainable biomass supply chain network design. *Computer Modeling in Engineering & Sciences, 129*(2), 927–951. DOI: 10.32604/cmes.2021.017511

Fallah, M., & Nozari, H. (2021). Quantitative analysis of cyber risks in IoT-based supply chain (FMCG industries). *Journal of Decisions and Operations Research, 5*(4), 510–521.

Ghahremani-Nahr, J., Nozari, H., & Szmelter-Jarosz, A. (2024). Designing a humanitarian relief logistics network considering the cost of deprivation using a robust-fuzzy-probabilistic planning method. *Journal of International Humanitarian Action*, *9*(1), 19. DOI: 10.1186/s41018-024-00163-8

Han, Y., Niyato, D., Leung, C., Kim, D. I., Zhu, K., Feng, S., Shen, X., & Miao, C. (2022). A dynamic hierarchical framework for IoT-assisted digital twin synchronization in the metaverse. *IEEE Internet of Things Journal*, *10*(1), 268–284. DOI: 10.1109/JIOT.2022.3201082

Kovacova, M., Oláh, J., & Popescu, G. H. (2022). Digital Twin simulation and modeling tools, deep learning object detection technology, and visual perception and sensor fusion algorithms in the metaverse commerce. Economics. *Management and Financial Markets*, *17*(3), 9–24.

Mourtzis, D. (2023). Digital twin inception in the Era of industrial metaverse. *Frontiers in Manufacturing Technology*, *3*, 1155735. DOI: 10.3389/fmtec.2023.1155735

Movahed, A. B., Movahed, A. B., & Nozari, H. (2024). Marketing 6.0 Conceptualization. In Advanced Businesses in Industry 6.0 (pp. 15-31). IGI Global.

Movahed, A. B., Movahed, A. B., & Nozari, H. (2024). Opportunities and challenges of marketing 5.0. Smart and Sustainable Interactive Marketing, 1-21.

Najafi, S. E., Nozari, H., & Edalatpanah, S. A. (2022). Investigating the key parameters affecting sustainable IoT-based marketing. In *Computational Intelligence Methodologies Applied to Sustainable Development Goals* (pp. 51–61). Springer International Publishing. DOI: 10.1007/978-3-030-97344-5_4

Nozari, H. (Ed.). (2025). *Dynamic and Safe Economy in the Age of Smart Technologies*. IGI Global. DOI: 10.4018/979-8-3693-4369-2

Nozari, H. (2025). Cognitive Targeting and Neuromarketing Applications in AI-Driven Digital Advertising. *Applied Innovations in Industrial Management*, *5*(2), 52–58. DOI: 10.63630/aiim.52.52

Nozari, H. (2025). NeuroTwinceutics™ as a Neuromorphic Digital Twin Model for Predictive and Personalized Pharmacotherapy. *Transformative Science*, *1*(1), 1–8.

Nozari, H., Abdi, H., & Jahangard, S. (2025). Quantum Cognitive Intelligence Network Q-CIN as a Transformative Framework for Industry 6.0. *ALL Bioscience*, *1*(1), 27–37.

Nozari, H., Abdi, H., & Rafiei, K. (2025). Edge Computing and Marketing in the Smart Economy: Processing Consumer Data in Real-Time. In Dynamic and Safe Economy in the Age of Smart Technologies (pp. 191-208). IGI Global Scientific Publishing.

Nozari, H., Rahmaty, M., & Szmelter-Jarosz, A. (2024). A framework for AIoT-based smart sustainable marketing system. In *Artificial Intelligence of Things for Achieving Sustainable Development Goals* (pp. 255–271). Springer Nature Switzerland. DOI: 10.1007/978-3-031-53433-1_13

Nozari, H., & Samadi, S. (2025). Digital Twin-Enhanced Sentiment Analysis for Targeted Marketing Optimization. In Dynamic and Safe Economy in the Age of Smart Technologies (pp. 121-138). IGI Global Scientific Publishing. DOI: 10.4018/979-8-3693-4369-2.ch008

Nozari, H., Szmelter-Jarosz, A., & Ghahremani-Nahr, J. (2021). The ideas of sustainable and green marketing based on the internet of everything—The case of the dairy industry. *Future Internet*, *13*(10), 266. DOI: 10.3390/fi13100266

Nozari, H., Szmelter-Jarosz, A., & Rahmaty, M. (2024). Smart marketing based on artificial intelligence of things (AIoT) and Blockchain and evaluating critical success factors. In *Smart and Sustainable Interactive Marketing* (pp. 68–82). IGI Global Scientific Publishing. DOI: 10.4018/979-8-3693-1339-8.ch005

Nozari, H., Tavakkoli-Moghaddam, R., & Dolgui, A. (2024, September). Analysis of Critical Success Factors of Sustainable and Resilient Aioe-based Supply Chain in Industry 5.0. In IFIP International Conference on Advances in Production Management Systems (pp. 76-90). Cham: Springer Nature Switzerland. DOI: 10.1007/978-3-031-65894-5_6

Oskounejad, M. M., & Nozari, H. (Eds.). (2024). *Advanced Businesses in Industry 6.0*. IGI Global. DOI: 10.4018/979-8-3693-3108-8

Panagiotakopoulos, D., Marentakis, G., Metzitakos, R., Deliyannis, I., & Dedes, F. (2022). Digital scent technology: Toward the internet of senses and the metaverse. *IT Professional*, *24*(3), 52–59. DOI: 10.1109/MITP.2022.3177292

Prabhakaran, A., Mahamadu, A. M., Adekunle, S., Manu, P., Booth, C. A., & Aigbavboa, C. (2025). 24 Towards a Metaverse Platform for Immersive Collaborative Design. Applications of Immersive Technology in Architecture, Engineering and Construction: A Handbook, 24.

Rane, N., Choudhary, S., & Rane, J. (2023). Metaverse marketing strategies: enhancing customer experience and analysing consumer behaviour through leading-edge Metaverse technologies, platforms, and models. Platforms, and Models (November 3, 2023).

Sai, S., Prasad, M., Garg, A., & Chamola, V. (2024). Synergizing digital twins and metaverse for consumer health: A case study approach. *IEEE Transactions on Consumer Electronics*, *70*(1), 2137–2144. DOI: 10.1109/TCE.2024.3367929

Wallace, S. (2023). Digital Twin and Metaverse Technologies, Geospatial Simulation and Sensor Fusion Tools, and Object Perception and Motion Control Algorithms in Immersive Hyper-Connected Virtual Spaces. *Linguistic and Philosophical Investigations*, (22), 264–280.

Yang, W., Tan, F., Bai, Y., & Ryu, J. H. (2024, November). Exploring Experiential Marketing Strategies of Luxury Fashion Brands in the Metaverse: An In-Depth Analysis of Immersive Consumer Engagement. In International Conference on Services Computing (pp. 100-113). Cham: Springer Nature Switzerland.

Yordanova, Z., & Nozari, H. (2025). Harnessing Cyber-Physical Systems and Digital Twins for Industrial Innovation and Economic Resilience. In Dynamic and Safe Economy in the Age of Smart Technologies (pp. 33-48). IGI Global Scientific Publishing. DOI: 10.4018/979-8-3693-4369-2.ch003

Chapter 13
Neuromorphic Models for Dynamic Customer Segmentation in Digital Marketing

Hamed Nozari
https://orcid.org/0000-0002-6500-6708
Bio10, Dubai, UAE

ABSTRACT

This research investigates the application of neuromorphic models in dynamic and real-time customer segmentation in digital marketing. By designing a spiky neural network, user behavioral data was analyzed and categorized in real time. The results showed that the neuromorphic model, compared to traditional methods such as K-means, has greater accuracy, speed, and flexibility, and is capable of identifying changing behavioral patterns. This model can be an effective step in the development of intelligent and personalized marketing systems.

1- INTRODUCTION

In recent decades, the spread of digital technologies has led to a profound transformation in marketing models. Digital marketing is no longer limited to displaying advertisements on web pages or sending mass emails, but has become an intelligent, personalized, and data-driven system that continuously adapts to the changing behavior and needs of consumers (Movahed, Movahed, & Nozari, 2024). One of the fundamental pillars of this transformation is the analysis of customer behavior based on their interactive and productive data in online spaces. In this context, customer

DOI: 10.4018/979-8-3373-3775-3.ch013

segmentation is recognized as one of the most important decision-making strategies in digital marketing; because by dividing users into groups with similar behavioral characteristics, it allows for more precise targeting and personalized offers (Najafi, Nozari, & Edalatpanah, 2022).

However, traditional segmentation, which is mainly based on static algorithms such as K-means, decision trees, or hierarchical clustering, faces several challenges. These methods often lack the flexibility to adapt to the changing dynamics of user behavior and cannot keep up with the dynamics of digital consumer behavior (Movahed, Movahed, & Nozari, 2024). In the real world, user behavior changes continuously and abruptly, and understanding this dynamic requires approaches that go beyond traditional, static frameworks.

In this regard, the use of advanced artificial intelligence models, especially neuromorphic models, has provided a new perspective in behavioral data analysis and dynamic segmentation. Inspired by the structure of biological neurons in the human brain, neuromorphic models are able to process data in real time and generate adaptive responses (Nozari, Abdi, & Jahangard, 2025). Unlike classical neural networks, which are based on continuous and symmetric information transmission, neuromorphic networks (such as Spiking Neural Networks or SNNs) use pulsed and temporal systems for data transmission that are more similar to the natural processing of the brain (Nozari, 2023). This feature allows them to be used in dynamic and complex environments such as digital marketing with less energy consumption, faster response, and higher adaptability.

In such environments, real-time analysis of user interaction data, including clicks, scrolls, time spent on pages, and navigation paths, can provide invaluable insights into user states of mind and interests (Nozari, 2024). When combined with an intelligent neuromorphic system, this data can be used to identify behavioral segments in real time, without the need to completely retrain the model. In other words, these systems can learn, predict, and adapt—three key features that are critical to the success of campaigns in modern marketing.

On the other hand, neuromorphic models are not only efficient at identifying behavioral groups, but also highly robust in the face of noise, incomplete data, and sudden changes (Nozari, 2025). These features make them an attractive option for dynamic segmentation in platforms such as online stores, content platforms, and social networks. Furthermore, the possibility of implementing these models in hardware optimized for neural processing, such as neuromorphic chips, has opened new avenues for their implementation on an industrial scale (Nozari, Rahmaty, & Szmelter-Jarosz, 2024).

Given this theoretical and technical background, the present research seeks to answer the central question: Can neuromorphic models perform better than traditional methods in dynamic and real-time customer segmentation in digital marketing? To answer this question, a model based on spiking neural networks has been designed and implemented that receives customer behavioral data live and identifies different behavioral groups in real time. This model has not only been tested against classical segmentation algorithms, but has also been evaluated in terms of accuracy, processing speed, and adaptation to changes.

In the following, the structure of the article will be presented as follows: In the second section, theoretical foundations and a review of previous literature in the field of neuromorphic models and digital segmentation are presented. The third section is dedicated to describing the research methodology, which includes model design, data collection method, and evaluation criteria. The fourth section presents empirical results and comparative analysis. Then, in the fifth section, the findings are interpreted and their impact on improving the digital marketing process is examined. Finally, in the sixth section, conclusions are drawn and suggestions for future research will be presented.

2- LITERATURE REVIEW

Digital transformation has been expanding at an unprecedented pace in recent years, affecting traditional marketing structures and approaches, and the need for new, more accurate, and more flexible models for analyzing customer behavior is increasingly felt. In this context, the concept of customer segmentation as one of the pillars of decision-making in digital marketing has always played a key role. The purpose of segmentation is to identify homogeneous groups among customers based on behavioral, demographic, or psychographic characteristics, so that marketing strategies can be adjusted to be more effective (Aliahmadi, Nozari, Ghahremani-Nahr, & Szmelter-Jarosz, 2022). However, classic models in this field, such as K-means clustering or decision tree-based algorithms, are generally static and have little ability to understand the dynamics of consumers' digital behavior.

With the growth of online interactions, the dynamics of customer behavior have become one of the most important analytical challenges in the marketing space. Today's customers may switch between different roles, such as searcher, comparator, or buyer, in a matter of minutes. Such changes require algorithms that not only recognize behavioral patterns, but also react to these changes in real time and with high accuracy (Nozari, 2025). This is where the use of artificial intelligence, and especially its newer subfields such as neuromorphic computing, comes as an innovative solution.

Neuromorphic models are inspired by the human nervous system and try to simulate the natural way the brain processes and learns. One of the most prominent features of these models is the use of spiking neurons instead of classical neurons in neural networks. Instead of sending continuous signals, these neurons transmit information in the form of time pulses, thereby enabling real-time processing with low energy consumption (Nozari & Chobar, 2024). These features have made neuromorphic models attractive in applications such as object recognition, neural signal analysis, and more recently in behavioral data processing in digital environments.

In the field of digital marketing, although much of the research has focused on the use of machine learning algorithms, the use of neuromorphic architectures is still emerging and has rarely been explored in depth in the context of dynamic segmentation. However, some early studies have shown that spiking neural networks, due to their ability to recognize temporal patterns, can model changing customer behaviors better than traditional neural networks (Rahmaty & Nozari, 2023). Also, due to their impulse structure, these models are able to perform more consistently in environments with sparse, discontinuous, or noisy data.

From an application perspective, analyzing customer behavior with digital data involves a set of challenges. The data is usually heterogeneous, voluminous, and often unstructured. Traditional models require complex and often time-consuming preprocessing to analyze such data. In contrast, neuromorphic models can receive data as it is and respond to it quickly through continuous and adaptive learning (Aliahmadi & Nozari, 2023). This ability allows neuromorphic-based marketing systems to respond much faster to behavioral changes and provide more personalized recommendations.

Another important point that has been considered in research related to neuromorphic models is the ability of these models to be integrated with specialized hardware such as neuromorphic chips. These chips, which also have similarities to the brain in terms of physical structure, enable the parallel execution of neuromorphic algorithms with very low energy consumption. This feature has led to these chips being seriously used in some industries, including in the design of robotic systems and smart sensors (Movahed, Aliahmadi, Parsanejad, & Nozari, 2023). In the field of digital marketing, this can also pave the way for the deployment of intelligent models at the edge of the network (Edge Computing); Where data analysis is done directly at the point of production, avoiding the time-consuming transfer to central servers.

From a methodological perspective, it is also very important to pay attention to the architecture and structure of neuromorphic models compared to other models. Unlike classical models that have a predetermined structure, neuromorphic models can dynamically change their structure according to the inputs. This provides significant flexibility in analyzing nonlinear and complex behaviors, which are abundantly observed in customer visits to digital platforms (Irani & Nozari, 2024).

Despite all these advantages, research on the application of neuromorphic models in digital marketing is still in its infancy. Most of the existing studies have either focused on biological and engineering applications or have only addressed the theoretical aspects of the models and have neglected their practical testing in real-world contexts. For this reason, there is an urgent need for empirical research to investigate the real-world effectiveness of these models in identifying behavioral patterns, dynamic segmentation, and increasing conversion rates in marketing campaigns (Nozari, Ghahremani-Nahr, & Szmelter-Jarosz, 2024).

The present study is designed to address this gap and attempts to take a practical step in this direction by designing and implementing a neuromorphic model for real-time customer segmentation in the digital marketing environment. This model is designed based on real-world behavioral data, such as interaction time, clicks, and navigation patterns, and is compared with classical models such as K-means and traditional neural networks. Initial results show that the neuromorphic model is not only capable of recognizing more complex patterns, but also performs better in terms of speed and flexibility (Nozari, Szmelter-Jarosz, & Ghahremani-Nahr, 2021).

Finally, a review of the existing literature suggests that combining the computational capabilities of neuromorphic models with the analytical requirements of digital marketing could lead to a new generation of intelligent marketing systems; systems that not only analyze data, but also actively and adaptively play a role in decision-making (Nozari, Fallah, Szmelter-Jarosz, & Krzemiński, 2021). This combination promises a future in which human-machine interaction in marketing reaches a level of shared cognitive understanding; a level in which the customer experience is no longer simply a product of reacting to inputs, but rather a product of prediction, learning, and moment-to-moment personalization.

3- METHODOLOGY

This research aims to investigate and analyze the application of neuromorphic models for dynamic and real-time customer segmentation in digital marketing. The approach of this research is designed to be practical and based on real-world data analysis and includes various stages of data collection, neuromorphic model design, and performance evaluation. In this section, the research process is explained in detail and a conceptual flow chart (Figure 1) is provided for a better understanding of the process.

Figure 1. Research methodology diagram

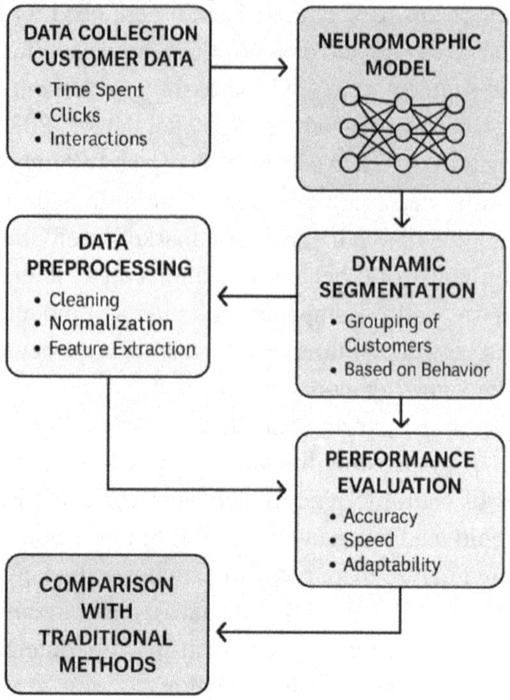

- ***Data Collection***

In the first step, customer behavioral data was obtained from a digital marketing platform. This data included information such as the number of page views, time spent on each page, number of clicks, user navigation paths, and their interactions with the content. This data was used as the primary source to identify customer behavioral patterns. The goal of this step was to collect valid and sufficient data to design and train the neuromorphic model.

- ***Data Preprocessing***

To prepare the data, a preprocessing process was performed, including data cleaning, removal of missing values, and standardization of values. The behavioral data was converted into a set of interpretable features, which included various indicators such as average interaction time, click rate, number of pages viewed, and navigation paths. These features were used as input to the neuromorphic model. Proper data preprocessing plays a key role in improving the accuracy and stability of the model.

- ***Neuromorphic Model Design***

In this step, a neuromorphic model based on Spiking Neural Networks (SNNs) was designed. These networks are capable of instantaneous and real-time data processing due to their structure inspired by the brain's nervous system. The model structure included input layers to receive feature data, hidden layers to process data using spiking neurons, and an output layer to produce dynamic segmentation results. Each neuron in this network was configured to be able to learn from customer behavior patterns.

To optimize the model's performance and prevent overfitting, methods such as adjusting neuron weights, reinforcement learning, and gradual reduction of the learning rate were used. This approach allowed the model to dynamically adapt to changes in customer behavior.

- ***Dynamic and Real-Time Segmentation***

The designed neuromorphic model processes incoming behavioral data in real-time and divides customers into different segments based on their behavioral characteristics. This dynamic segmentation means that customers are moved to new segments based on changes in their behavior in real-time. For example, a customer may be moved from one segment to another if their behavior (such as interaction duration or number of clicks) changes significantly.

- ***Model Performance Evaluation***

After the model was designed and implemented, its performance was evaluated using several key metrics. These metrics include:

Segmentation Accuracy: The extent to which the model's segmentation matches actual customer behavior patterns.
Processing Speed: The time required to process and segment new data.
Adaptability: The ability of the model to adapt to real-time changes in customer behavior.

- ***Comparison with Traditional Methods***

To evaluate the effectiveness of the neuromorphic model, its results were compared with traditional customer segmentation methods such as K-means and classical neural networks. This comparison included examining the accuracy, processing time, and the model's capability in dynamic segmentation. The results clearly showed that the neuromorphic model performs better in dynamic and real-time customer segmentation.

4- RESULTS

This section presents and analyzes the results of implementing a neuromorphic model for dynamic and real-time customer segmentation in digital marketing. The results are divided into two main sections: First, the performance of the neuromorphic model in dynamic segmentation and identifying customer behavior patterns is examined, and then these results are compared with traditional segmentation methods. To better present the results, three figures and two tables are used.

4.1 Performance of Neuromorphic Model in Dynamic Segmentation

The designed neuromorphic model was run using customer behavioral data. The model was able to segment customers into different segments in real time, which were defined based on behavioral characteristics such as interaction duration, number of clicks, and customer navigation paths. Figure 2 shows an example of the model output, where customers are divided into different groups based on similar behaviors.

Figure 2. Dynamic customer segmentation using the neuromorphic model

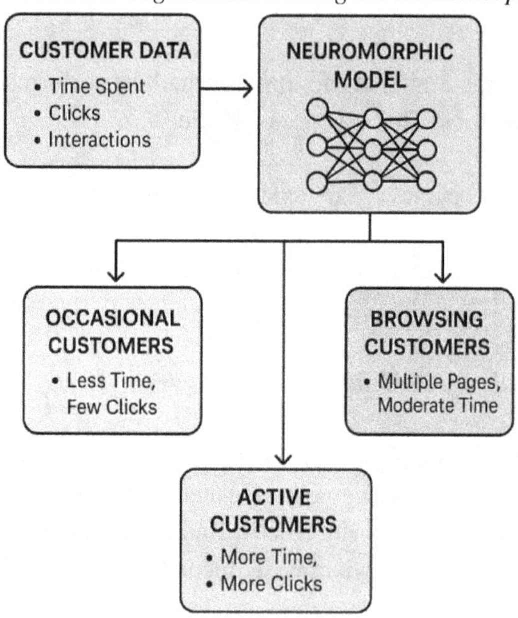

This graph shows that the neuromorphic model is able to identify different groups of customers dynamically and in real time. For example, customers who spend more time on product pages and have more clicks are grouped into the "active customers" group, while customers who have only viewed one or two pages are categorized as "occasional customers."

4.2 Detailed Customer Segmentation Analysis

In order to investigate this further, the neuromorphic model was tested on various datasets and its performance was evaluated based on the criteria of accuracy, speed, and flexibility. Table 1 shows the results of this evaluation.

Table 1. Performance of the neuromorphic model in dynamic segmentation

Metric	Neuromorphic Model	K-means	Neural Network
Accuracy	92.3%	78.5%	84.7%
Processing Speed	0.02 seconds	0.15 seconds	0.08 seconds
Adaptability	High	Medium	Low

This table clearly shows that the neuromorphic model outperforms traditional methods such as K-means and classical neural networks. Higher accuracy, faster processing speed, and the ability to dynamically adapt to changes in customer behavior are among the advantages of this model.

4.3 Analyzing Customer Behavior in Different Segments

To more accurately analyze the created segments, the neuromorphic model monitored changes in customer behavior in real time. Figure 3 shows the trend of customer behavior changes in one of the dynamic segments over a specific time period.

Figure 3. Trends in customer behavior changes in the "Active Customers" group

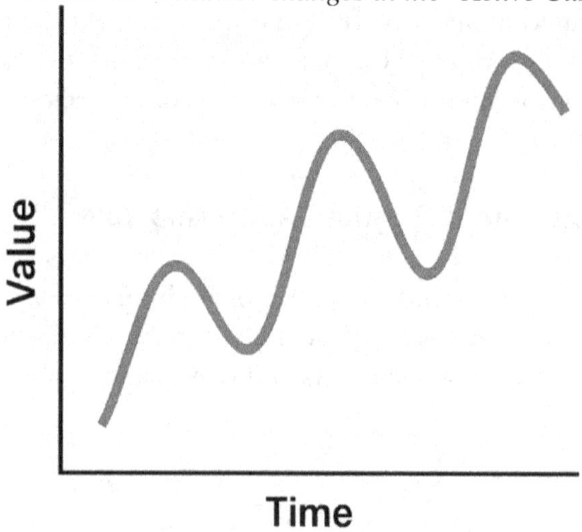

This diagram shows that the neuromorphic model continuously monitors customer behavior and updates segmentations as their behavior changes. This feature allows for dynamic, real-time segmentation that is not possible with traditional methods.

4.4 Comparison of the Performance of the Neuromorphic Model With Traditional Methods

For a more comprehensive review, the neuromorphic model was compared with traditional methods such as K-means and traditional neural networks. Table 2 shows the results of this comparison.

Table 2. Comparison of neuromorphic model performance with traditional methods

Metric	Neuromorphic Model	K-means	Neural Network
Dynamic Segmentation	Yes	No	No
Real-Time Processing	Yes	No	No
Accuracy	92.3%	78.5%	84.7%
Processing Speed	0.02 seconds	0.15 seconds	0.08 seconds
Adaptability	High	Medium	Low

This table clearly shows that the neuromorphic model outperforms traditional methods with real-time processing capabilities, high flexibility, and greater accuracy in dynamic segmentation.

4.5 Qualitative Analysis of Dynamic Segmentation

To qualitatively examine the performance of the model, a deeper analysis of customer behavior in each segment was performed. Figure 4 shows an example of a heatmap of customer interactions in the "Active Customers" group.

Figure 4. Heatmap of active customer interactions

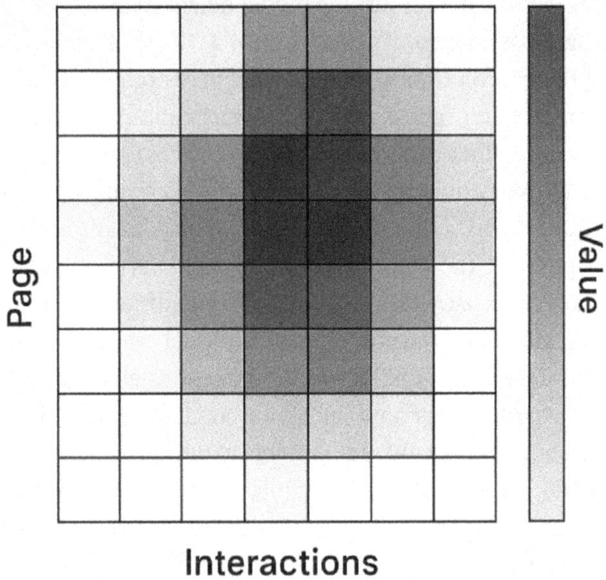

This heat map shows that active customers are most engaged on product pages and purchase-related sections. This qualitative analysis demonstrates the power of the neuromorphic model in identifying behavioral patterns and dynamic and accurate segmentation.

Quantitative and qualitative results show that the neuromorphic model is not only able to accurately identify dynamic segments, but also adapts to momentary changes in customer behavior. This model can be used as an efficient tool in digital marketing, where customer behavior changes rapidly and real-time adaptation is required.

5- DISCUSSION

The results of this study show that the designed neuromorphic model has effectively improved the dynamic and real-time segmentation of customers in the digital marketing environment. By utilizing spiking neural networks (SNNs), this model is able to analyze and process customer behavioral data in real time and create segments with high accuracy and remarkable flexibility. This feature is particularly prominent compared to traditional methods such as K-means and conventional neural networks, as these classical methods have performed poorly due to their static nature and inability to identify instantaneous changes in customer behavior.

Comparing the performance of the neuromorphic model with traditional segmentation methods shows the clear superiority of this model. For example, the segmentation accuracy of the neuromorphic model reached 92.3%, while K-means was only 78.5% and the classical neural network was 84.7%. This difference indicates the higher ability of the neuromorphic model to identify complex behavioral patterns. In addition, the processing speed of the neuromorphic model (0.02 seconds) was significantly faster than that of K-means (0.15 seconds) and neural network (0.08 seconds). This improvement in speed is due to the neuromorphic structure and its real-time architecture, which allows for instantaneous data processing.

Another advantage of the neuromorphic model is its flexibility in adapting to instantaneous changes in customer behavior. Unlike traditional methods that segment only based on a fixed pattern, the neuromorphic model is able to continuously adapt to changes in customer behavior. This feature is especially important in dynamic digital environments where customer behavior changes rapidly. This flexibility allows the model to continuously move customers to the appropriate segments without the need for manual adjustment. For example, customers who were initially in the "transient customers" category can be moved to the "active customers" category if their interactions increase.

The analysis of the results also shows that the neuromorphic model was successfully able to identify different behavioral segments of customers based on their interaction characteristics. This segmentation included the groups of "passive customers", "active customers" and "interested in browsing". Among them, the "active customers" group had the highest interaction with the platform content, which is clearly visible in the heat map (Figure 4). This heat map shows the concentration of active customer interactions in specific sections of the platform, which can be used as a basis for optimizing marketing content.

From an applied perspective, these findings show that the use of the neuromorphic model can help improve digital marketing strategies. By taking advantage of this model, brands and companies can dynamically segment their customers and intelligently adjust their content for each segment. For example, customers who are identified as "active customers" can receive more targeted content and special promotions, while transient customers will be presented with more familiar content and invitations to engage.

The study also points out some limitations that should be addressed in future research. First, the neuromorphic model is designed for behavioral data and may require further tuning when dealing with more complex data such as images or videos. Furthermore, while the neuromorphic model has performed well in dynamic segmentation, real-time processing of the data requires high-performance hardware. This can be challenging for small companies with limited resources.

In future research, it is suggested that the neuromorphic model be tested with multimodal data such as a combination of text, images, and audio. This approach could help identify customer behavior patterns more accurately. Also, the use of more advanced architectures such as Hybrid Neuromorphic Models that have self-adaptive learning capabilities can further increase segmentation accuracy. For example, combining a neuromorphic model with reinforcement learning algorithms can help this model continuously learn from customer behavior and adapt to their changes.

Finally, the findings of this research show that the neuromorphic model can be used as an efficient and advanced tool in dynamic and real-time customer segmentation in digital marketing. With its high capabilities in identifying and analyzing customer behavior, this model can help improve marketing strategies, increase customer interactions, and improve conversion rates. These results can be the basis for developing intelligent digital marketing systems and designing more targeted campaigns in the future.

6- CONCLUSION

The present study aimed to investigate the capabilities of neuromorphic models in dynamic and real-time customer segmentation in the digital marketing space and showed that these models, especially spiky neural networks (SNN), can create a fundamental transformation in understanding and analyzing user behavior. The neuromorphic model that was designed and implemented, using a structure inspired by the human brain, was able to process customer behavioral data in real time and form meaningful groupings based on real interaction patterns. Unlike traditional methods that typically operate based on static clustering, this model was able to adaptively and continuously update customer segmentation.

The quantitative and qualitative results of the study showed that the neuromorphic model outperforms methods such as K-means and conventional neural networks in terms of segmentation accuracy, response speed, and flexibility. The model's 92% accuracy, 1/100th of a second processing speed, and ability to adapt to real-time changes in user behavior clearly demonstrate the superiority of this approach. In addition, heat maps and behavioral graphs also showed that the model is capable of providing deep and actionable insights into user interactions on digital platforms.

From a practical perspective, this model can provide digital marketers with a powerful tool to adjust their strategies more accurately and quickly. By leveraging dynamic segmentation, companies can deliver their messages, offers, and content to their audiences in a more targeted manner, which ultimately leads to increased engagement rates, improved user experience, and improved marketing campaign effectiveness. This ability to personalize on a mass scale is a competitive advantage in modern marketing.

At the same time, it should be noted that the development and deployment of such models requires appropriate processing infrastructure and access to high-quality data. Although the neuromorphic model was successfully implemented in this study, its implementation on an industrial scale requires further studies from the perspective of operation, cost, and integration with other digital marketing systems.

Overall, it can be said that neuromorphic models have the potential to become the backbone of the next generation of intelligent marketing systems. This study was a first step towards utilizing this approach in digital marketing and paves the way for deeper research in areas such as multimodal data fusion, adaptive learning, and neural intelligence-based personalization. The future of digital marketing, under the shadow of such models, will move towards better understanding of humans and more intelligently responding to individual needs and interests.

REFERENCES

Aliahmadi, A., & Nozari, H. (2023, January). Evaluation of security metrics in AIoT and blockchain-based supply chain by Neutrosophic decision-making method. In Supply chain forum: an international journal (Vol. 24, No. 1, pp. 31-42). Taylor & Francis. DOI: 10.1080/16258312.2022.2101898

Aliahmadi, A., Nozari, H., Ghahremani-Nahr, J., & Szmelter-Jarosz, A. (2022). Evaluation of key impression of resilient supply chain based on artificial intelligence of things (AIoT). arXiv preprint arXiv:2207.13174.

Irani, H. R., & Nozari, H. (Eds.). (2024). *Smart and Sustainable Interactive Marketing*. IGI Global. DOI: 10.4018/979-8-3693-1339-8

Movahed, A. B., Aliahmadi, A., Parsanejad, M., & Nozari, H. (2023). A systematic review of collaboration in supply chain 4.0 with meta-synthesis method. *Supply Chain Analytics*, *4*, 100052. DOI: 10.1016/j.sca.2023.100052

Movahed, A. B., Movahed, A. B., & Nozari, H. (2024). Opportunities and challenges of marketing 5.0. Smart and Sustainable Interactive Marketing, 1-21.

Movahed, A. B., Movahed, A. B., & Nozari, H. (2024). Marketing 6.0 Conceptualization. In Advanced Businesses in Industry 6.0 (pp. 15-31). IGI Global.

Najafi, S. E., Nozari, H., & Edalatpanah, S. A. (2022). Artificial Intelligence of Things (AIoT) and Industry 4.0–Based Supply Chain (FMCG Industry). A roadmap for enabling industry 4.0 by artificial intelligence, 31-41.

Nozari, H. (Ed.). (2023). *Building Smart and Sustainable Businesses with Transformative Technologies*. IGI Global. DOI: 10.4018/979-8-3693-0210-1

Nozari, H. (2024). Green Supply Chain Management based on Artificial Intelligence of Everything. *Journal of Economics and Management*, *46*, 171–188. DOI: 10.22367/jem.2024.46.07

Nozari, H. (2025). NeuroTwinceutics™ as a Neuromorphic Digital Twin Model for Predictive and Personalized Pharmacotherapy. *Transformative Science*, *1*(1), 1–8.

Nozari, H. (2025). Cognitive Targeting and Neuromarketing Applications in AI-Driven Digital Advertising. *Applied Innovations in Industrial Management*, *5*(2), 52–58. DOI: 10.63630/aiim.52.52

Nozari, H., Abdi, H., & Jahangard, S. (2025). Quantum Cognitive Intelligence Network Q-CIN as a Transformative Framework for Industry 6.0. *ALL Bioscience*, *1*(1), 27–37.

Nozari, H., & Chobar, A. P. (2024). The Dimensions and Components of Marketing 5.0: Introduction to Marketing 6.0. In Advanced Businesses in Industry 6.0 (pp. 75-86). IGI Global.

Nozari, H., Fallah, M., Szmelter-Jarosz, A., & Krzemiński, M. (2021). Analysis of security criteria for IoT-based supply chain: a case study of FMCG industries. Central European Management Journal, 29(4).

Nozari, H., Ghahremani-Nahr, J., & Szmelter-Jarosz, A. (2024). AI and machine learning for real-world problems. [). Elsevier.]. *Advances in Computers*, *134*, 1–12. DOI: 10.1016/bs.adcom.2023.02.001

Nozari, H., Rahmaty, M., & Szmelter-Jarosz, A. (2024). A framework for AIoT-based smart sustainable marketing system. In *Artificial Intelligence of Things for Achieving Sustainable Development Goals* (pp. 255–271). Springer Nature Switzerland. DOI: 10.1007/978-3-031-53433-1_13

Nozari, H., Szmelter-Jarosz, A., & Ghahremani-Nahr, J. (2021). The ideas of sustainable and green marketing based on the internet of everything—The case of the dairy industry. *Future Internet*, *13*(10), 266. DOI: 10.3390/fi13100266

Rahmaty, M., & Nozari, H. (2023). Optimization of the hierarchical supply chain in the pharmaceutical industry. *Edelweiss Applied Science and Technology*, *7*(2), 104–123. DOI: 10.55214/25768484.v7i2.376

Chapter 14
Impact of Digital Marketing on Consumer Engagement Through Cognitive AI:
A Critical Review of the Hospitality Industry

Earnest Anand
https://orcid.org/0009-0006-4298-2323
Lovely Professional University, India

Sanjeev Kumar
https://orcid.org/0000-0002-7375-7341
Lovely Professional University, India

Geetha Manoharan
https://orcid.org/0000-0002-8644-8871
SR University, India

ABSTRACT

With the usage of grown technologies, the hospitality area is continuously converting. Among them, virtual advertising has revolutionized patron interplay thanks to cognitive synthetic intelligence (AI). This observe examines how AI-powered digital advertising methods enhance consumer satisfaction, increase brand loyalty, and propel employer growth in the hotel industry. Cognitive AI describes artificial intelligence (AI) structures that use information analytics, system learning, and herbal language processing (NLP) to simulate human cognitive techniques. Cognitive AI

DOI: 10.4018/979-8-3373-3775-3.ch014

aids in studying customer conduct, forecasting preferences, and customizing encounters in virtual advertising. Chatbots driven with the aid of AI offer actual-time aid, efficiently handling reservations, purchaser complaints, and questions. AI makes use of patron facts analysis to personalize offerings and advertising and marketing messaging. Actual-time communique is made feasible via AI, which guarantees activate solutions to customer questions.

INTRODUCTION

Any advertising and marketing campaign that makes use of an electronic tool or the internet is taken into consideration virtual marketing. To communicate with each present and potential client, corporations use digital platforms which include web sites, social media, electronic email, and search engines like Google. Different names for this include "internet advertising," "net advertising," and "on line advertising." making use of a variety of virtual strategies and systems to have interaction with customers in which they spend a big quantity of time on-line is called digital advertising and marketing (Kannan & Li, 2017). The term "digital marketing" incorporates a extensive variety of strategies, from websites to a enterprise's online branding belongings, together with virtual advertising, e-mail marketing, online brochures, and extra. The promotion of products or services using virtual technology, more often than not the net but additionally mobile devices, show commercials, and other virtual media, is known as digital advertising. the use of digital advertising techniques like SEO, SEM, content material advertising and marketing, influencer advertising, content automation, campaign advertising, data-pushed marketing, e-commerce advertising, social media advertising and marketing, social media optimization, direct marketing via mails, direct advertising, show advertising, e-books, optical disks, and games is growing in popularity as generation advances (Goldfarb & Tucker, 2019). Nowadays, digital advertising and marketing consists of non-internet platforms that offer digital media, such callback, on-preserve mobile ring tones, and mobile phones (SMS and MMS). Era development and digital advertising improvement are inextricably connected. Ray Tomlinson sent the primary electronic mail in 1971, and his invention created the framework that enabled record transfers among computers. Instead of the usage of limited list brokers, corporations commenced making use of internet techniques like database marketing. Groups had been able to better song purchaser information way to these databases, which modified the consumer-seller dynamic. But the guide approach wasn't very effective in deliver greater commercial enterprise (Piñeiro-Otero & Martínez-Rolán, 2016).

Whilst the phrase "virtual advertising" becomes first used inside the Nineties, the introduction of server/client structure and the massive use of private computer systems led to the rise in importance of consumer relationship management (CRM) software program in advertising and marketing generation (Parsons et al., 1998). Providers were pressured by fierce competition to provide new services, which include advertising and marketing, income, and service packages, to their software. With the appearance of the internet, marketers may also access vast amounts of on-line consumer data with e-CRM software. Organizations may get the concern of their clients' experiences and update the records about their demands. In the 2000s and 2010s, as the wide variety of devices that would get admission to digital media extended dramatically, virtual advertising advanced. Virtual advertising persisted to upward push, in line with records from 2012 and 2013. As social media structures like Facebook, YouTube, LinkedIn, and Twitter grew in popularity in the 2000s, human being's normal lives have become more and more reliant on virtual gadgets (Morris, 2009). They expected a smooth consumer experience while searching for product data across numerous channels. The form of advertising and marketing technology turned into improved via the shift in patron conduct. By way of representing facts in bits, digital technology lowers the prices associated with amassing, storing, and processing client information. The five major costs have decreased as a result of this: search, replication, monitoring, transportation, and verification prices (Peter & Dalla Vecchia, 2021). Virtual products don't have any competition. One individual can eat them without lowering the quantity or caliber that is accessible to others. A non-rival good is fire. One person can ignite another person's fire using the fire they started, without putting out their own. Digital products' non-competitive nature has significant marketing ramifications, especially in regards to copyright and privacy(Chaffey & Smith, 2022).

REVIEW OF LITERATURE

AI adoption emphasizes the significance of data-driven decision-making for a customer-centric approach, continuous learning, and ethical issues when combined with the current technologies. AI's effects on digital marketing include improved consumer experiences, better productivity, competitive advantage, and ethical and legal issues (Prentice et al., 2020). Predictive analytics, chatbots, recommendation systems, and dynamic content creation are just a few of the technologies that allow marketers to provide highly relevant and timely interactions that increase customer pleasure, loyalty, and conversion rates (Y. Gupta & Khan, 2024). AI makes every customer connection more personalized, enabling real-time communication and meeting the modern consumer's demand for individualized attention. By using chatbots and sentiment analysis to track client feedback in real time, virtual assistants offer individualized financial advice (Bag et al., 2022). Purchaser pride, loyalty, and organization overall performance are therefore the outcomes of a successful AI integration. So that you can develop compelling advertising and marketing messages, AI and neuroscience integration in advertising involves identifying emotions, comparing sentiments, and presenting tailor-made content material relying on user preferences and cognitive reactions. AI can personalize advertising procedures to optimize efficacy through comprehending how the brain interprets statistics and reacts to stimuli (Hao, 2020). Campaigns which can be greater engaging and centered can affect consumer conduct thanks to the combination of neuroscience and generation. However it additionally tackles subjects like facts safety, safety, and ethics, as well as the problems in integrating AI and the requirement for brand spanking new metrics to gauge AI-powered advertising strategies. Groups want to concentrate on ability development; efficacy assessment, integration tactics, and ethical AI use (Li, Wang, et al., 2024). The privateness Calculus theory describes how clients make decisions by using balancing the blessings of individualized services against possible privacy dangers. Even though AI can improve person revel in, it wishes sturdy privateness safeguards and open facts policies to be depended on. Corporations may also correctly appoint AI technology to offer individualized reviews at the same time as maintaining customer accept as true with in their privateness regulations by means of putting a balance between those criteria (Perez-Vega et al., 2021).

Keeping consumer self-assurance requires striking stability between the benefits of individualized service and privacy worries. Agencies need to be looking for ethical problems as AI technologies broaden similarly. AI integration in digital advertising gives a number of blessings, including higher client experiences, elevated operational effectiveness, and tailored interactions that improve consumer happiness and engagement (Chen et al., 2021). Recommendation engines, chatbots, and predictive analytics are examples of technology that help marketers in correctly engaging purchasers, which will increase purchaser happiness and loyalty. Groups must, however, triumph over barriers together with records safety, security problems, moral dilemmas, and the difficulties of integrating AI (Alam et al., 2024). Obvious statistics coping with, non-stop talent improvement and ethical AI methods are essential. AI-pushed customization makes use of state-of-the-art device gaining knowledge of algorithms that go past conventional records analytics to forecast and alter person behavior in actual time, customizing advertising efforts for man or woman customers. Large amounts of statistics from sources like social media, purchase histories, and surfing histories are processed via AI structures (Mariani & Borghi, 2021). AI generates precise predictions via identifying a distinct set of user styles through the analysis of this statistics. This long-time period flexibility distinguishes AI-pushed customization from traditional techniques. By using growing tailored and pertinent records for clients based totally on their demographics, interests, and conduct, dynamic content introduction raises consumer happiness, increases conversion charges, and improves consumer engagement (Behera et al., 2024). By tracking humans's on line activities, behavioral targeting makes use of the information to expose those tailor-made classified ads or content that suits with their choices.

Through grouping statistics in line with similarities and variations, segmentation and clustering algorithms make it feasible to find patterns and insights. Businesses may also higher recognise patron remarks and make facts-pushed picks with the aid of using sentiment analysis, which utilizes gadget mastering and herbal language processing to discover emotional tone in messages (Ku, 2024). Via making cloth greater visible, applicable, and tasty for engines like google, content material optimization raises a bit's search engine rating. Groups may customize their advertising and marketing campaigns to target specific areas and demographics by using the use of geo-focused on, which distributes facts or ads to particular audiences relying on their geographic area (Zahidi et al., 2024). User adventure mapping gives a complete photograph of the user experience through graphically representing the moves a user plays whilst interacting with an amazing or provider. As a consequence, by means of improving productivity, customer happiness, and customization, AI technology are remodeling advertising strategies. They provide corporations the ability to be expecting customer needs, offer tailored stories, maximize the exposure of facts, goal unique demographics, and effectively have interaction with ability customers (Maduku et al., 2024). however, to assure the sustainable and accountable use of AI in marketing, organising consider and enduring purchaser connections, problems including records privacy worries, ethical implications, and educated humans control have to be resolved. AI integration in marketing creates aggressive advantage further to improving client engagement and operational performance (rather, 2024). The use of AI to customise content material involves adjusting offers, advertisements, and marketing messages for precise users according to their demographics, options, and conduct. This approach has been proven to be pretty a success in raising customer involvement. By way of improving purchaser interaction and choice-making, synthetic intelligence (AI) has absolutely converted the advertising sector (Bilro et al., 2019). Primarily based on consumer demographics, conduct, and alternatives, it could offer tailor-made advertising messages, commercials, and content material.

IMPACT OF COGNITIVE AI IN HOSPITALITY INDUSTRY

The lodge sector is changing its carrier models because of AIoT generation. By way of combining A IoT generation with hospitality carrier robots, a brand new carrier model has been created in which robots cope with cleansing, meals and beverage transport, tourist welcome, and navigation on their personal (Chung & Tan, 2025).

these robots enhance operational performance and carrier fine via making use of technological era along with artificial intelligence (AI), the net of things (IoT), and sensor-based totally systems. Service robots and different systems can talk seamlessly due to the fact to A IoT's multisystem cooperation abilities, which move beyond self-reliant operation. Mainly, the A IoT framework permits customized provider shipping this is desirable to purchaser needs with the aid of integrating carrier robots with clever hospitality equipment like lighting, climate control, and safety systems (Han et al., 2024). in accordance to analyze, A IoT-powered hospitality systems enhance patron happiness and improve the emblem price of hospitality companies by means of dynamically adjusting service settings relying on tourist preferences. Three key regions were the main emphasis of AIoT adoption in the hotel sector: enhancing commercial enterprise model innovation, maximizing information use, and growing service efficiency. First, A IoT-enabled service robots greatly reduce down on room service wait instances for customers and enhance order accuracy at some stage in durations of high occupancy; this generation successfully relieves the strain of human personnel (Ruel & Njoku, 2021). 2nd, through combining real-time behavioral insights with beyond customer facts, AIoT structures optimize data use with the aid of generating tailored service pointers. Artificial Intelligence (AI) has being adopted by means of the hotel zone to improve the visitor enjoy via personalizing it. AI equipment like device getting to know algorithms are important for analyzing vacationer data and tailoring hospitality services in keeping with personal tastes and patterns of conduct (S. Gupta et al., 2022).

It diagnosed how nicely AI-powered advice systems work to boom traveler delight and cultivate repeat business, two matters which are important to a emblem's achievement. Issues over traveller privateness and safeguarding non-public information were also introduced up by means of the observe, underscoring the moral conundrum faced with the aid of hospitality vendors as they try for awesome individualized carrier (El-Akhras et al., 2025). those problems highlight how critical it's far to use AI inside the business in a balanced manner, making sure that vacationer studies decorate and respect individual limitations while reminding the target audience of the ethical troubles worried in integrating AI. The dynamics of open innovation range in step with enterprise, which includes collective intelligence, mobile payments, and transport structures (El-Akhras et al., 2025). Thru cooperation between telecom providers, economic establishments, and regulators, mobile payment systems including M-Pesa in Kenya serve as an instance of ways open innovation contributes to economic inclusion.

DIGITAL MARKETING ON CONSUMER ENGAGEMENT THROUGH COGNITIVE AI

Cognitive Artificial Intelligence (AI) revolutionizing in the digital marketing by significantly enhancing consumer engagement; personalized, intelligent, and adaptive interactions. Unlike traditional AI, cognitive AI mimics human thought processes such as reasoning, learning, & decision-making, enabling marketers to create deeply contextualized experiences that resonate with individual consumer preferences. It one of the most profound impacts of cognitive AI in digital marketing is the development of intelligent customer journeys. Through natural language processing, sentiment analysis, and behavioral prediction, brands can understand not just what consumers do, but why they do it. This allows for highly targeted content delivery across platforms—emails, social media, chatbots, and personalized recommendations—tailored to emotional and situational cues. Tools like IBM Watson and Salesforce Einstein are leading the charge by enabling real-time data processing to optimize marketing strategies dynamically. In addition, chatbots powered by cognitive AI provide human-like conversations that enhance customer satisfaction and reduce churn. These bots can resolve queries, offer product advice, and even predict needs, fostering deeper engagement and loyalty. On social media, AI-powered listening tools analyze consumer feedback and trends to tailor brand communication with exceptional precision. Cognitive AI also enhances visual and voice search capabilities, creating new interactive experiences. Brands using AI to predict what consumers might want next—based on context, mood, or history seeing higher click-through rates, dwell time, and conversion metrics. On the other hand, successful implementation requires ethical considerations such as data privacy, transparency, and consent, as misuse can erode trust. In the era of hyper-digitalization, the fusion of cognitive AI and digital marketing is not just a competitive advantage it is becoming an essential strategy for meaningful, sustained consumer engagement.

FACTORS EFFECTING THE AI IMPLICATION IN HOSPITALITY INDUSTRY

Inspecting the technology adoption models that theoretically explain the recognition of latest technology is vital to comprehending the major elements riding the lodge enterprise's adoption of AI. Inspecting those fashions serves as a foundation for the use of an analytical method that advances our information of the variables affecting the adoption of AI (Bhuiyan et al., 2024). This segment summarizes the various models of era adoption and mainly makes use of the era-organization-environment (TOE) paradigm as the muse for explaining how AI is being followed within the resort sector. The use of AI as a digital ordering mechanism has multiplied due to the meals service industry's growing demand for transport and takeout services. Each purchasers and eating place owners have benefited from this (Flavián et al., 2024). Customers can also locate eating places, book reservations, order takeout, and get pertinent records concerning get dressed policies at these establishments with the help of chatbots. Using artificial intelligence might provide restaurant owners a competitive edge in communication as compared to alternative ordering methods, as well as enhance profitability, efficiency, and labor expenses (Gao et al., 2022). Due to the fact they will have to treat the AI device as an intelligent being based on their personal social norms and beliefs, customers may similarly justify their opposition to using AI devices in service delivery via assuming that interacting with an AI device will possibly require extra attempt than interacting with a human employee (Wu et al., 2016). Being a humanoid means that effort comes from two assets: the effort had to recognize a technical system and the effort needed to engage with an actual human. Consequently, anthropomorphic traits ought to make users sense that making use of AI devices calls for extra paintings. The implementation of Artificial Intelligence (AI) in the hospitality industry providing the new shape to hospitality sector in terms of; service delivery, guest experience, and operational efficiency. However, its adoption is influenced by a multitude of technological, organizational, economic, and human-centric factors. Research highlights both the enablers (like enhanced data availability, demand for personalization, and cost reduction) and barriers (such as workforce resistance, privacy concerns, and infrastructure readiness). This synthesis presents major factors affecting AI implementation in the hospitality sector, grounded in academic literature.

Although numerous media outlets have extensively covered the advantages of this new AI tool for businesses, it is crucial to comprehend the limitations of generative AI models, which can result in reputational and legal risks, the use of offensive or copyrighted content, privacy loss, fraudulent transactions, and the dissemination of false information (Himanshu et al., 2025). Organizations must comprehend, control, and reduce the risks associated with implementing AI.

From the standpoint of AI risk management, the theory offers a method for settling disputes by using a flexible, outcome-driven lens to create and evaluate policies at every phase of the risk management cycle. In a similar vein, the contextual significance of AI adoption (in each sector for a particular application) can help AI developers, organizations preparing to implement AI, and even policy makers make practical and ethical decisions by comprehending and balancing the advantages and disadvantages (Lee & Lu, 2024). Therefore, in order to make socially responsible decisions that will assist assure a deliberate, careful, rational, and ethical approach of using generative AI, AI risk management frameworks and ethical theory viewpoints should be combined. Although clients generally expect the basic factors—which form the foundation of the product/service offering—to be fulfilled, this is not a sufficient requirement for customer happiness (Jung & Yoon, 2016). Since high performance suggests a smaller benefit in terms of overall happiness than poor performance, the link between these elements' performance and satisfaction is asymmetrical. It is possible to view AI-powered service operations as a way to simultaneously improve customer satisfaction, service quality, and productivity (Li, Zhou, et al., 2024). This suggests that the use of service robots enables service organizations to attain cost-effective service excellence, that is, service excellence at low unit costs, rather than necessarily resulting in a trade-off between productivity and satisfaction.

The main focus areas of AI Implementation in the Hospitality Industry are:

I. Technological Readiness and Infrastructure
II. Employee Perception and Resistance
III. Customer Acceptance and Trust
IV. Organizational Culture and Leadership Support
V. Economic and Cost Considerations
VI. Legal and Ethical Issues
VII. Data Security and Privacy
VIII. AI Maturity and Use Case Development
IX. Training and Skills Development
X. Post-COVID Acceleration and Contactless Trends

AI implementation in hospitality is a complex, multidimensional process, shaped by a variety of internal and external forces. While it promises efficiency and innovation, it also requires careful alignment with human, technical, and ethical dimensions. Hospitality businesses that prepare strategically—investing in infrastructure, training, and trust—are better positioned to harness AI's full potential.

FUTURE TRENDS IN AI POWERED HOSPITALITY INDUSTRY

AI has thc potential to completely transform personalized marketing by producing highly tailored content via the use of technologies like natural language generation (NLG) and natural language processing (NLP). By crafting customized product descriptions, messaging, and offers that speak to specific clients on a deep level, this will increase customer engagement and conversion rates (Saleh, 2025). By examining enormous volumes of data, different customer groups will be found based on their interactions, preferences, and behaviors, leading to improved customer segmentation. Marketing materials will stay current and interesting thanks to real-time dynamic content optimization, which will allow for real-time campaign modifications depending on customer feedback (Ahmed, 2025). Hyper-personalized content and communications are being produced using generative AI, including OpenAI's GPT-4, which has resulted in notable increases in engagement rates and cost savings. More advanced AI-powered virtual assistants are giving individualized customer support by making customized suggestions, responding to consumer inquiries, and gathering insightful information about their preferences and actions (Huang et al., 2024). Consumer privacy and ethical issues will receive increasing attention when AI is used into marketing. Businesses want to ensure they make use of AI sensibly, putting stability among user privacy and personalization at the same time as adhering to information protection laws (Battour et al., 2024). It's far predicted that future traits in AI generation will provide even greater advanced personalization functions, bearing in mind greater customization and interactivity, enhancing marketing marketing campaign efficacy, and building closer relationships with customers (Irani, 2024). As AI develops in addition, its application to tailor-made advertising will become more and more essential for obtaining a aggressive benefit within the digital market (Parvez et al., 2025).

The future of the AI-powered hospitality industry is poised for transformational growth, with trends focusing on hyper-personalization, contactless guest experiences, emotion-aware service robots, and AI-driven sustainability initiatives. As machine learning and natural language processing advance, hotels will deploy intelligent virtual concierges, predictive maintenance systems, and adaptive pricing algorithms tailored to individual guest behaviors. Integration with the Internet of Things (IoT) will enable seamless automation across rooms and facilities, enhancing operational efficiency. Moreover, ethical AI and privacy-preserving designs will become pivotal as guests demand more control over their data. These innovations will not only elevate customer satisfaction but also redefine competitive advantage in the sector.

ISSUES AND CHALLENGES DIGITAL MARKETING ON CONSUMER ENGAGEMENT THROUGH COGNITIVE AI

The integration of cognitive AI into digital marketing for consumer engagement offers transformative potential, yet it presents several critical issues and challenges that businesses must navigate carefully. One of the foremost concerns is data privacy and security. Cognitive AI thrives on analyzing vast datasets, including sensitive personal and behavioral information. However, with rising consumer awareness and strict regulations like GDPR and CCPA, marketers must ensure ethical data collection, transparency, and consent mechanisms to avoid legal and reputational risks. Another major challenges algorithmic bias and ethical decision-making. Cognitive AI systems can inadvertently perpetuate biases present in training data, leading to discriminatory targeting, exclusionary messaging, or skewed personalization. It is not only hampers inclusive engagement but can alienate consumer segments. Ensuring fairness and inclusivity in AI-driven campaigns requires constant human oversight, auditing, and refinement of AI models. Integration complexity is another hurdle. Most organizations struggle to seamlessly combine cognitive AI with their existing CRM systems, data warehouses, and multichannel marketing platforms. It demands high technological maturity, skilled personnel, and substantial investment. Smaller businesses may lack the infrastructure or resources to implement such advanced AI solutions effectively. Additionally, loss of human touch remains a critical concern. While AI enhances efficiency, over-automation can lead to impersonal interactions. Consumers may feel disconnected if brands rely too heavily on AI-driven chatbots or recommendation engines without human backup, especially in scenarios requiring empathy or nuanced understanding. Finally, interpretability and trust in AI decisions pose a challenge. Marketers and consumers alike may not fully understand how AI systems arrive at certain conclusions or suggestions. This "black box" problem can lead to skepticism or resistance, undermining campaign effectiveness and consumer trust. To address these challenges, businesses must adopt a human-centric AI strategy—one that balances automation with empathy, transparency with innovation, and personalization with privacy. Only then can digital marketing truly leverage cognitive AI for meaningful and ethical consumer engagement.

DYNAMIC CUSTOMER SEGMENTATION IN DIGITAL MARKETING

Dynamic customer segmentation is an advanced approach in digital marketing that leverages AI and machine learning to categorize consumers based on real-time behaviors, preferences, and interactions rather than static demographic profiles. Unlike traditional segmentation methods, which rely on fixed variables like age, gender, or geography, dynamic segmentation evolves continuously as customers engage with a brand across multiple touch-points. By utilizing machine learning algorithms, marketers can analyze large volumes of data—including browsing patterns, purchase history, social media activity, and sentiment to create granular and adaptive customer segments. These segments are not predefined but are shaped dynamically by the consumer's journey, allowing for more relevant and personalized marketing strategies. For example, a customer who shifts from casual browsing to active interest in high-value products might be automatically reclassified into a high-intent buyer segment, triggering tailored content and promotions. This approach significantly enhances campaign performance, as it enables hyper-personalization at scale. AI models can predict future behavior and preferences, facilitating the delivery of the right message, at the right time, through the right channel. It also allows for real-time re-segmentation, which is crucial in today's fast-paced, data-driven marketing landscape. On the other hand, implementing dynamic segmentation requires robust data infrastructure, integration across systems (CRM, social media, e-commerce), and strict adherence to privacy regulations. When executed effectively, it empowers marketers to move from reactive to proactive strategies, deepening customer engagement and loyalty. In essence, dynamic customer segmentation transforms digital marketing from a one-size-fits-all approach to a continuously evolving, insight-driven practice that aligns with individual customer needs and behaviors in real time.

CONCLUSION

Through improving patron interaction with custom designed records, artificial intelligence (AI) has completely converted personalized virtual advertising. AI offers marketers a comprehensive hold close of the specific necessities and options of each consumer by evaluating good sized volumes of records using system studying, natural language processing, and predictive analytics. Because of this know-how, quite custom designed content material that appeals to clients is produced, increasing logo loyalty and standard consumer satisfaction. AI-powered customization strategies have revolutionized conventional advertising and marketing techniques by using emphasizing tailored advertising and marketing. Advice engines, dynamic content material manufacturing, and chatbots pushed with the aid of synthetic intelligence have confirmed efficacy in providing timely and pertinent interactions, boosting customer engagement and conversion costs. However, there are obstacles to integrating AI in digital marketing, including issues with data security, privacy, and channel consistency. Companies must spend money on ongoing AI algorithm monitoring and upgrading as well as staff training to manage the intricacies of AI technology. With developments in AI technologies like generative AI and real-time dynamic content optimization, the use of AI in customized marketing has a bright future.

REFERENCES

Ahmed, M. (2025). AI Revolutionizing Hospitality: Insights from the MENA. In Azoury, N., & Yahchouchi, G. (Eds.), *AI in the Middle East for Growth and Business* (pp. 217–236). Springer Nature Switzerland., DOI: 10.1007/978-3-031-75589-7_13

Alam, S. S., Masukujjaman, M., Mohamed Makhbul, Z. K., Helmi Ali, M., Ahmad, I., & Al Mamun, A. (2024). Experience, Trust, eWOM Engagement and Usage Intention of AI Enabled Services in Hospitality and Tourism Industry: Moderating Mediating Analysis. *Journal of Quality Assurance in Hospitality & Tourism*, *25*(6), 1635–1663. DOI: 10.1080/1528008X.2023.2167762

Bag, S., Srivastava, G., Bashir, M. M. A., Kumari, S., Giannakis, M., & Chowdhury, A. H. (2022). Journey of customers in this digital era: Understanding the role of artificial intelligence technologies in user engagement and conversion. *Benchmarking*, *29*(7), 2074–2098. DOI: 10.1108/BIJ-07-2021-0415

Battour, M., Salaheldeen, M., Mady, K., & Ratnasari, R. T. (2024). ChatGPT and Halal Travel: An Overview of Current Trends and Future Research Directions. In Khamis, R., & Buallay, A. (Eds.), *AI in Business: Opportunities and Limitations* (Vol. 515, pp. 23–31). Springer Nature Switzerland., DOI: 10.1007/978-3-031-48479-7_3

Behera, R. K., Bala, P. K., Rana, N. P., Algharabat, R. S., & Kumar, K. (2024). Transforming customer engagement with artificial intelligence E-marketing: An E-retailer perspective in the era of retail 4.0. *Marketing Intelligence & Planning*, *42*(7), 1141–1168. DOI: 10.1108/MIP-04-2023-0145

Bhuiyan, K. H., Ahmed, S., & Jahan, I. (2024). Consumer attitude toward using artificial intelligence (AI) devices in hospitality services. *Journal of Hospitality and Tourism Insights*, *7*(2), 968–985. DOI: 10.1108/JHTI-08-2023-0551

Bilro, R. G., Loureiro, S. M. C., & Guerreiro, J. (2019). Exploring online customer engagement with hospitality products and its relationship with involvement, emotional states, experience and brand advocacy. *Journal of Hospitality Marketing & Management*, *28*(2), 147–171. DOI: 10.1080/19368623.2018.1506375

Chaffey, D., & Smith, P. (2022). *Digital Marketing Excellence: Planning, Optimizing and Integrating Online Marketing* (6th ed.). Routledge., DOI: 10.4324/9781003009498

Chen, S., Han, X., Bilgihan, A., & Okumus, F. (2021). Customer engagement research in hospitality and tourism: A systematic review. *Journal of Hospitality Marketing & Management*, *30*(7), 871–904. DOI: 10.1080/19368623.2021.1903644

Chung, K. C., & Tan, P. J. B. (2025). Artificial intelligence and internet of things to improve smart hospitality services. *Internet of Things : Engineering Cyber Physical Human Systems, 31*, 101544. DOI: 10.1016/j.iot.2025.101544

El-Akhras, H. A., Abd El-Wahab, M. A., Saghier, E. G., & Selem, K. M. (2025). ChatGPT adoption risks and cognitive achievement among tourism and hospitality college students: From faculty member perspective. *Journal of Hospitality and Tourism Insights, 8*(4), 1288–1307. DOI: 10.1108/JHTI-04-2024-0292

Flavián, C., Tussyadiah, I. P., & Orús, C. (2024). How immersive technologies are re-defining the customer journey. Guest editorial. *International Journal of Contemporary Hospitality Management, 36*(11), 3557–3565. DOI: 10.1108/IJCHM-11-2024-215

Gao, J., Ren, L., Yang, Y., Zhang, D., & Li, L. (2022). The impact of artificial intelligence technology stimuli on smart customer experience and the moderating effect of technology readiness. *International Journal of Emerging Markets, 17*(4), 1123–1142. DOI: 10.1108/IJOEM-06-2021-0975

Goldfarb, A., & Tucker, C. (2019). Digital marketing. In *Handbook of the Economics of Marketing* (Vol. 1, pp. 259–290). Elsevier., DOI: 10.1016/bs.hem.2019.04.004

Gupta, S., Modgil, S., Lee, C.-K., Cho, M., & Park, Y. (2022). Artificial intelligence enabled robots for stay experience in the hospitality industry in a smart city. *Industrial Management & Data Systems, 122*(10), 2331–2350. DOI: 10.1108/IMDS-10-2021-0621

Gupta, Y., & Khan, F. M. (2024). Role of artificial intelligence in customer engagement: A systematic review and future research directions. *Journal of Modelling in Management, 19*(5), 1535–1565. DOI: 10.1108/JM2-01-2023-0016

Han, H., Kim, S., Hailu, T. B., Al-Ansi, A., Lee, J., & Kim, J. J. (2024). Effects of cognitive, affective and normative drivers of artificial intelligence ChatGPT on continuous use intention. *Journal of Hospitality and Tourism Technology, 15*(4), 629–647. DOI: 10.1108/JHTT-11-2023-0363

Hao, F. (2020). The landscape of customer engagement in hospitality and tourism: A systematic review. *International Journal of Contemporary Hospitality Management, 32*(5), 1837–1860. DOI: 10.1108/IJCHM-09-2019-0765

Himanshu, A., Aggarwal, R., Gupta, S., Dhingra, S., & Kumar, A. (2025). The virtual voyage: Understanding the factors affecting metaverse adoption in the tourism and hospitality industry. *Current Issues in Tourism*, •••, 1–21. DOI: 10.1080/13683500.2025.2475491

Huang, A., Ozturk, A. B., Zhang, T., De La Mora Velasco, E., & Haney, A. (2024). Unpacking AI for hospitality and tourism services: Exploring the role of perceived enjoyment on future use intentions. *International Journal of Hospitality Management*, *119*, 103693. DOI: 10.1016/j.ijhm.2024.103693

Irani, F. (2024). Exploring the future of tourism: A qualitative study on the integration of robotics in North Cyprus hospitality and destination development. *Worldwide Hospitality and Tourism Themes*, *16*(6), 694–705. DOI: 10.1108/WHATT-05-2024-0097

Jung, H. S., & Yoon, H. H. (2016). Why is employees' emotional intelligence important?: The effects of EI on stress-coping styles and job satisfaction in the hospitality industry. *International Journal of Contemporary Hospitality Management*, *28*(8), 1649–1675. DOI: 10.1108/IJCHM-10-2014-0509

Kannan, P. K., & Li, H. (2017). Digital marketing: A framework, review and research agenda. *International Journal of Research in Marketing*, *34*(1), 22–45. DOI: 10.1016/j.ijresmar.2016.11.006

Ku, E. C. S. (2024). Digital marketing innovation and industrial marketing: Evidence from restaurants' service robots. *Asia Pacific Journal of Marketing and Logistics*, *36*(11), 3099–3117. DOI: 10.1108/APJML-02-2024-0185

Lee, W., & Lu, L. (2024). The hospitable thought that counts: An emerging theory of "AI consciousness" in genuine hospitality. *International Journal of Hospitality Management*, *123*, 103928. DOI: 10.1016/j.ijhm.2024.103928

Li, Y., Wang, S., & Li, Z. (2024). Animating arousal and engagement: Empirical insights into AI-enhanced robotic performances and consumer reactions. *Journal of Hospitality and Tourism Technology*, *15*(5), 737–768. DOI: 10.1108/JHTT-01-2024-0053

Li, Y., Zhou, X., Jiang, X., Fan, F., & Song, B. (2024). How service robots' human-like appearance impacts consumer trust: A study across diverse cultures and service settings. *International Journal of Contemporary Hospitality Management*, *36*(9), 3151–3167. DOI: 10.1108/IJCHM-06-2023-0845

Maduku, D. K., Rana, N. P., Mpinganjira, M., Thusi, P., Mkhize, N. H.-B., & Ledikwe, A. (2024). Do AI-powered digital assistants influence customer emotions, engagement and loyalty? An empirical investigation. *Asia Pacific Journal of Marketing and Logistics*, *36*(11), 2849–2868. DOI: 10.1108/APJML-09-2023-0935

Mariani, M., & Borghi, M. (2021). Customers' evaluation of mechanical artificial intelligence in hospitality services: A study using online reviews analytics. *International Journal of Contemporary Hospitality Management*, *33*(11), 3956–3976. DOI: 10.1108/IJCHM-06-2020-0622

Morris, N. (2009). Understanding Digital Marketing: Marketing Strategies for Engaging the Digital Generation. *Journal of Direct, Data and Digital Marketing Practice*, *10*(4), 384–387. DOI: 10.1057/dddmp.2009.7

Parsons, A., Zeisser, M., & Waitman, R. (1998). Organizing today for the digital marketing of tomorrow. *Journal of Interactive Marketing*, *12*(1), 31–46. DOI: 10.1002/(SICI)1520-6653(199824)12:1<31::AID-DIR4>3.0.CO;2-X

Parvez, M. O., Hossain, M. S., Islam, M. S., & Eluwole, K. K. (2025). Customers' acceptance of AI-powered robot chefs in casual dining restaurants. *Journal of Hospitality and Tourism Insights*, *8*(4), 1564–1581. DOI: 10.1108/JHTI-04-2024-0347

Perez-Vega, R., Kaartemo, V., Lages, C. R., Borghei Razavi, N., & Männistö, J. (2021). Reshaping the contexts of online customer engagement behavior via artificial intelligence: A conceptual framework. *Journal of Business Research*, *129*, 902–910. DOI: 10.1016/j.jbusres.2020.11.002

Peter, M. K., & Dalla Vecchia, M. (2021). The Digital Marketing Toolkit: A Literature Review for the Identification of Digital Marketing Channels and Platforms. In Dornberger, R. (Ed.), *New Trends in Business Information Systems and Technology* (Vol. 294, pp. 251–265). Springer International Publishing., DOI: 10.1007/978-3-030-48332-6_17

Piñeiro-Otero, T., & Martínez-Rolán, X. (2016). Understanding Digital Marketing—Basics and Actions. In Machado, C., & Davim, J. P. (Eds.), *MBA* (pp. 37–74). Springer International Publishing., DOI: 10.1007/978-3-319-28281-7_2

Prentice, C., Weaven, S., & Wong, I. A. (2020). Linking AI quality performance and customer engagement: The moderating effect of AI preference. *International Journal of Hospitality Management*, *90*, 102629. DOI: 10.1016/j.ijhm.2020.102629

Rather, R. A. (2024). AI-powered ChatGPT in the hospitality and tourism industry: Benefits, challenges, theoretical framework, propositions and future research directions. *Tourism Recreation Research*, •••, 1–11. DOI: 10.1080/02508281.2023.2287799

Ruel, H., & Njoku, E. (2021). AI redefining the hospitality industry. *Journal of Tourism Futures*, *7*(1), 53–66. DOI: 10.1108/JTF-03-2020-0032

Saleh, M. I. (2025). Generative artificial intelligence in hospitality and tourism: Future capabilities, AI prompts and real-world applications. *Journal of Hospitality Marketing & Management, 34*(4), 1–32. DOI: 10.1080/19368623.2025.2458603

Wu, H.-C., Ai, C.-H., & Cheng, C.-C. (2016). Synthesizing the effects of green experiential quality, green equity, green image and green experiential satisfaction on green switching intention. *International Journal of Contemporary Hospitality Management, 28*(9), 2080–2107. DOI: 10.1108/IJCHM-03-2015-0163

Zahidi, F., Kaluvilla, B. B., & Mulla, T. (2024). Embracing the new era: Artificial intelligence and its multifaceted impact on the hospitality industry. *Journal of Open Innovation, 10*(4), 100390. DOI: 10.1016/j.joitmc.2024.100390

Compilation of References

Abdi, H., & Nozari, H. (2025). Blockchain-Powered Multiobjective Portfolio Optimization under Uncertainty. *Journal of Future Digital Optimization*, *1*(1), 62–70.

Abhiseka, M., R., Alex, Y., Saputra, R., & Setiawan, A. (2024). AI for Digital Marketing. *Apollo: Journal of Tourism and Business*. .DOI: 10.58905/apollo.v2i2.298

Abtahi, A., Shafique, T., Haque, T., Siam, S. A. J., & Rahman, A. (2023). Exploring consumer preferences: The significance of personalization in e-commerce. Malaysian E Commerce Journal (MECJ), 8(1), 01-07.

Adeyinka, K. I., Takunda, C. O., & Adeyinka, T. I. (2024). Artificial Intelligence (AI) Algorithms in Nigeria's Integrated Marketing Communications. In *AI-Driven Marketing Research and Data Analytics* (pp. 67–81). IGI Global. DOI: 10.4018/979-8-3693-2165-2.ch004

Adwan, A. (2024). Can companies in digital marketing benefit from artificial intelligence in content creation? *International Journal of Data and Network Science*. .DOI: 10.5267/j.ijdns.2023.12.024

Agbo-Adediran, I., Adeusi, O. C., Bello, A. B., & Afolabi, O. N. (2025). Analyzing the Impact of AI adoption and ICT Platforms in improving Customer Engagement of Small and Medium-Sized Enterprises (SMEs). *Applied Sciences, Computing, and Energy*, *2*(2), 284–298.

Aggarwal, D., Sharma, D., & Saxena, A. B. (2024). *Exploring the role of AI for enhancement of social media marketing*. Journal of Media. *Culture and Communication*, *4*(5), 1–11. DOI: 10.55529/jmcc.45.1.11

Ahmed, M. (2025). AI Revolutionizing Hospitality: Insights from the MENA. In Azoury, N., & Yahchouchi, G. (Eds.), *AI in the Middle East for Growth and Business* (pp. 217–236). Springer Nature Switzerland., DOI: 10.1007/978-3-031-75589-7_13

Ait Hammou, K., Galib, M. H., & Melloul, J. (2013). The contributions of neuromarketing in marketing research. *Journal of Management Research, 5*(4), 20. DOI: 10.5296/jmr.v5i4.4023

Akbarossadat, S. M., & Esmaeilpour, B. (2022). An Overview of Bankruptcy Detection Methods Using Artificial Intelligence. *Intelligent Knowledge Exploration and Processing, 2*(6), 20–41. DOI: 10.30508/kdip.2022.349333.1044

Akpatsa, S. K., Addo, P. C., Lei, H., Li, X., Dorgbefu, M.Jr, Fiawoo, D. D., & Dagadu, J. C. (2022). Sentiment analysis and topic modeling of Twitter data: a text mining approach to the US-Afghan war crisis. Available at *SSRN* 4064560. DOI: 10.2139/ssrn.4064560

Akter, S., Dwivedi, Y., Sajib, S., Biswas, K., Bandara, R., & Michael, K. (2022). Algorithmic bias in machine learning-based marketing models. *Journal of Business Research, 144*, 201–216. Advance online publication. DOI: 10.1016/j.jbusres.2022.01.083

Al Zami, M. B., Shaon, S., Quy, V. K., & Nguyen, D. C. (2025). Digital Twin in Industries: A Comprehensive Survey. *IEEE Access : Practical Innovations, Open Solutions.*

Alam, S. S., Masukujjaman, M., Mohamed Makhbul, Z. K., Helmi Ali, M., Ahmad, I., & Al Mamun, A. (2024). Experience, Trust, eWOM Engagement and Usage Intention of AI Enabled Services in Hospitality and Tourism Industry: Moderating Mediating Analysis. *Journal of Quality Assurance in Hospitality & Tourism, 25*(6), 1635–1663. DOI: 10.1080/1528008X.2023.2167762

Ala-Pietilä, P., & Smuha, N. A. (2021). A framework for global cooperation on artificial intelligence and its governance. *Reflections on artificial intelligence for humanity*, 237-265. https://doi.org/DOI: 10.1007/978-3-030-69128-8_15

Aliahmadi, A., & Nozari, H. (2023, January). Evaluation of security metrics in AIoT and blockchain-based supply chain by Neutrosophic decision-making method. In Supply chain forum: an international journal (Vol. 24, No. 1, pp. 31-42). Taylor & Francis. DOI: 10.1080/16258312.2022.2101898

Aliahmadi, A., Nozari, H., Ghahremani-Nahr, J., & Szmelter-Jarosz, A. (2022). Evaluation of key impression of resilient supply chain based on artificial intelligence of things (AIoT). *arXiv preprint arXiv:2207.13174.*

Alidoust Ghahfarokhi, E., & Dehghan Ghahfarokhi, A. (2024). (in press). Blockchain Technology and the Future of Sports Industry. *New Approaches in Sports Mmanagement. Articles.* Advance online publication. DOI: 10.22034/ntsmj.2024.2030428.1028

Aljumah, A. I., Nuseir, M. T., & Alam, M. M. (2021). Traditional marketing analytics, big data analytics and big data system quality and the success of new product development. *Business Process Management Journal*, *27*(4), 1108–1125. DOI: 10.1108/BPMJ-11-2020-0527

Allioui, H., & Mourdi, Y. (2023). Unleashing the potential of AI: Investigating cutting-edge technologies that are transforming businesses. [IJCEDS]. *International Journal of Computer Engineering and Data Science*, *3*(2), 1–12.

Aloqaily, M., Bouachir, O., Karray, F., Al Ridhawi, I., & El Saddik, A. (2022). Integrating digital twin and advanced intelligent technologies to realize the metaverse. *IEEE Consumer Electronics Magazine*, *12*(6), 47–55. DOI: 10.1109/MCE.2022.3212570

Alsharif, A. H., Salleh, N. Z. M., Abdullah, M., Khraiwish, A., & Ashaari, A. (2023). Neuromarketing tools used in the marketing mix: A systematic literature and future research agenda. *SAGE Open*, *13*(1), 21582440231156563. DOI: 10.1177/21582440231156563

Alsharif, A., Salleh, N., Baharun, R., & Safaei, M. E. H. D. I. (2020). Neuromarketing approach: An overview and future research directions. *Journal of Theoretical and Applied Information Technology*, *98*(7).

Alvarez, J. M., Colmenarejo, A. B., Elobaid, A., Fabbrizzi, S., Fahimi, M., Ferrara, A., Ghodsi, S., Mougan, C., Papageorgiou, I., Reyero, P., Russo, M., Scott, K. M., State, L., Zhao, X., & Ruggieri, S. (2024). Policy advice and best practices on bias and fairness in AI. *Ethics and Information Technology*, *26*(1), 31–45. DOI: 10.1007/s10676-024-09746-w

Amuda-Kannike, A., & Amuda-Kannike, Y. (2025). A Critical Examination of the Legal and Institutional Framework for Protection of E-Consumers Rights in Nigeria. *Journal of Commercial and Property Law*, *12*(1), 24–36.

Anantrasirichai, N., & Bull, D. (2020). Artificial intelligence in the creative industries: A review. *Artificial Intelligence Review*, *55*(1), 589–656. DOI: 10.1007/s10462-021-10039-7

Anthony, D. R., Gordon, S., & Gucciardi, D. F. (2020). A qualitative exploration of mentally tough behaviour in Australian football. *Journal of Sports Sciences*, *38*(3), 308–319. DOI: 10.1080/02640414.2019.1698002 PMID: 31783717

Arce, C., Valderrama, D., Barragán, G., & Santillán, J. (2023). Optimizing Business Performance: Marketing Strategies for Small and Medium Businesses Using Artificial Intelligence Tools. *Migration Letters : An International Journal of Migration Studies*, *21*(S1), 193–201. Advance online publication. DOI: 10.59670/ml.v21iS1.6008

Ariely, D., & Berns, G. S. (2010). Neuromarketing: The hope and hype of neuroimaging in business. *Nature Reviews. Neuroscience, 11*(4), 284–292. DOI: 10.1038/nrn2795 PMID: 20197790

Aslan, Z. "Emotion Detection via BERT-Based Deep Learning Approaches in Natural Language Processing," International Journal of Energy and Engineering Sciences, vol. 9, no. 2, pp. 103–114, Dec. 2024. [Online]. Available: https://dergipark.org.tr/en/pub/ijees/issue/85059/1524075.DergiPark

Awad, N. F., & Krishnan, M. S. (2006). The personalization privacy paradox: An empirical evaluation of information transparency and the willingness to be profiled online for personalization. *Management Information Systems Quarterly, 30*(1), 13–28. DOI: 10.2307/25148715

Ayyappa, Y., Kumar, B. V., Priya, S. P., Akhila, S., Reddy, T. P. V., & Goush, S. M. (2023, April). Forecasting Equity Prices using LSTM and BERT with Sentiment Analysis. In *2023 International Conference on Inventive Computation Technologies (ICICT)* (pp. 643-648). IEEE. DOI: 10.1109/ICICT57646.2023.10134443

Babadoğan, B. (2024). *Unveiling the Power of AI-Driven Personalization: Transforming Consumer Behavior in the Age of Digital Marketing*. Next Frontier For Life Sciences and AI., DOI: 10.62802/fj43xy18

Babatunde, S., Odejide, O., Edunjobi, T., & Ogundipe, D. (2024). The Role Of Ai In Marketing Personalization: A Theoretical Exploration Of Consumer Engagement Strategies. *International Journal of Management & Entrepreneurship Research.* .DOI: 10.51594/ijmer.v6i3.964

Babics, I., & Jermolajeva, E. (2024). Development of Social Platforms and New Opportunities in Digital Marketing. *Complex Systems Informatics and Modeling Quarterly*, (41), 22–39. DOI: 10.7250/csimq.2024-41.02

Bag, S., Pretorius, J. H. C., Gupta, S., & Dwivedi, Y. K. (2021). Role of institutional pressures and resources in the adoption of big data analytics powered artificial intelligence, sustainable manufacturing practices and circular economy capabilities. *Technological Forecasting and Social Change, 163*, 120420. DOI: 10.1016/j.techfore.2020.120420

Bag, S., Srivastava, G., Bashir, M. M. A., Kumari, S., Giannakis, M., & Chowdhury, A. H. (2022). Journey of customers in this digital era: Understanding the role of artificial intelligence technologies in user engagement and conversion. *Benchmarking, 29*(7), 2074–2098. DOI: 10.1108/BIJ-07-2021-0415

Bag, S., & Wood, L. C. (2022). Guest editorial: Human resource development in the digital age: recent issues and future research directions. *International Journal of Manpower, 43*(2), 253–262. DOI: 10.1108/IJM-05-2022-561

Baker, C. R., Pease, M., Sexton, D. P., Abumoussa, A., & Chambless, L. B. (2024). Artificial intelligence innovations in neurosurgical oncology: A narrative review. *Journal of Neuro-Oncology, 169*(3), 489–496. DOI: 10.1007/s11060-024-04757-5 PMID: 38958849

Bastray, T. (2025). The Integration of AI in Digital Marketing: Opportunities and Challenges. *Journal of Informatics Education and Research.* .DOI: 10.52783/jier.v5i1.2111

Battour, M., Salaheldeen, M., Mady, K., & Ratnasari, R. T. (2024). ChatGPT and Halal Travel: An Overview of Current Trends and Future Research Directions. In Khamis, R., & Buallay, A. (Eds.), *AI in Business: Opportunities and Limitations* (Vol. 515, pp. 23–31). Springer Nature Switzerland., DOI: 10.1007/978-3-031-48479-7_3

Bayindir, M. (2024). The Role of Mobile Applications and Social Media in Increasing Fan Loyalty. *Turkish Journal of Sports Informatics and Technology, 1*(1), 1–13.

Bechara, A., & Damasio, A. R. (2005). The somatic marker hypothesis: A neural theory of economic decision. *Games and Economic Behavior, 52*(2), 336–372. DOI: 10.1016/j.geb.2004.06.010

Behera, R. K., Bala, P. K., Rana, N. P., Algharabat, R. S., & Kumar, K. (2024). Transforming customer engagement with artificial intelligence E-marketing: An E-retailer perspective in the era of retail 4.0. *Marketing Intelligence & Planning, 42*(7), 1141–1168. DOI: 10.1108/MIP-04-2023-0145

Bello, A., Ng, S.-C., & Leung, M.-F. (2023, January). A BERT Framework to Sentiment Analysis of Tweets. *Sensors (Basel), 23*(1), 506. DOI: 10.3390/s23010506 PMID: 36617101

Bercea, M. D. (2012, August). Anatomy of methodologies for measuring consumer behavior in neuromarketing research. In *Proceedings of the Lupcon Center for Business Research (LCBR) European Marketing Conference.* Ebermannstadt, Germany.

Berryman, D. R. (2012). Augmented reality: A review. *Medical Reference Services Quarterly, 31*(2), 212–218. DOI: 10.1080/02763869.2012.670604 PMID: 22559183

Bhattacharyya, S. S. (2023). Monetization of customer futures through machine learning and artificial intelligence based persuasive technologies. Journal of science and technology policy management, 14(4), 734-757.

Bholat, D., Gharbawi, A., & Thew, O. (2018). Artificial intelligence and the future of finance. *Bank of England Quarterly Bulletin*, *58*(3), 1–12.

Bhuiyan, K. H., Ahmed, S., & Jahan, I. (2024). Consumer attitude toward using artificial intelligence (AI) devices in hospitality services. *Journal of Hospitality and Tourism Insights*, *7*(2), 968–985. DOI: 10.1108/JHTI-08-2023-0551

Bilgin, F., Hadziahmetovic, N., & Tandir, N. (2025). From Compensation to Commitment: Dynamic Capabilities as Bridges to Ethical Climates in Nigerian Private Education. *Compensation and Benefits Review*, *57*(2), 08863687251320140. DOI: 10.1177/08863687251320140

Bilro, R. G., Loureiro, S. M. C., & Guerreiro, J. (2019). Exploring online customer engagement with hospitality products and its relationship with involvement, emotional states, experience and brand advocacy. *Journal of Hospitality Marketing & Management*, *28*(2), 147–171. DOI: 10.1080/19368623.2018.1506375

Binsaeed, R. H., Yousaf, Z., Grigorescu, A., Chitescu, R. I., Nassani, A. A., & Samoila, A. (2023). Customer engagement and customer relationship management capabilities' effects on innovation performance and customer distrust's moderating role. *Sustainability*, *15*(12), 9475.

Black, D., & Hibbeln, M. (2019). Sport and contemporary international political economy. *The Palgrave Handbook of Contemporary International Political Economy*, 651-665. https://doi.org/DOI: 10.1057/978-1-137-45443-0_40

Blackburn, R., Lurz, K., Priese, B., Göb, R., & Darkow, I. (2015). A predictive analytics approach for demand forecasting in the process industry. *International Transactions in Operational Research*, *22*(3), 407–428. DOI: 10.1111/itor.12122

Blümel, J., Zaki, M., & Bohné, T. (2023). Personal touch in digital customer service: A conceptual framework of relational personalization for conversational AI. *Journal of Service Theory and Practice*. Advance online publication. DOI: 10.1108/JSTP-03-2023-0098

Bolboli Qadikolaei, S., & Parsania, H. (2023). A systematic review of the ethical implications of using artificial intelligence in digital technologies and its relationship with the ethics of flourishing. *Socio-Cultural Strategy*, *12*(3), 771–798. DOI: 10.22034/scs.2022.160772

Bonta, R. (2022). California consumer privacy act (CCPA). Retrieved from State of California Department of Justice: https://oag. ca. gov/privacy/ccpa.

Bormane, S., & Blaus, E. (2024). Artificial intelligence in the context of digital marketing communication. *Frontiers in Communication, 9*, 1411226. Advance online publication. DOI: 10.3389/fcomm.2024.1411226

Bossuwé, E. (2023). *AI-DRIVEN BUSINESS MODELS AIMED AT PROMOTING A CIRCULAR ECONOMY* (Doctoral dissertation, Ghent University).

Bozkurt, S., Uğursoy, A. S., & Meral, S. P. (2025). The Impact of Personalized Messages and Designs on Consumer Experiences and Marketing Communications in Technology: Hyper-Personalization. In *Impact of Contemporary Technology on Art and Design* (pp. 135–164). IGI Global.

Bradley, S. (2024). Comparative Analysis of Two Data Privacy Regulatory Schemes: The GDPR and the CCPA.

Bruce, M. R., Adekoya, A. F., Boateng, S., & Appiahene, P. (2023). Prevalent user-centered monetization techniques in social media. *International Review of Management and Marketing, 13*(1), 19–28.

Büchi, M., Fosch-Villaronga, E., Lutz, C., Tamó-Larrieux, A., & Velidi, S. (2021). Making sense of algorithmic profiling: User perceptions on Facebook. *Information Communication and Society, 26*(4), 809–825. DOI: 10.1080/1369118X.2021.1989011

Buhalis, D., Leung, D., & Lin, M. (2023). Metaverse as a disruptive technology revolutionising tourism management and marketing. *Tourism Management, 97*, 104724. DOI: 10.1016/j.tourman.2023.104724

Buiten, M. (2019). Towards Intelligent Regulation of Artificial Intelligence. *European Journal of Risk Regulation, 10*(1), 41–59. DOI: 10.1017/err.2019.8

Calefato, F., Lanubile, F., & Novielli, N. (2019). Emotions and personality traits in developer–client interactions for trust prediction. *Empirical Software Engineering, 24*(4), 2243–2271. DOI: 10.1007/s10664-018-9671-5

Calefato, F., Lanubile, F., & Novielli, N. (2020). Sentiment analysis for software engineering: How far can we go? *IEEE Software, 38*(1), 30–37. DOI: 10.1109/MS.2020.2983737

Campbell, C., Sands, S., Ferraro, C., Tsao, H. Y. J., & Mavrommatis, A. (2020). From data to action: How marketers can leverage AI. *Business Horizons, 63*(2), 227–243. DOI: 10.1016/j.bushor.2019.12.002

Cao, L. (2021). Artificial intelligence in retail: Applications and value creation logics. *International Journal of Retail & Distribution Management, 49*(7), 958–976. DOI: 10.1108/IJRDM-09-2020-0350

Chaffey, D., & Smith, P. (2022). *Digital Marketing Excellence: Planning, Optimizing and Integrating Online Marketing* (6th ed.). Routledge., DOI: 10.4324/9781003009498

Chang, X. (2023). *Gender Bias in Hiring: An Analysis of the Impact of Amazon's Recruiting Algorithm*. Advances in Economics, Management, and Political Sciences., DOI: 10.54254/2754-1169/23/20230367

Chatterjee, P., Das, D., Rawat, D. B., Ghosh, U., Banerjee, S., & Al-Numay, M. S. (2024). Digital Twins and Blockchain Fusion for Security in Metaverse-Driven Consumer Supply Chains. *IEEE Transactions on Consumer Electronics, 70*(3), 5688–5697. DOI: 10.1109/TCE.2024.3477297

Chatterjee, S., Rana, N. P., Tamilmani, K., & Sharma, A. (2022). Understanding the role of AI-enabled emotion detection in customer service: A review and research agenda. *Journal of Business Research, 142*, 1020–1032. DOI: 10.1016/j.jbusres.2021.12.055

Cheah, J. H., Lim, X. J., Ting, H., Liu, Y., & Quach, S. (2022). Are privacy concerns still relevant? Revisiting consumer behaviour in omnichannel retailing. *Journal of Retailing and Consumer Services, 65*, 102242. DOI: 10.1016/j.jretconser.2020.102242

Cheng, C. F., Huang, C. C., Lin, M. C., & Chen, T. C. (2023). Exploring effectiveness of relationship marketing on artificial intelligence adopting intention. *SAGE Open, 13*(4), 21582440231222760.

Chen, H., Chiang, R. H. L., & Storey, V. C. (2012). Business intelligence and analytics: From big data to big impact. *Management Information Systems Quarterly, 36*(4), 1165–1188. DOI: 10.2307/41703503

Chen, S.-H., & Ahmed, F. (2025). The transformative power of AI and AR in customer-centric services in the tourism and hospitality sector: Looking back to predict the future outlook. In *Managing customer-centric strategies in the digital landscape* (pp. 105–138). IGI Global.

Chen, S., Han, X., Bilgihan, A., & Okumus, F. (2021). Customer engagement research in hospitality and tourism: A systematic review. *Journal of Hospitality Marketing & Management, 30*(7), 871–904. DOI: 10.1080/19368623.2021.1903644

Cherian, M., Manoja, K., &, A. (2025). Leveraging AI for Predicting Marketing and Customer Insights Overview. *Journal of Informatics Education and Research*. .DOI: 10.52783/jier.v5i1.2050

Cheung, M. L., Pires, G. D., Rosenberger, P. J., Leung, W. K. S., & Salehhuddin Sharipudin, M.-N. (2021). The role of consumer-consumer interaction and consumer-brand interaction in driving consumer-brand engagement and behavioral intentions. *Journal of Retailing and Consumer Services, 61*, 102574. DOI: 10.1016/j.jretconser.2021.102574

Chew, P., & Gilani, H. (2024). Artificial Intelligence in Marketing Education. In *Decolonizing Marketing Theory and Practice* (pp. 218–236). Routledge. DOI: 10.4324/9781032698083-15

Chintalapati, S., & Pandey, S. (2021). Artificial intelligence in marketing: A systematic literature review. *International Journal of Market Research, 64*(1), 38–68. DOI: 10.1177/14707853211018428

Choi, K. H. M. (2020). *A Critical Juncture in Data Protection Standards: Comparing Data Protection Legislation in the United States and the European Union*].

Choi, J., & Lim, K. (2020). Identifying machine learning techniques for classification of target advertising. *ICT Express, 6*(3), 175–180. DOI: 10.1016/j.icte.2020.04.012

Chung, K. C., & Tan, P. J. B. (2025). Artificial intelligence and internet of things to improve smart hospitality services. *Internet of Things : Engineering Cyber Physical Human Systems, 31*, 101544. DOI: 10.1016/j.iot.2025.101544

Chung, M., Ko, E., Joung, H., & Kim, S. J. (2020). Chatbot e-service and customer satisfaction regarding luxury brands. *Journal of Business Research, 117*, 587–595. DOI: 10.1016/j.jbusres.2018.10.004

Chung, T. S., Wedel, M., & Rust, R. T. (2016). Adaptive personalization using social networks. *Journal of the Academy of Marketing Science, 44*(1), 66–87. DOI: 10.1007/s11747-015-0441-x

Cialdini, R. B. (2009). *Influence: Science and practice* (5th ed.). Pearson Education.

Collins, L., & Collins, D. (2013). Decision making and risk management in adventure sports coaching. *Quest, 65*(1), 72–82. DOI: 10.1080/00336297.2012.727373

Corren, E. (2022). The Consent Burden in Consumer and Digital Markets. *Harv JL & Tech*, (36), 551.

Cossich, V. R., Carlgren, D., Holash, R. J., & Katz, L. (2023). Technological breakthroughs in sport: Current practice and future potential of artificial intelligence, virtual reality, augmented reality, and modern data visualization in performance analysis. *Applied Sciences (Basel, Switzerland), 13*(23), 12965. DOI: 10.3390/app132312965

Cowie, R., Douglas-Cowie, E., Tsapatsoulis, N., Votsis, G., Kollias, S., Fellenz, W., & Taylor, J. G. (2001). Emotion recognition in human-computer interaction. *IEEE Signal Processing Magazine*, *18*(1), 32–80. DOI: 10.1109/79.911197

Crawford, K., & Calo, R. (2016). There is a blind spot in AI research. *Nature*, *538*(7625), 311–313. DOI: 10.1038/538311a PMID: 27762391

Cruz-Neira, C., Sandin, D. J., DeFanti, T. A., Kenyon, R. V., & Hart, J. C. (1992). The CAVE: Audio visual experience automatic virtual environment. *Communications of the ACM*, *35*(6), 64–73. DOI: 10.1145/129888.129892

Cutler, K. (2024). The evolution of digital marketing in the era of AI. *Applied Marketing Analytics: The Peer-Reviewed Journal*. .DOI: 10.69554/UNDG1907

Dai, C. P. (2023). *Enhancing learning achievements and self-efficacy for preservice teachers using model-based support in simulation-based learning with artificial intelligence-powered virtual agents*. The Florida State University.

Damasio, A. R. (1994). *Descartes' error: Emotion, reason and the human brain*. Avon Books.

Davenport, T., Guha, A., Grewal, D., & Bressgott, T. (2020). How artificial intelligence will change the future of marketing. *Journal of the Academy of Marketing Science*, *48*(1), 24–42. DOI: 10.1007/s11747-019-00696-0

Davtyan, N. (2024). AI in Consumer Behavior Analysis and Digital Marketing: A Strategic Approach. *The Integration of AI and Technology in Modern Business Practices*. .DOI: 10.70301/CONF.SBS-JABR.2024.1/1.5

De Bruyn, A., Viswanathan, V., Beh, Y., Brock, J., & Von Wangenheim, F. (2020). Artificial Intelligence and Marketing: Pitfalls and Opportunities. *Journal of Interactive Marketing*, *51*(1), 91–105. DOI: 10.1016/j.intmar.2020.04.007

De Cremer, D., & Kasparov, G. (2021). AI should augment human intelligence, not replace it. *Harvard Business Review*. https://hbr.org/2021/01/ai-should-augment-human-intelligence-not-replace-it

De Keyzer, F., Van Noort, G., & Kruikemeier, S. (2022). Going too far? How consumers respond to personalized advertising from different sources. *Journal of electronic commerce research.-Long Beach, Calif.,[200-], currens, 23*(3), 138-159.

Dehghanpouri, H., Soltani, Z., & Rostamzadeh, R. (2020). The impact of trust, privacy and quality of service on the success of E-CRM: The mediating role of customer satisfaction. *Journal of Business and Industrial Marketing*, *35*(11), 1831–1847. DOI: 10.1108/JBIM-07-2019-0325

Deloitte. (2021). *Chatbots and virtual assistants: Driving the digital transformation*. Deloitte Insights. https://www2.deloitte.com/

Deng, B., Wong, I. A., & Lian, Q. L. (2024). From metaverse experience to physical travel: The role of the digital twin in metaverse design. *Tourism Review*, *79*(5), 1076–1087. DOI: 10.1108/TR-05-2023-0315

Deng, J., & Liu, Y. (2025, February). Research on Sentiment Analysis of Online Public Opinion Based on RoBERTa–BiLSTM–Attention Model. *Applied Sciences (Basel, Switzerland)*, *15*(4), 2148. DOI: 10.3390/app15042148

Deshpande, S. B., Velrani, K. S., Bhagyalakshmi, A., Vani, M. S., Ananthi, S., & Sahu, D. (2024). Neural Networks for Natural Language Processing. 2024 Asian Conference on Intelligent Technologies (ACOIT), Dimeo, P. (2014). Why Lance Armstrong? Historical context and key turning points in the 'cleaning up'of professional cycling. *The International Journal of the History of Sport*, *31*(8), 951–968. DOI: 10.1080/09523367.2013.879858

Devlin, J., Chang, M. W., Lee, K., & Toutanova, K. (2019). *BERT: Pre-training of deep bidirectional transformers for language understanding*. In *Proceedings of NAACL-HLT* (pp. 4171–4186). DOI: 10.48550/arXiv.1810.04805

Diekson, Z. A., Prakoso, M. R. B., Putra, M. S. Q., Syaputra, M. S. A. F., Achmad, S., & Sutoyo, R. (2023). Sentiment analysis for customer review: Case study of Traveloka. *Procedia Computer Science*, *216*, 682–690. DOI: 10.1016/j.procs.2022.12.184

Du, J., Pifer, N. D., & Gulavani, S. S. (2023). Harnessing the power of machine learning in sport consumer behavior research. In *Sports Sponsorship and Branding* (pp. 165–183). Routledge., DOI: 10.4324/9781003458890-12

Duque-Hurtado, P., Samboni-Rodriguez, V., Castro-Garcia, M., Montoya-Restrepo, L. A., & Montoya-Restrepo, I. A. (2020). Neuromarketing: Its current status and research perspectives. Estudios gerenciales, 36(157), 525-539.

Durana, P., Vochozka, M., Tucmeanu, A. I., & Tudosă, P. (2022). Digital Twin-enabled Industrial Internet of Things, Multi-Sensory Extended Reality and Immersive Holographic Imaging Technologies, and 3D Modeling and Virtual Simulation Tools across Blockchain-based Decentralized Metaverse Systems. Economics. *Management and Financial Markets*, *17*(4), 43–57.

Dwivedi, Y. K.. (2021). Artificial intelligence: Emerging challenges. *International Journal of Information Management*, *57*, 101994. DOI: 10.1016/j.ijinfomgt.2019.08.002

Dwivedi, Y., Ismagilova, E., Hughes, D., Carlson, J., Filieri, R., Jacobson, J., Jain, V., Karjaluoto, H., Kefi, H., Krishen, A., Kumar, V., Rahman, M., Raman, R., Rauschnabel, P., Rowley, J., Salo, J., Tran, G., & Wang, Y. (2020). Setting the future of digital and social media marketing research: Perspectives and research propositions. *International Journal of Information Management*, *59*, 102168. DOI: 10.1016/j.ijinfomgt.2020.102168

Efendioglu, I. (2023). *The evaluation of AI integration in innovative digital marketing strategies*. Pressacademia., DOI: 10.17261/Pressacademia.2023.1820

Egbuhuzor, N. S., Ajayi, A. J., Akhigbe, E. E., Agbede, O. O., Ewim, C. P. M., & Ajiga, D. I. (2025). AI and data-driven insights: Transforming customer relationship management (CRM) in financial services. *Gulf Journal of Advance Business Research*, *3*(2), 483–511.

El-Akhras, H. A., Abd El-Wahab, M. A., Saghier, E. G., & Selem, K. M. (2025). ChatGPT adoption risks and cognitive achievement among tourism and hospitality college students: From faculty member perspective. *Journal of Hospitality and Tourism Insights*, *8*(4), 1288–1307. DOI: 10.1108/JHTI-04-2024-0292

Elhai, W. (2020). Regulating digital harm across Borders: Exploring a content platform commission. Paper read at International Conference on Social Media and Society.

Elkhatibi, Y., & Benabdelouhed, R. (2024). Digital Marketing and Artificial Intelligence: Towards a Better Understanding of the Two Strategies. *International Journal of Advanced Multidisciplinary Research and Studies*. .DOI: 10.62225/2583049X.2024.4.3.2847

Erevelles, S., Fukawa, N., & Swayne, L. (2016). Big Data consumer analytics and the transformation of marketing. *Journal of Business Research*, *69*(2), 897–904. DOI: 10.1016/j.jbusres.2015.07.001

Esmaeili, A., Mohammadi, N., & Emami, F. (2021). A Model of Factors Affecting the Behavioral Intentions of Premier League Football Fans Using Grounded Theory. *Strategic Studies on Youth and Sports*, *20*(53), 93–112. DOI: 10.22034/ssys.2021.458

Ezeife, E., Kokogho, E., Odio, P. E., & Adeyanju, M. O. (2025). Agile tax technology development in the US: A conceptual framework for scalable and efficient enterprise solutions. *Gulf Journal of Advance Business Research*, *3*(2), 512–526.

Fakeyede, O. G., Okeleke, P. A., Hassan, A., Iwuanyanwu, U., Adaramodu, O. R., & Oyewole, O. O. (2023). Navigating data privacy through IT audits: GDPR, CCPA, and beyond. *International Journal of Research in Engineering and Science*, *11*(11).

Fallah, M., & Nozari, H. (2021). Neutrosophic mathematical programming for optimization of multi-objective sustainable biomass supply chain network design. *Computer Modeling in Engineering & Sciences*, *129*(2), 927–951. DOI: 10.32604/cmes.2021.017511

Fallah, M., & Nozari, H. (2021). Quantitative analysis of cyber risks in IoT-based supply chain (FMCG industries). *Journal of Decisions and Operations Research*, *5*(4), 510–521.

Fathi, S., & Motlag, M. (2011). Globalization and Generation Gap (A social study of generation gap by focusing on information and communication technologies). *Strategic Studies of public policy*, *2*(5), 145-177. https://sspp.iranjournals.ir/article_2481_e28e739c320baaac1ca139e35ddbc449.pdf

Fatokun, B. O. (2023). *Customers' Affective Responses Towards the Key Factors Influencing E-Commerce Adoption: Extended Technology Acceptance Model (TAM) Approach*. Liverpool John Moores University.

Fazeli, F., Mahmoudi, A., & Askarian, F. (2024). (in press). Blockchain Technology: Advantages, Challenges, and Development Strategies in the Sports Industry Services Sector. *Sport Management Journal. Articles*. Advance online publication. DOI: 10.22059/jsm.2024.373644.3269

Feijóo, C., Kwon, Y., Bauer, J. M., Bohlin, E., Howell, B., Jain, R., Potgieter, P., Vu, K., Whalley, J., & Xia, J. (2020). Harnessing artificial intelligence (AI) to increase wellbeing for all: The case for a new technology diplomacy. *Telecommunications Policy*, *44*(6), 101988. DOI: 10.1016/j.telpol.2020.101988 PMID: 32377031

Fekrat, A., & Jaberi, A. (2024). Phenomenology of the role of artificial intelligence marketing on increasing sales and exports of Iranian sports goods. *Sports Marketing Studies*, *5*(2), 1–15. DOI: 10.22034/sms.2024.139803.1254

Festinger, L. (1957). *A theory of cognitive dissonance*. Stanford University Press. DOI: 10.1515/9781503620766

Flavián, C., Tussyadiah, I. P., & Orús, C. (2024). How immersive technologies are redefining the customer journey. Guest editorial. *International Journal of Contemporary Hospitality Management*, *36*(11), 3557–3565. DOI: 10.1108/IJCHM-11-2024-215

Fugate, D. L. (2008). Marketing services more effectively with neuromarketing research: A look into the future. *Journal of Services Marketing*, *22*(2), 170–173. DOI: 10.1108/08876040810862903

Gade, R., Merler, M., Thomas, G., & Moeslund, T. B. (2024). The (Computer) Vision of Sports: Recent Trends in Research and Commercial Systems for Sport Analytics. *Computer Vision*, 296-311. https://doi.org/DOI: 10.1201/9781003328957-14

Gani, M. O., & Faroque, A. R. (2021). Digital marketing. In *Cross-border E-commerce marketing and management* (pp. 172–202). IGI Global Scientific Publishing., DOI: 10.4018/978-1-7998-5823-2.ch008

Gao, B., Wang, Y., Xie, H., Hu, Y., & Hu, Y. (2023). Artificial intelligence in advertising: Advancements, challenges, and ethical considerations in targeting, personalization, content creation, and ad optimization. *SAGE Open*, *13*(4), 21582440231210759. Advance online publication. DOI: 10.1177/21582440231210759

Gao, J., Ren, L., Yang, Y., Zhang, D., & Li, L. (2022). The impact of artificial intelligence technology stimuli on smart customer experience and the moderating effect of technology readiness. *International Journal of Emerging Markets*, *17*(4), 1123–1142. DOI: 10.1108/IJOEM-06-2021-0975

Gao, Y., & Liu, H. (2023). Artificial intelligence-enabled personalization in interactive marketing: A customer journey perspective. *Journal of Research in Interactive Marketing*, *17*(5), 663–680. DOI: 10.1108/JRIM-01-2022-0023

García-Hernández, R. A., Luna-García, H., Celaya-Padilla, J. M., García-Hernández, A., Reveles-Gómez, L. C., Flores-Chaires, L. A., Delgado-Contreras, J. R., Rondon, D., & Villalba-Condori, K. O. (2024, August). A Systematic Literature Review of Modalities, Trends, and Limitations in Emotion Recognition, Affective Computing, and Sentiment Analysis. *Applied Sciences (Basel, Switzerland)*, *14*(16), 7165. DOI: 10.3390/app14167165

Garcia, J. R., & Saad, G. (2008). Evolutionary neuromarketing: Darwinizing the neuroimaging paradigm for consumer behavior. *Journal of Consumer Behaviour*, *7*(4-5), 397–414. DOI: 10.1002/cb.259

Genovard, F., Muñoz, J., Petchamé, J., & Solanellas, F. (2025). Risk management approaches in sports organisations: A scoping review. *Heliyon*, *11*(3), e42270. Advance online publication. DOI: 10.1016/j.heliyon.2025.e42270 PMID: 39968147

Gentsch, P. (2019). *AI in marketing, sales and service: How marketers without a data science degree can use AI, big data and bots*. Palgrave Macmillan. DOI: 10.1007/978-3-319-89957-2

Ghafarzadeh Malasi, M. R., & Ismaili Shahzandi, M. R. (2022). *Risk management in sports and sports organizations* The 8th National Conference of Sport Sciences and Physical Education of Iran, Tehran. https://civilica.com/doc/1649667

Ghahremani-Nahr, J., Nozari, H., & Szmelter-Jarosz, A. (2024). Designing a humanitarian relief logistics network considering the cost of deprivation using a robust-fuzzy-probabilistic planning method. *Journal of International Humanitarian Action*, *9*(1), 19. DOI: 10.1186/s41018-024-00163-8

Ghasemi Abyaneh, A., Bakhshi Movahed, A., Abyari, A., Nodehfarahani, A., & Khakbazan, M. (2025). Evaluating the RFID Technology in Costco Company: A Focus on Logistics and Supply Chain Management. *Applied Innovations in Industrial Management*, *5*(2), 34–51. DOI: 10.63630/aiim.52.34

Ghorbani Ghader, A., Hashemi Nasab, M., & Hedayati, M. S. (2024). Designing a Customer Behavior Prediction Model Using Artificial Intelligence Algorithms and Neural Networks. *Journal of Intelligent Strategic Management*, *3*(2), 39–56. https://doi.org/bumara.3.2.15564.35879841478

Gkikas, D. C., & Theodoridis, P. K. (2022). AI in consumer behavior. *Advances in Artificial Intelligence-based Technologies: Selected Papers in Honour of Professor Nikolaos G. Bourbakis*, *1*, 147–176.

Gkikas, D., & Theodoridis, P. (2024). Predicting Online Shopping Behavior: Using Machine Learning and Google Analytics to Classify User Engagement. *Applied Sciences (Basel, Switzerland)*, *14*(23), 11403. Advance online publication. DOI: 10.3390/app142311403

Glikson, E., & Woolley, A. W. (2020). Human trust in artificial intelligence: Review of empirical research. *The Academy of Management Annals*, *14*(2), 627–660. DOI: 10.5465/annals.2018.0057

Gnewuch, U., Morana, S., & Maedche, A. (2017). Towards designing cooperative and social conversational agents for customer service. *Proceedings of the International Conference on Information Systems (ICIS)*.

Goldfarb, A., & Tucker, C. (2019). Digital marketing. In *Handbook of the Economics of Marketing* (Vol. 1, pp. 259–290). Elsevier., DOI: 10.1016/bs.hem.2019.04.004

Golmohammadi, H., Ghadami, S., Pashaie, S., & Zolfi, H. (2025). Identification and Analysis of Prominent Concepts in Digital Marketing and Sports. *Sports Marketing Studies*, *5*(4), -. https://doi.org/DOI: 10.22034/sms.2024.140983.1328

Gross, M. (2006). 'Not cricket': A'nexus of silence'over the cricket match-fixing scandal.

Gu, F., Gao, J., Zhu, X., & Ye, J. (2023). The impact of digital inclusive finance on SMEs' technological innovation activities—Empirical analysis based on the data of new third board enterprises. *PLoS One*, *18*(11), e0293500.

Guingrich, R. E., & Graziano, M. S. A. (2024). Ascribing consciousness to artificial intelligence: Human-AI interaction and its carry-over effects on human-human interaction. *Frontiers in Psychology, 15*, 1322781. Advance online publication. DOI: 10.3389/fpsyg.2024.1322781 PMID: 38605842

Gujar, P., Paliwal, G., & Panyam, S. (2024). Generative AI and the Future of Interactive and Immersive Advertising. *2024 IEEE Eighth Ecuador Technical Chapters Meeting (ETCM)*, 1-6. DOI: 10.1109/ETCM63562.2024.10746166

Gündüzyeli, B. (2024). Artificial Intelligence in Digital Marketing Within the Framework of Sustainable Management. *Sustainability (Basel), 16*(23), 10511. Advance online publication. DOI: 10.3390/su162310511

Gungunawat, A., Khandelwal, N., & Gupta, N. (2024). *AI-Powered Personalization in Digital Marketing: Transforming Consumer Engagement and Strategy*. RESEARCH REVIEW International Journal of Multidisciplinary., DOI: 10.31305/rrijm.2024.v09.n11.026

Gupta, S., Modgil, S., Lee, C.-K., Cho, M., & Park, Y. (2022). Artificial intelligence enabled robots for stay experience in the hospitality industry in a smart city. *Industrial Management & Data Systems, 122*(10), 2331–2350. DOI: 10.1108/IMDS-10-2021-0621

Gupta, Y., & Khan, F. M. (2024). Role of artificial intelligence in customer engagement: A systematic review and future research directions. *Journal of Modelling in Management, 19*(5), 1535–1565. DOI: 10.1108/JM2-01-2023-0016

Gutierrez, N. (2023). The ballad of morton heilig: On VR's mythic past. *JCMS: Journal of Cinema and Media Studies, 62*(3), 86–106. DOI: 10.1353/cj.2023.0027

Habbat, N., Nouri, H., Anoun, H., & Hassouni, L. (2023). Sentiment analysis of imbalanced datasets using BERT and ensemble stacking for deep learning. *Engineering Applications of Artificial Intelligence, 126*, 106999. DOI: 10.1016/j.engappai.2023.106999

Halchin, L. E., & Rollins, J. W. (2017). The 2016 Olympic Games: Health, security, environmental, and doping issues. *Current Politics and Economics of South and Central America, 10*(2), 203–249.

Haleem, A., Javaid, M., Qadri, M. A., Singh, R. P., & Suman, R. (2022). Artificial intelligence (AI) applications for marketing: A literature-based study. *International Journal of Intelligent Networks, 3*, 119–132. DOI: 10.1016/j.ijin.2022.08.005

Hameed, H. (2025). Developing Cost-Effective AI Algorithms for Resource-Constrained Devices. *International Journal of Computers and Informatics*. .DOI: 10.59992/IJCI.2025.v4n1p3

Han, H., Kim, S., Hailu, T. B., Al-Ansi, A., Lee, J., & Kim, J. J. (2024). Effects of cognitive, affective and normative drivers of artificial intelligence ChatGPT on continuous use intention. *Journal of Hospitality and Tourism Technology*, *15*(4), 629–647. DOI: 10.1108/JHTT-11-2023-0363

Han, R., Lam, H., Zhan, Y., Wang, Y., Dwivedi, Y., & Tan, K. (2021). Artificial intelligence in business-to-business marketing: A bibliometric analysis of current research status, development, and future directions. *Industrial Management & Data Systems*, *121*(12), 2467–2497. DOI: 10.1108/IMDS-05-2021-0300

Han, Y., Niyato, D., Leung, C., Kim, D. I., Zhu, K., Feng, S., Shen, X., & Miao, C. (2022). A dynamic hierarchical framework for IoT-assisted digital twin synchronization in the metaverse. *IEEE Internet of Things Journal*, *10*(1), 268–284. DOI: 10.1109/JIOT.2022.3201082

Hao, F. (2020). The landscape of customer engagement in hospitality and tourism: A systematic review. *International Journal of Contemporary Hospitality Management*, *32*(5), 1837–1860. DOI: 10.1108/IJCHM-09-2019-0765

Heidari, L., Aghaei, N., & Akbari Yazdi, H. (2024). The Role of Team Identification and Sentiment Analysis of Iranian Football Clubs' Fans in Twitter Social Media with Natural Language Processing. *Journal of Intelligent Marketing Management*, *5*(4), 77–97. https://doi.org/Jabm.3.2.15564.35887879085849695

Herath, D., Ode, E., & Herath, G. (2025). Can AI replace humans? Comparing the capabilities of AI tools and human performance in a business management education scenario. *British Educational Research Journal*, berj.4111. Advance online publication. DOI: 10.1002/berj.4111

Himanshu, A., Aggarwal, R., Gupta, S., Dhingra, S., & Kumar, A. (2025). The virtual voyage: Understanding the factors affecting metaverse adoption in the tourism and hospitality industry. *Current Issues in Tourism*, •••, 1–21. DOI: 10.1080/13683500.2025.2475491

Holzinger, A., Zatloukal, K., & Müller, H. (2024). Is Human Oversight to AI Systems still possible? *New Biotechnology*, *85*(25), 59–62. DOI: 10.1016/j.nbt.2024.12.003 PMID: 39675423

Hossain, M. A., & Kim, M. (2020). The effect of AI-powered recommendation systems on consumer decision-making. *Journal of Consumer Behaviour, 19*(3), 239–254. DOI: 10.1002/cb.1813

Hossain, M. B. (2023). Acquiring an awareness of the latest regulatory developments concerning digital assets and anti-money laundering. *Journal of Money Laundering Control, 26*(6), 1261–1268.

Hoy, M. B. (2018). Alexa, Siri, Cortana, and more: An introduction to voice assistants. *Medical Reference Services Quarterly, 37*(1), 81–88. DOI: 10.1080/02763869.2018.1404391 PMID: 29327988

Huang, A., Ozturk, A. B., Zhang, T., De La Mora Velasco, E., & Haney, A. (2024). Unpacking AI for hospitality and tourism services: Exploring the role of perceived enjoyment on future use intentions. *International Journal of Hospitality Management, 119*, 103693. DOI: 10.1016/j.ijhm.2024.103693

Huang, C., Jiang, W., Wu, J., & Wang, G. (2020). Personalized review recommendation based on users' aspect sentiment. *ACM Transactions on Internet Technology, 20*(4), 1–26. DOI: 10.1145/3414841

Huang, M. H., & Rust, R. T. (2021). Artificial intelligence in service. *Journal of Service Research, 24*(1), 3–20. DOI: 10.1177/1094670520902266

Huang, M., & Rust, R. (2020). A strategic framework for artificial intelligence in marketing. *Journal of the Academy of Marketing Science, 49*(1), 30–50. DOI: 10.1007/s11747-020-00749-9

Hussain, H. N., Alabdullah, T. T. Y., Ries, E., & Jamal, K. A. M. (2023). Implementing Technology for Competitive Advantage in Digital Marketing. *International Journal of Scientific and Management Research, 6*(6), 95–114. DOI: 10.37502/IJSMR.2023.6607

Ikenga, U. G., & Egbule, C. N. (2024). Strategic Model for Effective Digital Entrepreneurship for Small Business. In *New Strategy Models in Digital Entrepreneurship* (pp. 53–70). IGI Global. DOI: 10.4018/979-8-3693-3743-1.ch004

Ip, K. (2023). Revolutionizing content recommendation: The impact of AI in marketing. *Journal of AI, Robotics & Workplace Automation*. .DOI: 10.69554/AMHI2323

Iqbal, M. N., & Jan, M. T. (2025). AI-Powered Business Strategies for Enhancing Consumer Behavior and Brand Loyalty in the Bancassurance Sector. In *Elevating Brand Loyalty With Optimized Marketing Analytics and AI* (pp. 101–132). IGI Global Scientific Publishing. DOI: 10.4018/979-8-3693-9954-5.ch006

Irani, F. (2024). Exploring the future of tourism: A qualitative study on the integration of robotics in North Cyprus hospitality and destination development. *Worldwide Hospitality and Tourism Themes*, *16*(6), 694–705. DOI: 10.1108/WHATT-05-2024-0097

Irani, H. R., & Nozari, H. (Eds.). (2024). *Smart and Sustainable Interactive Marketing*. IGI Global. DOI: 10.4018/979-8-3693-1339-8

Iroka, N. A., & Nwaizugbo, I. C. (2024). Digital marketing channels and customer patronage of online shops. *UNIZIK Journal of Marketing*, *1*(4), 53–76.

Islam, M., Sourav, M., & Reza, J. (2024). *The impact of data protection regulations on business analytics*. World Journal of Advanced Research and Reviews., DOI: 10.30574/wjarr.2024.24.2.3503

Istasse, M., Somers, V., Elancheliyan, P., De, J., & Zambrano, D. (2023). DeepSportradar-v2: A multi-sport computer vision dataset for sport understandings. Proceedings of the 6th International Workshop on Multimedia Content Analysis in Sports, Jaiwant, S. V., & Kureethara, J. V. (2024). Sports Marketing Analytics: Digital Evolution in Shaping the Sports Industry. In *Sports Analytics: Data-Driven Sports and Decision Intelligence* (pp. 221-235). Springer. https://doi.org/DOI: 10.1145/3606038.3616160

Jain, G., Paul, J., & Shrivastava, A. (2021). Hyper-personalization, co-creation, digital clienteling and transformation. *Journal of Business Research*, *124*, 12–23. DOI: 10.1016/j.jbusres.2020.11.034

Jalal, M., & Elmaghraby, A. (2024). Analyzing the Dynamics of Customer Behavior: A New Perspective on Personalized Marketing through Counterfactual Analysis. *Journal of Theoretical and Applied Electronic Commerce Research*, *19*(3), 1660–1681. DOI: 10.3390/jtaer19030081

Jana, A. K. (2016). Dynamic simulation, numerical control and analysis of a novel bottom flashing scheme in batch distillation. *Computers & Chemical Engineering*, *89*, 166–171. DOI: 10.1016/j.compchemeng.2016.04.010

Janice, N., & Kusumawati, N. (2024). *Harmonizing Algorithms and User Satisfaction: Evaluating The Impact of Spotify's Discover Weekly on Customer Loyalty*. Journal Integration of Management Studies., DOI: 10.58229/jims.v2i2.168

Jastacia, B., & Akbar, D. (2023). Potential Use Of Artificial Intelligence For Digital Promotional Video: Neuromarketing Approach. *Jurnal Studi Inovasi*. .DOI: 10.52000/jsi.v3i4.140

Javor, A., Koller, M., Lee, N., Chamberlain, L., & Ransmayr, G. (2013). Neuromarketing and consumer neuroscience: Contributions to neurology. *BMC Neurology*, *13*(1), 1–12. DOI: 10.1186/1471-2377-13-13 PMID: 23383650

Jobin, A., Ienca, M., & Vayena, E. (2019). The global landscape of AI ethics guidelines. *Nature Machine Intelligence*, *1*(9), 389–399. DOI: 10.1038/s42256-019-0088-2

Jung, H. S., & Yoon, H. H. (2016). Why is employees' emotional intelligence important?: The effects of EI on stress-coping styles and job satisfaction in the hospitality industry. *International Journal of Contemporary Hospitality Management*, *28*(8), 1649–1675. DOI: 10.1108/IJCHM-10-2014-0509

Kahneman, D. (2011). *Thinking, fast and slow*. Farrar, Straus and Giroux.

Kalogeras, S. (2021). Transmedia Storytelling Edutainment and the New Testament Lesson. In Handbook of Research on Contemporary Storytelling Methods Across New Media and Disciplines (pp. 392-406). IGI Global Scientific Publishing. DOI: 10.4018/978-1-7998-6605-3.ch020

Kalogeras, S. (2019). The practice of transmedia storytelling edutainment in media-rich learning environments. In *Technology-supported teaching and research methods for educators* (pp. 149–164). IGI Global. DOI: 10.4018/978-1-5225-5915-3.ch008

Kalogeras, S. (2025). A Smart Framework for Making Stories Smarter through Transmedia and Real User Interaction. *Applied Innovations in Industrial Management*, *5*(2), 59–66. DOI: 10.63630/aiim.52.59

Kamal, M., & Himel, A. S. (2023). Redefining modern marketing: An analysis of AI and NLP's influence on consumer engagement, strategy, and beyond. *Eigenpub Review of Science and Technology*, *7*(1), 203–223.

Kandipati, A. (2025). A Systematic Literature Review on Artificial Intelligence Based Techniques for Nurturing Operations in Real Estate Sector. *Journal of Real Estate Literature*, •••, 1–26. DOI: 10.1080/09277544.2025.2466370

Kannan, P. K., & Li, H. (2017). Digital marketing: A framework, review and research agenda. *International Journal of Research in Marketing*, *34*(1), 22–45. DOI: 10.1016/j.ijresmar.2016.11.006

Kaplan, A., & Haenlein, M. (2020). Rulers of the world, unite! The challenges and opportunities of artificial intelligence. *Business Horizons*, *63*(1), 37–50. DOI: 10.1016/j.bushor.2019.09.003

Kapoor, H., Dwivedi, Y. K., Piercy, N. F., & Reynolds, N. (2020). AI-based emotional intelligence: A conceptual framework. *Technological Forecasting and Social Change*, *158*, 120118. DOI: 10.1016/j.techfore.2020.120118

Karami, A., Shemshaki, M., & Ghazanfar, M. (2024). *Exploring the Ethical Implications of AI-Powered Personalization in Digital Marketing. Data Intelligence*. In-Press., DOI: 10.3724/2096-7004.di.2024.0055

Karimi, J., Pashaie, S., & Golmohammadi, H. (2025). Artificial Intelligence (AI) and the Future of Sports Marketing: Exploring New Challenges and Opportunities. *Journal of Advanced Sport Technology*. https://doi.org/DOI: 10.22098/jast.2025.15830.1374

Karimi, M. (2025). The Role of Artificial Intelligence in Reducing Risks and Managing Risk in the Futured. *Research in Safety, Health and Environment Quarterly, 2*(7), 63-71. https://hse.ihu.ac.ir/article_209704_ac817f999c644467abd07373a78f934d.pdf

K, D. T. (2024, August 31). K, T. (2024). AI-DRIVEN CUSTOMER SEGMENTATION: TARGETING AND RETARGETING STRATEGIES IN DIGITAL MARKETING. *Donglixue Yu Kongzhi Xuebao*, 400–415. Advance online publication. DOI: 10.71058/jodac.v8i8027

Kedi, W. E., Ejimuda, C., Idemudia, C., & Ijomah, T. I. (2024). AI software for personalized marketing automation in SMEs: Enhancing customer experience and sales. *World Journal of Advanced Research and Reviews*, *23*(1), 1981–1990. DOI: 10.30574/wjarr.2024.23.1.2159

Kiani, M. S. (2024). An in-depth look at the future of sports with artificial intelligence, virtual reality, and data visualization to improve athlete performance analysis. *Intelligent Knowledge Exploration and Processing*, *4*(12), 8–35. DOI: 10.30508/kdip.2024.451951.1100

Kietzmann, J., Paschen, J., & Treen, E. (2018). Artificial intelligence in advertising: Personalization and targeting. *Journal of Business Research*, *92*, 180–194. DOI: 10.1016/j.jbusres.2018.07.008

Kim, C. M. (2020). *Social media campaigns: Strategies for public relations and marketing*. Routledge. DOI: 10.4324/9781003020196

King, N. (2016). *Sport governance: An introduction*. Routledge. DOI: 10.4324/9781315623313

Knowles, B., Richards, J., & Kroeger, F. (2022). The Many Facets of Trust in AI: Formalizing the Relation Between Trust and Fairness, Accountability, and Transparency. *ArXiv*, abs/2208.00681. https://doi.org//arXiv.2208.00681.DOI: 10.48550

Kobets, K., Terentieva, N., Shkvyria, N., Lysytsia, N., & Siemak, I. (2024). Digitalization and its impact on the development of contemporary marketing strategies. *Economic Affairs*, *69*(2), 1021–1040.

Koob, C. (2023). Consumers' Preferences for Digital Corporate Content on Company Websites: A Best-Worst Scaling Analysis. *Journal of Theoretical and Applied Electronic Commerce Research*, *18*(3), 1301–1319. DOI: 10.3390/jtaer18030066

Kovacova, M., Oláh, J., & Popescu, G. H. (2022). Digital Twin simulation and modeling tools, deep learning object detection technology, and visual perception and sensor fusion algorithms in the metaverse commerce. Economics. *Management and Financial Markets*, *17*(3), 9–24.

Krishnan, C., Gupta, A., Gupta, A., & Singh, G. (2022). Impact of artificial intelligence-based chatbots on customer engagement and business growth. In *Deep learning for social media data analytics* (pp. 195–210). Springer., DOI: 10.1007/978-3-031-10869-3_11

Kubovics, M. (2024). Innovative Content Production in Marketing Communication Through AI. *European Conference on Innovation and Entrepreneurship*. DOI: 10.34190/ecie.19.1.2877

Ku, E. C. S. (2024). Digital marketing innovation and industrial marketing: Evidence from restaurants' service robots. *Asia Pacific Journal of Marketing and Logistics*, *36*(11), 3099–3117. DOI: 10.1108/APJML-02-2024-0185

Kufel, J., Bargieł-Łączek, K., Kocot, S., Koźlik, M., Bartnikowska, W., Janik, M., Czogalik, Ł., Dudek, P., Magiera, M., Lis, A., Paszkiewicz, I., Nawrat, Z., Cebula, M., & Gruszczyńska, K. (2023). What is machine learning, artificial neural networks and deep learning?—Examples of practical applications in medicine. *Diagnostics (Basel)*, *13*(15), 2582. DOI: 10.3390/diagnostics13152582 PMID: 37568945

Kumar, A., Dixit, A., Javalgi, R. G., Dass, M., & Kamboj, S. (2021). Digital transformation of sustainability: A review and research agenda. *Technological Forecasting and Social Change*, *166*, 120602. DOI: 10.1016/j.techfore.2021.120602

Kumar, A., Sharma, R., & Singh, R. (2022). AI-based content personalization. *Journal of Business Research*, *139*, 1225–1236. DOI: 10.1016/j.jbusres.2021.10.045

Kumar, D., & Suthar, N. (2024). Ethical and legal challenges of AI in marketing: An exploration of solutions. *Journal of Information. Communication and Ethics in Society*, *22*(1), 124–144. DOI: 10.1108/JICES-05-2023-0068

Kumar, H., & Singh, P. (2015). Neuromarketing: An emerging tool of market research. [IJEMR]. *International Journal of Engineering and Management Research, 5*(6), 530–535.

Kumari, P. (2024). To study the impact of ai on digital marketing strategy. [IJRAR]. *IJRAR-International Journal of Research and Analytical Reviews, 11*(2), 286–320.

Kumar, V., & Abdul, R. (2024). AI-powered marketing: What, where, and how? *International Journal of Information Management, 77*, 102783. DOI: 10.1016/j.ijinfomgt.2024.102783

Lambrecht, A., & Tucker, C. (2021). Algorithm-Based Advertising: Unintended Effects and the Tricky Business of Mitigating Adverse Outcomes. *NIM Marketing Intelligence Review, 13*(1), 24–29. DOI: 10.2478/nimmir-2021-0004

Lanier, J. (1992). Virtual reality: The promise of the future. *Interactive Learning International, 8*(4), 275–279. DOI: 10.5555/155259.155263

Laroche, D., & Corbett, R. (2010). . Risk management guide for community sport organizations. *2010 Legacies Now.*

Lee, N., Broderick, A. J., & Chamberlain, L. (2007). What is 'neuromarketing'? A discussion and agenda for future research. *International Journal of Psychophysiology, 63*(2), 199–204. DOI: 10.1016/j.ijpsycho.2006.03.007 PMID: 16769143

Lee, W., & Lu, L. (2024). The hospitable thought that counts: An emerging theory of "AI consciousness" in genuine hospitality. *International Journal of Hospitality Management, 123*, 103928. DOI: 10.1016/j.ijhm.2024.103928

Liu, X. (2023). Deep learning in marketing: A review and research agenda. *Artificial Intelligence in Marketing*, 239-271. https://doi.org/DOI: 10.1108/S1548-643520230000020014

Liu, B. (2015). *Sentiment analysis: Mining opinions, sentiments, and emotions.* Cambridge University Press. DOI: 10.1017/CBO9781139084789

Liu, Y., Soroka, A., Han, L., Jian, J., & Tang, M. (2020). Cloud-based big data analytics for customer insight-driven design innovation in SMEs. *International Journal of Information Management, 51*, 102034. DOI: 10.1016/j.ijinfomgt.2019.11.002

Li, Y., Wang, S., & Li, Z. (2024). Animating arousal and engagement: Empirical insights into AI-enhanced robotic performances and consumer reactions. *Journal of Hospitality and Tourism Technology, 15*(5), 737–768. DOI: 10.1108/JHTT-01-2024-0053

Li, Y., Zhou, X., Jiang, X., Fan, F., & Song, B. (2024). How service robots' human-like appearance impacts consumer trust: A study across diverse cultures and service settings. *International Journal of Contemporary Hospitality Management, 36*(9), 3151–3167. DOI: 10.1108/IJCHM-06-2023-0845

Luo, X., Tong, S., Fang, Z., & Qu, Z. (2019). Machines versus humans: The impact of artificial intelligence chatbot disclosure on customer purchases. *Marketing Science, 38*(6), 937–947. DOI: 10.1287/mksc.2019.1182

Lv, C., Wang, Y., & Ma, Y. (2022). Construction of business innovation model for sports industry using a deep learning algorithm. *Soft Computing, 26*(20), 10753–10763. DOI: 10.1007/s00500-022-06962-8

Lyu, X., Jia, F., & Zhao, B. (2023). Impact of big data and cloud-driven learning technologies in healthy and smart cities on marketing automation. *Soft Computing, 27*(7), 4209–4222. DOI: 10.1007/s00500-022-07031-w

Ma, F., ... "Generative Technology for Human Emotion Recognition: A Scope Review," *arXiv preprint*, arXiv:2407.03640, Jul. 2024. [Online]. Available: https://arxiv.org/abs/2407.03640.arXiv DOI: 10.2139/ssrn.4889990

Maduku, D. K., Rana, N. P., Mpinganjira, M., Thusi, P., Mkhize, N. H.-B., & Ledikwe, A. (2024). Do AI-powered digital assistants influence customer emotions, engagement and loyalty? An empirical investigation. *Asia Pacific Journal of Marketing and Logistics, 36*(11), 2849–2868. DOI: 10.1108/APJML-09-2023-0935

Mahmoudian, A., Mohammadi, S., & Wang, W. (2024). Fan Engagement Management: Fan Response to Brand Image Attributes of Professional Athletes on Instagram. *Journal of Global Sport Management*, 1-19.

Ma, L., & Sun, B. (2020). Machine learning and AI in marketing–Connecting computing power to human insights. *International Journal of Research in Marketing, 37*(3), 481–504. DOI: 10.1016/j.ijresmar.2020.04.005

Malekmahmoodi, V., Mondalizadeh, Z., & Zohrevandian, K. (2022). The Effect of Innovation Capability on Innovative Performance of Sport Clubs [Research]. *New Trends in Sport Management, 9*(35), 29-44. http://ntsmj.issma.ir/article-1-1462-fa .html

Mandapuram, M., Gutlapalli, S. S., Reddy, M., & Bodepudi, A. (2020). Application of artificial intelligence (AI) technologies to accelerate market segmentation. *Global Disclosure of Economics and Business, 9*(2), 141–150. DOI: 10.18034/gdeb.v9i2.662

Manyika, J. (2022). The state of AI in 2022—and a half-decade in review. *McKinsey & Company*. https://www.mckinsey.com/featured-insights/artificial-intelligence/the-state-of-ai-in-2022-and-a-half-decade-in-review

Manzouri, H., & Khalili, A. J. (2023). Investigating the effect of perceived convenience, personalization and improvement of service quality on the formation of customers' experience of using artificial intelligence through the mediating variable of trust. *Management Science in Industry*, *2*(1), 227–239.

Mariani, M., & Borghi, M. (2021). Customers' evaluation of mechanical artificial intelligence in hospitality services: A study using online reviews analytics. *International Journal of Contemporary Hospitality Management*, *33*(11), 3956–3976. DOI: 10.1108/IJCHM-06-2020-0622

Marion, T. J., & Fixson, S. K. (2021). The transformation of the innovation process: How digital tools are changing work, collaboration, and organizations in new product development. *Journal of Product Innovation Management*, *38*(1), 192–215. DOI: 10.1111/jpim.12547

Martinoli, A., & Vuković, V. (2024). *Personalized distribution of media content: AI algorithms and enhancement of user experience*. Kultura., DOI: 10.5937/kultura2484057M

Maslow, A. H. (1943). A theory of human motivation. *Psychological Review*, *50*(4), 370–396. DOI: 10.1037/h0054346

Matthew, U. O., Kazaure, A. S., Kazaure, J. S., Hassan, I. M., Nwanakwaugwu, A. C., & Okafor, N. U. (2022). Educational technology adaptation & implication for media technology adoption in the period of COVID-19. *Journal of Trends in Computer Science and Smart Technology*, *4*(4), 226–245.

Matthew, U. O., Kazaure, J. S., & Haruna, K. (2020). Multimedia information system (MIS) for knowledge generation and ICT policy framework in education: Innovative sustainable educational investment. [IJICTHD]. *International Journal of Information Communication Technologies and Human Development*, *12*(3), 28–58.

Matthew, U. O., Kazaure, J. S., John, O., & Haruna, K. (2021). Telecommunication Business Information System and Investment Ecosystem in a Growing Economy: A Review of Telecom Investment in Nigeria. [IJICTHD]. *International Journal of Information Communication Technologies and Human Development*, *13*(2), 1–20.

Matthew, U. O., Kazaure, J. S., Kazaure, A. S., Nwamouh, U. C., & Chinonso, A. (2022). ICT Policy Implementation as Correlate for Achieving Educational Sustainability: Approaching Development in Multi ICT Dimensions. *Journal of Information Technology*, *4*(4), 250–269.

Matthew, U. O., Kazaure, J. S., Ndukwu, C. C., Ebong, G. N., Nwanakwaugwu, A. C., & Nwamouh, U. C. (2024). Artificial Intelligence Educational Pedagogy Development: ICT Pedagogy Development for Education 5.0. In *Educational Perspectives on Digital Technologies in Modeling and Management* (pp. 65–93). IGI Global. DOI: 10.4018/979-8-3693-2314-4.ch003

McDuff, D., El Kaliouby, R., & Picard, R. (2019). Affective computing and sentiment analysis. In *The Oxford Handbook of Affective Computing* (pp. 240–254). Oxford University Press.

Medina-Ortiz, D., Contreras, S., Quiroz, C., Asenjo, J. A., Medina-Ortiz, D., Contreras, S., Quiroz, C., Asenjo, J. A., & Olivera-Nappa, Á. (2020). Dmakit: A user-friendly web platform for bringing state-of-the-art data analysis techniques to non-specific users. *Information Systems*, *93*, 101557.

Mensah, G. (2024). *Artificial Intelligence and Ethics: A Comprehensive Review of Bias Mitigation, Transparency, and Accountability in AI Systems*. Africa Journal For Regulatory Affairs., DOI: 10.62839/AJFRA/2024.v1.I1.32-45

Mero, J., Leinonen, M., Makkonen, H., & Karjaluoto, H. (2022). Agile logic for SaaS implementation: Capitalizing on marketing automation software in a start-up. *Journal of Business Research*, *145*, 583–594. Advance online publication. DOI: 10.1016/j.jbusres.2022.03.026

Meshrarm, D., & Bekouni, A. (2021). Prediction and classification of customer behavior in electronic marketing using data mining and neural network (A case study of network marketing companies). *Applied Innovations in Industrial Management*, *1*(2), 1–7.

Mileti, A., Guido, G., & Prete, M. I. (2016). Nanomarketing: A new frontier for neuromarketing. *Psychology and Marketing*, *33*(8), 664–674. DOI: 10.1002/mar.20907

Mishra, S., Afaq, A., Mishra, T. K., & Mathur, N. (2025). Integrating Generative AI-Driven Learning Programs to Enhance Marketing Skills. In *Generative Artificial Intelligence and Ethics: Standards, Guidelines, and Best Practices* (pp. 189-226). IGI Global.

Modi, T. B. (2023). Artificial Intelligence Ethics and Fairness: A study to address bias and fairness issues in AI systems, and the ethical implications of AI applications. *Revista Review Index Journal of Multidisciplinary*, *3*(2), 24–35. DOI: 10.31305/rrijm2023.v03.n02.004

Mohammadi, S., Pashaie, S., & Ghaffarisadr, S. I. (2025). Aesthetics and Football: Aesthetics. In *Global Perspectives on Soccer and the Media and Entertainment Industry* (pp. 237-282). IGI Global Scientific Publishing. https://doi.org/DOI: 10.4018/979-8-3693-4298-5.ch009

Mohammadi, S., Siani, M. G., Abdolmaleki, H., & Sato, M. COVID-19 Pandemic and Sporting Events: Tokyo 2020 Olympics–Challenges and Solutions. In *Crisis Management and Sports* (pp. 182-195). Routledge.

Mohammadi, S., Pashaie, S., Ghaffarisadr, S. I., & Rayner, M. (2025a). Opportunities and Challenges of Leveraging Artificial Intelligence (AI) in Sport Marketing. *Advancing the Marketing Technology (MarTech). Advances in Marketing, Customer Relationship Management, and E-Services*, •••, 233–272. DOI: 10.4018/979-8-3693-4361-6.ch009

Mohammed, A. H., & Ali, A. H. (2021). (in press). Survey of bert (bidirectional encoder representation transformer) types. Journal of Physics: Conference Series, Moradi, E. (2025). Tracing the Evolution of Sport Marketing and Sponsorship: A Bibliometric Analysis of Trends and Scholarly Impact in a Leading Journal. *Sports Business Journal. Articles*. Advance online publication. DOI: 10.22051/sbj.2025.49152.1194

Moradipour, T., Nikbakhsh, R., Farahani, A., & Safani, A. M. (2021). Investigating the cognitive and social behaviors of fans and the effect of these behaviors on their enthusiasm to attend the stadium. *New Trends in Sport Management*, *9*(34), 85–99.

More, A., & Unnikrishnan, R. (2024). AI-Powered Analytics in Product Marketing Optimizing Customer Experience and Market Segmentation. *Journal Of Multidisciplinary*, *4*(11), 12–19.

Morris, N. (2009). Understanding Digital Marketing: Marketing Strategies for Engaging the Digital Generation. *Journal of Direct, Data and Digital Marketing Practice*, *10*(4), 384–387. DOI: 10.1057/dddmp.2009.7

Mourtzis, D. (2023). Digital twin inception in the Era of industrial metaverse. *Frontiers in Manufacturing Technology*, *3*, 1155735. DOI: 10.3389/fmtec.2023.1155735

Movahed, A. B., Abyaneh, A. G., Khakbazan, M., & Movahed, A. B. (2025). Smart Economy Cybersecurity: AI-Driven Risk Management in Digital Markets. In *Dynamic and Safe Economy in the Age of Smart Technologies* (pp. 49-72). IGI Global Scientific Publishing. DOI: DOI: 10.4018/979-8-3693-4369-2.ch004

Movahed, A. B., Movahed, A. B., & Nozari, H. (2024). Marketing 6.0 Conceptualization. In Advanced Businesses in Industry 6.0 (pp. 15-31). IGI Global.

Movahed, A. B., Movahed, A. B., & Nozari, H. (2024). Opportunities and challenges of marketing 5.0. Smart and Sustainable Interactive Marketing, 1-21.

Movahed, A. B., Movahed, A. B., & Nozari, H. (2024). Opportunities and challenges of smart supply chain in Industry 5.0. *Information Logistics for Organizational Empowerment and Effective Supply Chain Management*, 108-138.

Movahed, A. B., Aliahmadi, A., Parsanejad, M., & Nozari, H. (2023). A systematic review of collaboration in supply chain 4.0 with meta-synthesis method. *Supply Chain Analytics*, *4*, 100052. DOI: 10.1016/j.sca.2023.100052

Murár, P., & Kubovics, M. (2023). Using AI to Create Content Designed for Marketing Communications. *European Conference on Innovation and Entrepreneurship*. DOI: 10.34190/ecie.18.1.1638

Murthy, G. S. N., Allu, S. R., Andhavarapu, B., Bagadi, M., & Belusonti, M. (2020). Text based sentiment analysis using LSTM. *Int. J. Eng. Res. Tech. Res*, *9*(05), 299–303.

Nadler, A., & McGuigan, L. (2018). An impulse to exploit: The behavioral turn in data-driven marketing. *Critical Studies in Media Communication*, *35*(2), 151–165.

Nair, K., & Gupta, R. (2021). Application of AI technology in modern digital marketing environment. *World Journal of Entrepreneurship, Management and Sustainable Development*, *ahead-of-print*(ahead-of-print). Advance online publication. DOI: 10.1108/WJEMSD-08-2020-0099

Najafi, S. E., Nozari, H., & Edalatpanah, S. A. (2022). Artificial Intelligence of Things (AIoT) and Industry 4.0–Based Supply Chain (FMCG Industry). A roadmap for enabling industry 4.0 by artificial intelligence, 31-41.

Najafi, S. E., Nozari, H., & Edalatpanah, S. A. (2022). Investigating the key parameters affecting sustainable IoT-based marketing. In *Computational Intelligence Methodologies Applied to Sustainable Development Goals* (pp. 51–61). Springer International Publishing. DOI: 10.1007/978-3-030-97344-5_4

Nalbant, K. G., & Aydın, S. (2022). Literature review on the relationship between artificial intelligence technologies with digital sports marketing and sports management. *Indonesian Journal of Sport Management, 2*(2), 135–143. DOI: 10.31949/ijsm.v2i2.2876

Na, S., Heo, S., Han, S., Shin, Y., & Roh, Y. (2022). Acceptance model of artificial intelligence (AI)-based technologies in construction firms: Applying the Technology Acceptance Model (TAM) in combination with the Technology–Organisation–Environment (TOE) framework. *Buildings (Basel, Switzerland), 12*(2), 90.

Neumann, D. L., Moffitt, R. L., Thomas, P. R., Loveday, K., Watling, D. P., Lombard, C. L., Antonova, S., & Tremeer, M. A. (2018). A systematic review of the application of interactive virtual reality to sport. *Virtual Reality (Waltham Cross), 22*(3), 183–198. DOI: 10.1007/s10055-017-0320-5

Ngai, E., Lee, M., Luo, M., Chan, P., & Liang, T. (2021). An intelligent knowledge-based chatbot for customer service. *Electronic Commerce Research and Applications, 50*, 101098. DOI: 10.1016/j.elerap.2021.101098

Nguyen, Q., Sidorova, A., & Torres, R. (2021). User interactions with chatbot interfaces vs. Menu-based interfaces: An empirical study. *Computers in Human Behavior, 128*, 107093. DOI: 10.1016/j.chb.2021.107093

Nimbalkar, A., & Singh, A. (2024). *A Study of the Impact of Artificial Intelligence on Digital Marketing - A Systematic Review of Literature*. JOURNAL OF MANAGEMENT AND ENTREPRENEURSHIP., DOI: 10.70906/20241803001008

Niyozov, N., Saburov, S., Ganiyev, S., & Olimov, S. (2023). AI-powered learning: revolutionizing technical higher education institutions through advanced power supply fundamentals. In *E3S Web of Conferences* (Vol. 461, p. 01092). EDP Sciences. DOI: 10.1051/e3sconf/202346101092

Nourian, H. (2021). *Artificial Intelligence and its Management Risks*. hosseinnourian.com

Nozari, H., & Chobar, A. P. (2024). The Dimensions and Components of Marketing 5.0: Introduction to Marketing 6.0. In Advanced Businesses in Industry 6.0 (pp. 75-86). IGI Global.

Nozari, H., & Samadi, S. (2025). Digital Twin-Enhanced Sentiment Analysis for Targeted Marketing Optimization. In Dynamic and Safe Economy in the Age of Smart Technologies (pp. 121-138). IGI Global Scientific Publishing. DOI: 10.4018/979-8-3693-4369-2.ch008

Nozari, H., Abdi, H., & Rafiei, K. (2025). Edge Computing and Marketing in the Smart Economy: Processing Consumer Data in Real-Time. In Dynamic and Safe Economy in the Age of Smart Technologies (pp. 191-208). IGI Global Scientific Publishing.

Nozari, H., Abdi, H., & Szmelter-Jarosz, A. (2025). Goat Optimization Algorithm: A Novel Bio-Inspired Metaheuristic for Global Optimization. arXiv preprint arXiv:2503.02331.

Nozari, H., Fallah, M., Szmelter-Jarosz, A., & Krzemiński, M. (2021). Analysis of security criteria for IoT-based supply chain: a case study of FMCG industries. Central European Management Journal, 29(4).

Nozari, H., Ghahremani-Nahr, J., & Najafi, E. (2023). The role of Internet of things and Blockchain in the development of agile and sustainable supply chains. In *Digital Supply Chain, Disruptive Environments, and the Impact on Retailers* (pp. 271-282). IGI Global. DOI: 10.4018/978-1-6684-7298-9.ch015

Nozari, H., Irani, H. R., & Rahmaty, M. (2023, November). Investigating Critical Success Factors in IoT-Based Marketing Systems. In International Conference on Optimization and Data Science in Industrial Engineering (pp. 259-271). Cham: Springer Nature Switzerland.

Nozari, H., Tavakkoli-Moghaddam, R., & Dolgui, A. (2024, September). Analysis of Critical Success Factors of Sustainable and Resilient Aioe-based Supply Chain in Industry 5.0. In IFIP International Conference on Advances in Production Management Systems (pp. 76-90). Cham: Springer Nature Switzerland. DOI: 10.1007/978-3-031-65894-5_6

Nozari, H. (2024). Green Supply Chain Management based on Artificial Intelligence of Everything. *Journal of Economics and Management*, *46*, 171–188. DOI: 10.22367/jem.2024.46.07

Nozari, H. (2025). Cognitive Targeting and Neuromarketing Applications in AI-Driven Digital Advertising. *Applied Innovations in Industrial Management*, *5*(2), 52–58. DOI: 10.63630/aiim.52.52

Nozari, H. (2025). NeuroTwinceutics™ as a Neuromorphic Digital Twin Model for Predictive and Personalized Pharmacotherapy. *Transformative Science*, *1*(1), 1–8.

Nozari, H. (Ed.). (2023). *Building Smart and Sustainable Businesses with Transformative Technologies*. IGI Global. DOI: 10.4018/979-8-3693-0210-1

Nozari, H., Abdi, H., & Jahangard, S. (2025). Quantum Cognitive Intelligence Network Q-CIN as a Transformative Framework for Industry 6.0. *ALL Bioscience*, *1*(1), 27–37.

Nozari, H., Abdi, H., & Rafiei, K. (2025). Edge Computing and Marketing in the Smart Economy: Processing Consumer Data in Real-Time. In Nozari, H. (Ed.), *Dynamic and Safe Economy in the Age of Smart Technologies* (pp. 191–208). IGI Global Scientific Publishing., DOI: 10.4018/979-8-3693-4369-2.ch012

Nozari, H., & Aliahmadi, A. (2023). Analysis of critical success factors in a food agile supply chain by a fuzzy hybrid decision-making method. [Formerly known as Iranian Journal of Management Studies]. *Interdisciplinary Journal of Management Studies*, *16*(4), 905–926.

Nozari, H., & Edalatpanah, S. A. (2023). Smart systems risk management in IoT-based supply chain. In *Advances in reliability, failure and risk analysis* (pp. 251–268). Springer Nature Singapore. DOI: 10.1007/978-981-19-9909-3_11

Nozari, H., Fallah, M., Kazemipoor, H., & Najafi, S. E. (2021). Big data analysis of IoT-based supply chain management considering FMCG industries. *Бизнес-информатика*, *15*(1, 1 (eng)), 78–96. DOI: 10.17323/2587-814X.2021.1.78.96

Nozari, H., Ghahremani-Nahr, J., & Szmelter-Jarosz, A. (2023). A multi-stage stochastic inventory management model for transport companies including several different transport modes. *International Journal of Management Science and Engineering Management*, *18*(2), 134–144. DOI: 10.1080/17509653.2022.2042747

Nozari, H., Ghahremani-Nahr, J., & Szmelter-Jarosz, A. (2024). AI and machine learning for real-world problems. [). Elsevier.]. *Advances in Computers*, *134*, 1–12. DOI: 10.1016/bs.adcom.2023.02.001

Nozari, H., Movahed, A. B., & Movahed, A. B. (2024). The AIoE Revolution: Redefining Organizational Maturity in a Hyper-Connected World. *Applied Innovations in Industrial Management*, *4*(1), 10–17.

Nozari, H., Najafi, E., Fallah, M., & Hosseinzadeh Lotfi, F. (2019). Quantitative analysis of key performance indicators of green supply chain in FMCG industries using non-linear fuzzy method. *Mathematics*, *7*(11), 1020. DOI: 10.3390/math7111020

Nozari, H., Rahmaty, M., & Szmelter-Jarosz, A. (2024). A framework for AIoT-based smart sustainable marketing system. In *Artificial Intelligence of Things for Achieving Sustainable Development Goals* (pp. 255–271). Springer Nature Switzerland. DOI: 10.1007/978-3-031-53433-1_13

Nozari, H., Szmelter-Jarosz, A., & Ghahremani-Nahr, J. (2021). The ideas of sustainable and green marketing based on the internet of everything—The case of the dairy industry. *Future Internet*, *13*(10), 266. DOI: 10.3390/fi13100266

Nozari, H., Szmelter-Jarosz, A., & Ghahremani-Nahr, J. (2022). Analysis of the challenges of artificial intelligence of things (AIoT) for the smart supply chain (case study: FMCG industries). *Sensors (Basel), 22*(8), 2931. DOI: 10.3390/s22082931 PMID: 35458916

Nozari, H., Tavakkoli-Moghaddam, R., & Gharemani-Nahr, J. (2022). A neutrosophic fuzzy programming method to solve a multi-depot vehicle routing model under uncertainty during the covid-19 pandemic. *International Journal of Engineering, 35*(2), 360–371.

Nurgalieva, L., Frik, A., & Doherty, G. (2023). A narrative review of factors affecting the implementation of privacy and security practices in software development. *ACM Computing Surveys, 55*(14s), 1–27.

Nwanakwaugwu, A. C., Matthew, U. O., Kazaure, A. A., & Haruna, K. (2023). Data Mining Business Intelligence Applications in Retail Services Using Artificial Neural Networks. In *Handbook of Research on Cybersecurity Risk in Contemporary Business Systems* (pp. 186–210). IGI Global. DOI: 10.4018/978-1-6684-7207-1.ch010

Obia, V. (2025). Digital policy and Nigeria's Platform Code of Practice: Towards a radical co-regulatory turn. *Data & Policy, 7*(7), e12. DOI: 10.1017/dap.2025.1

Ogabu, J. (2024). The Future of Finance is Intelligent: Exploring the Positive Impact of AI Education on Efficiency, Innovation, and Profitability in the Financial Sector. *International Journal of Research and Scientific Innovation*. .DOI: 10.51244/IJRSI.2024.11110084

Oğuz, A. (2024). Consumer Behavior in the Era of AI-Driven Marketing. *Human-Computer Interaction, 8*(1), 147. Advance online publication. DOI: 10.62802/h9frxh42

Okazaki, S., Eisend, M., Plangger, K., de Ruyter, K., & Grewal, D. (2020). Understanding the strategic consequences of customer privacy concerns: A meta-analytic review. *Journal of Retailing, 96*(4), 458–473. DOI: 10.1016/j.jretai.2020.05.007

Okeleke, P. A., Ajiga, D., Folorunsho, S. O., & Ezeigweneme, C. (2024). Predictive analytics for market trends using AI: A study in consumer behavior. *International Journal of Engineering Research Updates, 7*(1), 36–49. DOI: 10.53430/ijeru.2024.7.1.0032

Okwudili, U. M., & Kazaure, J. S. (2020). Digital activism and digital revolution in objective journalism. [IJICST]. *International Journal of Interactive Communication Systems and Technologies, 10*(2), 39–56.

Oladiran, O., & Dickins, L. (2024). *PropTech and Real Estate Innovations: A Guide to Digital Technologies and Solutions in the Built Environment*. Taylor & Francis. DOI: 10.1201/9781003262725

Olatunji, F., Sajuyigbe, A. S., Tella, R. A., Oke, O. D., Babalola, O. A., & Adebayo, W. (2025). Assessing The Impact of Financial Service Digitalization on SME Businesses In Lagos, Nigeria. *Journal of Entrepreneurship and Business*, *6*(1), 94–118.

Olsen, G. D., & Pracejus, J. W. (2020). Customized advertising: Allowing consumers to directly tailor messages leads to better outcomes for the brand. *Journal of Business Research*, *116*, 245–257. DOI: 10.1016/j.jbusres.2020.04.054

Olson, E., Olson, K., Czaplewski, A., & Key, T. (2021). Business strategy and the management of digital marketing. *Business Horizons*, *64*(2), 285–293. Advance online publication. DOI: 10.1016/j.bushor.2020.12.004

Oskounejad, M. M., & Nozari, H. (Eds.). (2024). *Advanced Businesses in Industry 6.0*. IGI Global. DOI: 10.4018/979-8-3693-3108-8

Oyedokun, T. T. (2025). Digitally Enhanced World of Realities: Immersive Technologies and Innovative Business Models. In *AI-Driven Business Model Innovation* (pp. 37–70). IGI Global Scientific Publishing. DOI: 10.4018/979-8-3693-9571-4.ch002

Oyekunle, D. O. T., Okwudili Matthew, U., Preston, D., & Boohene, D. (2024). Trust beyond technology algorithms: A theoretical exploration of consumer trust and behavior in technological consumption and AI projects. *Journal of Computer and Communications*, *12*(06), 10–4236.

Palle, R. R. (2021). Discuss the role of data analytics in extracting meaningful insights from social media data, influencing marketing strategies and user engagement. *Journal of Artificial Intelligence and Machine Learning in Management*, *5*(1), 64–69.

Panagiotakopoulos, D., Marentakis, G., Metzitakos, R., Deliyannis, I., & Dedes, F. (2022). Digital scent technology: Toward the internet of senses and the metaverse. *IT Professional*, *24*(3), 52–59. DOI: 10.1109/MITP.2022.3177292

Pangeran, A., Afra, I., & Lenando, T. (2024). *Maximizing the Impact of Digital Marketing: AI Integration for More Precise and Effective Strategies*. INTERNATIONAL JOURNAL OF MULTIDISCIPLINARY RESEARCH AND ANALYSIS., DOI: 10.47191/ijmra/v7-i06-35

Parsons, A., Zeisser, M., & Waitman, R. (1998). Organizing today for the digital marketing of tomorrow. *Journal of Interactive Marketing*, *12*(1), 31–46. DOI: 10.1002/(SICI)1520-6653(199824)12:1<31::AID-DIR4>3.0.CO;2-X

Parvez, M. O., Hossain, M. S., Islam, M. S., & Eluwole, K. K. (2025). Customers' acceptance of AI-powered robot chefs in casual dining restaurants. *Journal of Hospitality and Tourism Insights*, *8*(4), 1564–1581. DOI: 10.1108/JHTI-04-2024-0347

Pashaie, S., Mohammadi, S., & Golmohammadi, H. (2024). Unlocking athlete potential: The evolution of coaching strategies through artificial intelligence. *Proceedings of the Institution of Mechanical Engineers, Part P: Journal of Sports Engineering and Technology*, 17543371241300889. https://doi.org/DOI: 10.1177/17543371241300889

Pashaie, S., & Golmohammadi, H. (2024). Exploring the Influence of E-CRM on the innovation capabilities of sports venues: The moderating role of covid-19. *Sports Marketing Studies*, *4*(3), 108–128. DOI: 10.22034/sms.2024.139773.1253

Pashaie, S., Golmohammadi, H., & Zakhirani, E. (2024). Digital Transformation in Sports Marketing: The Impact of Artificial Intelligence on Personalization and Customer Engagement. *International Journal of Innovation in Management. Economics and Social Sciences*, *4*(4), 42–58. DOI: 10.59615/ijimes.4.4.42

Pashaie, S., & Nasirpour, M. (2024). (in press). The Impact of Observability and Compatibility on Consumers' Attitudes Towards AI-Generated Sports Marketing Content and Its Effect on Purchase Intent. *Sports Marketing Studies. Articles*. Advance online publication. DOI: 10.22034/sms.2024.141529.1367

Pathan, M., Jarad, R., Bhavsar, D., Yadav, M., Suryavanshi, P., & Moholkar, N. (2024). Artificial intelligence in social media marketing. *International Journal of Research Publication and Reviews*, *5*(12), 2780–2784.

Patil, D. 2024. "Generative Artificial Intelligence In Marketing And Advertising: Advancing Personalization And Optimizing Consumer Engagement Strategies." *Available at SSRN* 5057404.

Pereira, A. M., Moura, J. A. B., Costa, E. D. B., Vieira, T., Landim, A. R., Bazaki, E., & Wanick, V. (2022). Customer models for artificial intelligence-based decision support in fashion online retail supply chains. *Decision Support Systems*, *158*, 113795. DOI: 10.1016/j.dss.2022.113795

Perez-Vega, R., Kaartemo, V., Lages, C. R., Borghei Razavi, N., & Männistö, J. (2021). Reshaping the contexts of online customer engagement behavior via artificial intelligence: A conceptual framework. *Journal of Business Research*, *129*, 902–910. DOI: 10.1016/j.jbusres.2020.11.002

Peter, M. K., & Dalla Vecchia, M. (2021). The Digital Marketing Toolkit: A Literature Review for the Identification of Digital Marketing Channels and Platforms. In Dornberger, R. (Ed.), *New Trends in Business Information Systems and Technology* (Vol. 294, pp. 251–265). Springer International Publishing., DOI: 10.1007/978-3-030-48332-6_17

Piñeiro-Otero, T., & Martínez-Rolán, X. (2016). Understanding Digital Marketing—Basics and Actions. In Machado, C., & Davim, J. P. (Eds.), *MBA* (pp. 37–74). Springer International Publishing., DOI: 10.1007/978-3-319-28281-7_2

Plutchik, R. (2001). The nature of emotions. *American Scientist*, *89*(4), 344–350. https://www.jstor.org/stable/27857503. DOI: 10.1511/2001.28.344

Podobed, N. A. (2024). Integrated marketing communications: electronic educational-methodical complex for specialties: 6-05-0412-04" Marketing", 1-26 02 03" Marketing"/Institute of Business BSU, Department of marketing; comp. NA Podobed.–Minsk: BSU, 2024.–106 p.–Bibliogr.: p. 105–106.

Ponomarenko, I. (2024). Artificial intelligence in digital marketing. *Scientia fructuosa*. .DOI: 10.31617/1.2024(155)04

Poria, S., Cambria, E., Bajpai, R., & Hussain, A. (2017). A review of affective computing: From unimodal analysis to multimodal fusion. *Information Fusion*, *37*, 98–125. DOI: 10.1016/j.inffus.2017.02.003

Potla, R. T., & Pottla, V. K. (2024). AI-Powered Personalization in Salesforce: Enhancing Customer Engagement through Machine Learning Models. Valley International Journal Digital Library, 1388-1420.

Potwora, M., Zakryzhevska, I., Mostova, A., Kyrkovskyi, V., & Saienko, V. (2023). Marketing strategies in e-commerce: Personalised content, recommendations, and increased customer trust. *Financial and Credit Activity: Problems of Theory and Practice*, *5*(52), 562–573

Prabhakaran, A., Mahamadu, A. M., Adekunle, S., Manu, P., Booth, C. A., & Aigbavboa, C. (2025). 24 Towards a Metaverse Platform for Immersive Collaborative Design. Applications of Immersive Technology in Architecture, Engineering and Construction: A Handbook, 24.

Prasad, K., Xavier, L., Jain, S., Subba, R., Mittal, S., & Anute, N. (2024). AI-Driven Chatbots for E-Commerce Customer Support. *2024 International Conference on Advances in Computing, Communication and Applied Informatics (ACCAI)*, 1-5. DOI: 10.1109/ACCAI61061.2024.10602261

Prasetyo, Y. T., Susanto, K. C., Chuang, K.-H., Yin, R.-T., Chen, J.-W., Zhang, Y.-X., Benito, O. P., & John A Belmonte, Z. (2025). Factors influencing the perceived usability of line pay: An extended technology acceptance model approach. *Acta Psychologica, 255*, 104924. DOI: 10.1016/j.actpsy.2025.104924 PMID: 40090060

Prentice, C., Dominique Lopes, S., & Wang, X. (2020). The impact of artificial intelligence and employee service quality on customer satisfaction and loyalty. *Journal of Hospitality Marketing & Management, 29*(7), 739–756. DOI: 10.1080/19368623.2020.1722304

Prentice, C., Weaven, S., & Wong, I. A. (2020). Linking AI quality performance and customer engagement: The moderating effect of AI preference. *International Journal of Hospitality Management, 90*, 102629. DOI: 10.1016/j.ijhm.2020.102629

Purwanto, A., Fauzan, M., Widya, T., & Azzaky, N. (2024). Ethical Implications and Challenges of AI Implementation in Business Operations. *TechComp Innovations. Journal of Computer Science and Technology, 1*(2), 68–82. Advance online publication. DOI: 10.70063/techcompinnovations.v1i2.52

Quach, S., Thaichon, P., Martin, K. D., Weaven, S., & Palmatier, R. W. (2022). Digital technologies: Tensions in privacy and data. *Journal of the Academy of Marketing Science, 50*(6), 1299–1323. DOI: 10.1007/s11747-022-00845-y PMID: 35281634

Raaj, A., & Premnath, D. (2023). A Case Study on the Impact of ChatGPT On Personalised Marketing and Customer Engagement at Different Stages of the Purchase Process.

Rahimi Kolour, H., & Ghasemi Hamedani, I. (2023). Investigating the role of artificial intelligence-based risk management in increasing the agility and capabilities of supply chain reengineering. *Science and Technology Policy Letters, 13*(3), 5–23.

Rahmani, M., Majedi, N., Hemmatinejad, M., & Jamshidi, A. (2024). Application of Artificial Intelligence in the Sports Industry: A Review Article. *AI and Tech in Behavioral and Social Sciences, 2*(2), 20–27. DOI: 10.61838/kman.aitech.2.2.4

Rahmaty, M., & Nozari, H. (2023). Optimization of the hierarchical supply chain in the pharmaceutical industry. *Edelweiss Applied Science and Technology, 7*(2), 104–123. DOI: 10.55214/25768484.v7i2.376

Rane, N., Choudhary, S., & Rane, J. (2023). Metaverse marketing strategies: enhancing customer experience and analysing consumer behaviour through leading-edge Metaverse technologies, platforms, and models. Platforms, and Models (November 3, 2023).

Rane, N. (2023). Enhancing customer loyalty through Artificial Intelligence (AI), Internet of Things (IoT), and Big Data technologies: improving customer satisfaction, engagement, relationship, and experience. *Internet of Things (IoT), and Big Data Technologies: Improving Customer Satisfaction, Engagement, Relationship, and Experience*. https://doi.org/DOI: 10.2139/ssrn.4616051

Rane, N., Choudhary, S., & Rane, J. (2023). Hyper-personalization for enhancing customer loyalty and satisfaction in Customer Relationship Management (CRM) systems. *Available at SSRN* 4641044. DOI: 10.2139/ssrn.4641044

Rather, R. A. (2024). AI-powered ChatGPT in the hospitality and tourism industry: Benefits, challenges, theoretical framework, propositions and future research directions. *Tourism Recreation Research*, •••, 1–11. DOI: 10.1080/02508281.2023.2287799

Rauschnabel, P. A., Felix, R., Hinsch, C., Shahab, H., & Alt, F. (2022). What is XR? Towards a framework for augmented and virtual reality. *Computers in Human Behavior*, *133*, 107289. DOI: 10.1016/j.chb.2022.107289

Rautaray, S. S., & Agrawal, A. (2015). Vision based hand gesture recognition for human computer interaction: A survey. *Artificial Intelligence Review*, *43*(1), 1–54. DOI: 10.1007/s10462-012-9356-9

Raut, S., Chandel, A., & Mittal, S. (2025). Enhancing marketing and brand communication with AI-driven content creation. In *AI, corporate social responsibility, and marketing in modern organizations* (pp. 139–172). IGI Global Scientific Publishing.

Rodgers, S., & Nguyen, T. (2023). *Ethical AI in digital marketing: Addressing bias & privacy concerns*. Digital Ethics Review., DOI: 10.1007/s12345-023-00123-4

R, S., Mujahid, M., Rustam, F., Shafique, R., Chunduri, V., Villar, M. G., Ballester, J. B., Diez, I. T., & Ashraf, I.S. R et al. (2023, September). Analyzing Sentiments Regarding ChatGPT Using Novel BERT: A Machine Learning Approach. *Information (Basel)*, *14*(9), 474. DOI: 10.3390/info14090474

Ruel, H., & Njoku, E. (2021). AI redefining the hospitality industry. *Journal of Tourism Futures*, *7*(1), 53–66. DOI: 10.1108/JTF-03-2020-0032

Saboune, F. (2024). AI-Driven Marketing Strategies: Unlocking Growth Potential and Operational Efficiency in the Digital Communication Landscape. *2024 International Conference on Intelligent Computing, Communication, Networking and Services (ICCNS)*, 295-301. DOI: 10.1109/ICCNS62192.2024.10776195

Saif, W. Q. A., Alshammari, M. K., Mohammed, B. A., & Sallam, A. A. (2024, October). Enhancing Emotion Detection in Textual Data: A Comparative Analysis of Machine Learning Models and Feature Extraction Techniques. *Engineering, Technology & Applied Science Research, 14*(5), 16471–16477. . DOI: 10.48084/etasr.7806

Sai, S., Prasad, M., Garg, A., & Chamola, V. (2024). Synergizing digital twins and metaverse for consumer health: A case study approach. *IEEE Transactions on Consumer Electronics, 70*(1), 2137–2144. DOI: 10.1109/TCE.2024.3367929

Saleh, M. I. (2025). Generative artificial intelligence in hospitality and tourism: Future capabilities, AI prompts and real-world applications. *Journal of Hospitality Marketing & Management, 34*(4), 1–32. DOI: 10.1080/19368623.2025.2458603

Saragih, H., & Manurung, J. (2024). Leveraging the BERT model for enhanced sentiment analysis in multicontextual social media content. *Jurnal Teknik Informatika CIT Medicom, 16*(2), 82–89. DOI: 10.35335/cit.Vol16.2024.766.pp82-89

Sathyavani, B., Kalyan, N. B., Peddinti, D. R., Bihade, V., & Tiwari, A. (2025). Next-Generation CRM: AI, IoT, and the Future of Customer Relationship Management. Paper read at 2025 International Conference on Pervasive Computational Technologies (ICPCT).

Saura, J. R., Škare, V., & Ozretić Došen, Đ. (2024). Is AI-based digital marketing ethical? Assessing a new data privacy paradox. *Journal of Innovation & Knowledge, 9*(4), 100597. DOI: 10.1016/j.jik.2024.100597

Saura, J., Palacios-Marqués, D., & Ribeiro-Soriano, D. (2021). Digital marketing in SMEs via data-driven strategies: Reviewing the current state of research. *Journal of Small Business Management, 61*(3), 1278–1313. DOI: 10.1080/00472778.2021.1955127

Sbrighi, A. (2024a). *Leveraging The Power Of Deep Tech Within The Realm Of Digital Marketing: An Explorative Insight Into The Relationship Between Artificial Intelligence And Sports Fan Engagement* Università Ca' Foscari]. Italy.

Sbrighi, A. (2024b). Leveraging The Power Of Deep Tech Within The Realm Of Digital Marketing: An Explorative Insight Into The Relationship Between Artificial Intelligence And Sports Fan Engagement. https://doi.org/DOI: 10579/26168

Schwartz, S. H. (1992). Universals in the content and structure of values: Theoretical advances and empirical tests. *Advances in Experimental Social Psychology, 25*, 1–65. DOI: 10.1016/S0065-2601(08)60281-6

Scullen, T., Amenta, P. S., Nerva, J. D., & Dumont, A. S. (2020). Commentary: Predicting long-term outcomes after poor-grade aneurysmal subarachnoid hemorrhage using decision tree modeling. *Neurosurgery, 87*(3), E293–E295. DOI: 10.1093/neuros/nyaa074 PMID: 32195548

Segun-Falade, O. D., Osundare, O. S., Kedi, W. E., Okeleke, P. A., Ijomah, T. I., & Abdul-Azeez, O. Y.Osinachi Deborah Segun-FaladeOlajide Soji OsundareWagobera Edgar KediPatrick Azuka OkelekeTochukwu Ignatius IjomahOluwatosin Yetunde Abdul-Azeez. (2024). Utilizing machine learning algorithms to enhance predictive analytics in customer behavior studies. *International Journal of Scholarly Research in Engineering and Technology, 4*(1), 1–18. DOI: 10.56781/ijsret.2024.4.1.0018

Semerádová, T., & Weinlich, P. (2019). Computer Estimation of Customer Similarity With Facebook Lookalikes: Advantages and Disadvantages of Hyper-Targeting. *IEEE Access : Practical Innovations, Open Solutions, 7*, 153365–153377. DOI: 10.1109/ACCESS.2019.2948401

Semwal, R., Tripathi, N., Rana, A., Dafouti, B. S., Bairwa, M. K., & Mathur, V. (2024, May). AI-Powered Personalization and Emotional Intelligence Integration for Enhanced Service Marketing in Transformative Tourism Experiences. In *2024 International Conference on Communication, Computer Sciences and Engineering (IC3SE)* (pp. 1851-1856). IEEE. DOI: 10.1109/IC3SE62002.2024.10592909

Shah Alam, S., & Mohamed Sayuti, N. (2011). Applying the Theory of Planned Behavior (TPB) in halal food purchasing. *International Journal of Commerce and Management, 21*(1), 8–20. DOI: 10.1108/10569211111111676

Shah, A. M., Zahoor, S. Z., & Qureshi, I. H. (2019). Social media and purchasing behavior: A study of the mediating effect of customer relationships. *Journal of Global Marketing, 32*(2), 93–115. Advance online publication. DOI: 10.1080/08911762.2018.1497243

Shah, K., & LaPlaca, P. J. (1981). Assessing risks in strategic planning. *Industrial Marketing Management, 10*(2), 77–91. DOI: 10.1016/0019-8501(81)90001-8

Shahpar Tofigh, A., Deldar, E., Eghbali, K., & Aflatoon, S. (2022). Identification and ranking of socio-cultural factors affecting making culture in sport of Iran. *Applied Research in Sport Management, 10*(4), 49–61. DOI: 10.30473/arsm.2022.8957

Shanahan, T., Tran, T., & Taylor, E. (2019). Getting to know you: Social media personalization as a means of enhancing brand loyalty and perceived quality. *Journal of Retailing and Consumer Services, 47*, 57–65. Advance online publication. DOI: 10.1016/j.jretconser.2018.10.007

Shanmugam, G., Rajendran, D., Thanarajan, T., Murugaraj, S. S., & Rajendran, S. (2023). Artificial Intelligence as a Catalyst in Digital Marketing: Enhancing Profitability and Market Potential. *Ingénierie des Systèmes d'Information, 28*(6).

Sharbati, A., Bakhshi Movahed, A., Ghasemi Abyaneh, A., & Rahmanian, F. (2025). Risk Assessment of Healthcare Systems Using the FMEA Method: Medication Management Process. *Journal of Future Digital Optimization, 1*(1), 71–85.

Sharifan, M. S. (2023). Providing a framework for reducing artificial intelligence risks in finance and banking (with considerations of passive defense). In *Proceedings of the 7th National Conference on New Horizons in Management*. Economics, and Computer Science., https://civilica.com/doc/2015030

Sharma, K., Tomar, M., & Tadimarri, A. (2023). Unlocking Sales Potential: How AI Revolutionizes Marketing Strategies. *Journal of Knowledge Learning and Science Technology ISSN: 2959-6386 (online)*. DOI: 10.60087/jklst.vol2.n2.p250

Sharma, A. K., & Sharma, R. (2024). How artificial intelligence is transforming social media marketing: Analysing its potential and addressing concerns. *Journal of Cultural Marketing Strategy, 9*(1), 75–90.

Shayeg, M. M. (2023). Future research on artificial intelligence in the sports industry. *Paya Shahr Specialized Scientific Monthly, 1*, 1–17.

Shen, A. (2024). AI Ethics and Governance at International Standards. *International IT Journal of Research, ISSN: 3007-6706, 2*(1), 8-14.

Shi, F., Ning, H., Huangfu, W., Zhang, F., Wei, D., Hong, T., & Daneshmand, M. (2020). Recent progress on the convergence of the Internet of Things and artificial intelligence. *IEEE Network, 34*(5), 8–15. DOI: 10.1109/MNET.011.2000009

Shrestha, Y., Krishna, V., & Krogh, G. (2020). Augmenting Organizational Decision-Making with Deep Learning Algorithms: Principles, Promises, and Challenges. *ArXiv*, abs/2011.02834. .DOI: 10.1016/j.jbusres.2020.09.068

Shrotri, N. V., Tiwari, A., Karthikeya, E., Ahmed, S., & Shukla, P. (2024, December). Effective Use of AI Tools for Engineering and Management Education for Experiential Learning. In *2024 IEEE International Conference on Teaching, Assessment and Learning for Engineering (TALE)* (pp. 1-7). IEEE. DOI: 10.1109/TALE62452.2024.10834327

Siles, I., Espinoza-Rojas, J., Naranjo, A., & Tristán, M. (2019). The Mutual Domestication of Users and Algorithmic Recommendations on Netflix. *Communication, Culture & Critique*, tcz025. Advance online publication. DOI: 10.1093/ccc/tcz025

Singh, A. K. (2023). Applications of the internet of things and machine learning using python in digital marketing. In *Global Applications of the Internet of Things in Digital Marketing* (pp. 213–232). IGI Global., DOI: 10.4018/978-1-6684-8166-0.ch011

Singh, B., & Kaunert, C. (2024). Future of Digital Marketing: Hyper-Personalized Customer Dynamic Experience with AI-Based Predictive Models. In *Revolutionizing the AI-Digital Landscape* (pp. 189–203). Productivity Press. DOI: 10.4324/9781032688305-14

Singh, N., & Adhikari, D. (2023). Challenges and Solutions in Integrating AI with Legacy Inventory Systems. *International Journal for Research in Applied Science and Engineering Technology, 11*(12), 609–613. Advance online publication. DOI: 10.22214/ijraset.2023.57376

Singh, P., Das, L., Bahubal, D., Rani, S., & Kumar, A. (2023). AI/ML Revolutionizing social media and Business: A Comprehensive Study. In *Security and Risk Analysis for Intelligent Cloud Computing* (pp. 252–279). CRC Press.

Sinnett, A., Ho, C., & Malcolm, B. (2016). Expanding a dairy business affects business and financial risk. *Animal Production Science, 57*(10), 2167–2174. DOI: 10.1071/AN15041

Smuha, N. A. (2021). Beyond the individual: Governing AI's societal harm. *Internet Policy Review, 10*(3). Advance online publication. DOI: 10.14763/2021.3.1574

Sodiya, E., Umoga, U., Amoo, O., & Atadoga, A. (2024). *AI-driven warehouse automation: A comprehensive review of systems*. GSC Advanced Research and Reviews., DOI: 10.30574/gscarr.2024.18.2.0063

Solomon, M. R. (2020). *Consumer behavior: Buying, having, and being* (13th ed.). Pearson Education.

Somosi, Z. (2022). THE ROLE OF ARTIFICIAL INTELLIGENCE IN CONTENT CREATION AND CHECKING ITS EFFECTIVENESS IN THE GOOGLE ADS ADVERTISING SYSTEM. *The Annals of the University of Oradea. Economic Sciences*. .DOI: 10.47535/1991AUOES31(2)025

Stone, M., Aravopoulou, E., Ekinci, Y., Evans, G., Hobbs, M., Labib, A., Laughlin, P., Machtynger, J., & Machtynger, L. (2020). Artificial intelligence (AI) in strategic marketing decision-making: A research agenda. *The Bottom Line (New York, N.Y.), 33*(2), 183–200. DOI: 10.1108/BL-03-2020-0022

Sung, E., Bae, S., Han, D., & Kwon, O. (2021). Consumer engagement via interactive artificial intelligence and mixed reality. *International Journal of Information Management*, *60*, 102382. DOI: 10.1016/j.ijinfomgt.2021.102382

Sutherland, I. E. (1968). A head-mounted three dimensional display. Proceedings of the December 9-11, 1968, fall joint computer conference, part I, Sylvia IV, J. (2024). The Data Renaissance: Analyzing the Disciplinary Effects of Big Data, Artificial Intelligence, and Beyond. DOI: 10.1145/1476589.1476686

Syrotkina, O., Bhatta, S., & Jacob, K. (2023). Recency-Frequency-Monetary Analysis and Recommendation System using Apriori Algorithm on E-Commerce Sales Data. *2023 13th International Conference on Advanced Computer Information Technologies (ACIT)*, 321-326. DOI: 10.1109/ACIT58437.2023.10275513

Tadimarri, A., Jangoan, S., Sharma, K. K., & Gurusamy, A. AI-Powered Marketing: Transforming Consumer Engagement and Brand Growth.

Talaat, A. S. (2023, June). Sentiment Analysis Classification System Using Hybrid BERT Models. *Journal of Big Data*, *10*(110), 110. Advance online publication. DOI: 10.1186/s40537-023-00781-w

Tang, C. S., Bai, J., So, K. C., Chen, X. M., & Wang, H. (2016). Coordinating supply and demand on an on-demand platform: Price, wage, and payout ratio. SSRN *Electronic Journal*. DOI: 10.2139/ssrn.2831794

Tanveer, M., Ahmad, A. R., Mahmood, H., & Haq, I. U. (2021). Role of ethical marketing in driving consumer brand relationships and brand loyalty: A sustainable marketing approach. *Sustainability (Basel)*, *13*(12), 6839. DOI: 10.3390/su13126839

Tashtemirovich, A. O., Balbaa, M. E., Ibrohimjon, F., & Batirova, N. (2024). Investigating the Impact of Artificial Intelligence on Digital Marketing Tactics Strategies Using Neutrosophic Set. [IJNS]. *International Journal of Neutrosophic Science*, *23*(3).

Tcharnetsky, M., & Vogt, F. (2023). An Artificial Intelligence Cycle Model Against the Shortage of Skilled Professionals - An AI-based Holistic Solution Approach for Human Resources. [JAES]. *Journal of Applied Economic Sciences*, *18*(16), 108. Advance online publication. DOI: 10.57017/jaes.v18.2(80).05

Thalpage, N. (2023). Unlocking the black box: Explainable artificial intelligence (XAI) for trust and transparency in ai systems. *J. Digit. Art Humanit*, *4*(1), 31–36. DOI: 10.33847/2712-8148.4.1_4

Topbaş, A., Jamil, A., Hameed, A. A., Ali, S. M., Bazai, S., & Shah, S. A. (2021, October). Sentiment analysis for covid-19 tweets using recurrent neural network (rnn) and bidirectional encoder representations (bert) models. In 2021 International Conference on Computing, Electronic and Electrical Engineering (ICE Cube) (pp. 1-6). IEEE.

Torres, A. I., Darkio, L. S. P., Santos, J. D., & Pires, P. B. (2025). Return on AI: Mapping and Exploring ROI. In *Tangible Measures." In Leveraging AI for Effective Digital Relationship Marketing* (pp. 353–384). IGI Global.

Troy, L. C. (2025). Enhancing Marketing Student Success with AI-Guided Experiential Learning: A Case Study.

Turing, A. M. (2009). *Computing machinery and intelligence*. Springer. DOI: 10.1007/978-1-4020-6710-5_3

Ulman, Y. I., Cakar, T., & Yildiz, G. (2015). Ethical issues in neuromarketing:"I consume, therefore I am!". *Science and Engineering Ethics*, *21*(5), 1271–1284. DOI: 10.1007/s11948-014-9581-5 PMID: 25150848

Umamaheswari, D. D. (2024). Role of Artificial Intelligence in Marketing Strategies and Performance. *Migration Letters : An International Journal of Migration Studies*, *21*(S4), 1589–1599.

Umoh, E. (2024). "The Impact of Artificial Intelligence on Public Administration in the Public Sector: Opportunities and Challenges." *The Impact of Artificial Intelligence on Public Administration in the Public Sector: Opportunities and Challenges (November 11, 2024).*

Uzomah, M. M., & Eruetemu, P. O. (2024). Artificial intelligence and digital economy and the economic state of Nigerians. *Journal of Emerging Technologies*, *4*(1), 26–35.

Van Esch, P., & Black, S. (2021). Artificial Intelligence (AI): Revolutionizing Digital Marketing. *Australasian Marketing Journal*, *29*(3), 199–203. DOI: 10.1177/18393349211037684

Varona, D., & Suárez, J. L. (2022). Discrimination, bias, fairness, and trustworthy AI. *Applied Sciences (Basel, Switzerland)*, *12*(12), 5826. DOI: 10.3390/app12125826

Verma, N., Mishra, P., & Purohit, N. (2020). Development of a knowledge based decision tree classifier using hybrid polarimetric SAR observables. *International Journal of Remote Sensing*, *41*(4), 1302–1320. DOI: 10.1080/01431161.2019.1666314

Verver, J. (2015). Lessons from the FIFA corruption scandal. *Risk Management*, *62*(7), 16–18.

Vesper, H. W., Wang, Y., Vidal, M., Botelho, J. C., & Caudill, S. P. (2015). Serum total testosterone concentrations in the US household population from the NHANES 2011–2012 study population. *Clinical Chemistry*, *61*(12), 1495–1504. DOI: 10.1373/clinchem.2015.245969 PMID: 26510959

Vieira, M., Paulo, H., Pinto-Varela, T., & Barbosa-Póvoa, A. P. (2021). Assessment of financial risk in the design and scheduling of multipurpose plants under demand uncertainty. *International Journal of Production Research*, *59*(20), 6125–6145. DOI: 10.1080/00207543.2020.1804638

Vlačić, B., Corbo, L., Silva, S., & Dabić, M. (2021). The evolving role of artificial intelligence in marketing: A review and research agenda. *Journal of Business Research*, *128*, 187–203. DOI: 10.1016/j.jbusres.2021.01.055

Von Eschenbach, W. J. (2021). Transparency and the black box problem: Why we do not trust AI. *Philosophy & Technology*, *34*(4), 1607–1622. DOI: 10.1007/s13347-021-00477-0

Wagner, G., Schramm-Klein, H., & Steinmann, S. (2020). Online retailing across e-channels and e-channel touchpoints: Empirical studies of consumer behavior in the multichannel e-commerce environment. *Journal of Business Research*, *107*, 256–270. DOI: 10.1016/j.jbusres.2018.10.048

Wallace, S. (2023). Digital Twin and Metaverse Technologies, Geospatial Simulation and Sensor Fusion Tools, and Object Perception and Motion Control Algorithms in Immersive Hyper-Connected Virtual Spaces. *Linguistic and Philosophical Investigations*, (22), 264–280.

Wamba-Taguimdje, S. L., Wamba, S. F., Kamdjoug, J. R. K., & Wanko, C. E. T. (2020). Influence of artificial intelligence (AI) on firm performance: The business value of AI-based transformation projects. *Business Process Management Journal*, *26*(7), 1893–1924. DOI: 10.1108/BPMJ-10-2019-0411

Wang, M. C.-H., & Tang, Y.-Y. (2018). Examining the antecedents of sport team brand equity: A dual-identification perspective. *Sport Management Review*, *21*(3), 293–306. DOI: 10.1016/j.smr.2017.07.010

Wei, Y., & Tyson, G. (2024). Human vs. AI content: Engagement analysis. *Journal of Interactive Marketing*. Advance online publication. DOI: 10.1016/j.intmar.2023.01.001

Westerbeek, H. (2025). Algorithmic fandom: How generative AI is reshaping sports marketing, fan engagement, and the integrity of sport. *Frontiers in Sports and Active Living*, *7*, 1597444. DOI: 10.3389/fspor.2025.1597444 PMID: 40406423

Williamson, S., & Prybutok, V. (2024). Balancing Privacy and Progress: A Review of Privacy Challenges, Systemic Oversight, and Patient Perceptions in AI-Driven Healthcare. *Applied Sciences (Basel, Switzerland)*, *14*(2), 675. Advance online publication. DOI: 10.3390/app14020675

Wu, Y., ... "Research on the Application of Deep Learning-Based BERT Model in Sentiment Analysis," *arXiv preprint*, arXiv:2403.08217, Mar. 2024. [Online]. Available: https://arxiv.org/abs/2403.08217.arXiv

Wu, H.-C., Ai, C.-H., & Cheng, C.-C. (2016). Synthesizing the effects of green experiential quality, green equity, green image and green experiential satisfaction on green switching intention. *International Journal of Contemporary Hospitality Management*, *28*(9), 2080–2107. DOI: 10.1108/IJCHM-03-2015-0163

Wu, S., Yau, W., Ong, T., & Chong, S. (2021). Integrated Churn Prediction and Customer Segmentation Framework for Telco Business. *IEEE Access : Practical Innovations, Open Solutions*, *9*, 62118–62136. DOI: 10.1109/ACCESS.2021.3073776

Xia, Y., Liu, Z., Wang, S., Huang, C., & Zhao, W. (2024). Unlocking the impact of user experience on AI-powered mobile advertising engagement. *Journal of the Knowledge Economy*, *16*(1), 1–37. DOI: 10.1007/s13132-024-02153-y

Xue, H., ... "E-chat: Emotion-Sensitive Spoken Dialogue System with Large Language Models," arXiv preprint, arXiv:2401.00475, Dec. 2023. [Online]. Available: https://arxiv.org/abs/2401.00475

Xu, T., & Baghaei, S. (2025). Reshaping the future of sports with artificial intelligence: Challenges and opportunities in performance enhancement, fan engagement, and strategic decision-making. *Engineering Applications of Artificial Intelligence*, *142*, 109912. DOI: 10.1016/j.engappai.2024.109912

Yadav, A., & Pandita, D. (2024). A Decision Model for Revolutionizing Digital Marketing Campaigns Powered by AI and Predictive Analytics. *2024 ASU International Conference in Emerging Technologies for Sustainability and Intelligent Systems (ICETSIS)*, 791-795. DOI: 10.1109/ICETSIS61505.2024.10459608

Yang, W., Tan, F., Bai, Y., & Ryu, J. H. (2024, November). Exploring Experiential Marketing Strategies of Luxury Fashion Brands in the Metaverse: An In-Depth Analysis of Immersive Consumer Engagement. In International Conference on Services Computing (pp. 100-113). Cham: Springer Nature Switzerland.

Yashveer Raghav, Y., Tipu, R. K., Bhakhar, R., Gupta, T., & Sharma, K. (2024). The Future of Digital Marketing: Leveraging Artificial Intelligence for Competitive Strategies and Tactics. In Teixeira, S., & Remondes, J. (Eds.), *The Use of Artificial Intelligence in Digital Marketing: Competitive Strategies and Tactics* (pp. 249–274). IGI Global Scientific Publishing., DOI: 10.4018/978-1-6684-9324-3.ch011

Yau, A.. (2021). AI-driven marketing automation: Customer trust and satisfaction. *Journal of Business Research, 124*, 569–578. DOI: 10.1016/j.jbusres.2020.11.045

Yeboah, D., Osei-Wusu, F., Asiedu, W., Asante, G., Antwi, E. S., Muntanka, S. A., ... & Olowookere, G. (2025). A Framework for Intelligent Color Processing and Design Optimization in UI/UX Systems.

Yordanova, Z., & Nozari, H. (2025). Harnessing Cyber-Physical Systems and Digital Twins for Industrial Innovation and Economic Resilience. In Dynamic and Safe Economy in the Age of Smart Technologies (pp. 33-48). IGI Global Scientific Publishing. DOI: 10.4018/979-8-3693-4369-2.ch003

Young, P. C., & Wendit, J. T. (2017). GOVERNANCE IN SPORTS GOVERNING BODIES: A RISK MANAGEMENT PERSPECTIVE. *International Sports Law Review Pandektis, 12*.

Zahidi, F., Kaluvilla, B. B., & Mulla, T. (2024). Embracing the new era: Artificial intelligence and its multifaceted impact on the hospitality industry. *Journal of Open Innovation, 10*(4), 100390. DOI: 10.1016/j.joitmc.2024.100390

Zhang, C., & Lu, Y. (2021). Study on artificial intelligence: The state of the art and future prospects. *Journal of Industrial Information Integration, 23*, 100224. DOI: 10.1016/j.jii.2021.100224

Zhang, J., Hassandoust, F., & Williams, J. (2020). Online Customer Trust in the General Data Protection Regulation (GDPR) Context. *Pac. Asia J. Assoc. Inf. Syst., 12*, 4. DOI: 10.17705/1pais.12104

Zhang, J., & Li, X. (2019). Sentiment analysis in AI marketing. *The Journal of Consumer Research, 46*(5), 805–822. DOI: 10.1093/jcr/ucz020

Zhang, S., Zhang, S., Huang, T., Gao, W., & Qiao, Y. (2022). Emotion recognition in conversation: Research challenges, datasets, and recent advances. *IEEE Transactions on Affective Computing*. Advance online publication. DOI: 10.1109/TAFFC.2022.3168459

Zhao, Y. (2021). [Retracted] Sports Enterprise Marketing and Financial Risk Management Based on Decision Tree and Data Mining. *Journal of Healthcare Engineering, 2021*(1), 7632110. DOI: 10.1155/2021/7632110 PMID: 34691380

Zheng, K., Shen, Z., Chen, Z., Che, C., & Zhu, H. (2024). Application of AI-empowered scenario-based simulation teaching mode in cardiovascular disease education. *BMC Medical Education, 24*(1), 1003. DOI: 10.1186/s12909-024-05977-z PMID: 39272041

Zhong, Y., Li, Y., Ding, J., & Liao, Y. (2021). Risk management: Exploring emerging Human Resource issues during the COVID-19 pandemic. *Journal of Risk and Financial Management, 14*(5), 228. DOI: 10.3390/jrfm14050228

Ziakis, C., & Vlachopoulou, M. (2023). Artificial Intelligence in Digital Marketing: Insights from a Comprehensive Review. *Information (Basel), 14*(12), 664. DOI: 10.3390/info14120664

Ziakis, C., & Vlachopoulou, M. (2023). The evolution of AI-driven user profiling: Privacy challenges and regulatory responses. *AI & Society, 38*(2), 275–294. DOI: 10.1007/s00146-022-01453-9

About the Contributors

Oyedemi Oluyemisi Adenike is a lectuer in the Department of Computer Science/Cybersecurity, University of Ilesa, Ilesa, Osun State, Nigeria. She is currently on postdoctoral study in the Department of Computer Science, Federal University of Lavras, Brazil. Her research interest is in the area of Machine learning, IoT context and Cybersecurity. In the area of Machine learning, she has worked on intelligent system to detect Cyberthreat. She is currently exploring the world of connected devices and the intricacies of sensor networks in IoT platforms.

Earnest Anand is a Professor in Lovely Professional University Punjab India. He received Undergraduate in Hotel Management from Manipal University, Postgraduate in Tourism Management from Madurai Kamaraj University. He completed Doctor of Philosophy in Hospitality Management in 2023 from G D Goenka University Gurugram India. His research areas lies in food Service Industry, his research focuses on Alcoholic beverages, Event management and Sustainable Management Practices, Front Office operation, Event Management, Tourism Ethics, Destination Marketing. Dr Earnest is an active researcher and has published numerous research articles in prestigious national and international journals and books. He has participated in various National and International Conferences as a Session Chair and Resource person and he also reviewed the various papers and book chapters in renowned publication houses.

Godwin Nse Ebong is a scholarly AI enthusiast with a strong academic record and years of experience in machine learning research. I specialize in applying statistics and data mining techniques to develop decision-making systems that drive strategic improvements and predict future trends for businesses. With a deep understanding of Hadoop and text analytics, I excel in extracting valuable insights.

Ogheneruona Maria Esegbona-Isikeh is a Data Journalist with years of experience in uncovering compelling stories through data analysis and visualization.

She specializes in using Python, R, and SQL to mine large datasets and distill complex information into clear, engaging narratives. Ogheneruona's work often explores social justice, economic trends, and public policy, with a particular focus on making data accessible to a broad audience. Her investigative reporting has been featured in leading publications such as News agency of Nigeria (NAN), The Guardian, UrbanKapital Magazine agmonst others. She has written multiple health data stories. Ogheneruona holds a Master's degree in Data Journalism from Birmingham City University(BCU), United Kingdom and a Bachelor's degree in Mass Communication from Delta State University, Abraka In Nigeria.When she's not crunching numbers, Jane enjoys mentoring aspiring data journalists and speaking at industry conferences about the importance of transparency in data storytel

Kritika Gupta is an experienced academician with over 13 years in the education sector. She holds a Ph.D. in Business Management and is currently an Assistant Professor at the University Business School, Chandigarh University. Her research contributions include publications in reputed Q1 journals indexed in SCOPUS and Web of Science. Dr. Gupta is passionate about delivering quality education and advancing academic research, consistently striving to enhance learning outcomes and contribute to the development of knowledge in the field of business management.

Praise Akinsipe is a dedicated Quality Assurance (QA) Engineer with a robust background in software testing and a profound commitment to enhancing human health through technology. Holding a B.Sc. in Microbiology and an MSc in Public Health Management, Praise seamlessly integrates expertise in health management with technological proficiency to drive innovations in software quality assurance. At Ground Control Limited, Praise has been instrumental in leading comprehensive QA processes for product releases. Their expertise encompasses test planning, execution, and reporting, ensuring that all deliverables meet stringent quality standards before deployment. A notable achievement includes the enhancement of internal scheduling and billing applications, where Praise proactively identified system defects and mitigated risks across desktop, web, and mobile platforms. By maintaining a scalable automated testing framework using Selenium integrated with CI/CD pipelines, they have significantly improved testing efficiency and ensured continuous quality validation. In collaboration with cross-functional teams, including Product Management, Development, and Design Praise has defined clear acceptance criteria, reducing ambiguity and complexity. They have also provided actionable feedback to ensure testability and alignment with business objectives. Their leadership extends to mentoring a team of junior QA engineers, and individuals delving into careers in Information Technology fostering a culture of continuous improvement through knowledge-sharing sessions and the adoption of new testing methodologies and tools. Praise earned a Bachelor of Science degree in Microbiology from Redeemer's University and furthering their commitment to public health, they obtained an MSc in Public Health Management. This advanced degree has equipped Praise with critical skills in data analysis, health policy development, and program planning. These competencies are invaluable in assessing software systems designed for health-related applications. The integration of public health principles into their QA practice ensures that software solutions are not only technically sound but also aligned with health standards and user needs. Driven by a passion for technology's role in human health and nutrition, Praise actively explores how technological advancements can improve health outcomes. They are particularly interested in the development and testing of applications that promote healthy lifestyles, facilitate nutritional education, and provide accessible health monitoring tools. By leveraging their combined expertise in public health and software quality assurance, contributes to creating reliable, user-friendly health technologies that empower individuals to make informed decisions about their well-being. Praise's unique blend of public health insight and technological acumen positions them as a forward-thinking professional dedicated to advancing software quality in the health, nutrition and environmental sectors.

Amit Kumar Jain earned his B.Tech. in Electronics & Communication from Rajasthan Technical University, Kota, followed by an M.Tech. from Jagannath University, Jaipur, Rajasthan. He later completed his Ph.D. in Wireless Communication at Poornima University, Jaipur, Rajasthan. With 14 years of experience, he currently serves as an Associate Professor in the Electrical & Electronics Engineering Department at Poornima Group, Jaipur. His research interests include Antennas, Wireless Communication, Machine Learning, and Artificial Intelligence.

Sanjeev Kumar is a Professor in Lovely Professional University Punjab India. He received Undergraduate in Hotel Management from Osmania University, Postgraduate in Tourism Management from Madurai Kamaraj University. He completed Doctor of Philosophy in Hospitality Management in 2019 from Amity University Jaipur India. His research areas lies in food Service Industry, his research focuses on Alcoholic beverages, Event management and Sustainable Management Practices, Metaverse, AI Machine Learning and Artificial Intelligence. He published more than 60 research papers, articles and chapters in Scopus Indexed, UGC Approved and peer reviewed Journals and books. Dr. Sanjeev Kumar participated and acted as resource person in various National and International conferences, seminars, session chair, research workshops and industry talks and his work has been widely cited. Dr. Sanjeev also edited more than 12 books with various International Publishers such as IGI Global, Cambridge Scholars, Emerald, CABI, Bentham Science, Taylor & Francis. Dr Sanjeev is an active researcher and has published numerous research articles in prestigious national and international journals and books.

Geetha Manoharan is currently working in Telangana as an assistant professor at SR University. She is the university-level PhD program coordinator and has also been given the additional responsibility of In Charge Director of Publications and Patents under the Research Division at SR University.

Ugochukwu O. Matthew, presently is an Academic scholar with Hussaini Adamu Federal Polytechnic, Nigeria, in the Department of Computer Science with specialty in AI, Big Data Science, Cloud Computing, Internet of Things, Data Mining, Multimedia and E-Learning Education. A Member of Nigeria Computer Society (NCS), Nigeria Institute of Management (NIM), International Association of Computer Science & Information Technology (IACSIT), European Alliance for Innovation(EAI) and also a member of Teaching & Education Research Association (TERA). Ugochukwu O. Matthew hold Masters in Computer Applications from Bayero University Kano, Nigeria. Ugochukwu O. Matthew had reviewed several Journals and a member of Review Board Committee of Journals Indexed by Scopus and Web of Science including IEEE Access, SN Computer Science (Springer), International Journal of Information Communication Technologies & Human Development(IJICTHD), International Journal of Business Data Communications and Networking (IJBDCN), International Journal of Cloud Applications and Computing (IJCAC). Ugochukwu O. Matthew is a cofounder of U&J Digital Consult Limited, an IT and Educational Consulting Firm in Nigeria.

Amaonwu Onyebuchi is a lecturer in the Department of Computer Science, Hussaini Adamu Federal Polytechnic Kazaure, Jigawa State, Nigeria. Onyebuchi is a seasoned IT professional, registered with Nigeria Computer Society (NCS) with speciality in Artificial Intelligence, Cloud Technology Management, Information System Security, Internet of Things and E-Learning Education. Onyebuchi hold Masters of Science Degree in Computer Science from Kampala University Uganda.

David Oyekunle is AI and data science expert with extensive experience in scaling and expanding product-led digital technology businesses and projects. David is rooted in a deep commitment to driving innovation, harnessing the power of artificial intelligence, and delivering transformative project solutions across multiple industries. Focused to growth of digital technology products by combining a strategic mindset with a hands-on approach to project which spans emerging trends in AI, the future of work, Industry 5.0, risk and ethics

P. Selvakumar is currently an Associate Professor in the Department of Science and Humanities at Nehru Institute of Technology, Coimbatore, Tamil Nadu, India. Prior to joining Nehru Institute of Technology, he held positions as an Assistant Professor in the Department of Science and Humanities various engineering colleges in Coimbatore, Tamil Nadu, India, spanning from 2011 to 2023. Dr.P. Selvakumar's academic and research interests lie primarily in the field of phytochemistry. He has made significant contributions to his field, with an impressive record that includes 30 journal publications, 12 patents, and 20 conference papers. Additionally, he has organized 5 seminars and conferences, further demonstrating his commitment to academic and scientific exchange. Throughout his career, Dr. P.Selvakumar has been recognized for his dedication and excellence in teaching, having been honored with several awards, including the Best Teacher Awards. He holds a prominent position in the academic community, contributing actively to research.

Sajjad Pashaie an Assistant Professor of Sports Marketing Management, University of Tabriz, Tabriz, Iran, a researcher, and an inventor. As a top graduate of the National Elite Foundation, I was recognized as a Young Assistant Professor by the same foundation in 2024. His expertise in research methods, CRM, sports marketing, and technology drives advancements in sports management, evident in his numerous published articles and authored books. Additionally, His have expertise in AI, VR, AR, organizational behavior. Beyond my research activities, I contribute to the academic community by serving on the editorial board and as a reviewer for several journals. I have been a member of the Scientific Committee and a Scientific Reviewer for numerous international and national conferences. I am also a member of the International Federation of Inventors' Association.

Mike Rayner is an Associate Professor and Head of the School of Psychology, Sport, and Health Sciences. Dr Mike Rayner is a National Teaching Fellow of the Higher Education Academy (HEA), Fellow of The Institute of Leadership and Management (ILM), Fellow of the Chartered Institute for the Management of Sport and Physical Activity (CIMSPA), a Senior Fellow of the Higher Education Academy and a registered practitioner with the Chartered Management Institute (CIM) and the Chartered Institute of Marketing (CIM). Mike is currently the section-editor for the Sport Section of the Cogent Social Sciences Journal and sits on the editorial boards of Managing Sport and Leisure, Business and Management and The International Journal for Business and Social Science Journals. He is a reviewer for the Newton Fund, Sports Management Review, Managing Sport and Leisure and The International Journal for Sport and Society. As a Sports Management practitioner, Mike's consultancy work spans a diverse range of clients including elite athletes, coaches and support staff, business executives, National Governing Bodies, Professional Sports Clubs and Government Agencies.

Index

E

F

H

I

L

M

N

P

R

S

T

U

www.ingramcontent.com/pod-product-compliance
Lightning Source LLC
LaVergne TN
LVHW080342011026
849161LV00009B/2163
* 9 7 9 8 3 3 7 3 3 7 7 5 3 *